THE BOG BODY FROM TUMBEAGH

The bog body from Tumbeagh

By

Nóra Bermingham and Máire Delaney

Wordwell

First published in 2006 by
Wordwell Ltd
PO Box 69, Bray, Co. Wicklow
www.wordwellbooks.com

Copyright © The authors

All rights reserved. No part of this publication may be reproduced, stored in a retrieval system, or transmitted, in any form or by any means, electronic, mechanical, photocopying, recording or otherwise, without the prior permission in writing of the publisher.

This book is sold subject to the conditions that it shall not, by way of trade or otherwise, be lent, re-sold, hired out or otherwise circulated without the publisher's prior consent in any form of binding or cover other than that in which it is published and without a similar condition including this condition being imposed on the subsequent purchaser.

Library of Congress Cataloging-in-Publication Data are available for this book.

A CIP catalogue record for this book is available from the British Library.

ISBN 1869857 771

Cover design: Rachel Dunne, Wordwell Ltd

Centre-piece on cover drawn by Niamh Bermingham

Copy-editing: Aisling Flood
Typesetting and layout: Wordwell Ltd

Book design: Nick Maxwell

Printed by Graficas Castuera, Spain

Contents

Acknowledgements   *vii*
Contributors   *ix*

I. THE TUMBEAGH BOG BODY: DISCOVERY AND RESPONSE

1. Introduction   3
   Nóra Bermingham
2. 'Stripped bare by a turf cutter's spade'   5
   Nóra Bermingham
3. Body search: the field excavation   12
   Nóra Bermingham and Máire Delaney
4. A shin dig: the laboratory excavation   40
   Nóra Bermingham and Máire Delaney
5. The conservation of the Tumbeagh bog body   50
   Rolly Read
6. Resolving time: the radiocarbon dates   53
   W.A.B van der Sanden and J. van der Plicht

II. THE SURVIVING HUMAN REMAINS

7. Anatomy of the legs   59
   Máire Delaney
8. The radiographic examination of bog bodies   79
   Máire Delaney and D.P McInerney
9. Tissue samples and tests   90
   Máire Delaney
10. Preservation   98
    Máire Delaney

III. WIDENING THE VIEW

11. The bog at Tumbeagh   105
    Nóra Bermingham
12. Tumbeagh and Lemanaghan: an archaeological and historical perspective   109
    Nóra Bermingham
13. Tumbeagh Bog, Co. Offaly, an extremely wet landscape: 7500 years of peat growth reconstructed   119
    Wil A. Casparie
14. The beetles, the body and the bog   155
    Eileen Reilly
15. Trees, crops and bog plants   171
    David Weir

IV. PARALLELS, THOUGHTS AND POSSIBLE ANSWERS

16. Irish and European parallels   185
    Nóra Bermingham

17. A summary of explanations for the occurrence of bog bodies *Nóra Bermingham*	192
18. Assessing the evidence: the Tumbeagh body and its interpretation *Nóra Bermingham, Máire Delaney, Wil. A Casparie and Eileen Reilly*	195
19. 'Sure it's only a pair of legs': some concluding remarks *Nóra Bermingham and Máire Delaney*	204

REFERENCES 207

APPENDICES

Appendix 1. Supplementary list of Irish bog bodies noted since 1995 *Raghnall Ó Floinn*	217
Appendix 2: Coleopteran data *Eileen Reilly*	229

Acknowledgements

This publication represents the culmination of over six years of work that has relied on the cooperation and invaluable contribution of many individuals and numerous institutions and government agencies. Special thanks are due to some of those involved, without whom it is doubtful whether this project could have reached this point. It was my good fortune in taking on the excavation of the Tumbeagh remains that I came to meet and work closely with Dr Máire Delaney. Her enthusiasm and knowledge were welcome and essential to progressing the many phases of discovery and analysis that the project entailed. Her involvement continued up to her untimely passing, and this publication testifies to her immense contribution both to this project and to wider archaeological research. I have been greatly aided in preparing Máire's work for publication by her husband, Mr Pat O'Connell. For this I am very grateful. I also owe a debt of gratitude to Mr Donal Wynne of Bord na Móna and Dr Wil Casparie for their continuous support in this endeavour over the last six years.

The field and laboratory excavations were jointly funded by Bord na Móna and the Department of the Environment, Heritage and Local Government (DoEHLG) and were supported throughout by the National Museum of Ireland (NMI). These agencies are also responsible for funding this publication, assisted by the Heritage Council of Ireland Publication Grant Scheme 2004. Special thanks are due to Mr Donal Wynne (BNM), Dr Ann Lynch (DoEHLG) and Dr Raghnall Ó Floinn (NMI) for their support in this regard. Dr Wijnand van der Sanden generously provided the radiocarbon dates, with additional dates funded by the Heritage Council of Ireland and Bord na Móna.

The laboratory excavation took place in the Conservation Department of the NMI, Collins Barracks, expertly supported by Mr Rolly Read, Ms Carol Smith and Ms Lucia Hartnett. Many thanks are due to the field excavation team of Ms Cathy Moore, Mr Michael Stanley, Ms Abigail Brewer, Ms Joanne Hamilton, Ms Phillippa Joyce, Mr James Lyttleton, Ms Tina Murphy and Ms Margot Ryan. On-site logistical support was received from staff of Bord na Móna, Lemanaghan Works, in particular Mr Michael Guinan, Mr John Egan and Mr Ger Duffy and archaeological liaison officer Mr Aidan O'Hora.

This project has benefited enormously from specialist contributions, some of which were funded and some that were dependent on the generosity of the individuals and their institutions. The Heritage Council of Ireland funded aspects of the palaeoenvironmental investigations via the Archaeology Grant Scheme 2001, notably the palynological study completed by Dr David Weir of Queen's University Belfast and the coleopteran analysis undertaken by Ms Eileen Reilly. Early specialist involvement by Dr Karen Molloy, National University of Ireland, Galway, Ms Eileen Reilly and Dr Wil Casparie was funded through the original excavation budget, as was the work of Ms Ellen OCarroll, who provided the wood species identifications. Dr Wil Casparie generously and independently produced the results of his peat stratigraphic investigations for both report and publication stage. Magnetic resonance imaging of the human remains was provided by Dr David McInerney of the Royal College of Surgeons after Máire Delaney had convinced him of the project's merits. Máire herself conducted her research with the support of the Department of Anatomy, Trinity College Dublin (TCD). Others who kindly gave their time and expertise were Mr Conor Murphy of the State Laboratory, Dublin; Ms Claire

Murphy, Ms Siobhan Ward and Ms Philomena McAteer of the Department of Anatomy, TCD; Mr Mark Kavanagh, formerly of the Ecological Services Unit, TCD; and Mr Brian G. Scott and Mr Richard Warner of the Ulster Museum, Belfast, who were kind enough to comment on X-ray fluorescence spectroscopy results.

The photographic and illustration record derives from the efforts of a team of highly skilled illustrators and photographers. The NMI provided the photographic skills of Mr David Monaghan and later Mr Mark Moraghan, who captured wonderfully the progress and results of the laboratory excavation. Mr David Jennings, formerly of the Department of Archaeology, University College Dublin, contributed to the field excavation record. Mr Conor McHale finalised the excavation drawings, some of which were based on original drawings by Mr Michael O'Donoghue and Ms Katie Hyland of ADS Ltd. At times, technical assistance was provided by Mr John Garner of the Department of Geography in the University of Hull. Live recordings of the field and laboratory excavations were made by Ms Mary Harkin and her team from AvEdge, who persevered where their sound equipment could not.

For reading and commenting on early drafts of parts of this publication, thanks are due to Mr Pierce Bermingham, Professor Terry Barry, Dr Wijnand van der Sanden, Ms Claire Murphy, Dr Ben Gearey and Dr Catherine Dobson. Particularly invaluable discussions were had with Dr Wil Casparie and Ms Eileen Reilly. Beyond Ireland, further discussion and access to museum collections were provided in Denmark by Dr Mogens Schou Jørgensen, Dr Flemming Kaul, Ms Helga Schultz, Ms Birthe Gottlieb and Ms Annette Pedersen of the National Museum, Copenhagen; Dr Christian Fischer and Ms Anna Marie Grave of the Silkeborg Museum, Jutland; Dr Pia Bennike of the Biological Institute, Copenhagen; and Dr Flemming Rieck of the Maritime Institute, Roskilde. In the Netherlands, access to collections was arranged by Dr Wijnand van der Sanden in the Drents Museum. I would also like to acknowledge the work of Mr Nick Maxwell of Wordwell Ltd and Ms Aisling Flood in preparing this publication.

Contributors

Nóra Bermingham, Department of Geography, University of Hull, Hull, HU6 7RX, UK.

Wil Casparie, Saturnuslaan 5, 9742EA Groningen, the Netherlands.

Máire Delaney, RIP, Department of Anatomy, Trinity College Dublin, Dublin 2, Ireland.

David McInerney, MD, Dean, Faculty of Radiologists, Royal College of Surgeons, St Stephen's Green, Dublin 2, Ireland.

Raghnall Ó Floinn, National Museum of Ireland, Kildare Street, Dublin 2, Ireland.

Rolly Read, National Museum of Ireland, Collins Barracks, Benburb Street, Dublin 7, Ireland.

Eileen Reilly, Department of Botany, Trinity College Dublin, Dublin 2, Ireland.

Jans van der Plicht, University of Groningen, Groningen, the Netherlands.

Wijnand van der Sanden, Drents Plateau, Assen, the Netherlands.

David Weir, Research and Regional Services, The Queen's University of Belfast, Riddel Hall, 185 Stranmillis Road, Belfast, BT9 5EE, Northern Ireland.

In memory of Máire Delaney

I.

THE TUMBEAGH BOG BODY: DISCOVERY AND RESPONSE

1.
INTRODUCTION

Nóra Bermingham

Introduction

> The following…[is]…not so much founded on fact as in fact true. The events in each case relate either as they actually occurred or with a very slight dramatization and infusion of local and contemporaneous colour (O'Grady 1893).

So begins the preface to Standish O'Grady's collection of 'stories and sketches of Elizabethan Ireland'. The opening story provides the title for the compilation: *The bog of stars*. O'Grady recounts how a young drummer boy in the service of the Crown was captivated by the stars reflected in a bog pool. Startled by the brightness of the shining light, he beat his drum, thus alerting an Irish lord to the presence of an advancing force led by the lord deputy of Ireland. An empty hall was taken as a result. The drummer boy was condemned, and the bog that so swayed him appointed as his final resting place. The captain ordered that he be drowned in the bog.

> That evening a company of soldiers stood on a piece of firm ground above a dark pool in Mona Reulta [the bog of stars]. They had amongst them a lad pinioned hand and foot, with a stone fastened to his ankles. He was perfectly still and composed; there was even an expression of quiet pride in his illuminated countenance. He was to die a dog's death, but he had been true to his star. Two gigantic pike-men who had laid aside their defensive armour, but retained their helmets, raised him in their strong arms, while a third soldier simultaneously lifted the heavy stone. One, two, three, a splash, a rushing together in foam of displaced water, then comparative stillness, while bubbles continually rose to the surface and burst. Presently all was still as before, black and still (O'Grady 1893, 20–1).

This brutal death is reputed to have taken place in the sixteenth century, a period that forms the closing bracket to the narrative from Tumbeagh. It is quoted here because in this short passage we get a glimpse of people's attitudes to bogs.

We see that bogs are known to be dangerous: firm ground is sought out. The bog is viewed as ground fit only for traitors and other miscreants who could not be buried elsewhere. The bog then is a place to which people are condemned, in this case by someone else, but it could easily have been through their own folly or misfortune. This forms the central puzzle behind the presence of any body in a bog. The key question throughout the Tumbeagh investigation has been whether the body represents a deliberate burial or an accidental death.

In this book we relate the story of the Tumbeagh body's discovery and the ensuing archaeological and related investigations. Based on the evidence arising, we explore a range of possibilities about why and how this body came to rest in a relatively quiet corner of north-west Offaly. In many ways the book retains the structure of an excavation report. This is intentional, as details of the excavation of bog bodies are not numerous despite the numbers in which they have been found. This is, of course, a product of the nature of the discovery of bog bodies in general: chance finds brought up by a turf spade or a machine-driver's bucket. The structure, however, is also a reflection of the collaboration between researchers that this project has enjoyed.

2.
'Stripped bare by a turf cutter's spade'

Nóra Bermingham

'Stripped bare by a turf cutter's spade'
— *'Bog queen'* (Heaney 1998)

In September of 1998 an archaeological survey of a series of raised bogs in County Offaly was under way in a complex of industrial peatlands known as the Lemanaghan Group (Figs 1, 2; Pl. 1). The survey was designed to identify new and previously known archaeological sites in selected bogs that would be the focus of a programme of archaeological mitigation the following year. It was the first in a series of surveys funded by Bord na Móna and was conducted on its behalf by the Irish Archaeological Wetland Unit (IAWU).

Most of the crew had been in the field since June of that year, having completed new surveys of the Boora Bogs, which lay farther south in County Offaly. In the late afternoon of 17 September the focus of the survey was turned toward Tumbeagh Bog, one of eight bogs in the Lemanaghan Group (Fig. 2). The day was hot, and that afternoon a heavy heat haze clung to the brown bog surface. We were glad that we had to investigate only the western half of the bog. Under the sun, the survey pack of shovel, notebooks, camera, bamboos, lunch, water bottles and the compulsory raingear can feel more than its weight. We started at the northern end of the bog and moved south following the drains for about 1km. In the south some wooden structures were found before the crew faced north to complete the sweep. On the return leg a shout went up from Cathy Moore. Such shouts are generally reserved for special or unusual finds; trackways are marked up at the end of each drain and rarely generate such mid-survey alarm. Seconds later an explanation crackled over the walkie-talkie. It was Cathy: 'it looks like leather...there are yellow crumbs that look like butter'. That initial discovery was the first bog body to be found by an archaeologist and, at that time, the latest in Ireland since 1978.

Exposed on the field surface was a small, dark brown, leather-like flap, measuring about 0.10m by 0.10m. Its edges were ragged and dried by the sun (Pl. 2). Yellow, butter-like crumbs were mixed with the small damp balls of milled peat covering the field surface. A piece of wood and a blackened loose bone lay nearby. The exposure was limited, and the initial report to our Dublin base detailed the discovery of a suspected leather vessel containing bog butter. At this stage the loose bone was not recognised as human. From here, the discovery was reported to the National Museum of Ireland (NMI), as well as to Bord na Móna, so that milling in this part of Tumbeagh

The bog body from Tumbeagh

Fig. 1:
Map showing location of Tumbeagh in County Offaly.

Fig. 2:
The Lemanaghan complex of bogs with the location of the Tumbeagh bog body indicated. The map also shows the distribution of known archaeological sites in this complex and the surrounding dry land. Site locations are based on data derived from IAWU surveys, Bord na Móna excavations and the Record of Monuments and Places.

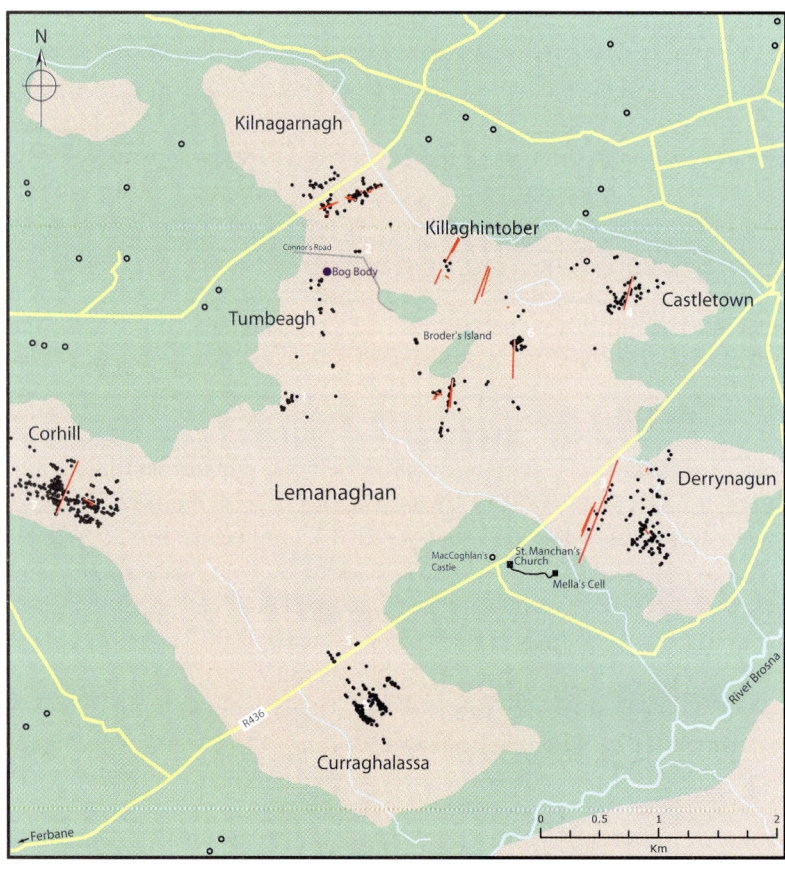

- ○ RMP site, dryland
- ● Raised-bog site
- — Long site

1. Togher AD 1410–1633
2. Togher AD 1217–1407
3. Multi-phase roadway AD 653–AD 1212+
4. Single-plank walkway AD 665
5. Multi-phase roadway AD 1219
6. Brushwood tracks AD 1292–1399
7. Coins AD 1279–1301

Pl. 1:
Looking east over Tumbeagh towards Killaghintober and Castletown bogs. The nearby upland lies just beyond the bottom of the photograph (photo: DoEHLG).

could be stopped. Having covered the find with peat and made note of its location, we departed from Tumbeagh in a contemplative humour. In previous years, artefacts discovered during IAWU field surveys were dealt with immediately. Generally any artefacts identified through survey were recorded and then removed. This particular survey, however, was taking place under a new regime. It had been commissioned by Bord na Móna, and at this time the intricacies of the developer's versus the state's responsibility were a matter of high-level discussion. In light of this, we made out the initial report and awaited further instruction. Since 1999, artefacts found during such surveys are reported to Bord na Móna, whose responsibility it is to arrange for their protection and recovery.

That evening the bone found next to the leather flap was the cause of some deep consideration. Finds of bones in bogs, either isolated or in association with artefacts or sites, were not common, and the combination of 'leather', bog butter, bone and wood was unusual. The evidence suggested that we were in fact dealing with a bog body.

Pl. 2:
The darker skin flap first identified with skin of both legs and the upper part of the left tibia after very loose milled peat had been removed (photo: David Jennings).

The next day the loose bone secured the previous day was retrieved, and a provisional identification as human was made. It was now late on Friday afternoon, and final verification would have to wait until the following Monday. That same afternoon, however, many phone calls were exchanged in order to arrange an on-site meeting for Monday morning to be attended by representatives of the heritage authorities, Bord na Móna and researchers known to have an interest in bogs and bodies.

The loose bone was bagged, tagged and brought to Dublin to be checked against bones from a comparative animal bone collection to ensure that the bone was still human and had not magically transformed into the bone of a pig or a sheep. The following Monday the bone was passed to Dr Máire Delaney for confirmation of its identification: she immediately identified it as human, adding that it was the navicular bone from a left foot.

The Tumbeagh discovery marks the only occasion when human remains were found by an archaeologist during an archaeological survey. Previously, all Irish, and indeed European, bog-body finds were chance discoveries. In addition, the circumstances of discovery at Tumbeagh allowed an immediate archaeological response. Generally bog bodies have been removed from the bog or had much of the surrounding peat dug away before an appropriate archaeological investigation could take place.

Before leaving the bog, on the afternoon of the discovery, we covered the find in loose peat, certain at least that it was a special find and that added precautions were necessary. The findspot was left unmarked, despite being relatively far into the bog and not obviously accessible. The nearest public road was $c.$ 600m to the north, and the bog extended for more than 1km to the south and east (Fig. 2). The closest upland area was $c.$ 200m to the west, but entry to the bog would have required negotiating peat faces and ditches, several metres high and wide, that result from domestic mechanical extraction of peat to make sausage turf. Normally the locations of sites found during a bog survey are flagged using a bamboo. Nevertheless, the findspot was not indicated, but a decoy marker was made $c.$ 30m to the south as an easy visual reminder.

With confirmation of the discovery as human, the probability that a quick, effective response was needed became a reality. In this instance responsibility for the find was shared between Bord na Móna, as the developer in whose production area the find was made, and the state, as legal custodian of all archaeological finds. This allowed for the rapid formation of a steering committee through which general project details such as financing were agreed. At this stage all of the agencies and individuals involved agreed not to release news of the discovery to the press in order to ensure the security of the find until everything was in place for the excavation.

Outlined in a method statement attached to the original licence application was a proposed excavation strategy. It had been designed to allow for the recovery of a complete body. The strategy was flexible as there was a chance that the body was incomplete. Milling had clearly impinged on the find for some time before its discovery: the exposed skin had ragged edges and was air dried and black, and crumbs of body fat were visible on the field surface (Pl. 2). In addition, the location of the body in the centre of the field, which was somewhat higher than the ground immediately flanking it, suggested that the body may have only partially survived.

Over the following two weeks the necessary logistical arrangements were made to allow the excavation to proceed as quickly as possible. Dúchas, The Heritage Service (now the Department of the Environment, Heritage and Local Government) agreed to expedite the licence application (98E452). Bord na Móna put a liaison officer in place and made available a range of personnel and equipment. In Dublin the Head of Conservation of the National Museum of Ireland, Mr Rolly Read, prepared for the arrival of a body, not least by purchasing a fridge large enough to hold it. Various specialists had been contacted and had made themselves available at short notice. The archaeological field team involved in the reassessment of the Lemanaghan bogs was diverted from the survey to the excavation.

Part of the response to the discovery involved satisfying the local police superintendent that the find was ancient. Though clearly damaged, the remains were found in undisturbed peats and had been uncovered as a result of the progressive removal through milling of drained peat from over the findspot. The skin was tanned, and the bone was blackened and decalcified. Though not exclusive to ancient bodies, such characteristics are indicative of bodies that have lain hidden in mire environments. Police officials from Birr, Co. Offaly, visited the site; once briefed and shown the exposed skin, the police acknowledged the archaeological character of the find, enabling the excavation to proceed.

The bog body from Tumbeagh

The unusual nature of the find prompted the incorporation in the overall project design of the filming of both the field excavation and the subsequent laboratory excavation. This was carried out by AvEdge and was financed by Dúchas. The film crew was present on the bog on three days and captured the exciting and not so pleasant aspects of carrying out an excavation of a body in a bog in Ireland in late autumn (Pl. 3). At times it was not certain that the sound equipment would survive the drenching rain that occasionally swept over the site. This footage is now archived in the offices of the Department of the Environment, Heritage and Local Government (DoEHLG).

Once the necessary arrangements had been finalised, the excavation was carried out between 29 September and 10 October 1998. Despite the intense rain and dense fog that greeted the team most mornings, the Tumbeagh bog body was lifted and transferred to the cold-storage unit of the National Museum.

Bodies found in strange places tend to attract attention from many different quarters. The treatment of the dead is a complicated and, for many, fascinating area of human behaviour. The media attention that the project attracted reinforced this attitude. Toward the end of the field excavation the local press was contacted and invited to visit the excavation. The *Tullamore Tribune* (17 October 1998) led with the somewhat overzealous headline: '2000 year old body unearthed in Offaly bog. Body could be victim of ritual sacrifice'. Later, while the laboratory excavation was in progress, an NMI press release outlining the progress of the laboratory excavation was picked up. The next day the laboratory was inundated with journalists and

Pl. 3: AvEdge—who covered aspects of both the field and the laboratory excavations—at work (photo: Nóra Bermingham).

photographers. Much to our surprise, we were front-page news the following day in the *Irish Times* (30 April 1999) and were featured in the *Irish Independent* (30 April 1999). Perhaps not surprisingly, the media focused on the most sensational interpretation of the then undated find. This foray into the national press aroused interest in the project from overseas. Café Productions was in the process of making a documentary for National Geographic on ancient and suspected current practices of human sacrifice in Peru against a background of past attitudes. Keen to include the most recent discoveries, the team flew from London to film in the museum and in Tumbeagh itself (Pl. 3). Footage from the bog (which temporarily claimed a cameraman) and details of the find itself made it into the final cut; the programme, entitled *Forbidden rites: human sacrifice*, was aired in 2000. But perhaps one of the most surprising consequences of the discovery was that it provided inspiration for an American crime-fiction writer, Erin Hart. In her novel *Haunted ground* (2003) a number of the characters seem strangely familiar, as if drawn from personalities associated with the Tumbeagh Bog Body Project.

3.
Body search: the field excavation

Nóra Bermingham and Máire Delaney

Introduction

The discovery of the Tumbeagh bog body provided the first opportunity in Ireland to investigate and retrieve a bog body using modern archaeological methods. Limited archaeological investigations had followed some earlier discoveries, most notably that from Baronstown, Co. Kildare, by Dr T.A. Lucas in 1953. The day after the discovery, Lucas undertook a one-day excavation, recovering the body of a man wrapped in a woollen shroud and overlain by sticks (Ó Floinn 1991). With the thorough and comprehensive approaches taken with earlier bog-body finds from Europe borne in mind, and in particular the approach taken at Lindow (Stead *et al.* [1986]), a strategy was devised that incorporated both rescue and research archaeological requirements. Recovery of all *in situ* archaeological material, human or otherwise, was a priority. The field in which the bog body lay was examined to determine the extent of the body's survival and the presence of any associated archaeological features. The find was made in an industrial peatland and had been damaged by milling. It was highly probable that parts of the body had been redeposited elsewhere (Pl. 4). Because the manner in which a bog is exploited was well understood, the zone within which such redeposition could have occurred was easily defined, and a series of 'search and rescue' measures were implemented. This included scrutiny of the nearby peat stockpile and adjacent fields, as well as an archaeologically supervised metal-detection survey of the same zone. To enable later study of the find in a wider cultural and environmental context, a programme of sampling for palaeoenvironmental purposes was incorporated in the overall project design. This involved on-site consultations with relevant specialists and sampling, which ran concurrently with the archaeological excavation.

Accounts of other bog-body discoveries show that a great emphasis was placed on removing the body from the bog as quickly as possible (Stead *et al.* [1986]). At Tumbeagh we had decided on a strategy that we knew could take between five and ten days. We were happy to allow this much time as we believed that leaving the remains enveloped in the peat was the best way to protect them. Questions of security were minimal, especially as word of the find had not reached the public domain at this stage and its location was not easily accessible without prior knowledge.

Body search: the field excavation

*Pl. 4:
Aerial view of the excavation and stockpile search in progress (photo: DoEHLG).*

The initial investigation

The human remains, visible as a small flap of damaged skin with crumbs of body fat, were situated on the field surface. They lay in the field centre, at the highest point across the width of the field (Pls 2, 4). This field was the primary focus of investigation, but adjacent fields were also included in the survey. To facilitate recording, each field was given a number (Fig. 3), and, within each field, individual context numbers were also assigned (e.g. Fig. 4).

The first stage of the excavation involved the establishment of a buffer zone around the visible remains until the extent to which they survived could be more closely determined. The zone had to be of sufficient size to allow for the presence of a complete body that may have lain in a number of different positions. An area measuring 3m by 3.5m (Cutting 1, Fig. 4) was considered large enough to accommodate a range of possibilities (see below). Within this cordon a second, smaller, buffer zone was established. This measured 1m by 1m and enclosed the visible remains and their projected line. The recovery of the foot bone just 0.80m south of the knee area, and the fact that this was the direction the tibia followed, suggested an approximate north–south orientation for the remains.

The bog body from Tumbeagh

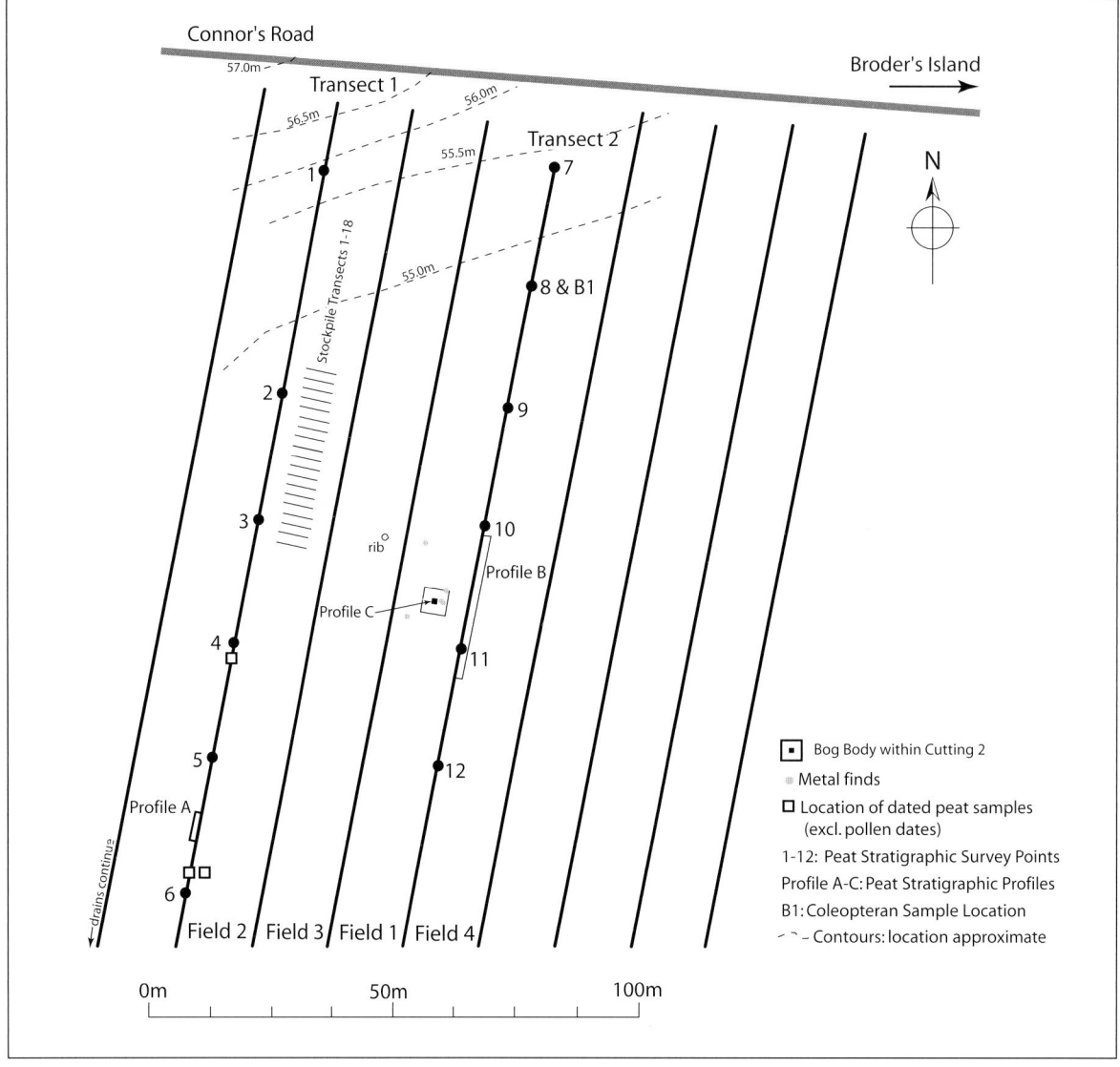

Fig. 3:
Map showing the location of the findspot and associated survey points.

Once the cordons were laid out, we concentrated on identifying the presence or absence of other archaeological features or finds in the immediate vicinity. A labour-intensive examination of the field surface took place. Working in a line moving away from Cutting 1, the team trowelled the field surface to either side of the cutting (Fig. 4). There was a light covering of loose milled peat on the surface. This was removed down to an apparently fresh, undisturbed level. Almost 270m² of the field surface was examined in this way, comprising 200m² to the north of Cutting 1 and 70m² to the south. The search was concentrated in the area north of the body because the milling machines generally moved over the field in this direction and, consequently, any disturbed material was likely to have been dragged northward.

Crumbs of body fat (adipocere) and fragments of wood were retrieved on both sides of the cutting. To the south, short pieces of worked hazel rods and a hazel withy were uncovered. To the north, parts of a pole and crumbs of body fat were found (Fig.

Body search: the field excavation

4). Most, but not all, of these finds had been displaced from their original contexts. Apart from these finds, trowelling had demonstrated the absence of other archaeological features or deposits.

It was anticipated that the field-surface examination would yield pieces of skin or skeletal elements torn from the corpse. Apart from crumbs of body fat, this proved not to be the case. This meant that any disturbed material still present on the bog was more likely to be found in the nearby peat stockpile. The transfer of milled peat from the field surface to the stockpile would have inadvertently included such material.

Fig. 4:
Plan showing the layout of the excavation.

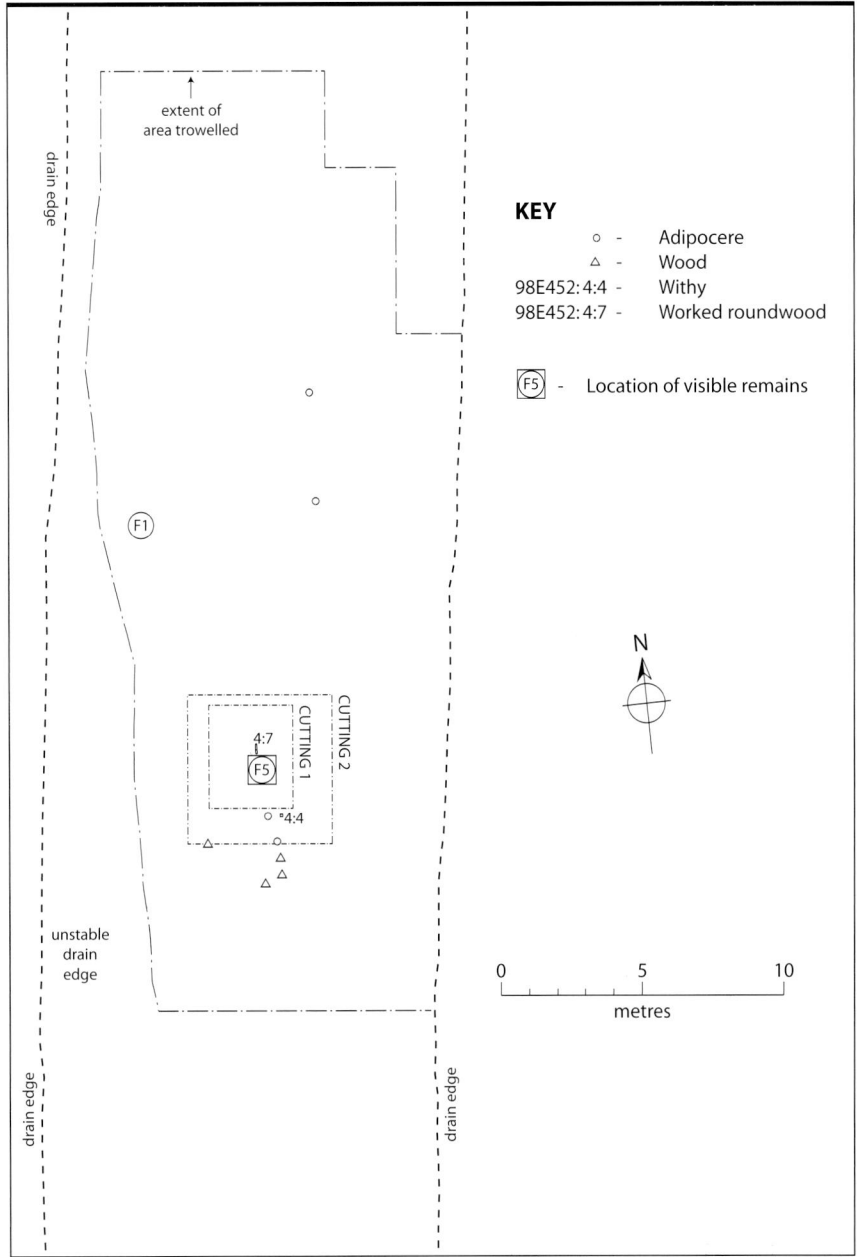

More than 120m² of the stockpile was searched by hand. The approach taken is described in more detail below; as the results have shown, it was worth the effort involved.

Defining the area to be excavated

Once the field surface had been checked, most of the team was moved off the field to concentrate on the stockpile search. Walking over the field surface was kept to a minimum. It was October now, and conditions on the bog could worsen if the weather turned. The western side of Field 1 lay low, and the adjacent drain was full of water. The potential for flooding was high, and, given that our intention was to excavate a 'water-free moat' around the findspot, the drain was mechanically excavated to release the water. As another precaution against deteriorating surface conditions, a plank walkway was laid down around Cutting 1 (Pl. 4). Within the trowelled zone, movement was restricted to the walkway, with the exception of planning and surveying. In this way further disturbance of the field surface was kept to a minimum. This was particularly important because a metal-detection survey of the field had yet to take place.

Once the field surface had been checked, excavation on Field 1 focused on Cutting 1. Although the knee area of the left leg had been identified, we still did not know the extent to which the body survived or in what position it lay. The torn skin and exposed bone showed that milling had damaged the body. The relationship between the bone and the flap of skin was obscured and sufficiently ambiguous to allow for several possible positions in which the body could have lain. The left leg lay on its side, so it was unlikely, but not impossible, that the body had originally been extended. The original flap of skin may have been from the left thigh of a crouched body or from part of the right lower leg of a flexed body. But where was the upper body? There were no surface indications of a torso or a head. They may have sunk deeper into the underlying peat. Alternatively, they may have originally lain higher in the bog and been removed by milling. Clearly, we now wondered if we were dealing with an incomplete body.

Testing for body parts

To reduce this ambiguity, a two-fold approach was taken. With the issues raised above taken into account, the maximum area in which the body could have lain was estimated. The position of the left leg was used to extrapolate the most likely position of the body. If the body was in an undisturbed extended position lying on its back, it could have occupied the space demonstrated in Fig. 5.

As a rough guide to the height of the body, the length of the tibia from the proximal (upper) limit of the shaft to the medial maleolus (inside of the ankle) would represent about one-fifth of the height of the individual. In the case of Tumbeagh, the upper epiphysis was missing and the lower end had not been exposed. Despite this, we had an indication of the position of the left foot, and a maximum height was

Fig. 5:
This is based on Leonardo da Vinci's 'Vitruvian Man', a composition based on Vitruvius's De Architectura, *book 3 chapter 1, describing the planning of temples and their relation to the proportions of the ideal human body.*

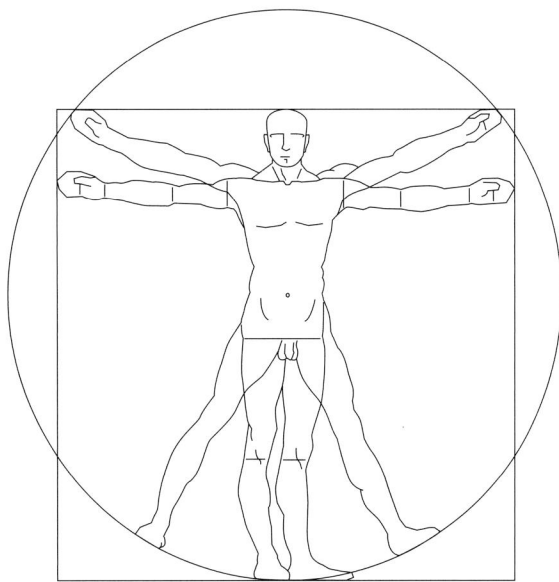

estimated. Though highly unlikely, the possibility of an arm or arms extending above the head was also taken into account. An added consideration was the possibility that the remains had been dragged northward as the machinery proceeded in that direction. Some of the toes had been displaced slightly to the south because of pressure from the massive machinery passing over the body. Indeed, that the remains were not fragmented by such a weight passing over them demonstrates the spongy and elastic nature of the bog, even when drained. Allowance was made for this displacement in the excavation design.

In repose the body takes up a position of flexion. Without external force, it is very unlikely that in death the limbs would rest in an outstretched position. The probable positions were drawn on graph paper, and, with Leonardo da Vinci's 'Vitruvian Man' kept in mind, the furthest possible extent of the limbs was estimated (Fig. 6). The first diagram (Fig. 6A) shows the probable position if the flap of skin originally exposed on the bog surface represented the left thigh. In this case the legs are strongly flexed and near to each other; the head faces to the left; and the arms are flexed in front of the body. The second diagram (Fig. 6B) is based on the supposition that the original skin flap represented the right leg. In this case the flexion of the legs is less and the body may have been extended.

The second part of the approach involved implementing a testing strategy. In Cutting 1 a series of small, hand-excavated test-pits were opened at 0.5m intervals (Fig. 7; Pl. 5). The pits were circular, measuring 0.10m in diameter, and 0.30m deep. This was considered wide enough to pick up a flattened body and deep enough to pick up any sunken remains.

Testing was concentrated on the northern side of the cutting as this was the most probable direction for the upper body to have lain in. The first pits were placed at the edge of the cutting, and progress was toward the centre. No new finds were made, and in a short time it became clear that testing was not required over the entire cutting.

The bog body from Tumbeagh

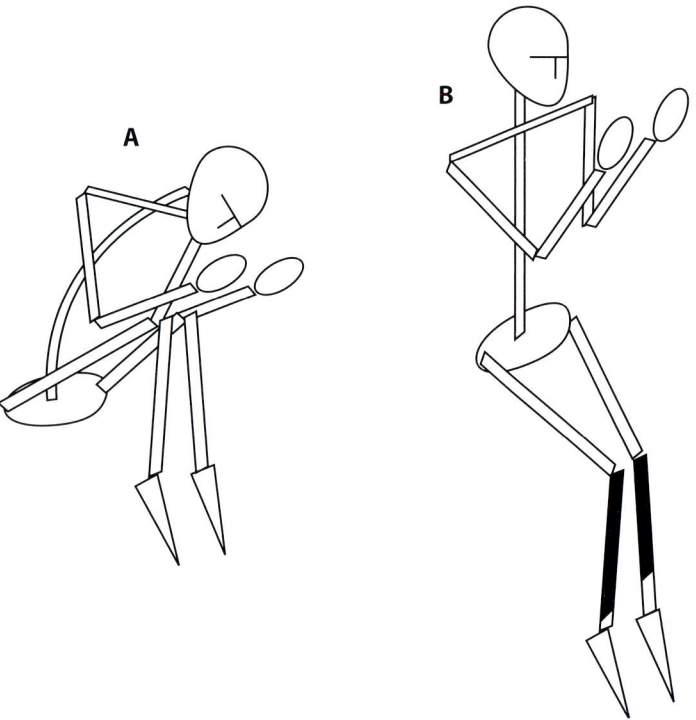

*Fig. 6:
Schematic figures indicating the most likely body positions.*

*Pl. 5:
Testing has been completed, showing the remains to be confined to the central 1m² (photo: Nóra Bermingham).*

Body search: the field excavation

The absence of the upper body on the northern side meant that testing was restricted to the three sides of the internal cordon in which the exposed remains were confined (F5).

Testing had shown that the upper body no longer survived. Immediately, we knew that the scale of the field excavation could be reduced and it could progress more rapidly. A complete body would have necessitated the removal of a larger block from the bog, involving greater labour and machine power. At this point we were able to notify the National Museum that we would be lifting a block no larger than 1m^3. On this basis we began to formulate our approach for the laboratory investigations.

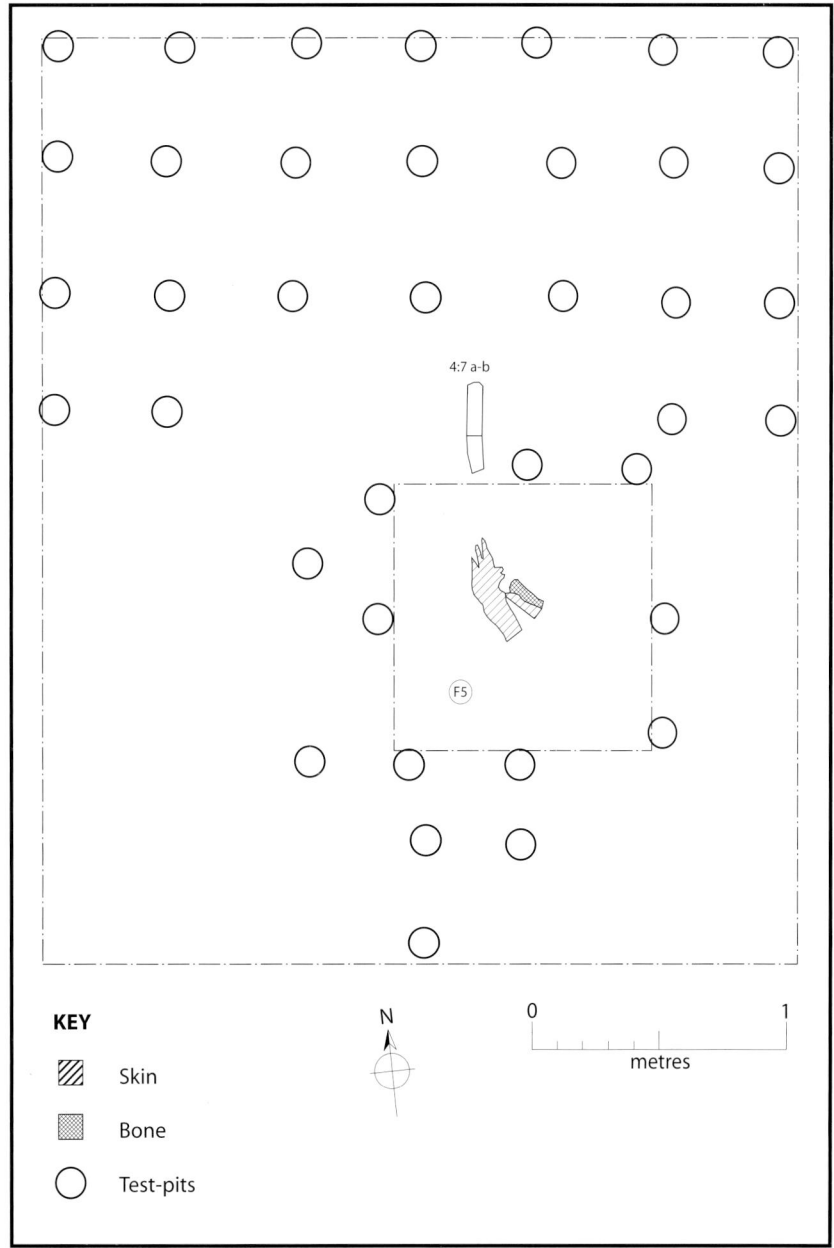

Fig. 7: Plan detailing the distribution of test-pits in Cutting 1 in relation to the visible human remains.

The area around the internal cordon was tested, and all loose milled peat within it was temporarily removed from over the exposed remains. Intact peats were left in place. More of the *in situ* material was revealed. On the northern side was the upper end of the left tibia (Pl. 2). This was dark brown and incomplete. Its proximal epiphysis was absent and had not fused with the tibial shaft. The flap of skin first noticed in the field survey was found to extend downward behind the bone. The distal end of the bone appeared to run under more skin. In the south-east corner another loose foot bone and a small piece of brushwood lay close to the field surface. This showed the surviving remains to have been oriented north-north-west/south-south-east, with the knee area lying in the north-north-west.

As a result of this examination the orientation of the remains was confirmed, and we now knew the direction in which the body lay. In addition, a picture of the individual preserved was emerging. The size of the tibial shaft and the loose navicular bone first found suggested that the body was that of a person approaching adulthood. That the tibial epiphysis had not fused provided further evidence that at death the person had been around 16–18 years of age.

Preparing the peat block

By this time, a few days into the investigation, the excavation focused on preparations for the extraction of the remains from the bog in a block of peat. The plan was to excavate a moat around the block in which the remains were isolated, leaving a free-standing block in the centre of the moat to which access could be gained from all sides and allowing the block to be secured and then lifted onto a forklift.

Before any more digging took place a metal-detection survey of the site was completed. Using a spectrum machine set at its greatest sensitivity, Mr Denis Lynch swept field surfaces, drain faces and spoilheaps for any trace of metal. Metal finds from raised bogs are known, despite the corrosive power of the peat, and other bog-body finds from Europe have had metal finds associated with them (van der Sanden 1996). The survey, which is described below, produced some intriguing, albeit frustrating, finds.

Once the metal-detection survey was completed, a new cutting was laid out around the findspot. Cutting 2 measured 5m by 5m; the central 1m^2 was occupied by the zone in which the human remains had been isolated (Fig. 8). The upper levels of peat in the cutting were removed by trowel, revealing more finds. On the southern and eastern sides more short lengths of worked brushwood were retrieved and the withy was better defined (Pl. 6). Additional skeletal elements were found on the northern side, but all of these had been pulled from their original positions. The bones found were the distal epiphysis of the right femur and a medial cuneiform bone from the left foot. The femoral epiphysis showed that the upper right leg was probably lost, demonstrating that significant damage had been done to the body and reinforcing the initial suspicion that only the lower legs had survived.

Once the area was cleared of artefacts, digging proceeded by hand until a moat, 2m wide and 1m deep, had been excavated, leaving a central pedestal that measured 1m^3 (Fig. 8; Pl. 7). The moat was excavated by hand rather than machine in case new

Fig. 8:
Plan showing Cutting 2 and the locations of the lifted peat block and associated finds.

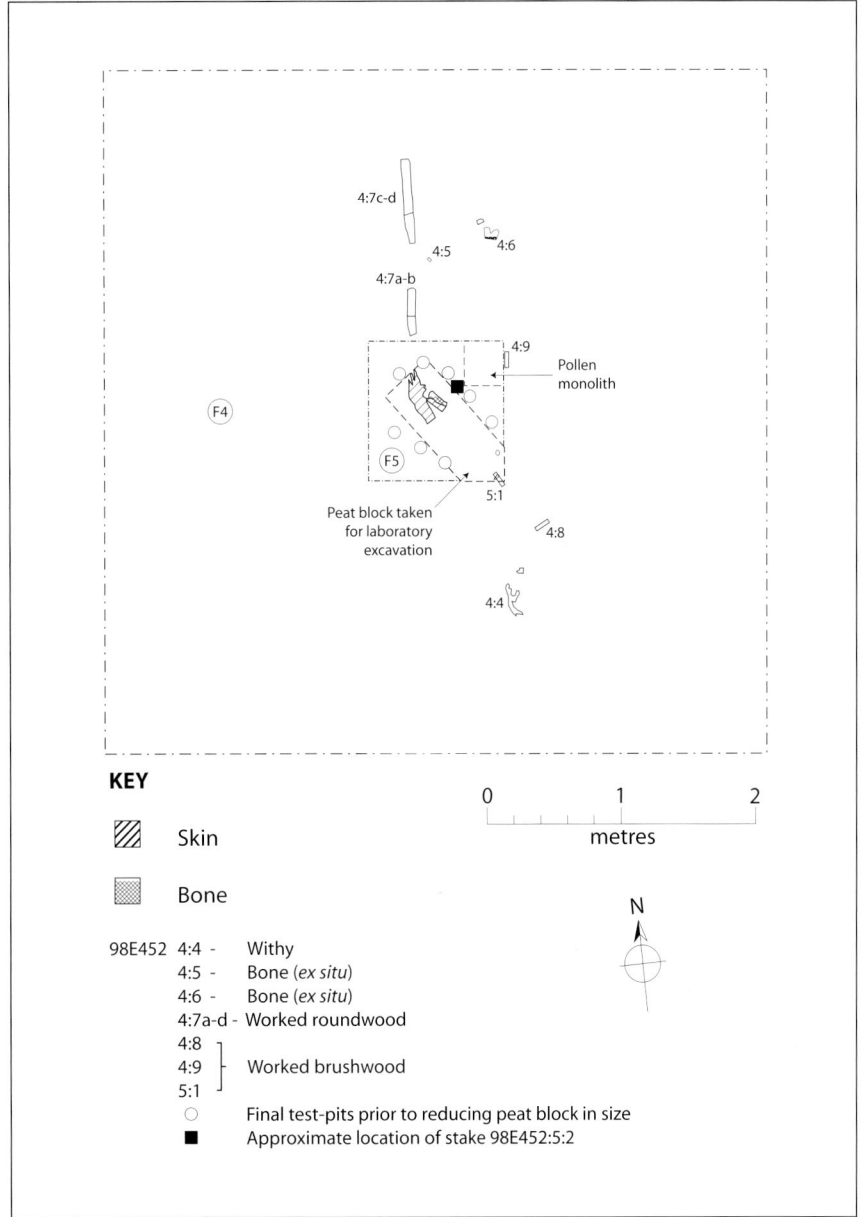

finds were made at a lower level. Initially it was intended to take a block this size to the museum for excavation. Its size was considered sufficient to provide protection for the *in situ* remains, as well as to allow for the possibility of new finds. It had also been intended to record and sample the peat for pollen in the laboratory. In discussion with the project's conservator, Mr Rolly Read, it soon became evident that extracting a block of this size brought some very practical problems. Firstly, there was the issue of weight. A cubic metre of peat weighs around 1 tonne, which does not make for easy lifting or subsequent manoeuvrability. At Lindow the block originally lifted from the bog was larger, and the excavators recorded it as being 'heavy and cumbersome and in danger of breaking up' (Turner [1986], 13). Secondly, there was the size. Given that

The bog body from Tumbeagh

Pl. 6:
The withy in situ. The tracks of milling machinery are clearly visible (photo: Nóra Bermingham).

the block was to be surrounded in a shell of foam and wood, its size would increase. Anything over 1m wide would not fit through the doors of the conservation department of the National Museum, nor would it fit into the walk-in fridge bought in response to the Tumbeagh discovery. At this time the department was housed in Collins Barracks. It has since moved to a modern, custom-designed building where the same problem would not arise. It was necessary, therefore, to reduce the size of the peat block in the field. Before this was done, the stratigraphy of the block was recorded (Casparie, Chapter 13) and a pollen monolith was taken from one corner of it.

Further testing and a new find

To allow the block to be reduced in size and for extraction of the pollen monolith, further definition of the area occupied by the surviving remains was required. A second series of test-pits were opened. The test-pits measured 0.05m in diameter and were 0.15m deep (Pl. 8; Fig. 8). This was considered sufficiently deep, as bog bodies tend to be flattened, the skin forming a leathery envelope that may or may not hold bones within. In peat deposits bones also tend to loose their robustness, and decalcification can make them spongy and susceptible to pressure. The test-pits were placed at the estimated maximum extent of *in situ* remains and where other body parts, if present, were likely to have lain. Care was taken to avoid disturbance of the

Pl. 7:
Excavation of the moat completed (photo: Nóra Bermingham).

peat immediately flanking the projected line of the legs. The test-pits did not reveal any new elements.

The removal of the monolith took place before the peat block was reduced. Its extraction led to one of the most significant discoveries made in relation to this body. It also provided one of those great excavation ironies that all projects seem to experience. The monolith measured 1m by 0.30m by 0.30m and was cut from the north-eastern corner of the peat block with a carving knife used by Bord na Móna operatives for freeing machine parts of tricky deposits of peat. When the peat column was pulled away we found that we had cut through the lower part of a stake. The top of the stake had not been visible, although its projected line suggested that it lay close to the left knee. Later, the laboratory excavation confirmed that two test-pits had in fact been opened to either side of the stake, its presence hidden until its lower half was so unexpectedly revealed. The stake threw open the on-site debate about how the body had come to be in the bog. Its presence suggested that other people may have been involved, that we were not dealing with a person who had become lost. With the remains undated, the stake allowed the possibility of a prehistoric origin for the body (see Chapter 4).

Lifting the block

The peat block, which originally measured 1m^3, was reduced to a size of 1.2m by

The bog body from Tumbeagh

0.6m by 0.5m by careful hand excavation of the excess peat; no new discoveries were made. A simple but extremely effective approach was taken to securing the block. Polyurethane foam was used to create a firm but lightweight protective shell around the block (Pl. 9). Conservators commonly use this foam when delicate or fragile objects are best lifted in blocks so that they can be worked on in a laboratory rather than in the field. Where peat and bodies were concerned, the Lindow project had shown this approach to be successful (Turner [1986]), and removal of the Tumbeagh withy in a small block allowed this approach to be first considered in the field.

At Tumbeagh, peat was first reapplied to the original field surface of the block in order to protect the skin and bone exposed in the field. The entire block was then wrapped in cling film. With a wooden frame in place, the expanding polyurethane foam was poured in (see Chapter 5, Pls 9, 10). This hardened to form a protective shell around the block that prevented dehydration and maintained its physical integrity. The block had already been undercut close to the bottom on all sides, leaving less peat to cut through when it was finally removed. The foam expanded into the space beneath the block and provided support without the block having to be inverted in order for more foam to be applied. When the foam had hardened the newly framed peat block was cut from the original pedestal using a saw. It was then twisted, inverted and finally lifted by a very determined team onto the back of a forklift (Pl. 10). After an overnight stay in the Lemanaghan Works, it was removed to refrigerated storage in Collins Barracks.

*Pl. 8:
Further testing within the 1m³ block was carried out to allow it to be reduced. The estimated limits of the surviving human remains are marked with string on the grid (photo: Nóra Bermingham).*

The stockpile search

Situated two fields to the west of the findspot was a stockpile of peat that had been amassed over the previous spring and summer milling seasons. Stockpiles are linear accumulations of loose peat formed by the transfer of milled peat onto a designated field. Peat is stored in this fashion until it is considered sufficiently dry to be transported to the relevant depot.

Harvesting occurs in a number of stages, as one stockpile is generally supplied from three fields on either side of the central stockpile. Peat from the farthest field is moved onto the adjacent field in the direction of the stockpile. This results in the combination of two sets of loose peat, which are then transferred to the next field closest to the stockpile. This process is repeated until the stockpile has been formed. Objects mixed up with the peat being transferred can also become deposited on the stockpile. In addition, the direction in which the harvesting machines work means that peat and other material are redeposited on the next field, several metres north or south of its original location. In the case of Tumbeagh, redeposition occurred in a northward direction.

The objective of the stockpile search was to retrieve any body parts or artefacts deposited as the stockpile was being accumulated. The search began in line with the findspot and continued northward. Eighteen 2m-wide transects were placed at right angles to the main axis of the stockpile (Fig. 3; Pl. 11). Peat was screened by hand,

Pl. 9:
The peat block is prepared for removal from the bog using a wooden frame and foam shell (photo: Nóra Bermingham).

starting at the bottom outside edge and working toward the middle, until each transect had been cleared. This was a particularly nasty job as the loose peat managed to invade clothing, footwear, hair and eyes (even with goggles). No amount of beach holidays had prepared the team for this. On the first day there was a high wind and slanting rain, but, because dried peat is not easily re-wetted, the rain only barely dampened the peat dust. These adverse conditions resulted in the search being interrupted until the following day.

Despite the poor conditions, four of the eighteen transects produced fragments of bone and skin. Another four yielded small, broken pieces of wood similar to that found close to the body. Transect 1 was *c.* 5m north of the line of the findspot. A search of this and Transect 2 did not reveal anything of significance. Transects 3 and 4 produced fragments of wood, and Transect 5 was blank. Transect 6, however, produced a shredded, desiccated fragment of skin and an almost complete lumbar vertebra. Transects 7–12 were free of human remains, but Transects 7 and 8 yielded fragments of wood. A patella was retrieved from Transect 13, and Transects 15 and 18 yielded the unfused proximal epiphyses of tibiae.

A total of 32.4 tonnes of peat was sifted in order to recover the loose bones. Though labour intensive, the search was fruitful and proved its worth. The skeletal elements recovered, in particular the vertebra, demonstrated that a body, or at least a body from the mid-torso down, had originally been present in the bog.

Further evidence in support of this was found on the field between the findspot of the body and the stockpile. Hopes were high that more finds would be made here, especially as, early in the field project, part of a human rib had been found on the field surface. The rib was found close to the drain edge, almost in line with the body findspot. The field itself had a heavy covering of redeposited peat over it. This was residue from the transfer of milled peat to the stockpile, and more stray finds may have been present. However, trowelling of this surface was impractical, and so rakes were used. These were effective in pulling back the peat cover, but the search did not produce any new finds. A recent peat transfer had more than likely removed any material to the stockpile.

Pl. 10 (opposite): The block is inverted before being lifted onto a forklift (photo: Nóra Bermingham).

Pl. 11 (opposite): The stockpile search in progress (photo: David Jennings).

The metal-detection survey

The metal-detection survey involved systematic sweeps of the field on which the bog body was found. The adjacent fields and drain faces, as well as the nearby stockpile and the excavation spoilheaps, were also swept. The survey began in Cutting 2. The area was swept in 0.50–0.75m-wide transects and included the findspot itself. Movement over the field surface was from north to south followed by east to west. In this way total coverage of the cutting was ensured. Here the survey produced three readings, all between 0.80m and 1.5m to the east of the human remains (Fig. 3; Pl. 12). Outside of the cutting the survey covered the extent of the earlier trowelling. Full coverage was achieved by making overlapping, 1m-wide sweeps up and down as well as across the field. Just over 4m to the west of the remains of the body a positive reading was obtained.

Before the positive readings were examined, the metal-detection survey was

Body search: the field excavation

completed over the rest of the site and the stockpile was swept. However, the survey did not produce any positive results apart from recovering one fragment of rusty and yellow-painted steel from the stockpile. The paint and the composition of the metal indicated that this fragment was from a Bord na Móna train or machine. These are generally painted yellow and made of steel.

Despite the recovery of the modern fragment, the proximity to the bog body of the positive readings seemed promising. Metal objects have been found in association with prehistoric and later bog bodies. For example, in Denmark a bronze brooch found with the Korselitse body provided a Roman date for it. An earlier Danish body, Borremose Woman, was accompanied by a bronze disc, and in Germany, at Obenaltendorf, two ornaments of silver were recovered (van der Sanden 1996). In Ireland, medieval and later finds of bodies have also included metal objects such as buttons, coins and a belt-buckle (Table 1). With good reason, then, we were hopeful that our survey would produce significant finds that might provide a date.

At a distance 4m west of the body, in an area of churned-up peat, a positive signal indicated the presence of metal. The spot was initially checked by hand, but nothing was recovered. Individual small lumps of peat were then passed over the detector. Successive passes allowed the lump to be reduced until there was only the piece of metal left. This was so small that it was unlikely to have been retrieved through hand excavation alone. As a result, it was decided to use the detector to examine the other positive readings in the same way. From Cutting 2 three small pieces of metal similar in size and shape to the first piece were recovered from the top 60mm of peat.

The pieces of metal recovered were in the form of small strips (Table 2). They shared similarities of shape, size and composition strongly suggestive of a common origin. They could not be readily identified as any sort of object fragment, although they looked like metal shavings. Until we could subject the metal to further analysis their origin and function remained indeterminate. At this stage their archaeological potential hinged on their proximity to the bog body and verification of their metallic composition.

After the field excavation, it was decided to carry out non-destructive analysis on the metal. Each piece was subject to X-ray fluorescence (XRF) analysis in the

Catalogue no.	Location	Find	Date
An3	Lockstown Bog, Co. Antrim	Metal buttons	Post-medieval or modern
Ar1	Charlemont Co. Armagh	Spurs of Elizabeth I	Post-medieval
De2	Flanders, Co. Derry	Dagger and weapons	Post-medieval
De6	Ballygudden, Co. Derry	Belt-buckle	Medieval or post-medieval
De13	Gortnamoyagh, Co. Derry	Armour, spears, horse trappings, stirrups	Post-medieval or modern
Dg2	Inver, Co. Donegal	Shoes with buckles	17th or 18th century
Lf1	Castlewilder, Co. Longford	Gold ornaments	?
Ma3	Cloonkee, Co. Mayo	Leather boot with nails	19th century
Of1	Cloghan Castle, Co. Offaly	Leather boot and spur	?
Sl1	Killerry, Co. Sligo	Silver coin	Early 17th century
Ty2	Kildress, Co. Tyrone	Brass buttons on coat	Post-medieval or modern

Table 1: List of Irish bog bodies with associated metal objects. Data extracted from Ó Floinn (Appendix 1; 1995a).

Body search: the field excavation

Pl. 12: Dennis Lynch sweeps the excavation zone for metal finds (photo: Nóra Bermingham).

Find no.	Length/ circumference	Width	Thickness	Cross-section	Shape
98E452:1:9	9mm	2.8mm	c. 0.1mm	Flat	Semicircular
98E452:4:1	31mm	1.1mm	c. 0.1mm	Flat	Twisted
98E452:4:2	11mm	1.2mm	c. 0.1mm	Flat	Twisted
98E452:4:3	17mm	c. 2mm	c. 0.1mm	Flat	Circular

Table 2: Dimensions of the metal strips.

laboratory at Collins Barracks. This was carried out by Carol Smith, one of the museum conservators. The metal was found to be magnetic and of iron (Table 3). The metallic composition of each piece is probably reflective of hardened steel (B.G. Scott, pers. comm.). This would suggest that the strips derived from Bord na Móna machinery, the most likely source of metal of this kind in Tumbeagh.

The modern origin of the metal strips was disappointing. It appears that their recovery close to the bog body should be taken as a coincidence of location. The use of metal detectors at archaeological sites in bogs has nonetheless proved to be useful, although some minor difficulties arose. Despite being set at its greatest sensitivity, the metal detector had difficulties working in such a waterlogged environment. The depth gauge on the detector indicated readings greater than actual depths. For example, where a depth of 0.20m was indicated, the actual depth was found to be less than 0.05m. In the case of very small objects there is a chance that such finds could be lost unless recovery was completed using a metal detector. The detector also indicated that the metal finds were non-ferrous, which was since shown not to be the case. At that stage we did not know the date of the body, and so the possibility that it dated from before the Iron Age had been quite engaging.

29

Find no.	Percentage metallic composition
98E452:1:9	(Metal) Fe 69.6, Co 2.7, Ti 4.2, Sb 17.6, Mn 1.7, In 2.5, Ag 1.6; (Corrosion) Fe 89.3, In 1.5, Mn 1.1, Sb 8.0
98E452:4:1	Fe 89.1, Mn 2.2, Sb 6.6, In 1.1, Co 1.0
98E452:4:2	Fe 93.9, Mn 2.7, Sb 3.3
98E452:4:3	Fe 91.0, Mn 3.3, Sb 5.0, Co 0.7

Table 3: Results of XRF analysis of the metal fragments.

Stakes, poles and a wooden rope

Alongside the human remains, a small collection of wooden artefacts was retrieved comprising both *in situ* and *ex situ* pieces. Truncation of the bog surface and the weight of the machines passing above had dislocated and damaged the wood to varying degrees. To the south and east of the body lay three short lengths of light hazel (*Corylus*) brushwood and a withy, also of hazel (Fig. 8; Pl. 6). The withy lay deeper in the peat and may have retained its original position. The brushwoods looked as if they had been recently disturbed; they lay in looser peat underlying the freshly exposed field surface. Extending northward from the human remains was a birch pole. Milling had broken it into four parts, which lay in a straight line separated by gaps made by machinery. The rest of the assemblage consists of three birch stakes found next to the knees of the body on the eastern side.

The criteria used for describing the worked ends are after O'Sullivan (1996). These include the category of worked end—whether it is a chisel, wedge or pencil point—and the nature of the facets on the worked surfaces. The degree of preservation and perhaps the species of wood have influenced the condition of the worked ends and thus the amount of information that they could yield. In addition, the individual elements amount to eight, a small assemblage without any immediate parallels.

Hazel brushwood

The three pieces of brushwood were short, 0.06–0.14m long, with diameters of 11–14mm. They had been taken from young hazel rods with four to five annual rings (Fig. 9). The end of one (98E452:4:8) was broken. It was not clear whether this had occurred in antiquity or more recently. Its other end was intact and retained a wedge point. Though poorly preserved, this retained flat facets, clean facet junctions and a minimum cutting angle of 10°. The shortest of the three pieces (98E452:4:9) had four worked surfaces, representing cuts and tears, a result of trimming the rod. One end was flat but damaged, and the other had been chopped or cut obliquely. A single-faceted chisel-pointed end survived on the third rod (98E452:5:1). The opposite end had been broken relatively recently. Unlike on the other worked ends, the woodworking on these was crisp: the facets were flat and with very shallow cutting angles.

The withy

About 1m south of the body, lying under a covering of loose peat, a withy was found, which was taken in a block of peat surrounded by polyurethane foam and excavated in the museum laboratory. Milling had impinged greatly on the integrity of the withy. Its

Fig. 9:
Hazel brushwood with worked ends.

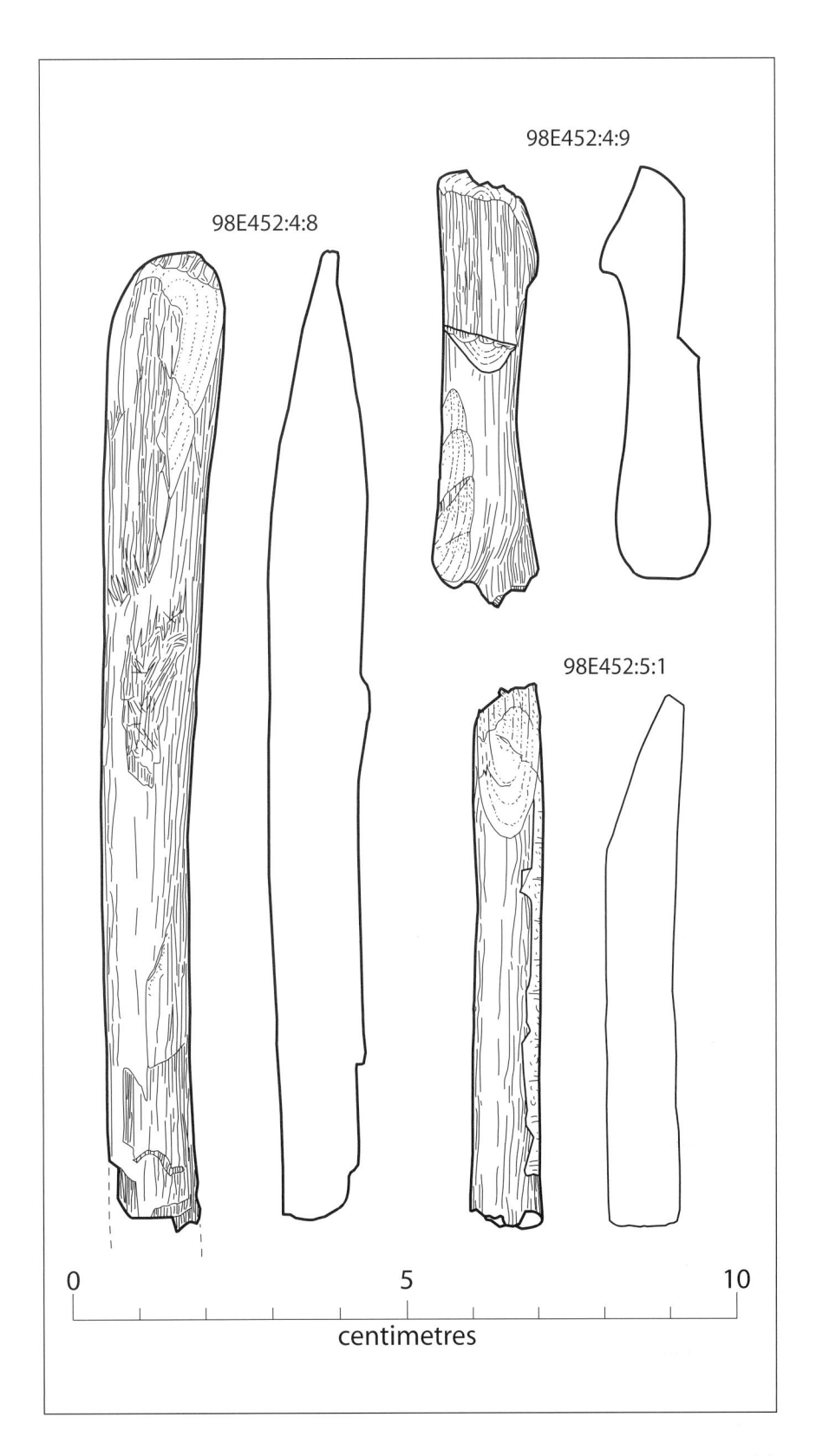

98E452:4:8

98E452:4:9

98E452:5:1

0   5   10
centimetres

Body search: the field excavation

The bog body from Tumbeagh

0   5   10
centimetres

Pl. 13 (right): The withy following excavation in the laboratory (photo: NMI).

Fig. 10 (left): The remains of the hazel withy, 98E452:4:4.

full length could not be determined, although its structural composition was retained for *c.* 0.23m of its length (Fig. 10; Pl. 13). It was composed of three twisted strands of hazel, two with diameters of 10mm and the third of only 4mm. The combined diameter was *c.* 30–40mm depending on the tightness of the twist. Annual ring counts were estimated as preservation made it difficult to obtain accurate figures. The two larger rods were 3 years old, and the smaller one was 1 year old. Bark had survived in various places, and a number of toolmarks were identified. One of the larger hazel rods retained a chisel-pointed end, which had a single, flat facet. Elsewhere, other toolmarks indicated that small side branches had been trimmed from the individual rods used to make the withy.

The birch pole
The initial discovery of the bog body included identification of a horizontally laid pole situated immediately to the north of the flap of skin first noticed on the field surface (Fig. 11). This birch (*Betula* sp.) pole was 60mm in diameter and *c.* 1.08m long. It was broken, with parts missing because of milling damage. The northern end retained a wedge point, but the southern end was not intact. The worked surfaces of the wedge point were multi-faceted, with facet widths of 25–40mm, indicating that the blade used was not less than 40mm wide. One corner of a jamb curve was identified toward the centre of the wood; it was rounded, and the curve was slightly concave. Facets were flat with, for the most part, clean junctions; cutting angles were shallow (30–35°). The individual parts of the pole had been sheared by the peat-milling machinery, and their upper surfaces were ragged and flattened.

The stakes
Extending downward and eastward from the knees were three stakes (Figs 11, 12; Pl. 14; Table 4). All were of birch (*Betula* sp.). The tops of the two longest elements had been broken relatively recently, and so their original lengths are not known. One (98E452:2) extended for nearly 1m into the peat, and all of the smallest stake lay within the peat.

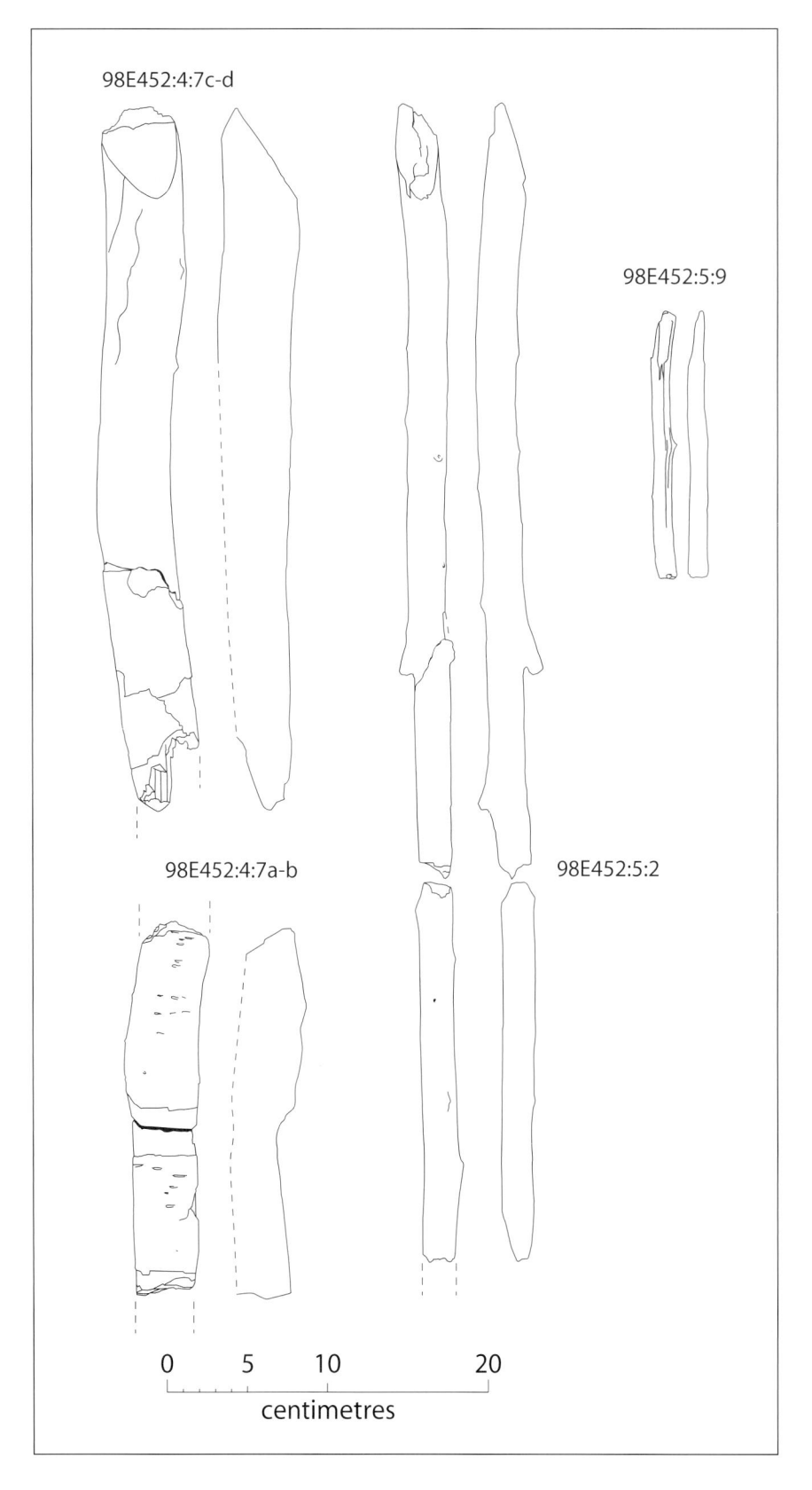

Fig. 11:
The broken birch pole (98E452:4:7a–d) and the birch stakes.

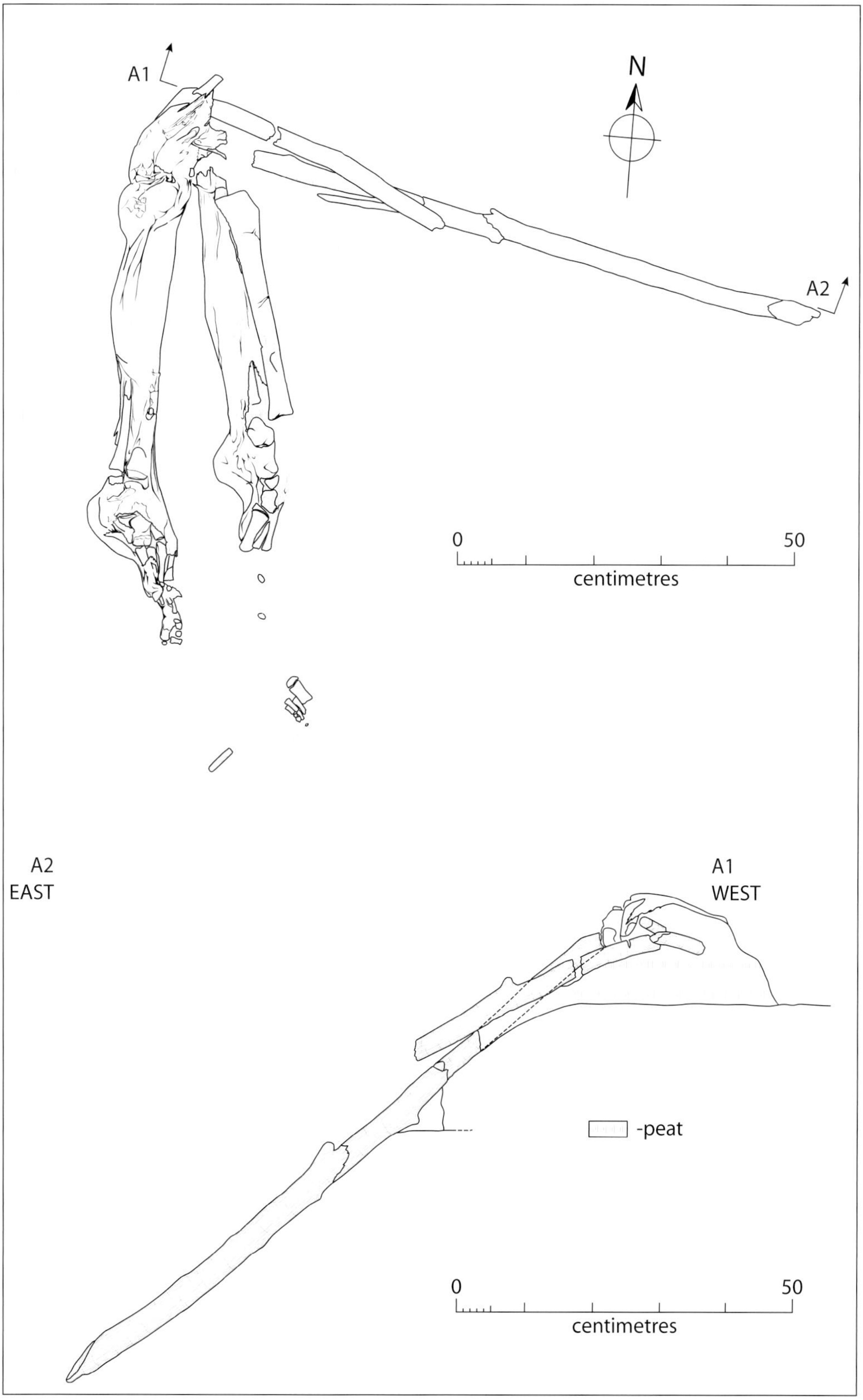

Fig. 12: Plan (top) and section (bottom) of the stakes in situ.

The bog body from Tumbeagh

The lightest of the three (98E452:5:9) had a single toolmark on its lower end, which, though broken, did not appear to have been fashioned into a point. The upper end appeared to have been torn. This stake was found *c.* 0.20m below the level of the left knee, immediately adjacent to stake 98E452:5:2. The latter had been cut through during the field excavation (see p. 21). The upper parts had been left *in situ* for excavation in the museum. The lower part was retrieved in the field. It had a wedge-pointed tip produced using a combination of chopping and tearing. Surviving

Find no.	Dimensions	No. of rings	Comments
98E452:5:9	15mm diam., 0.16m L	5	—
98E452:5:2	25–35mm diam., 0.97m L	8	Wide last ring
98E452:5:8	*c.* 25mm diam., *c.* 0.55m L	8	Wide last ring

Table 4: Dimensions and ring count for each stake.

Pl. 14:
A view of the stakes in situ *during the laboratory excavation (photo: NMI).*

facets were flat with shallow cutting angles of 30° and *c.* 45°. The shaft was very knotty, and side branches had been broken off. Approximately halfway along the stake was a break where the two halves were found to overlap, with signs of abrasion evident. The stake may have broken when it was driven into the peat, the weight of overlying peat causing the parts to rub and wear. Alternatively, the weight of machinery passing over it may have produced the same effect. The top of the stake was possibly broken. It lay next to the inverted distal femoral epiphysis of the left leg in an area obviously disturbed by the milling machines.

Lying adjacent to and crossing over this stake was a third (98E452:5:8). This stake provided the sample of wood submitted for radiocarbon dating (van der Sanden and van der Plicht, Chapter 6). This was in three parts and extended beneath the area of the left femur and the skin of the right thigh. It sat *c.* 45° off the vertical. Both ends were broken: the upper end recently, and the lower end in antiquity. A single, small facet was identified about midway along the shaft at the edge of a break caused by machine damage. The facet was perhaps a result of the shaft being nicked by a blade rather than chopped or cut through.

The two longest pieces were found to have 8 years' growth and a wide last ring. The latter may indicate that the wood was cut after the growing season, that is, at the end of autumn and before spring. If cut at the same time as the body ended up in the bog, it is possible that the event should be viewed as a late autumn occurrence. However, it is also possible the wood had been cut sometime before and does not indicate the season or timing of the body's immersion in the peat.

The wood assemblage—some comments

The wood assemblage, though small, provides information useful in placing the find within a broader context. The wood species represented are hazel (*Corylus avellana*) and birch (*Betula pendula* or *B. pubescens*). Both are native to Ireland and are frequently found in archaeological contexts, particularly wetland ones, from all periods. Hazel is mostly found as an under-storey tree in mixed oak woodland and can occur in hedges bordering agricultural land. Though tolerant of a wide range of conditions, hazel does not favour waterlogged situations. The two species of birch cannot be distinguished microscopically. Silver birch (*Betula pendula*) thrives in light, sandy soils, preferring dry conditions to wet, but can grow on the margins of raised bogs. Hairy birch (*B. pubescens*) inhabits poor and wet soils and can be found on raised bogs, especially those that may be drying out (Webb *et al.* 1996).

Recent wood-species studies have shown that structural wood found in bogs was more than likely taken from marginal woodlands fringing bogs and/or from the nearest upland (Stuijts 2001). The wood was gathered locally as this was more efficient than bringing wood from greater distances. This may also have been the case with the wood found in association with the bog body. Pollen analysis has shown that hazel was present in the landscape, albeit at a somewhat earlier date (Weir, Chapter 15). It may have been gathered at the margins before the journey into the bog; the withy was most likely made before the journey, with the hazel used taken from nearby woodland or agricultural land. Although the original amount of wood used is not known, the assemblage was relatively small and portable, so transporting it from farther afield may not have been an issue.

The wooden artefacts from Tumbeagh are some of the most intriguing pieces in the puzzle surrounding the presence of the body in Tumbeagh. Are they items carried by the person her-/himself? Were they brought onto the bog by a third party? Can they all be directly associated with the body? The use of stakes to secure a body in peat has prehistoric and medieval parallels in Ireland and elsewhere in Europe (see Chapter 16). These issues are returned to in Chapter 18, where the role that the stakes may have had is given deeper consideration.

A note on the palaeoenvironmental sampling strategy

There were three strands to on-site sampling for palaeoenvironmental purposes: pollen, Coleoptera (beetles) and ash content. Pollen in particular had been used in early bog-body studies (Glob 1969), but it was with Lindow that analyses of pollen and Coleoptera were established as essential elements in the study of bog bodies (Stead *et al.* [1986]; Turner and Scaife 1995). In addition, recent archaeological projects in Irish bogs have used the microscopic record to reconstruct past environments (Caseldine *et al.* 2004), informing the archaeological record and our interpretation of the physical evidence. Hence at Tumbeagh the palaeoenvironmental potential of the project was incorporated in the overall design from the outset. In order to get the most from the samples, the strategy adopted arose from on-site discussions with the relevant specialists.

In terms of pollen, a single peat column was taken from immediately adjacent to the surviving human remains. The objective of the sampling was to obtain pollen records from as close as possible to the surface on which the body lay. This would allow examination of the contemporaneous environment and, given that the column was 1m deep, provide new insight into the broader environment of the preceding centuries (Weir, Chapter 15).

Field samples for coleopteran analysis focused on locations that would elucidate the picture of bog development emerging from the peat stratigraphical survey. Two sample locations were chosen with direct reference to the stratigraphical record in terms of peat types, extent and overall bog development. The first column (B1) was taken from the drain immediately to the east of the findspot, where the development of Tumbeagh from fen to raised bog was preserved (Fig. 3). These deposits were more likely to produce a greater diversity of Coleoptera, providing a better picture of past environmental conditions. The second column (B2) was taken inside Cutting 2 (Fig. 3). The peat stratigraphy showed this area to have been a soak through which the bog drained. The fill of the soak was mainly poorly humified *Sphagnum*. The potential for wider environmental reconstruction from this type of deposit was significantly lower than from the deposits sampled at B1. As a result, analysis concentrated on the sequence at B1 (Reilly, Chapter 14).

The third set of field samples taken was for ash-content analysis. This would provide a measure of the amount of inorganic material in the deposits, allowing their origin to be more closely determined. Again, deposits were selected on the basis of the peat stratigraphical record. Six 1-litre peat samples were taken: three from horizons in the block in which the human remains had been initially isolated, and three from the fen peat and two phases of lake mud (Casparie, Chapter 13). The samples were submitted for analysis to Mr John Reilly of the Horticultural Division of Bord na Móna, with analysis funded by Bord na Móna Energy Ltd.

4.
A shin dig: the laboratory excavation

Nóra Bermingham and Máire Delaney

Protective measures

The laboratory excavation took place in two phases separated by just over three months. A laboratory in the Conservation Department of the National Museum of Ireland, Collins Barracks, hosted the excavation from 26 April to 13 May 1999 and again from 24 August to 3 September 1999. Staging the excavation in two phases enabled us to use the intervening period to evaluate the procedures used in Phase 1 and to make any necessary amendments to our approach.

In formulating the excavation strategy, concern for the preservation of the human remains was a priority. It was considered that storing the peat block in a fridge would keep the remains stable. Removal from the fridge and the reduction of the peat block necessary to retrieve the remains would expose them to decay. Consequently, in order to minimise deterioration, a series of inhibitive measures was devised.

The prevention of dehydration, which would result in shrinkage and make the remains vulnerable to attack from moulds and spores, was a primary concern. The peat block was stored in the fridge at 4°C. Once removed, its temperature was monitored: this never exceeded 13°C and on most days reached only 11°C.

Before the laboratory excavation, the rate of potential temperature increase was unknown. Initially it was envisaged that it might be necessary to return the peat block to the fridge perhaps every 30 to 60 minutes after removal. The remains and the peat, however, proved more resistant than anticipated, allowing longer exposure times, which greatly facilitated the progress of the excavation.

To prohibit dehydration, the peat block and the remains were regularly dampened with deionised water. At the end of every excavation session the block was covered with dampened cloths and polythene, which slowed the rate of evaporation. During daily breaks and at the end of each day the block was returned to the fridge. The cloths used had been soaked in deionised water and boiled in vinegar to extract any acid-soluble pigment. These were then boiled twice in deionised water to remove the vinegar. They were kitchen cloths designed not to shed fibre and were coloured, but the colour did not run on use.

Initially, sterile procedures were observed, but during the excavation it became clear that maintaining sterile conditions was not necessary beyond the usual hygienic standards. Surgical gloves were worn, and any implements used were sterilised and stored in 60% ethyl alcohol before use.

Excavation

To assist the recovery process, a series of X-rays of the entire block were taken before excavation. Unfortunately these yielded little information, leaving the exact layout of the structures within the block unclear (see Delaney and McInerney, Chapter 8). However, the X-rays, combined with the field survey, showed with reasonable certainty that no metal was present.

Before excavation the block was placed on a trolley that served as a platform for excavation and obviated the need to move the block itself, apart from when it was inverted. Initially the wooden frame and foam surround were only partially removed, and then only as necessary to allow the excavation to progress. In this way the stability of the block was ensured, and it was provided with continued protection from dehydration (Pl. 15).

Excavation was by hand and involved surface reduction of the peat block in spits of *c.* 10mm (Pl. 16). Plastic picnic knives and tweezers were used to pull the peat back from skin or bone where fingertips may have exerted too much pressure or in places inaccessible to fingers. If there was any possibility of damaging or displacing the remains, the peat was left in place. For this reason, the displaced toes were not fully exposed. Jets of water from the deionised water spray also helped to remove peat crumbs; we did not have a problem of excess water accumulating.

Phase 1 involved exposure of the upper side of the human remains and associated artefacts. On completion of the record, the remains were left *in situ* lying on the original bed of peat. They were then dampened, covered in damp cloths and wrapped in cling film. Peat retained from the excavation was then applied, and the block was covered in polythene and returned to the fridge.

So that the underside of the remains could be examined without their having to be lifted or disturbed, it was excavated from below. This involved inversion of the peat block through further excavation and the application of a new foam shell and was undertaken during Phase 2 of the excavation.

Before the block was inverted, the upper side was fully exposed so that the state of preservation could be checked. Conditions had not changed appreciably. The upper side was then directly covered with damp peat, and the entirety was wrapped in cling film and encased in a foam shell inside a cardboard frame. This proved simpler than the approach taken with Lindow Man (Stead [1986]), where a fibreglass mount made from bandages and quick-drying resin was used to support the body on inversion. With Tumbeagh the peat packing and the foam were easier to apply than bandages, and the peat ensured the continued protection of the remains from dehydration and contamination during the excavation of the underside. When hardened, the foam shell was cut from the original peat block and inverted. The mould of peat and foam absorbed any pressure exerted by the inverted peat block, so the human remains were

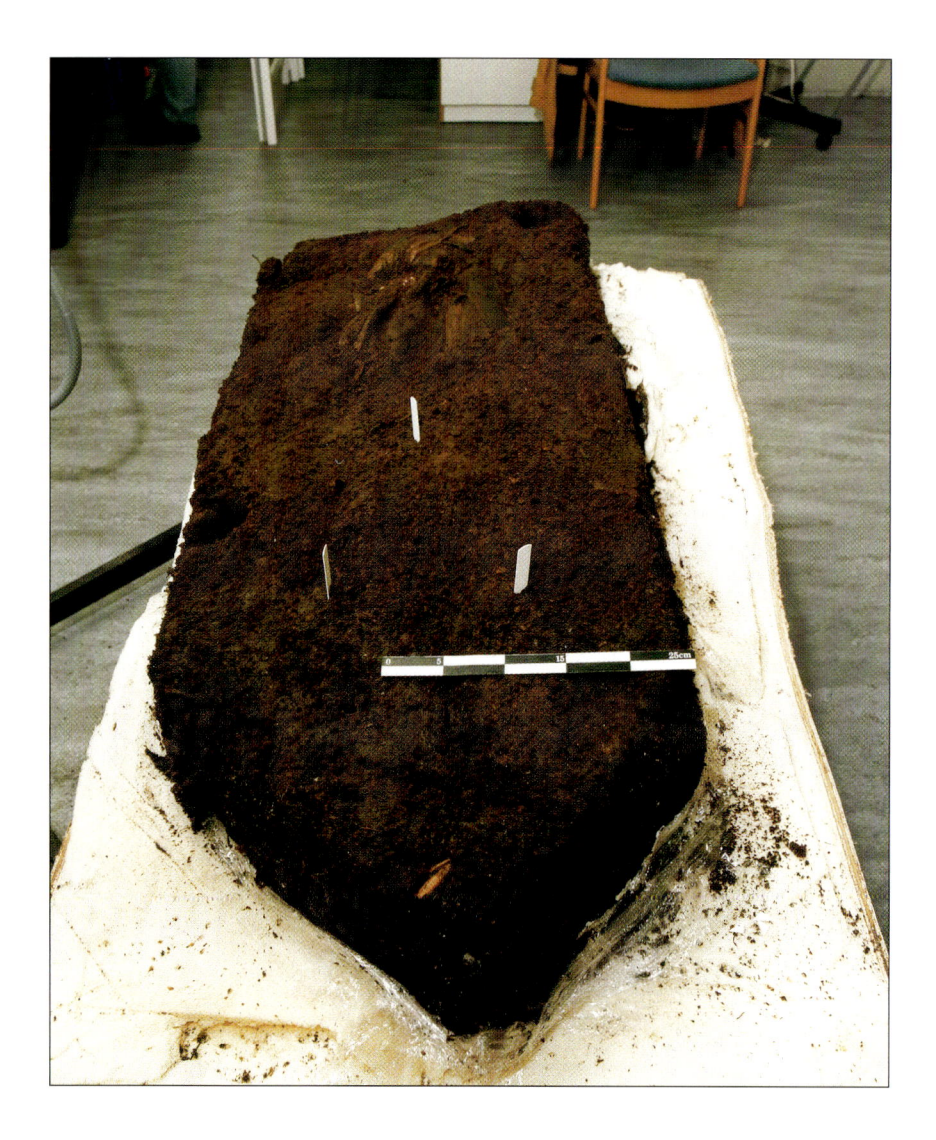

Pl. 15:
The foam shell has been removed and the peat surface prepared for further excavation. The three white tags mark pH test locations. A fragment of hazel brushwood is visible in the foreground (photo: NMI).

not put at risk of displacement or compression. There was some very slight compaction of the peat surrounding the human remains, but this did not impinge on them in any way.

The drawn record
Conventional archaeological drawing methods were employed to produce plans and profiles of the human remains after another method, which was hoped would require no physical contact with the surviving remains, was applied. Initially, a gridded perspex drawing board (1m by 1m by 0.01m) affixed to four legs was placed directly over the peat block in line with a set of fixed points. Small spirit levels on the corners of the board enabled a horizontal plane to be maintained. The underlying image was traced onto acetate with wipe-off felt markers and then onto the perspex itself. The image was then transferred onto permatrace to produce a pencil drawing, and the perspex was wiped clean, ready for reuse.

A shin dig: the laboratory excavation

This approach was only moderately successful, however. The image recorded was slightly distorted, as it proved difficult to maintain a vertical position over the peat block. To overcome this problem, a laser pen was then used in an attempt to ensure that the points recorded were consistently vertical. The laser pen was held in one hand while the other hand was used to mark with a dot the point selected for recording. The dots could then be joined freely. This procedure was awkward, however, and the drawings produced had a lesser but still unacceptable degree of distortion.

Because of the difficulties encountered, all subsequent drawings were completed using offsets. More time than originally envisaged was spent on completing the drawings. Though not ideal given the time involved (around 5 days), this approach did not have any apparent adverse affect on the human remains, as measures necessary for the continued protection and preservation of the remains were rigorously enforced. In addition, detailed accurate drawings of the physical remains were produced easily and at no great expense.

After the laboratory excavation, it was discovered that a mounted laser pen, acetate and a perspex drawing board are used with great success in the Maritime Institute, Roskilde, Denmark, for drawing ships' timbers (F. Rieck, pers. comm.). In terms of the Tumbeagh remains, it is probable that modification of the technique

Pl. 16:
Excavation proceeded from the edges of the block towards the middle (photo: NMI).

attempted—for example, by inserting the laser pen in a freestanding vertical mount as at Roskilde—would have worked well and produced accurate 1:1 drawings more quickly. The suitability to other bog bodies of a modified version of the first technique or of the drawing system finally used may depend on the preservation of the body and the facilities/resources available. More complex systems of recording have been employed elsewhere: for example, the use of photogrammetry in recording Lindow Man (Lindsey [1986]). In the case of Tumbeagh, where the surviving human remains were limited and lacked the complexity of a complete body, a simpler approach was both appropriate and sufficient. The drawings produced from the Tumbeagh find are distinguished in that few such drawings of bog bodies have been made or published.

Results

Phase 1
The peat block was rectangular, tapering to a point at the southern end, and was 1.18m long, 0.43m wide and *c.* 0.50m deep. The visible remains were concentrated in its northern end (Pl. 15). The proximal half of the left tibia, which lay directly on the skin of the left lower leg, was evident. Adjacent to this was the right leg, represented by the skin of the lower thigh and the shin and the proximal epiphyses of the right tibia. Near the apex of the southern end a small foot bone and a fragment of brushwood were present. The remains were oriented approximately north-north-west/south-south-east (Fig. 13).

On removal of the redeposited peat, it was observed that a very small patch of mould that had developed on the original exposed skin of the right thigh was no longer present. The chemical properties of the peat placed directly onto the affected skin prevented the continued development of the mould and caused it to die. The mould was not found during Phase 1 of the excavation.

Small white insect larvae were observed on the remains, particularly around the adipocere. They were present in the peat when the block was lifted in the field and were not recent contaminants. Within a short time of first being observed, the larvae were no longer visible. They have been provisionally identified as springtails (J. O'Connor, pers. comm.) and did not appear to have had a detrimental effect on the remains: storage in peat packing in a fridge had made them dormant. Springtails have been found on other types of bog finds—including bog butter, leather objects, wooden vessels and wood—that have been removed from the bog and stored elsewhere.

It was necessary to remove 30–50mm of peat to expose the full extent of the surviving remains. Initially, only the human remains were exposed (Pl. 17). The stake in the north-eastern corner was left covered until we were confident that its removal would not destabilise the peat block. Further excavation revealed additional brushwood fragments close to the knees.

Peat in direct contact with the human remains was sampled for coleopteran and dating analysis. Peat taken from off the right and the left leg was sampled separately, as was peat from the feet, in order to discern any differences in the nature of the bog and the conditions in which the body eventually became immersed (Reilly, Chapter 14).

Pl. 17:
The upper side of the surviving human remains (photo: NMI).

At the end of Phase 1 of the excavation the legs were covered with dampened cloths, wrapped in cling film and then covered in peat before being returned to the fridge. Damp cloths had been chosen as the protective covering to obviate the need to re-clean the remains in Phase 2 and to establish their effectiveness as a short-term protective measure. It was found that this approach was not satisfactory because the cloths quickly dried out and that peat placed directly on the legs provided the best protection.

The bog body from Tumbeagh

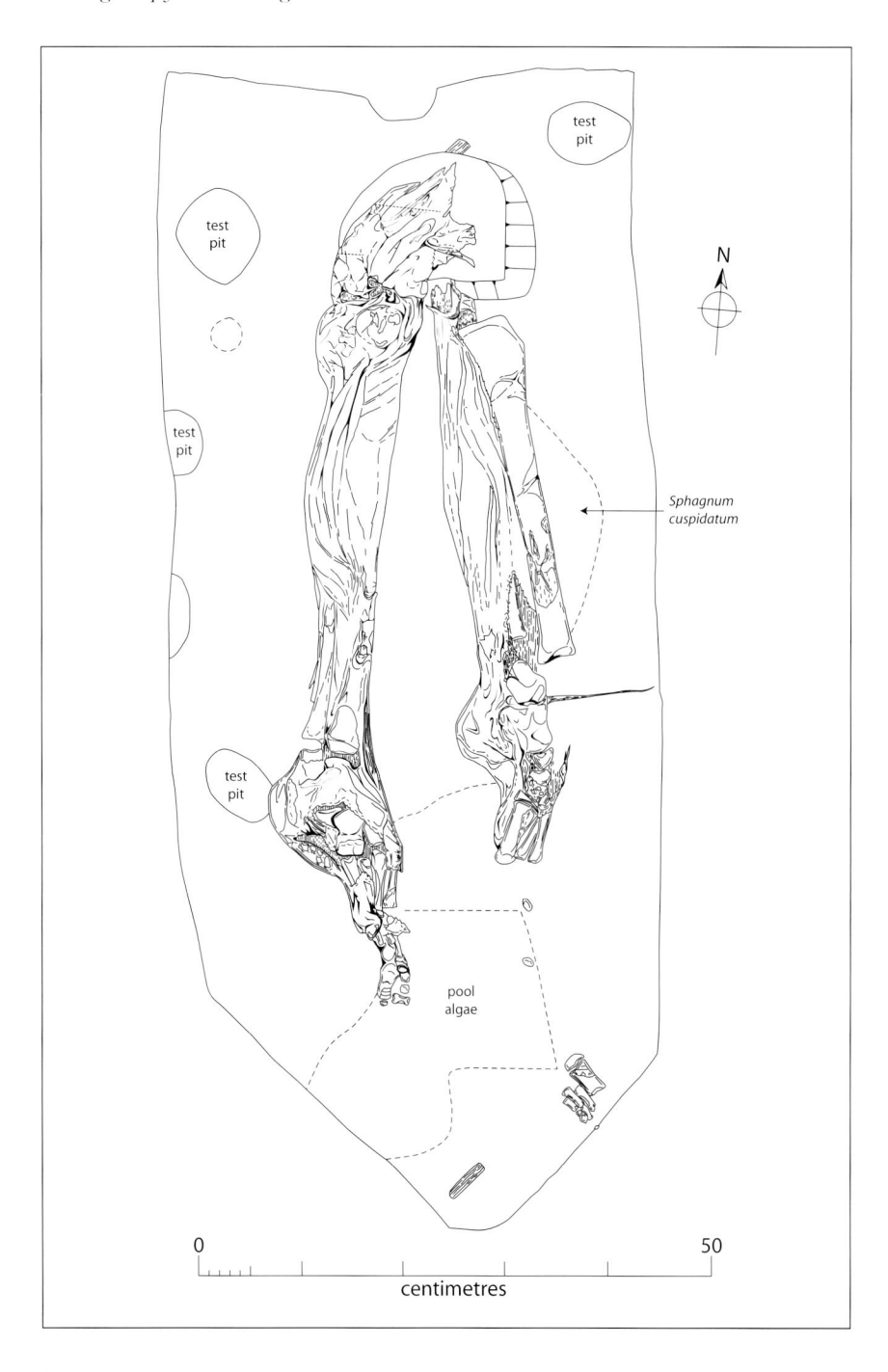

Fig. 13:
The upper side of the surviving human remains.

Phase 2
There was a period of just over three months between the two phases of excavation. On the removal of the protective layers of damp cloths and peat applied in Phase 1, minor superficial changes in the condition of the remains were observed. However, the overall condition had not significantly changed since the find was made in September 1998. There was a small patch of mould on the outer edge of the blackened skin of the right thigh and some minor surface dehydration of the

46

Fig. 14: The underside of the surviving human remains.

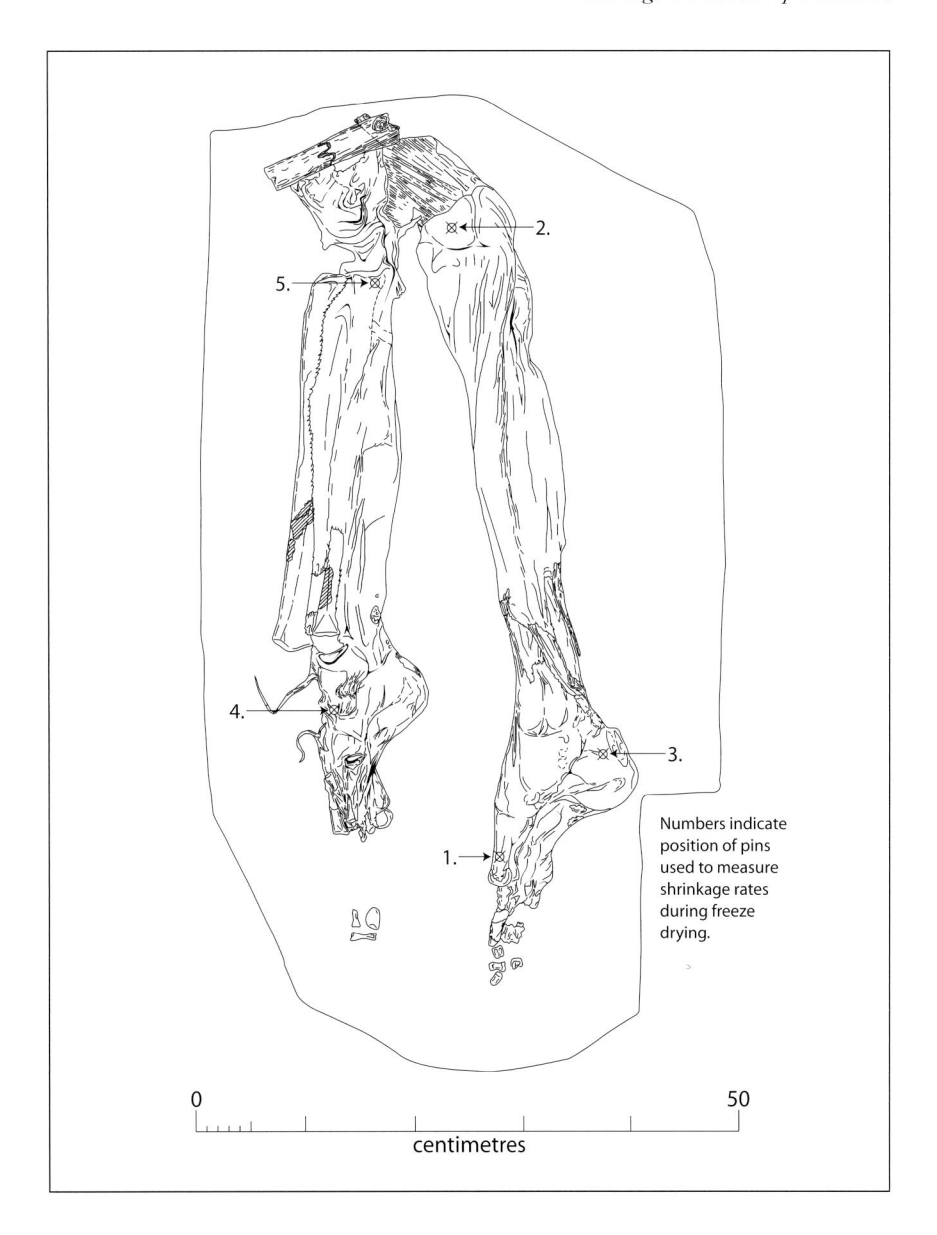

Numbers indicate position of pins used to measure shrinkage rates during freeze drying.

adipocere deposits in the right foot. Springtails were present in and around the depressions surrounding the right proximal tibia and associated adipocere, but they died off within 1.5 hours. Neither of the insect manifestations in Phases 1 and 2 caused visible deterioration of the remains. Their presence, however, should be kept in mind as a source of modern contamination when newer, more sophisticated methods of analysis are developed.

The inverted peat block was 0.86m long, 0.34m wide and *c.* 0.25m deep. Excavation and sampling followed the same procedures used in Phase 1 (Pl. 18). The lower surface of the legs was fully exposed, as were the pieces of wood that had been left *in situ* in Phase 1 (Pl. 18; Fig. 14). No additional artefacts were found.

The state of preservation of the underside was not significantly different from that of the upper side (Pls 17, 18). There was more skin cover over the foot soles and

The bog body from Tumbeagh

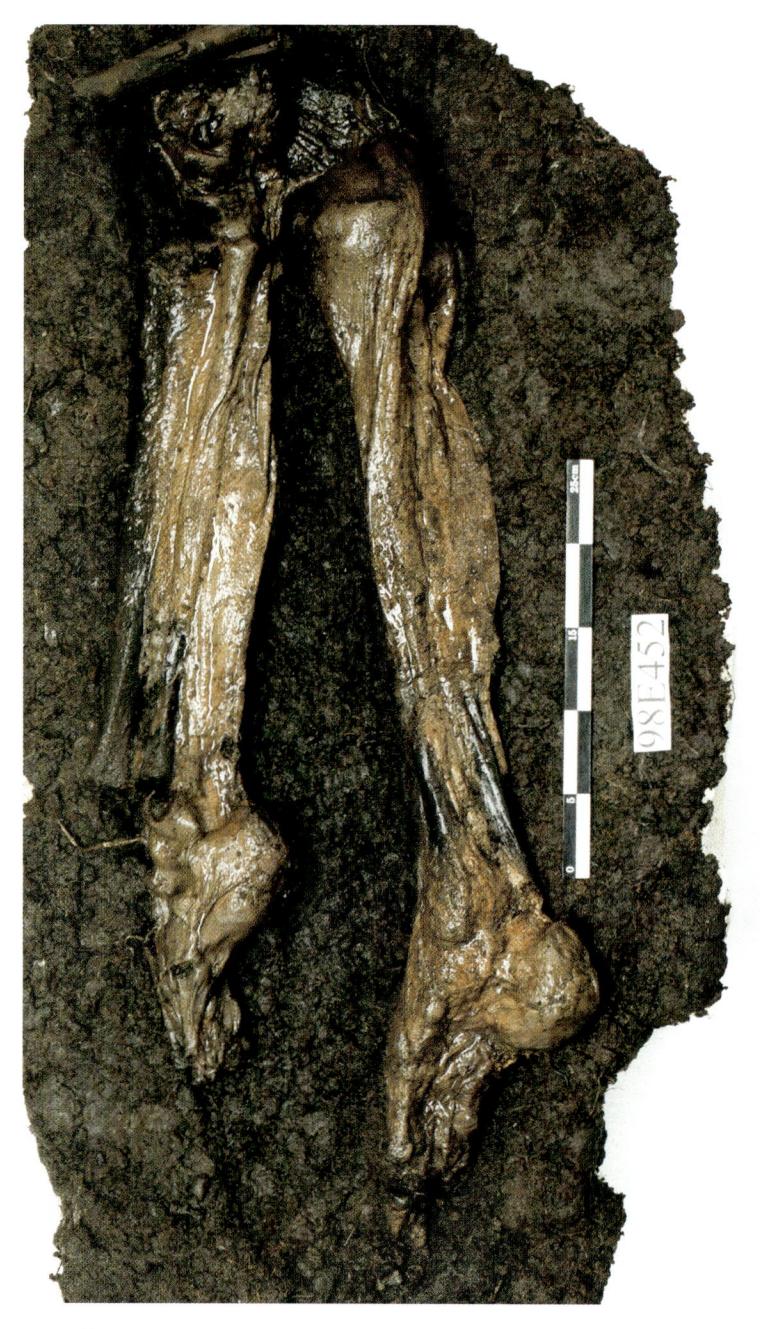

*Pl. 18:
The underside of the surviving human remains (photo: NMI).*

slightly more infiltration of peat into the skin. There were variations in the colour of the skin, with a slight overall difference between the two sides: both were beige/brown, but the underside had more yellow and pink tones (see Chapter 7).

Comments

The human remains had survived very well since first being exposed in April 1999. There was no marked shrinkage, distortion or discoloration. Covering them directly with wet peat was considered to provide a better protective mantle than dampened cloths and cling film as the peat prevents the growth of mould and retains moisture better than cloth.

Since the completion of Phase 2 of excavation, peat has been removed from parts of the surviving remains on at least three occasions. There has been no observable mould growth, dehydration or distortion through shrinkage, and springtails were not visible on these occasions. The covering peat is regularly dampened with deionised water and re-covered with black polythene, which traps evaporation and returns it to the peat block as condensation, a simple but effective way of maintaining moisture levels before conservation. In this way the remains are kept close to their original state, reducing the likelihood of interference with the applicability or results of tests or dating.

Several lessons were learned from the long and intermittent excavation process. There was no evidence that the non-sterile conditions of the field excavation had produced any deleterious effects. Sterile conditions, beyond usual hygienic standards, are not necessary for maintenance of the remains. Obviously, however, if samples were to be taken for microbial analysis, sterility of the material collected would be vital. In the presence of solid peat and deionised water, there is no need to maintain acidity artificially. Atmospheric and temperature variation did not cause deterioration, nor did the occasional presence of up to twelve people in the room (mostly visitors and press). All of the above proved possible as the human remains, altered by the preservation process, showed an inherent resistance to change. This allowed for flexibility in the scheduling of the laboratory analysis of the human remains, at least in the relative short term. In the future it will also allow speedier excavation and recording and enable remains from bogs to be rescued rapidly without the need to wait for ideal storage conditions (see Chapter 10). As a cautionary note, each body is likely to present different conditions of preservation. This, and the possibility of modern contamination, has to be assessed in each individual case. Nonetheless, the Tumbeagh excavations have provided some valuable lessons for modern approaches to the excavation of bog bodies.

5.
The conservation of the Tumbeagh bog body

Rolly Read

Shortly after its discovery, a conservator from the National Museum of Ireland supervised the lifting of the bog body from the find site. The approximate location of the remains had been worked out by digging a series of test-pits around it to define its limits (Fig. 7; Pl. 8), and it was decided to lift the body in a block of peat that could be excavated fully under laboratory conditions rather than excavate it in the field (see Chapter 3). To this end, during the excavation, the body was isolated on a pedestal of peat that was to be removed with it; this measured 1.2m by 0.6m by 0.5m. Weight was an important consideration owing to the density of waterlogged peat. The estimated weight of the block taken was approximately 350kg. Waterlogged peat weighs *c.* 1 tonne per cubic metre.

The pedestal of peat was undercut as far as was felt to be safe, given the working conditions, and the part of the pedestal containing the bog body was wrapped in a thick layer of cling film to act as an intervention layer. A box constructed from plywood was placed around the pedestal. The cavity between the pedestal and the plywood box was then filled with two-part expanding polyurethane foam (Pls 9, 10). This substance, initially mixed as two liquids in equal measure, expands to 30 times its original volume and sets into a rigid foam. The foam filled the gap between the pedestal and the box, gripping the pedestal, and formed a solid roof to the structure, which when inverted was capable of supporting the weight of peat to be taken with the body.

The base of the pedestal was then cut through using a knife and a saw, and the block of peat thus formed was quickly rolled over onto its back, resting securely in its nest of foam. The block was then lifted by hand (a particularly difficult undertaking) onto a forklift attachment fitted to a vehicle specially adapted for use on the bogs. After removal from the bog, the pedestal was transported to Dublin, where it was deposited in a walk-in fridge in the Conservation Department of the National Museum of Ireland.

It was decided to keep the bog body refrigerated but not to freeze it. This decision was based on anecdotal evidence that the last bog body to be dealt with in Ireland, Meenybraddan Woman, had suffered visible deterioration whenever it was thawed out from the frozen state in which it was kept while in storage. Instead, we tried to replicate the conditions that had given rise to the preservation of the remains in the first place. During storage, the bog body was kept encapsulated in waterlogged peat from the site at which it was found and wrapped in plastic to keep evaporation to a minimum. This maintained the body in a wet state and kept in constant supply the agents of preservation that were present in the peat. The body was kept refrigerated at 4°C to slow down the rate of evaporation of water, as well as any deterioration that may have occurred under these conditions. The peat was kept waterlogged by the addition of deionised water at regular intervals.

The upper side of the body was the first to be excavated in the laboratory by slowly cutting back the support (see Chapter 4). When recording was complete, the area of the remains that had been exposed was covered in wet peat and then cling film. A support of two-part expanding polyurethane foam was cast onto the block. This was considerably smaller than the first foam support that was produced in the field, since it followed the shape of the surviving remains rather than the area that was established as safe to lift without causing damage to the body.

The underside of the remains was then excavated. After excavation and recording, the bog body was covered in a thick layer of waterlogged peat and a layer of plastic sheeting to keep evaporation to a minimum. It was then returned to the fridge for storage, with periodic wetting of the peat with deionised water, while the conservation techniques to be used for its long-term preservation were investigated and prepared.

During four years of storage in these conditions, no visible deterioration of the bog body occurred. A colony of springtail larvae (a regular feature of wet bog finds in Ireland) that appeared in the three months after excavation was found to have vanished at the next viewing six months later, having done no apparent damage to the body. Mould was observed at various points on wooden stakes pushed into the peat around the body as reference points, but this did not extend to the peat or to the bog body, which appear to have continued their resistance to mould because of the maintenance of their burial environment. This is certainly the storage technique that we would use if faced with the same situation in the future.

When all of the investigative work had been completed, the bog body was conserved by freeze-drying according to the protocol established by the British Museum for the treatment of Lindow Man and Meenybraddan Woman (Omar *et al.* 1989). This decision was based on an informal survey of bog bodies from Europe, which had been conserved in a variety of ways (Brothwell 1986). Our survey concluded that freeze-drying was the most successful treatment that had been applied to such remains to date.

The bog body was uncovered from its peat and thoroughly cleaned using deionised water and hand tools. It was then covered in a layer of cling film to protect it while a support was made. The support was produced using Cellacast Xtra casting-tape bandages. These are resin-impregnated bandages, developed as a substitute for plaster of Paris in making casts for broken limbs and harden on contact with water. The bandages were applied to the upper surface of the remains in a number of layers, each running perpendicular to the last, to provide strength. The whole was then turned over onto the new support, and the other side was thoroughly cleaned.

The remains were held securely onto the resin bandage support by being covered in a fine, undyed polyester net bound with unbleached, undyed calico tape and then immersed in a solution of 15% polyethylene glycol (PEG) 400 in deionised water for impregnation. The 15% PEG 400 solution was selected as the most appropriate grade and percentage based on experimental work carried out on skin before the treatment of Lindow Man (Lindow II) and on bone (Ellam 1984).

The impregnation in 15% PEG 400 took 28 days, during which time the condition of the legs was regularly monitored. The PEG solution became discoloured as the peat stain leached slightly out of the remains. As a consequence, the net and calico tape were removed and repositioned on three occasions to avoid any risk of darker stripes appearing on the conserved remains.

At the end of the impregnation period the human remains were removed from the solution and the excess PEG was removed, together with the calico and netting. The remains were left on their resin bandage support. Stainless-steel entomological pins (too fine to leave a visible hole) were pushed into the remains at key locations, and the distances between them were measured to monitor shrinkage (Fig. 14).

The legs were frozen to −22°C and left for 24 hours at this temperature. A vacuum was applied, and they were then freeze-dried for a period of 31 days, with the specimen chamber maintained at a constant −22°C and the condensation chamber at −50°C. The remains were then removed from the freeze-drier and left to adjust to the ambient environment (controlled to 20°C and 55% relative humidity). Cleaning was then completed with the removal of fragments of peat that had become visible because of the treatment.

Overall, the treatment was very successful, with minimal shrinkage (*c.* 2 per cent), and produced remains that, though dry and less flexible than in the wet state, were visually very acceptable (Table 5). The texture of the skin and the even, pale brown hue typical of freshly uncovered bog bodies remained, although the body was lighter in colour. There was no visual dimensional change.

Six months after treatment, after storage in a dark, humidity-controlled store, there has been no visual change in the remains.

Points	Distance between points (cm) Before treatment	After treatment	% shrinkage
1–2	55.5	54.0	2.7
1–3	13.9	13.8	0.7
1–4	22.0	21.5	2.3
1–5	53.3	52.0	2.4
2–3	47.2	46.0	2.5
3–4	25.9	25.6	1.2
4–2	41.6	40.8	1.9
4–5	36.6	35.8	2.2

Table 5: Percentage shrinkage resulting from conservation.

6.
Resolving time: the radiocarbon dates

W.A.B. van der Sanden and J. van der Plicht

As is so often the case with bog bodies (van der Sanden 1996, 93), the human remains that were found in 1998 in Tumbeagh were not associated with datable objects. Research carried out by Ó Floinn (1995a; 1995b) indicates that a large proportion of Irish bog bodies are relatively young, that is, of late medieval or modern date. Ó Floinn came to this conclusion on the basis of research into surviving fragments of clothing and (in the case of the paper bodies, that is, bodies known from documentary record only) descriptions of associated artefacts and clothing. However, the modest number of radiocarbon dates from Irish bog bodies indicates that they cover a much longer time-span (Brindley and Lanting 1995). The earliest radiocarbon date is from the Neolithic (Stoney Island: 5210 ± 50 BP), and the latest one is from the medieval period (Meenybraddan: 730 ± 90 BP). The only way to obtain a reliable date for the Tumbeagh bog body, therefore, was ^{14}C analysis of a selected number of samples.

In 2001 three samples were submitted to the Centrum voor Isotopen Onderzoek (CIO) of Groningen University (Table 6):

(1) peat originating from directly under the calf of the left leg (98E452:30);
(2) a fragment of one of the brushwood stakes found under the lower right thigh (98E452:5:8b); its position beneath the remains is dubious as the stake was broken and may originally have lain above the remains (see Chapters 4 and 18);
(3) a fragment of skin from the body itself; the sample comes from the posterio-medial aspect of the right leg in the region of the knee or lower thigh (98E452:45).

Dating these three samples was part of a research project on the reliability of radiocarbon dates of bog bodies (van der Plicht *et al.* 2004). From the radiocarbon point of view, bog bodies comprise special material because the peat contains natural tanning agents. This indicates that contamination with foreign carbon (humics) is significant, resulting in continuing debates about the reliability of ^{14}C dates for bog bodies (Housley *et al.* 1995).

Radiocarbon samples routinely undergo chemical pre-treatment in order to select the datable fraction and to remove contamination by foreign carbon. Standard treatment is called AAA (acid/alkali/acid) (Mook and Streurman 1983). The first

Sample	Treatment	Lab code	^{14}C age (BP)	δ^{13}C (‰)
Peat	AAA	GrA-14393	765±35	−24.23
	None	GrA-14305	880±30	−25.85
Wood	AAA	GrA-15314	545±45	−25.37
	None	GrA-14304	345±30	−27.58
Skin	AAA	GrA-15627	430±60	−23.04
	None	GrA-15628	790±60	−25.47

Table 6: Accelerator mass spectrometry dating results.

(acid) step dissolves soil carbonates (containing old carbon) and infiltrated humic/fulvic acids from the sample; the second (alkali) step removes compounds such as infiltrated tannic acids; and the third (acid) step removes any CO_2 absorbed during the second step.

The carbon yield (%C) and the stable carbon isotope ratio (δ^{13}C) values are, in general, indicators of the quality of the pre-treatment and/or the reliability of the ^{14}C date.

We conclude that, not surprisingly, the fully treated (AAA) samples yield the most reliable results. All of the AAA-treated samples have higher δ^{13}C values than the corresponding untreated samples. Without treatment, the skin gives a much older measurement; this is expected, because the (older) humic contaminants are not removed. We consider the AAA-treated skin date as the best ^{14}C date obtainable; it is also a 'direct' date (that is, from the body itself). For the 'indirect' sample materials, the (AAA-treated) peat has the oldest date and the (AAA-treated) wood is older than the body. This makes it a consistent series. The radiocarbon dates are calibrated using INTCAL98 (Stuiver and van der Plicht 1998) in order to obtain calendar ages. The calibrated dates indicate that the peat was formed in the thirteenth century (cal. AD 1215–1290, 2-sigma range), the wood dates to the fourteenth to early fifteenth century (cal. AD 1305–1440) and the body dates to the fifteenth to seventeenth century (cal. AD 1405–1635). The last calibration is rather imprecise because of the large 'wiggle' in the calibration curve during this time period, hampering precise (calibrated) dating of samples from the last 500–600 years.

The conclusion of the radiocarbon dating is that the human remains found in Tumbeagh Bog are those of a relatively recent bog body. It does not belong to the group of prehistoric bodies that has been associated with ritual sacrifices (van der Sanden 1996). Tumbeagh Woman/Man lived in the fifteenth or sixteenth century AD (based on the middle of the dating range) and may have ended up in the bog for a variety of reasons (van der Sanden 2000).

A note on the radiocarbon dates from Tumbeagh
Nóra Bermingham

The samples returned from Groningen were the first samples from the excavation to be dated. A few years later, as part of the palaeoenvironmental component of the project, further dating of peat samples from the site was funded by the Heritage Council and Bord na Móna. Table 7 lists all of the dates obtained from Tumbeagh. The dates are presented to two standard deviations (2 sigma); at times throughout this book, however, the mid-point of the calibrated range is cited rather than the full dating range.

The results returned for the samples of skin and wood subjected to dating require some further discussion. The wood has returned a seemingly older date than the skin from the body. This may suggest that the wood pre-dates the body and cannot be associated with it. Given, however, the uncertainties presented by radiocarbon dating, the results are not inconsistent. Ideally, the dating ranges would overlap within 1 sigma (68%), and they almost do: 545–45=500 BP and 430+60=490 BP. They overlap within 2 sigma, and therefore the dates from the wood and the skin can be considered consistent within 2 sigma (J. van der Plicht, pers. comm.). Dating therefore shows that there is a 95% chance that the peat and the skin fall within the same dating range; therefore, they may be considered contemporaneous.

Sample type	Sample code	Lab. code	Years BP (uncalibrated)	Calibrated (2σ)	Calibrated mid-point	$\delta^{13}C$ (‰)
Peat	98E452-basal	†Wk-12086	5417±90	6400 BP–5950 BP	4300 BC	–29.00
Peat	98E452-1	†UCD-01108	2540±60	815 (779) 411 BC	779 BC	–23.00
Peat	TUM 84–9	*UB-4692	2390±44	760–392 BC	407 BC	–27.413
Peat	TUM 60–3	*UB-4693	1928±44	35 BC–AD 142	AD 73	–26.611
Peat	98E452-2	† UCD-01109	1800±60	AD 77–391	AD 240	–23.00
Peat	TUM 29–32	*UB-4694	1642±43	AD 260–543	AD 410	–26.937
Peat	98E452-3	†UCD-01110	1595±50	AD 344 (432) 598	AD 430	–23.00
Peat	98E452:30	°GrA-14393	765±35	AD 1215–1290	AD 1250	–24.23
Wood	98E452:8b	°GrA-15314	545±45	AD 1305–1440	AD 1370	–25.37
Skin	98E452:45	°GrA-15627	430±60	AD 1405–1635	AD 1500	–23.04

*Table 7: The full list of sample dates from Tumbeagh in chronological order. Calibration reference: Stuiver and Polach 1977. † = Stuiver and Reimer 1993; * = Stuiver and Pearson 1986; ° = Stuiver and van der Plicht 1998.*

II.

THE SURVIVING HUMAN REMAINS

7.
Anatomy of the legs

Máire Delaney

In this chapter a detailed description of the surviving remains from Tumbeagh is presented. These remains are the latest published fresh remains in Europe. The last bog-body find to be as carefully excavated and described was Lindow Man (Stead *et al.* [1986]). Meenybraddan Woman was discovered in 1978 but was not systematically excavated: the body was examined and described some seven years later, having been frozen in the interim (Delaney and Ó Floinn 1995). There are many similarities in the appearance of these bodies. One of the more interesting observations made of the Tumbeagh remains was that the skin retained a pinkish colour. Meenybraddan Woman, when investigated by the author in 1985, was dark and brownish. There was some lightening of the colour after freeze-drying in 1985, and the appearance had not changed radically when the remains were reinspected in 1992.

The medical description of the Tumbeagh remains is divided into a number of sections. A glossary of the terms used is presented first (Table 8). This is followed by a series of tables detailing the various elements revealed in both the field and the laboratory excavation (Tables 9–12). A summary description is then presented. Finally, for readers interested in greater anatomical detail, the upper and lower aspect of each leg is described separately; in each case the description proceeds from above the knee downward.

Terminology

Term	Definition
Proximal	The part or parts nearest the head
Distal	The part or parts farthest from the head
Anterior	Toward the front
Posterior	Toward the back
Superior	Toward the head
Inferior	Away from the head
Proximal	The part or parts nearest the head
Lateral	Toward or away from the mid-plane of the body

Table 8: The main terms used in the description.

Term	Definition
Medial	Toward or closer to the mid-plane of the body
Thigh	Area above the knee joint: minimal in this case
Knee region	The area around the knee joint: poorly delineated in these remains
Leg	The region between the knee and the ankle joint
Ankle region	The area around the ankle joint
Foot incl. toes	Tarses, metatarses and phalanges
Plantar flexion	The position of the foot when the toes are pointed or when standing on one's toes
Epiphysis	The end of an immature long bone that remains separate from the shaft until the bone matures and the ends fuse
Diaphysis	The shaft of the bone
Metaphysis	The end of the immature shaft adjacent to the epiphysis

Table 8 (contd): The main terms used in the description.

Results

Tables 9 and 10 list the parts of the body found *in situ*. These are not all intact: some have been observed either in initial X-ray or as impressions beneath overlying skin. Recent imaging has clarified the presence or absence of structures not visible to the naked eye (see Chapter 8).

Bone	Right	Left
Femur	a	a
Distal femoral epiphysis	a	p
Tibia	p	p
Proximal tibial epiphysis	a	a
Distal tibial epiphysis	p	p
Fibula (including epiphyses)	p	p
Calcaneus	p	p
Talus	p	p
Navicular	—	p
Cuboid	p	p*
Medial cuneiform	p*	a
Intermediate cuneiform	p*	p*
Lateral cuneiform	p	p
Metatarsal I	1	p
Metatarsal II	p	p
Metatarsal III	p	p
Metatarsal IV	p	p
Metatarsal V	p	p
Phalanges 1	I, II, III, IV	ex situ
Phalanges 2	ex situ	ex situ
Phalanges 3	ex situ	ex situ

Table 9: Parts of the body found in situ. *a = absent, p = present, ★ = presumed to be present.*

Type of tissue	Right	Left
Skin	Lower thigh	Lower thigh
	Knee	Knee
	Lower leg	Lower leg
	Foot	Foot
Adipocere	Knee	
	Ankle	Ankle
	Foot	Foot
Tendons	Unidentified long extensor and flexor tendons of the foot	Unidentified long extensor and flexor tendons of the foot
	Achilles tendon	Achilles tendon
Cartilage	Articular surface of head of first and fourth metatarsals	Lateral cuneiform and head of fourth metatarsal
	Distal phalanx of great toe	
Muscle	None identified	None identified
Nails	None *in situ*	None *in situ*

Table 10: Soft tissue parts present in situ.

The elements listed in Table 11 were found mostly in a slightly disturbed situation near their original position. These remains had been moved by natural shift and by the action of peat-milling machinery. Fragments found farther away are listed in Table 12.

Body part	Findspot
Right	
Distal epiphysis femur (fragment)	Close to field surface
Phalanges great toe	Slightly disturbed
Phalanges (middle and distal)	Slightly disturbed
Nail great toe and others unidentified	Among disturbed phalanges
Left	
Distal epiphysis femur (fragment)	Close to field surface
Navicular	Disturbed peat field surface
Medial cuneiform	Disturbed peat field surface
Intermediate cuneiform	Close to field surface
Phalanges great toe	Slightly disturbed
Phalanges (middle and distal)	Slightly disturbed
General/unsided	
Skin fragments	Disturbed peat field surface
Adipocere (several scattered crumbs)	Disturbed peat field surface

Table 11: Body parts found in the vicinity of the in situ *remains.*

Body part	Location
Right	
Tibia: fragment of proximal epiphysis and attached skin	Stockpile
Femur: distal epiphysis	Field 1
Left	
Patella	Stockpile
Tibia: proximal epiphysis	Stockpile
Intermediate cuneiform	Field 1
General/unsided	
Skin fragments	Stockpile and Field 1
Lumbar vertebra	Stockpile
Rib (side uncertain)	Adjacent field surface
Adipocere crumbs	Field 1

Table 12: Body parts found distant from the in situ *remains.*

Position

When the excavation was completed, it was clear that both legs were present. All that survived was from just above the knee downward (Figs 13, 14; Pls 17, 18). The legs lay on their left side with the left leg below the right. The right knee seemed to have lain almost directly above the left knee in the original position. The left leg was lying anterior to the right leg. The feet were plantar flexed, that is, they were pointing downward. The right leg was probably less flexed than the left. The right leg appeared longer than the left (Pl. 18). There were, however, no pathological indications that this had been the case in life. This appearance was enhanced by the obvious distraction of the toe bones. The most likely position that can be extrapolated from the remains is one of slight flexion lying on the left side (Fig. 6b).

General description of the tissues

The tissues identified were skin, bone, tendon and adipocere. Unidentified tissues were:

(a) probably hyaline cartilage represented by a tan, shiny substance seen on the articular surfaces of some phalanges; hyaline cartilage coats the articular surface of bones in a synovial joint, ensuring smooth movement of the joint (Pl. 19);
(b) probably periosteum represented by slightly raised, pale, soft patches on the shafts of some of the long bones (Pl. 20);
(c) a very fine, slimy membrane seen on parts of the shin, which remains unidentified.

The various tissues had a similar appearance wherever they occurred. The skin overall was pinkish-beige, although there were darker and lighter areas. Hair follicles were visible, but the hairs seemed to have fallen out. The follicles were arrow-shaped orange

Anatomy of the legs

Pl. 19: The upper side of the right foot. Hyaline cartilage is visible on the ends of the phalanx and carpal bones. The nail bed of the little toe is visible, and other toenails lie close to the tip of the foot (photo: NMI).

spots surrounded by slightly pearly, grey/pink areas. They were visible on the legs but not on the feet. Papillary ridges were visible on both feet. The skin was tough and pliable, with the consistency of Nubuk leather. The flap of skin that had been exposed in the bog was almost black and was hard but not brittle. This is similar to the skin of other bog bodies that have dried out naturally, a good example of which is the body from Gallagh (van der Sanden 1996).

The bone was dark brown. As with all bog bodies immersed in an acid environment, it was very decalcified and it bent on the application of pressure. There was no major deformation of the bone as sometimes occurs in the bog, especially if a heavy object such as a stake is placed over it, as seen in the Haraldskær body, also known as Queen Gunhild (van der Sanden 1996). The long bones had longitudinal striations. This is a common finding in bone recovered from the bog (M. Delaney, unpublished data).

63

Pl. 20:
Detail of the left tibia. A patch of what may be periosteum is visible close to the distal end of the bone (photo: NMI).

The tendons were beige but retained some of the iridescent quality that they have in life. A few toenails, notably the nail from the left great toe, were present. These were brown and soft and were found near but not in close association with the toes from which they came (Pl. 17). This displacement was also noted in the Lindow body (Brothwell 1986). In the case of the Tumbeagh body, the peat-milling machinery may have contributed to this.

Adipocere (fat that has undergone a chemical change called hydrolysis) was present in small quantities. The largest accumulations were on the sole of the foot, particularly the heel. In life this is an area of dense connective tissue that cushions the calcaneus (heel) bone. Adipocere was also noted in the region of the knee and the right ankle, but the amounts were not large. It had the usual dirty white, crumbly appearance of adipocere from bog bodies.

Apart from bone and adipocere, there seemed to be no bulky tissue beneath the skin. Muscle was apparently absent. This caused the skin to fall into longitudinal folds (Pl. 17). The combination of the overlying pressure of the bog, the virtual disappearance of muscle, and the settling of bone when released from the support of muscle and tendon had resulted in the legs being extremely flattened. They occupied less than 50mm in a vertical plane in the bog except where there were deep indentations as described below. This flattening is a feature of bog bodies and can be seen in most examples (Glob 1969; van der Sanden 1996). Damage to the remains seems to have occurred in the recent past rather than in the peri-mortem period or in antiquity.

Description of the surface uppermost in the bog

Right leg
The lateral aspect of the right leg was uppermost. Less bone was exposed than in the left leg, and it appeared that more of the right leg survived. The most proximal part surviving was the flap of skin that had been originally recognised in the bog. It was almost black and was hard but not brittle. This flap of skin was turned over like a cuff. The skin of the thigh was like an empty sleeve (Pl. 17). It was angled forward above the knee. This is not a natural anatomical position and was probably the result of the shearing effect of the peat-cutting machine. The upper extremity of the skin of the thigh was frayed and ragged. The skin on the back of the thigh was longer than the skin on the front. There is no evidence of the skin having been cut with a sharp instrument. A very thin, soft, pliable membrane was observed on the inner aspect of the skin of the thigh.

There was a deep hollow in the region of the knee. This measured 70mm by 50mm, narrowed from top to bottom and was deepest (60mm) behind the knee joint. The skin was broken on the inferior edge of the hollow (Pl. 21). Part of the right tibia, probably part of the epiphysis, and a small part of the head of the fibula were visible at the hollow. The tibia was covered with adipocere, to which the skin adhered. A small fragment of brushwood was retrieved from against the anterior edge of the hollow. The upper part of the right tibial shaft was outlined under the skin. It lay just below the area of damage described above. In the region of the knee there was a collection of adipocere measuring *c.* 35mm by 35mm. The skin anterior to the adipocere had a rounded edge; just superior to this the skin was frayed. The skin that would have covered the posterior aspect of the knee was also frayed.

Distal and posterior to this patch of adipocere there was a second, almost rectangular hollow, measuring 50mm in diameter and *c.* 15mm deep. Posterior to the tibia, just below the second hollow, there was a diagonal depression in the skin, *c.* 20mm wide, 60mm long and 8mm deep. This depression had a rounded bottom and was semicircular in cross-section (Pl. 21). It had distorted the skin of the calf on its upper posterior aspect. There was no indication of the cause of this depression, which wrinkled the skin and pulled it forward, but it probably occurred post-mortem.

There was a longitudinal wrinkle extending from the inferior edge of the large hollow at the knee to approximately halfway down the calf. It petered out nearer to the posterior aspect of the leg than the anterior aspect (Pl. 22). The outline of the

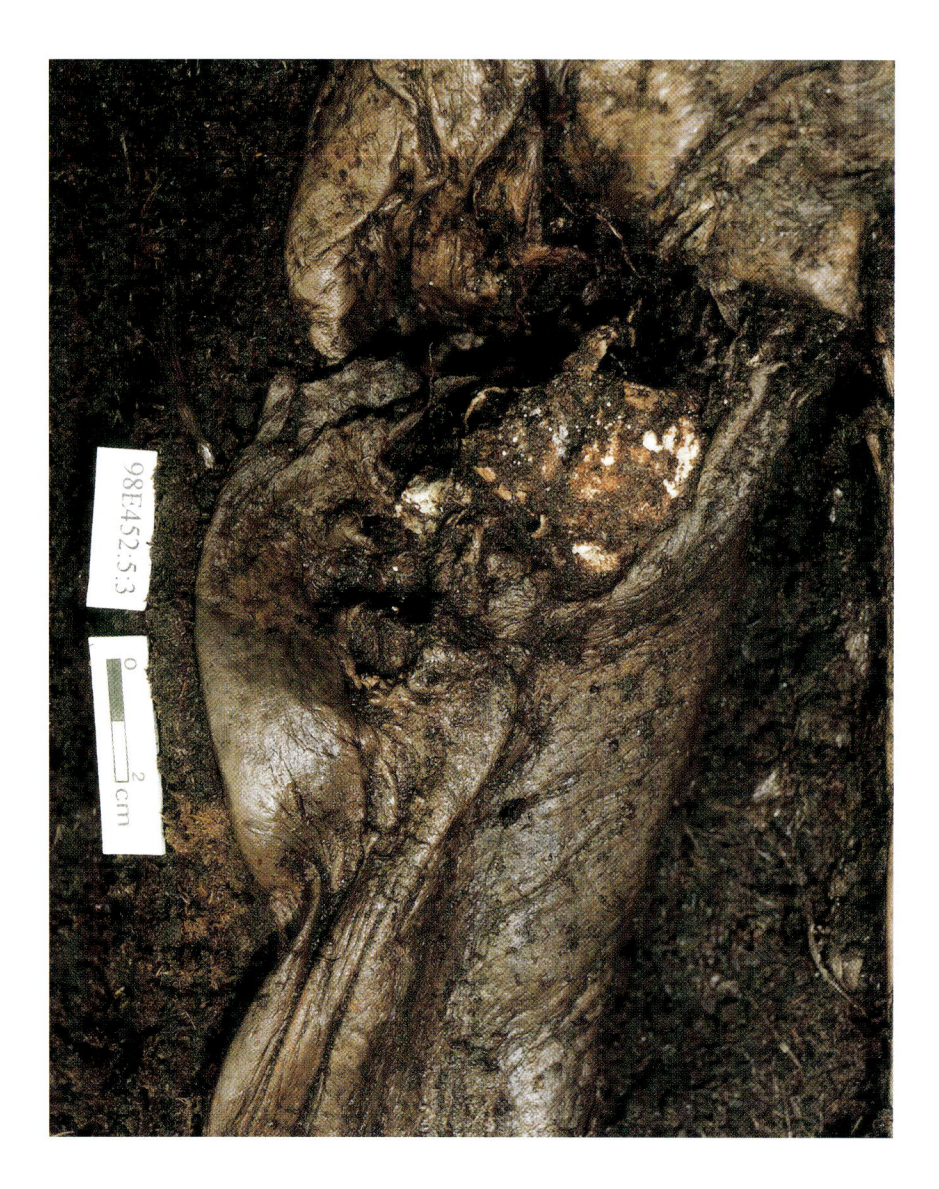

Pl. 21:
The proximal epiphysis of the right tibia, with adipocere adhering (photo: NMI).

anterior border of the tibia was visible beneath the skin of the shin. About 15mm from the lower end of the tibia there was no evidence of bone between the layers of skin in this region, an area characterised by a horizontal depression.

The skin on the posterior aspect of the calf tapered out at *c.* 120mm proximal to the distal end of the tibial metaphysis (Pl. 23). The lower few centimetres of the fibula were bare. A strip of skin could be seen behind the shaft of the fibula. In front of the shaft of the fibula the skin continued downward and then seemed to disappear, with an edge *c.* 150mm above the distal end of the bone. The lower end of the shaft of the tibia was bare, as were the tendons that ran over the front of the ankle joint. Thus there was a gap in the skin between the leg and the foot. The inferior border of the skin of the leg was indistinct. The skin was probably pulled apart at the same time as the bone.

The skin outlined the tibia below the depression described above. This outline was continuous with the exposed distal end of the shaft (Pl. 23). The lower part of the shaft

Pl. 22:
The skin of the right calf, under which the line of the tibia is visible (photo: NMI).

Pl. 23:
The distal half of the right fibula and the distal epiphysis of the tibia are visible through a defect in the skin (photo: NMI).

had been displaced forward slightly. Evidence from the underside showed that both bones were fractured in this region, but the cause of the fracture was not evident. The fibula was visible lying in an almost undisturbed position just below this depression. The shaft was fractured, and the cortical bone was very thin. It had well-defined edges but did not appear to have broken as fresh bone does. There were small defects in the bone below the fracture. There was no sign of healing, and these fractures probably occurred after the bone was decalcified. The fibula continued downward and terminated above the epiphysis of the lateral malleolus. There was a slight misalignment between the lateral malleolus and the diaphyseal part of the bone. The metaphysis met the epiphysis anteriorly, but posteriorly there was a gap of *c.* 20mm between them. This suggests slight shifting of the diaphysis as the epiphysis was *in situ*. The lateral malleolus was partially covered by skin on the lateral aspect.

Anterior to the fibula the skin continued down the tibia to a point *c.* 20mm above the epiphyseal junction. Here the skin became deficient and the bone was bare. The Achilles tendon ran posterior to the fibula for *c.* 100mm. It terminated in a frayed end *c.* 50mm above the lateral malleolus. Anterior to the tibia one of the extensor tendons was visible. Two other extensor tendons, which continued into the foot, were visible in front of the ankle joint (Pl. 24).

In the area of the fractured end of the fibula and the upper part of the subcutaneous block of tissue there was a roughly diagonal area slightly infiltrated by peat. It ran from the Achilles tendon posteriorly downward to the extensor tendons anteriorly. This coincided with the indistinct edges of the skin defect. Anteriorly, a small part of the tibial shaft was visible. It was fractured just below the upper level of the fibular fracture and was *c.* 55mm distal to a relatively firm bulge in the anterior surface of the shin skin. This probably represented the lower end of the proximal tibia shaft. The tibial epiphysis was present and visible. The alignment of the bone altered slightly at the fracture (see Chapter 8). There was no adipocere on the distal end of the tibia (Pl. 24).

The skin resumed on the foot (Pls 17, 19). Again, its upper edge was poorly defined. It continued over the dorsal aspect of the foot to the proximal end of the metatarsals (Pl. 24). The proximal end of the talus was visible in its correct position below the tibia. The cuboid bone was visible and devoid of skin. Its articulation with the calcaneus was visible. Most of the talus and calcaneus was covered with skin. Skin cover on the lateral side of the foot was patchy. A line of adipocere, measuring 65mm by 8mm, ran vertically from behind the lateral malleolus. It could be seen through a vertical defect in the skin. The skin covered most of the heel and extended forward onto the lateral aspect of the sole of the foot for *c.* 10mm (Pls 19, 24). Deep to the skin and extending forward on the lateral plantar surface (sole of the foot) for over 40mm was an area of adipocere *c.* 12mm thick (Pl. 24). There was a defect, *c.* 18mm wide, between the area of adipocere and the area of the tarsal bones. In life this gap would have been occupied by tendons and muscles.

Most of the metatarsals were devoid of skin. Metatarsals IV and V were present and had collapsed vertically; fragments of skin adhered to them. There was a small patch of skin on the proximal medial end of the third metatarsal (Pl. 19). Skin covered about one-quarter of the proximal end of the second metatarsal and about one-quarter of the distal end. The distal epiphysis was unfused, but the epiphysis itself was

Pl. 24:
Detail of the right ankle where skin is absent over the bone. The adipocere of the heel is clearly visible (photo: NMI).

not visible from this aspect. There was no other soft tissue adherent to this bone. The first metatarsal was not visible on this aspect. The skin of the sole of foot was visible just above the margin of the peat.

The little toe was present and flexed but slightly displaced. The impression of the nail was clearly visible, but the nail itself was not recovered (Pl. 19). The skin over the sole in this area and over the distal part of the fifth metatarsal was intact. The other toes had been disturbed. The first phalanx of the fourth toe was present and skeletal, protruding above the little toe. The first phalanx of the third toe was present and skeletal, with skin adhering to the proximal end. The first phalanx of the second toe was present, with skin visible on the plantar aspect. On the distal articular surface of the first phalanx of the great toe there was tissue that was interpreted as hyaline cartilage (Pl. 19); distal to this was a toenail, possibly that of the great toe. Distal to the toenail was a middle phalanx. Beneath the middle phalanx was another toenail. Immediately distal to this the base of the middle phalanx was visible.

Pl. 25:
Detail of the proximal left tibia with denting and warping visible (photo: NMI).

Left leg
The medial aspect of the left leg was uppermost in the bog (Pl. 17). The knee region was partly obscured by the flap of thigh skin from the right leg. Part of the anterior aspect of the distal femoral epiphysis was visible and was covered with adipocere. The skin appeared to overlie the lateral condyle. The epiphysis appeared to be lying facing into the peat, which suggests that the epiphysis had been rotated. The skin overlying the epiphysis had ragged edges; no clean cuts were apparent. This skin originally covered the lower thigh and knee region.

Most of the left tibia was exposed. Adipocere adhered to the proximal epiphyseal surface of the shaft. The skin present was posterior to the bone or slightly overlapping its posterior surface. No other soft tissues were visible in the leg. The upper proximal epiphysis had not fused and was missing (Pl. 25). A left tibial epiphysis was recovered from a peat stockpile during the field excavation. It is reasonable to assume that this belonged to the body (Table 12). The distal epiphysis was present but not fused. The

Pl. 26:
The upper side of the left foot (photo: NMI).

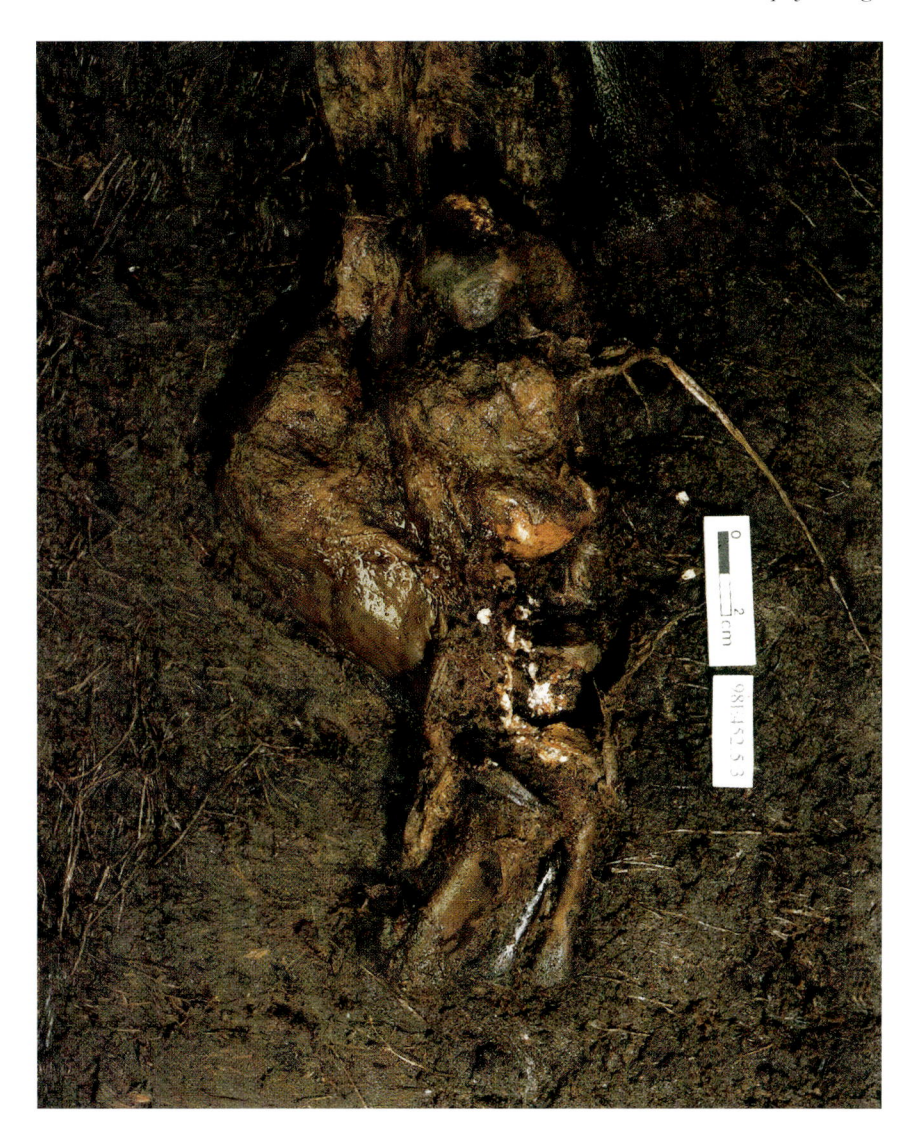

shaft of the tibia had moved forward, and the correct alignment with the distal epiphysis was lost (Pl. 17). This may be accounted for by soil shift or the weight of peat-milling machines.

At a point *c.* 70mm from the proximal end of the left tibia the bone was dented and warped (Pl. 25). There was a marked transverse groove across the bone, followed by an oblique diffuse dent. Approximately 160mm from the proximal end of the tibia was a second area of warping and grooving. This area was less diffuse than the upper one. A diagonal groove ran downward from the front of the bone for *c.* 20mm. This was joined at a right angle by a groove extending backward for *c.* 10mm. There was a small area of decay just above the diagonal groove, toward the front of the bone. Approximately 220mm from the proximal aspect of the tibia, on the medial aspect, was an area of fragmentation and warping, 40mm long (Pl. 20). This may have been caused recently. The skin behind it was more fragmented than in other areas in contact with the bone.

Two patches of lighter-coloured bone were visible on the medial aspect of the distal tibia. The first was on the antero-medial aspect (*c.* 250mm from the proximal end) and appeared to be an alteration of the colour of the bone itself. The second patch (*c.* 300mm from the proximal end) looked slightly raised and may represent the periosteum, or the very outer cortex of the bone (Pl. 20).

Some decay was identified on the medial aspect *c.* 300mm from the proximal end of the cortex. The skin that adhered to the bone had fallen away at this point. On the removal of peat from around the distal epiphysis, it was observed that peat had infiltrated the upper surface of the plate (Pl. 20). The distal epiphysis was separated from the diaphysis. Adipocere adhered to the medial malleolus.

A flap of skin emerged from under the peat *c.* 15mm below the exposed skin of the right leg (Pl. 17). This was upright to a height of *c.* 15–20mm and ran to the posterior aspect of the proximal tibia plate. This region was disturbed, and the original position of the flap was not determined. The skin of the calf emerged from under this flap. The skin retained the shape of the calf, but no muscle was present. The outline of the fibula could be seen running posterior and parallel to the tibia. The skin that once covered the tibia may have decayed, or the tibia may have thrust forward through it. The skin adhering to the bone had been infiltrated with peat. At a point *c.* 240mm from the proximal end of the tibia was the beginning of a triangular oblique defect in the skin (Pl. 17) through which part of the left fibula (*c.* 50mm) could be seen. The skin then covered the lower end of the bone.

The skin of the calf was continuous with the skin of the heel and the sole of the foot. There was, however, a continuous defect in the skin, reaching from the proximal end of the tibial shaft down the anterior aspect of the leg (Pl. 20). It extended onto the upper and medial surfaces of the foot, where the bones were exposed. All of this damage occurred post-mortem. Fine longitudinal folds were visible in the skin. These were not parallel to the bones but formed an angle of *c.* 45° (Pls 20, 25). The four large folds were probably formed by decay of the underlying tissues and subsequent collapse of the overlying skin.

The skin in the region of the left ankle was deficient anteriorly (Pl. 26). It continued down behind the ankle joint into the sole of the foot. The distal epiphysis was in place, and the ankle and foot seemed to be normally aligned. The distal epiphysis was bare, without skin cover, although the talus below it was covered by skin on its medial aspect, which was uppermost. The left navicular was missing. A compatible left navicular was retrieved in the field, not far from the foot. The skin covered the medial aspect of the calcaneus and ended at the distal end of the metatarsi. Skin was visible in the gap between the talus and the other, *in situ* tarsals.

One extensor tendon was visible at the ankle (Pl. 26), a pale, string-like structure extending at a right angle from the anterior aspect of the ankle. It had been displaced from its anatomical position during excavation.

The skin over the upper foot was deficient on the anterior and medial aspects of the metatarsals, although the sole of the foot seemed well preserved. There was no evidence of skin distal to the metatarsals, and the phalanges were not in their correct anatomical position. Adipocere was present between the distal tarsal bones and the metatarsals. The first, second and third metatarsals were visible. All had slightly collapsed downward. The proximal epiphysis of the first metatarsal was not fused.

Pl. 27:
The first phalanx of the left great toe, which had been pulled away from the foot by milling machines (photo: NMI).

Close to the southern apex of the peat block, on one side, were a number of bones that had been pulled away from the foot (Pl. 27). The first phalanx of the great toe was present. Its plantar aspect was visible, with skin adhering. The first phalanx and its epiphysis had been pulled away from the foot. Skin adhered to it, and a loose fragment of a toenail was present. Accompanying the first phalanx were fragments of the distal phalanx and the proximal end of another.

Description of the lower surface of the surviving human remains

Left leg

When the peat block was inverted, the left leg was then uppermost (Pl. 18). The fragmentary remains of the left thigh lay below the skin of the right thigh. More of the left thigh and knee region was visible on this aspect, although the tissues in the knee region were very distorted.

The proximal tibial epiphysis was absent. At *c.* 95mm from the proximal end of the tibia was a depression in the bone, *c.* 10mm long, that impinged on the anterior border. A longitudinal fracture, *c.* 90mm long, extended from this depression just lateral to the anterior border (Pl. 18). This seemed to be continuous with a defect described on the upper surface of the bone at this point. At a point *c.* 250mm from the proximal end of the tibia there was a diagonal fracture of the bone, *c.* 20mm long, which slanted downward anteriorly. The bone was not significantly distorted in overall shape. Its anterior surface was largely bare of skin, and the posterior aspect had a ragged covering of skin on the upper two-thirds.

As described above, the anatomical relationship of the fibula and the tibia had altered so that the fibula lay posterior to the tibia. The fibula, which was *c.* 330mm long, was visible under the skin for *c.* 235mm. The bone was exposed over its last 100mm. There was a pale patch on the fibula as it emerged from beneath the skin distally, which may have represented the periosteum. This was *c.* 20mm long and covered most of the shaft except the posterior aspect.

The skin between the fibula and the tibia was well preserved and extended distally for *c.* 270mm from the proximal end of the tibia but did not appear to have covered the proximal tibial epiphysis (Pl. 18). Whether this appearance was due to recent damage or was part of the decay process was unclear. The skin overlay the interosseus border of the tibia and the posterior aspect of the lateral surface. Fragments of what presumably was tendon protruded from the ragged anterior edge of the skin that lay on the distal tibial epiphysis (Pl. 28). There was defect in the skin *c.* 30mm above the attachment of the Achilles tendon to the calcaneus. The defect was oval, and its cause was unknown.

The skin was intact on the calf of the leg and was continuous with the skin of the foot (Pls 18, 28). There were major folds in the skin, which were longitudinal and were probably caused by the decay of muscle tissue and the subsequent collapse of the skin.

No hairs were visible on the skin, but hair follicles were obvious in the calf region. At a point *c.* 140mm distal to the proximal end of the shaft of the tibia there was a swelling under the skin of the calf, just behind the fibula. The swelling was 40mm long and 35mm wide and may have been associated with underlying tissue.

Behind the fibula, *c.* 100mm from its proximal end, there was a diagonal depression in the skin that reached out to the posterior border. This appeared to occur just below the slanting dent on the upper surface described above. Parallel to the defect above the Achilles tendon and *c.* 300mm from the proximal end of the tibia there was a transverse linear depression in the skin *c.* 1mm wide and *c.* 7mm long.

The left foot appeared to lie at a lower level in the bog. The arrangement of the bones of the foot prevented them from collapsing in the same way as the fibula and tibia (Pl. 28). The lateral malleolus was evident under the skin of the foot. The posterior, superior and anterior aspects of the calcaneus were visible under the skin. There was a defect in the skin over the lateral aspect of the head of the calcaneus, *c.* 30mm long and 17mm wide, with a jagged edge. In life the fat pad on the heel is situated beneath the calcaneus. Here it had moved forward slightly. There was one major crease, in an arc, in the skin on the lateral aspect of the foot, outlining the fat pad. This was probably caused by the decay of the muscles in the sole of the foot. The

Pl. 28: Detail of the underside of both feet. The distal end of the left fibula is visible in this view (photo: NMI).

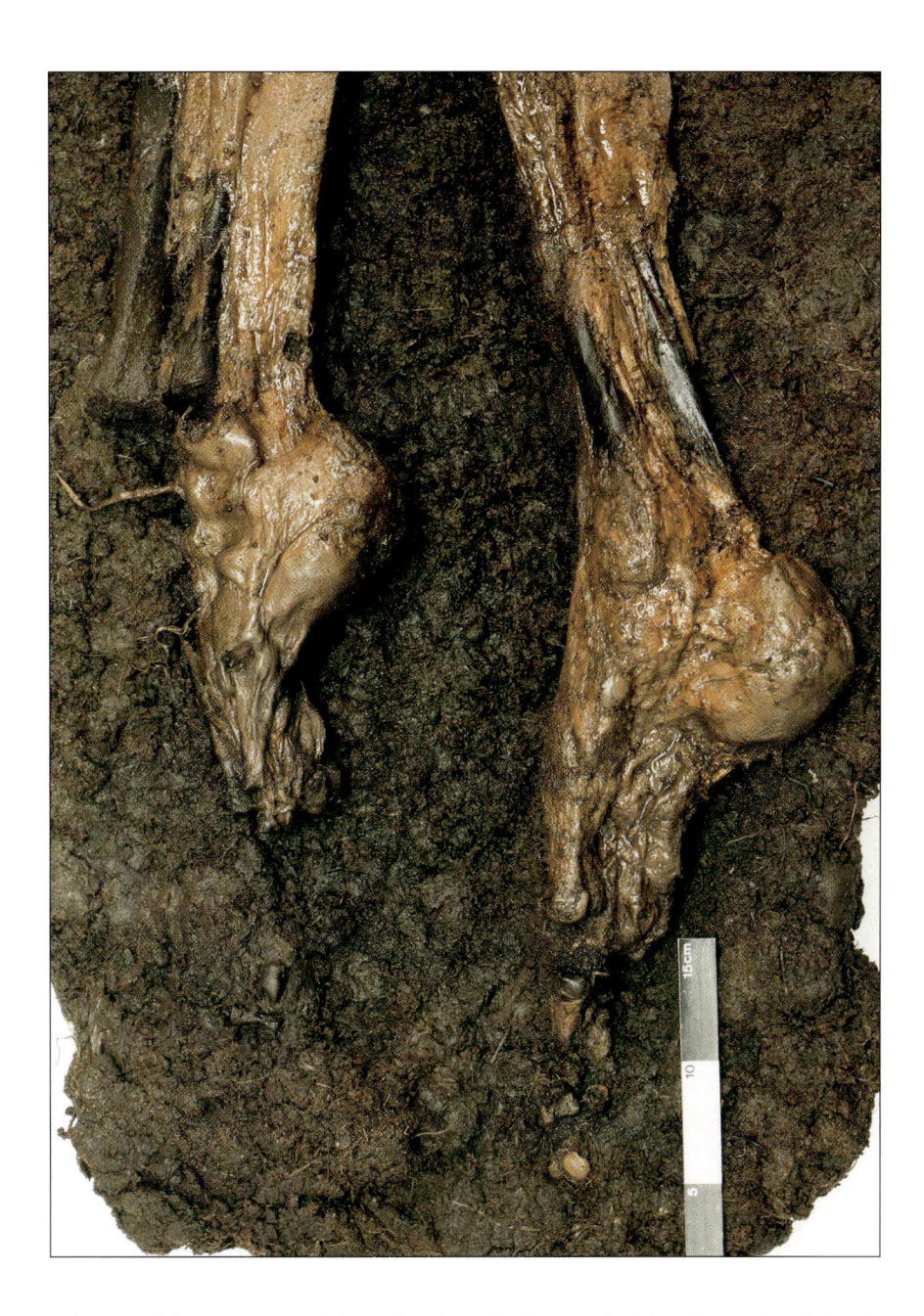

other tarsal bones were visible under the skin. The underside of a tendon (already described in the upper surface) was visible. The skin was intact over all of these.

The plantar surface of the foot was partially exposed. The skin was deficient over the distal row of tarsals and the proximal parts of the metatarsals. Metatarsals V, IV, III and II were visible on this view. The skin was patchy over the shafts of the second, third and fourth metatarsi. Some tendons were visible, which were ragged and thin. The skin was present on the lateral aspect of the fifth metatarsal and on the sole of the foot as far as the plantar surface of the heads of the metatarsals, except over the lateral cuneiform, where there was a small defect measuring 7mm by 7mm. A small area of the proximal fifth metatarsal was also visible through the defect. Tissue interpreted as articular hyaline cartilage covered the exposed articular surfaces of the lateral cuneiform and the head of the fourth metatarsal.

The skin of the left sole was a dirty grey/pink with small, dark brown blotches, which did not appear to be over pressure points. Similar blotches were present on the skin of both calves. The skin of the heel and the lateral aspect of the sole of the foot retained papillary ridges. This was more marked than on the right foot. The difference in colour between the sole and the heel may be explained by the natural difference in the texture of the skin.

The proximal and distal first phalanx and another proximal phalanx were visible but were not in their original position (Pl. 28).

Right leg
As on the superior surface, the skin of the right lower thigh swept forward above the knee. It was dark and hard on this aspect also, consistent with the appearance of the superior aspect. The tissues beneath the skin appeared to have decayed (Pl. 18).

The skin swept downward, with one major wrinkle and several striae, to a prominence that was roughly oblong. This corresponded with the depression on the upper surface at this point and was produced by the proximal end of the tibia. It appeared that the proximal tibia (until relatively recently) had lain in line with the skin of the thigh (Pl. 18). However, it seemed to have been pushed deeper into the peat by milling. This may explain the fracture visible in the tibia *c.* 130mm above the point of the medial malleolus. The direction of the shaft of the tibia changed at this point. If the shaft of the tibia were to have continued along the line of the medial malleolus, the proximal end of the tibia would have lain considerably higher in the bog.

The skin of the calf, other than that which covered the tibia, lay at a higher level in the bog than the skin of the left leg. Posterior to the tibia (*c.* 350mm proximal to the medial malleolus) was an indentation in the skin of the calf, *c.* 20mm wide. At a point *c.* 8mm from the proximal end of the tibia there was a slight depression, *c.* 20mm long. Below this indentation the calf skin appeared to be undisturbed up to a point *c.* 170mm above the medial malleolus on the posterior aspect, where the skin became defective.

The skin of the calf overlay the fibula to a point just above the tibia. Between the tibia and fibula it continued down and was ragged. The Achilles tendon was visible behind the posterior aspect of the fibula (Pl. 29). The skin was also defective over the tibia, from the level of the fracture to *c.* 40mm above the medial malleolus. Here the skin also had a ragged and indistinct edge, and tendons, including the tibialis posterior tendon, were visible.

The shaft of the tibia was beneath the skin to *c.* 185mm above the medial malleolus, where there appeared to be a defect in the bone, *c.* 65mm long. The skin in the area was transversely creased. There was an indentation on the posterior aspect of the calf that was also visible on the anterior aspect. The hair follicles, where present, were not so easily discernible on this aspect.

The impression of the proximal fibula could be seen beneath the skin behind the right tibia. The fibula was much decalcified and was not visible for *c.* 120mm of its

Pl. 29:
The lower calf and ankle area of the right leg with the tendon and fractured fibula visible (photo: NMI).

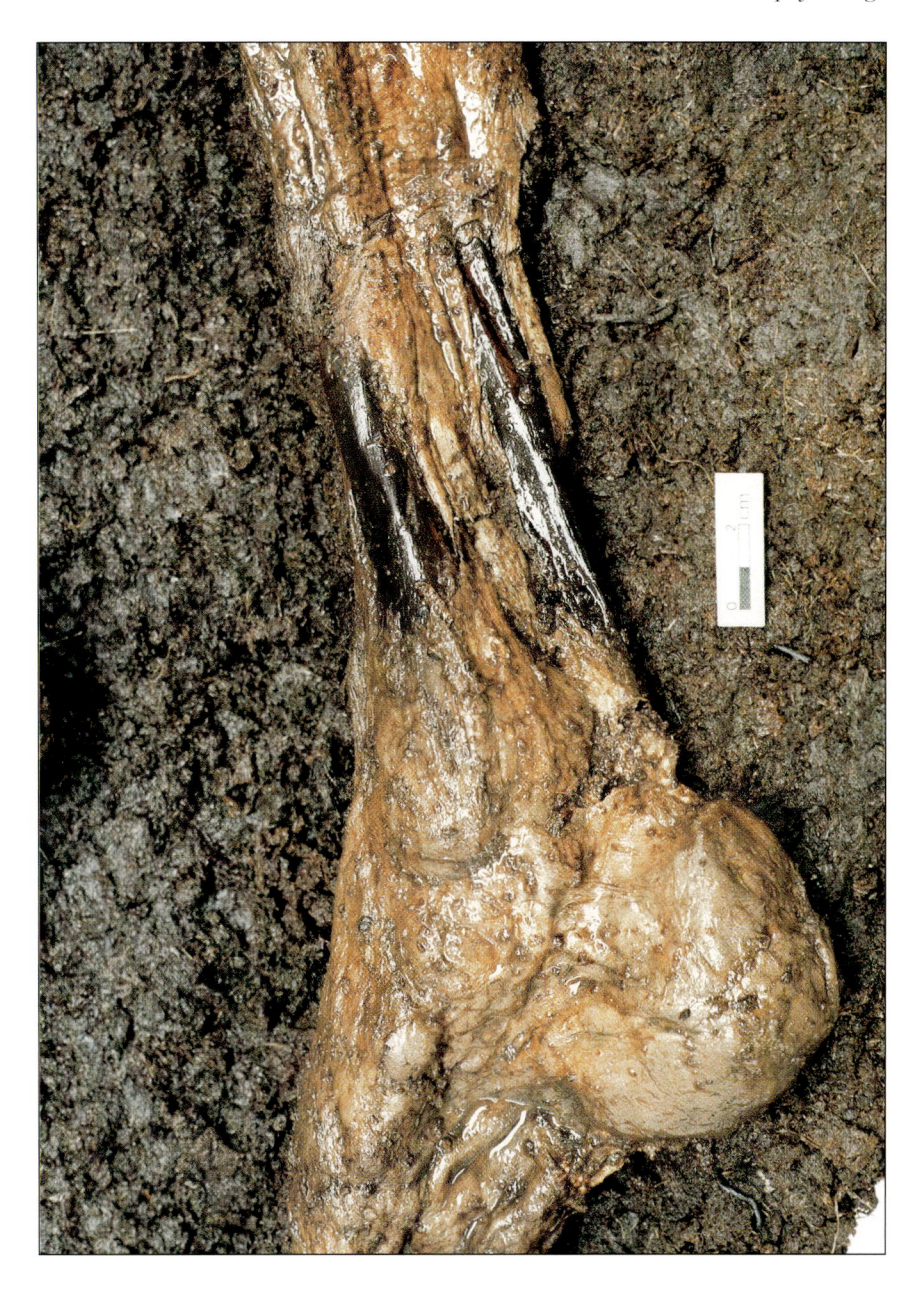

length (Pls 18, 29). The proximal end was not in line with the distal end, and the bone was bent upwards. This was probably caused by the same disturbance that had affected the proximal tibia. The skin posterior to the proximal fibula had also been pressed downward slightly.

The distal tibia was covered with skin and tendon with indistinct edges for 50–60mm. There was a depression in the skin between the tibia and the talus (Pl. 29). Adipocere and peat were visible over the distal fibula for 30–40mm. The lateral malleolus was not visible on this aspect.

Papillary ridges were visible on the sole of the foot (Pls 29, 30). The tarsals and metatarsals were covered with intact skin as far as the distal ends, except for an area

The bog body from Tumbeagh

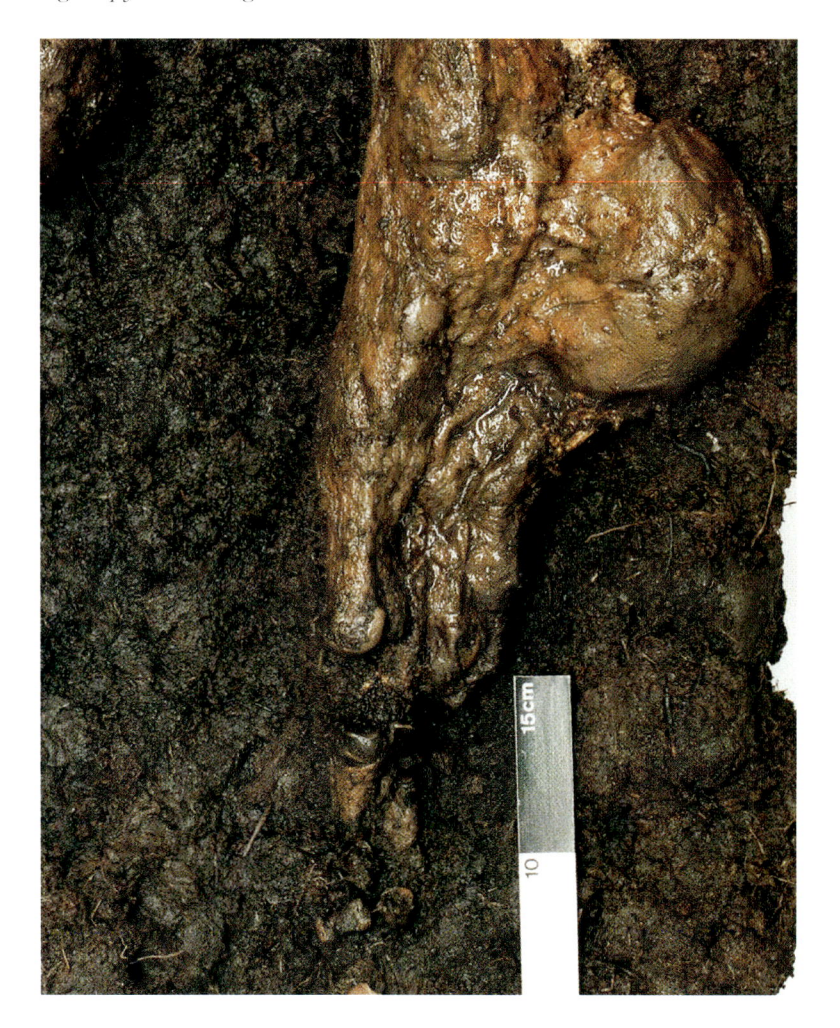

*Pl. 30:
The underside of the right foot. The metatarsals are exposed in this view, and the papillary ridges on the heel pad are visible (photo: NMI).*

of peat-infiltrated adipocere, *c.* 25mm in diameter and *c.* 55mm from the inferior posterior border of the calcaneus. The fat pad on the inferior surface of the calcaneus had maintained its anatomical position.

Tissue interpreted as articular hyaline cartilage was visible on the articulated surface on the head of the first and fourth metatarsals. Adipocere was visible just above the second metatarsal, and a fragment of tendon overlain by skin was also visible in this region. The first phalanx of the great toe had fallen slightly out of position. The middle phalanges and the nails were distal to the great toe, in a disturbed position (Pl. 18).

8.
The radiographic examination of bog bodies

Máire Delaney and D.P McInerney

Introduction

Although medical diagnosis has been the prime function of X-ray since its discovery by Roentgen in 1895 (Roentgen 1959), it has always been used for examining other objects, including human remains. Its property of penetrating solid material permits internal examination of objects without disrupting them. Imaging uses ionising radiation, non-ionising electromagnetic radiation and ultrasound to define the internal and external structures of the object being examined. The information produced by primary imaging methods can then be analysed by computers and used to synthesise more complex images, including three-dimensional, subtraction, variably enhanced and dynamic. Three-dimensional images of the body, in particular the head and face, have been valuable.

From the beginning of radiology, plain radiography has been the mainstay of bog-body imaging. With the development of radiological science, newer techniques that were developed for medical diagnosis are bringing a new dimension to bog-body studies. What is the purpose of imaging bog bodies? Firstly, it permits analysis of a block of material without disturbing or dissecting it. Secondly, it enables one to identify and describe the body parts. Observations may be made on the age, sex, physical condition and previous illnesses of the body, and one can conjecture the cause of death.

The great majority of mummies are preserved by freezing, drying or the application of chemicals (Rudenko 1970; Cockburn *et al.* 1998; Spindler 2001). In these various forms of mummification the physical properties and response to radiographic imaging depend on the type of mummification. The imaging results depend on the physical properties of the object being studied. Imaging of bog bodies is an intriguing challenge to radiology because the altered chemical composition of bog bodies profoundly changes the way they react to radiographic processes compared to normal bodies.

Of the considerable amount of literature on the radiological evaluation of ancient human remains, only a small fraction applies to bog bodies (Brothwell 1986; Brothwell and Bourke 1995; Delaney and Ó Floinn 1995; Garland 1995). This is because bog bodies represent only a tiny fraction of these remains. Their method of preservation is quite different from the others. Bog bodies are preserved in a wet and acid environment that causes progressive alteration of the body chemistry. The chemical composition of tissues is considerably altered, and, importantly, calcium and water concentrations are very different from those in living tissue (Painter 1995). The unsaturated fatty acids become hydrolysed, and the resulting material, called adipocere, is denser than fat; consequently, the radiographic contrast between fat and water density tissue is diminished. Many changes occur in bodies preserved in a bog environment (Bourke [1986]): the body parts are deformed owing to pressure; chemical changes lead to shrinkage of some organs, such as the brain (Brothwell 1986); other organs, such as muscles, virtually disappear (for example, Gallagh Man (M. Delaney, pers. comm.) and Damendorf Man (Glob 1969)); decalcification of bone occurs; but the collagen layer of the skin is preserved, as is collagen in tendons and in the matrix of bone and blood vessels (Connolly et al. [1986]).

Brief description of the surviving remains

The right leg, from the proximal tibial epiphysis to the foot, had been recovered. A fragment of a right distal femoral epiphysis had been found elsewhere. The distal tibial and fibular shafts were fractured, presumably post-mortem, as there was no evidence of healing. The Achilles tendon was present over a length of 100mm, terminating 50mm above the lateral malleolus. Several extensor tendons were present anterior to the lower tibia and ankle and could be traced into the foot. Tissue thought to be articular hyaline cartilage was visible on the articular surfaces of the lateral cuneiform and on the head of the fourth metatarsal. The first metacarpal had been pulled down and rotated distally.

In the left leg there was considerable displacement at the ankle joint. A left tibial epiphysis and a left navicular were recovered adjacent to the remains and are assumed to belong to this body. The lower left tibial epiphysis was unfused. The left first metacarpal was not found.

Conventional and digital radiography

Conventional radiography uses high-energy electromagnetic radiation produced by electron bombardment of a tungsten target anode. This ionising radiation is differentially absorbed by tissues in proportion to the atomic weight of the elements composing these tissues. Absorption is thus minimal in air, moderate in tissue of water density and great in tissue containing much calcium, because calcium has a much higher atomic weight than the other elements in tissue. The image is then captured either on a conventional photographic plate or, in the case of digital radiography, on a sensitised plate.

Conventional radiography is an excellent method of examining normal tissue, particularly when bony detail is sought. There is strong contrast between bone, soft tissue and air. Within soft tissue, there is poor to moderate contrast between tissue of water density and fatty density. In the case of bog bodies, these natural contrasts are obliterated. Extensive decalcification reduces the contrast of bone. Hydrolysis of fat increases its density to closer to that of water and thus reduces image contrast. Air in the tissues of the bog body does not have an anatomic distribution and merely degrades the image.

The shortcomings of conventional radiography in bog-body examination can be partly overcome by digital radiography. In this technique the X-ray film is replaced by a photosensitive plate on which the image is received. The image is read by an electronic processor and processed digitally. Computer analysis of the image allows differential enhancement and subsequently manipulation of different structures in the image.

The Tumbeagh body shows very poor detail on conventional radiography (Table 13). The remains were examined with digital radiography while contained within the dampened preservation peat material.

Digital radiography produces an improved but still unsatisfactory image. The lack of tissue contrast is so great that, in this case, this technique does not make a significant contribution (Pl. 31). The images are very poor, owing to lack of inherent contrast and interference caused by the surrounding preservative material, but are still substantially better than conventional radiography. There is virtually no bony contrast present. The limbs are faintly outlined by contrast between air and water density material. The bone is faint and decalcified. Soft-tissue detail is poor. Though not of great assistance in this study, in other cases, where they may be less decalcification and

Pl. 31.
Digital radiograph, coronal projection. The specimen is poorly seen as it is only slightly denser than the surrounding matrix. The bone outlines are faint.

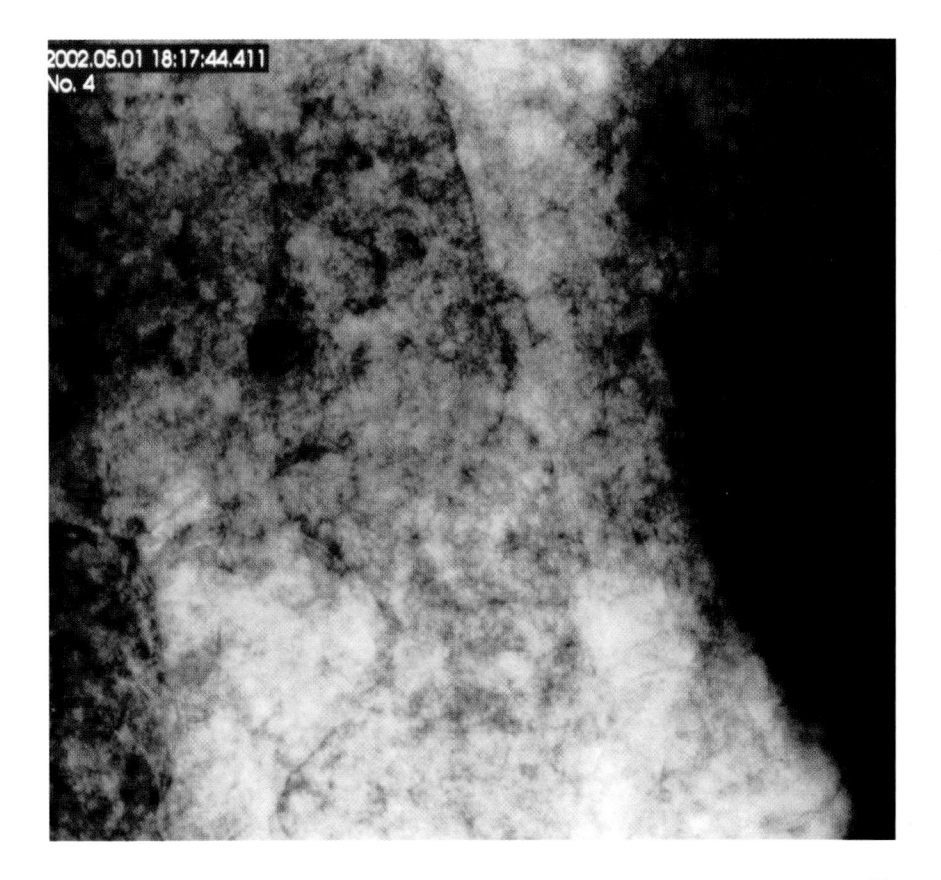

X-ray no.	No. of plates	kV, mA, seconds	Results
1	1	90kV, 5mA, 51 seconds	X-ray did not penetrate
2	1	90kV, 5mA, 25 seconds	X-ray did not penetrate
3	4	150kV, 5mA, 45 seconds	X-ray did not penetrate; the only image recorded is of metal staples securing the wooden frame.
4	4	136kV, 5mA, 70 seconds, with lead intensifier screens	X-ray did not penetrate
5	4	160kV, 5mA, 60 seconds, with lead intensifier	Some penetration; images blurred and unidentifiable
6	4	150kV, 5mA, 60 seconds	Possibly some penetration but no identifiable image

Table 13: *Conventional radiography of the peat block; kV (kilovolts) is the energy of the X-ray beam and thus its power to penetrate; mA (milliamps) indicates the quantity of radiation.*

distortion, digital radiography would be of value, allowing image manipulation with enhancement of contrast.

Xeroradiography, which is a variant of conventional radiography, has been used to study bog bodies; in the case of Lindow Man, better definition of decalcified bone and soft tissue was obtained (Reznek *et al.* [1986]). In xeroradiography the object is examined with a low-energy X-ray beam, and the image is captured as a pattern of electrostatic charges on a sensitised selenium plate. A fine powder is then blown across the plate, and this adheres differentially to areas of different charge, thus giving an image. The xerographic image is particularly sensitive to areas of sudden charge change, and thus there is edge enhancement. This technique is, however, suboptimal in bog bodies because of the inherently diminished physical contrast and has now largely been replaced by electronic methods of image enhancement.

Computed-tomography scanning

In computed-tomography (CT) scanning the object is placed within a circular gantry. An X-ray tube generating a pencil-thin beam of X-rays is rotated around the subject while a row of X-ray-sensitive detectors rotates on the opposite side of the gantry to record the differential absorption of X-rays. The data produced are analysed by computer to produce, in the first instance, axial or slice-like images of the object being examined. The data can then be further used to construct three-dimensional and other images of the object. The most modern scanners are called multi-slice scanners and allow rapid reconstruction of cross-sectional images in any projection, together with sophisticated image manipulation.

CT scanning is extremely sensitive to differences in tissue density. It can define and reconstruct objects within the tissue being examined even if there is only a slight density difference. In addition, CT scanning can give valid density measurements of tissue. It has

Pl. 32 (opposite): Axial CT image at the level of the right calcaneo-cuboid joint. Calcaneal trabeculation is well preserved. The joint space and articular margins are well defined.

Pl. 33 (opposite): Axial CT image at the level of the proximal part of the right talus. Bone density is variable and is no greater generally than adjacent tissues because virtually all of the calcium has been lost. Adipocere anterior to the talus is in fact of higher density than bone.

Pl. 34 (opposite): Axial CT image at the level of the upper tibial shafts. In the lower part of this image, on the left, an irregular density within the medulla of the left tibia may represent bone marrow. The calf muscles have been completely obliterated. The overlying skin layers are thus closely apposed, forming an apparently single layer.

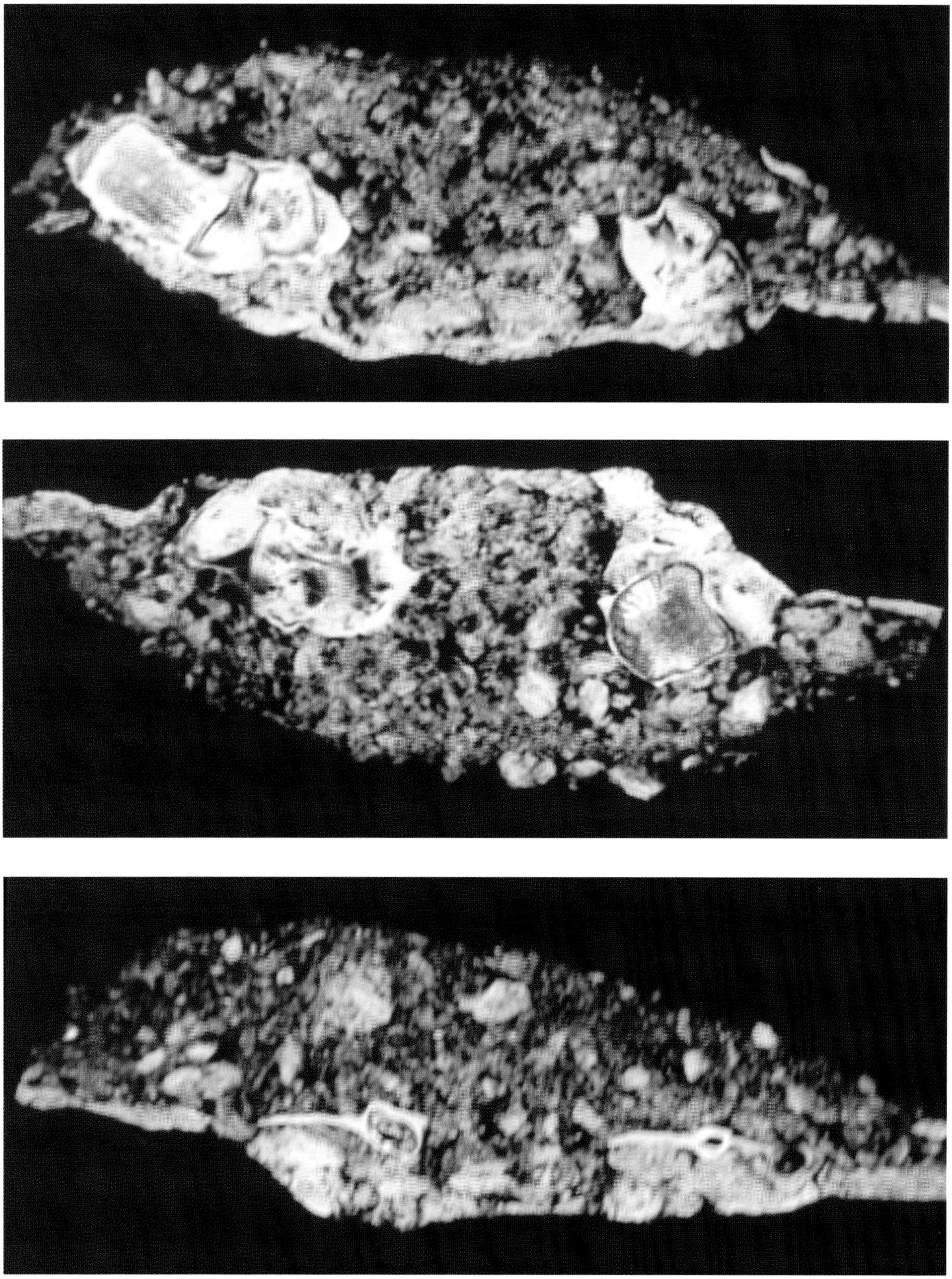

hitherto been considered an ideal imaging method for bog bodies (Reznek *et al.* [1986]).

CT scanning of the remains was done by axial imaging at 1mm intervals. There is a striking loss of bony contrast. Bone density is best retained in the calcaneus, which tends to be the densest bone in the human body. The trabecular structure is also best preserved in the calcaneus, where the longitudinal trabeculae are well seen (Pl. 32). The subtalar and calcaneo-cuboid joints are well visualised (Pls 32, 33).

The marked degree of flattening of the limbs is well shown by CT (Pl. 34). Material appears in the marrow cavity as a discrete opacity (Pl. 34) of equal density to the decalcified bone. The marrow cavity is interesting because in the intact bone it is sealed off from any particulate invasion from the outside world but still subject to chemical change. All of the muscle has gone. Skin material is retained and appears continuous on imaging with tendinous and vascular structures. The collagen of the tendon survives. On the upper CT sections, fragmentation of the upper tibia is shown and this is more marked on the left side. Most of the right upper tibial epiphysis is still *in situ*, but not the left.

CT imaging is markedly better than digital or conventional radiography but still relatively poor because of the loss of tissue-density contrast. Adipocere is denser than adjacent bone throughout much of the specimen (Pl. 33). Bone density measurements are in the range of 30–50HU (Hounsfield units); adipocere is 40–110HU; and skin and tendon are 50–100HU. This density measurement of bone is compatible with a total loss of calcium. Three-dimensional CT reconstruction is very poor because of the lack of tissue contrast.

Magnetic resonance imaging

In magnetic resonance (MR) imaging the object is placed in a very strong magnetic field. These fields are produced by large electrical currents passing through coils that have been cooled to extremely low temperatures. Radiofrequency radiation is induced in the object by pulsed electromagnetic radiation. By measuring radiofrequency emission from the different tissues, images in the form of cross-sectional slices are produced. MR does not depend on the physical density of an object but reflects the quantity of hydrogen nuclei and the tightness of their chemical bonds. By altering the technical parameters, two different types of signal can be induced in the object: T1-weighted and T2-weighted. In T1-weighted MR images the highest signal is from fat. In T2-weighted MR images the highest signal comes from areas of free (that is, not chemically bound) water. A further MR technique produces proton-density images, where the image also reflects the quantity of hydrogen nuclei within the slice.

MR imaging is an excellent method for examining bog bodies because of its capacity to differentiate soft tissues. Distinction can be made between bone cortex, medulla and articular cartilage, as well as skin, subcutaneous fat, tendons and blood vessels. In MR the skin and tendons produce a low signal and are therefore dark on T1- and T2-weighted imaging. Bone signal is variable depending on the quantity of free water associated with it; it does not depend on the presence of calcium.

On T2-weighted imaging adipocere gives a high signal because of hydrolysis of its

Pl. 35: Coronal MR image, T2-weighted, showing the right heel and ankle. The adipocere beneath the calcaneus is high signal as the fat has been hydrolysed.

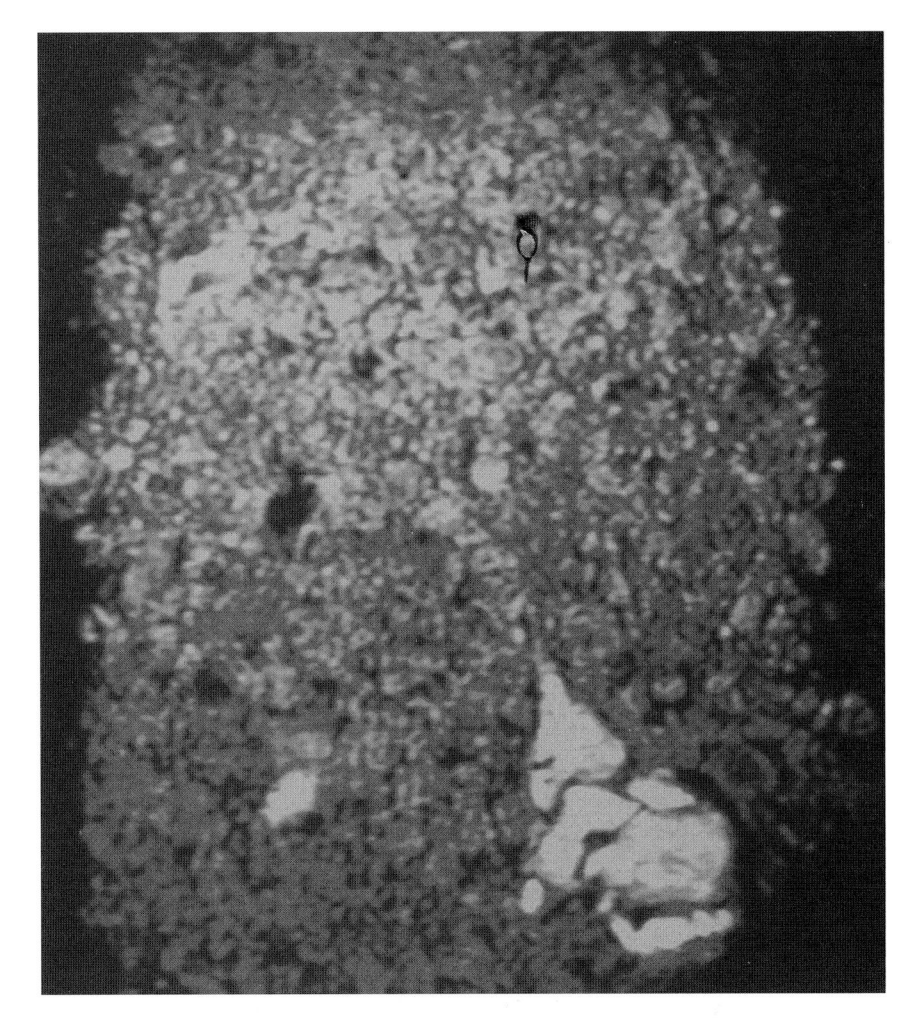

fat content (Pl. 35). The intracavitary object in the Tumbeagh body that was seen on CT (Pl. 34) was seen also on sagittal MR imaging, as an object of high signal on a STIR sequence (Pl. 36); this sequence is sensitive to unbound water molecules, similar to T2-weighting. This represented altered, shrunken bone marrow. The cavity of the fibula was dark on MR as it contained little or no marrow. The epiphyseal plates were well seen on MR imaging (Pl. 37). On T1-weighting the tendons were dark.

On T1-weighting the skin is low to medium signal and outlines well (Pl. 38). MR shows the state of fusion of the epiphyseal plates well when they are decalcified (Pl. 39). Tendons were better visualised on T2 than on T1. The epiphyseal plate was, again, well visualised on T2 (Pl. 35).

The separated right medial malleolus lay on the upper aspect of the left ankle. The right tibial shaft was broken at the junction of the middle and the lower one-third, and there was distraction over a segment c. 30mm long (Pl. 40).

The left tibia and fibula were dislocated anteriorly. The lower left tibial epiphysis was detached. The right tibia appeared to be longer than the left because of this distraction. The subtalar joints and sinus tarsi were well seen, and the epiphyseal plate at the base of the left first metatarsal appeared to be unfused (Pl. 37).

The bog body from Tumbeagh

*Pl. 36:
Coronal MR image, STIR sequence. This sequence suppresses fat signal and is sensitive to fluid. Bone cortex is lower signal than bone medulla. The object in the marrow cavity of the upper right tibial shaft is well visualised and of high signal, presumably marrow fat that is hydrolysed.*

*Pl. 37:
Coronal MR image, T1-weighted. A close-up view of the left first metatarsal shows that the epiphysis at the base is not yet united, a guide to age.*

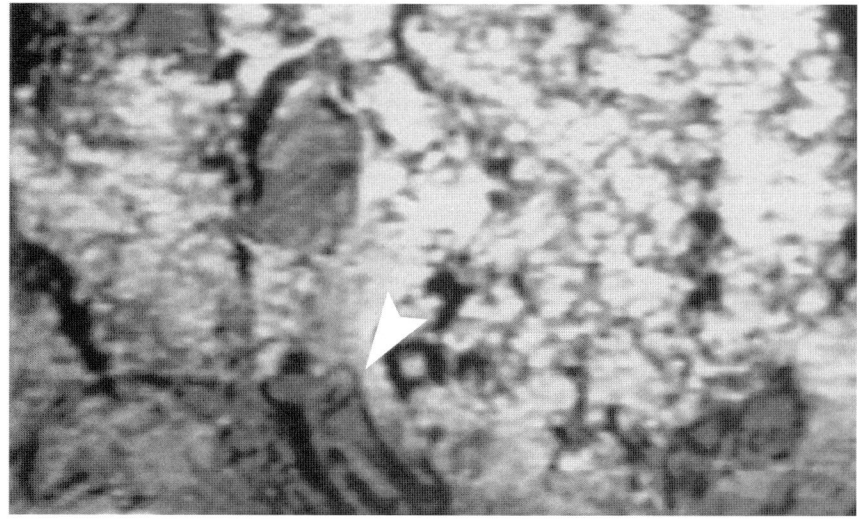

Pl. 38:
Coronal MR image, T1-weighted. Tendons and bone cortex are low signal and are well visualised.

Pl. 39:
Axial MR image, using gradient-echo FISP sequence, which enhances cartilage imaging. The right calcaneo-navicular joint is visualised, but its lining cartilage has been completely altered chemically and does not produce typical cartilage signal.

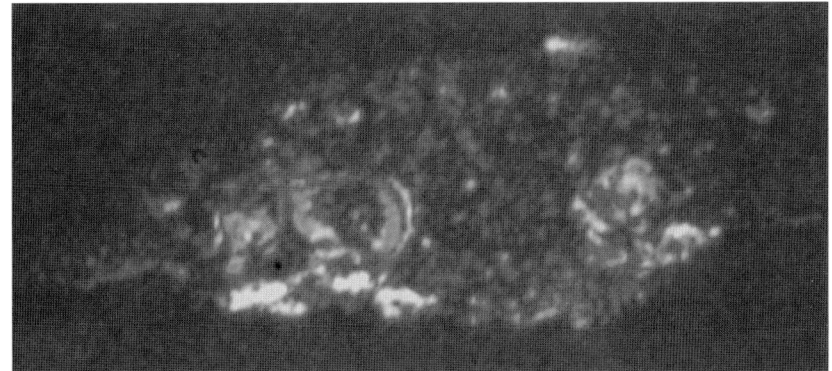

Pl. 40:
Coronal MR image, T2-weighted. The cortex of the long bones is dark, as water is still quite tightly bound in the protein matrix, after depletion of calcium. Skin layers are low signal.

Ultrasound imaging

In ultrasound imaging, sound waves are generated by crystals that are vibrated by the piezoelectric effect. The sound waves are inaudible because of the very high frequency (3–15Mhz) and can penetrate only liquid media; they are reflected by air. Normal human hearing detects only sound up to 20khz. The signal is differentially reflected from areas of different physical texture within the object and in particular is strongly reflected from sharp interfaces. High-frequency ultrasound requires a satisfactory air-free interface between the transducer producing and recording the radiation and the object being examined. Optimal ultrasound imaging is produced from objects containing regular interfaces and areas of homogeneous tissues. Bog bodies do not have homogeneous tissue masses, and the surfaces and interfaces are irregular and distorted. Useful images from the Tumbeagh bog body could not be obtained with high-frequency ultrasound using standard medical equipment.

Conclusion

Bog-body imaging uses techniques that have been developed for medical diagnosis. In this study the most striking radiographic finding was the magnitude of the chemical alteration in the tissues of the remains and the extent to which this altered the radiographic properties compared to normal human tissue. Medical imaging is undergoing a rapid and extensive revolution owing to advances in digital technology, and this will also enhance its contribution to the analysis of bog bodies. There will be further improvements in our ability to image and analyse objects without touching or dissecting them. CT and MR imaging will give further morphological detail that has not previously been available without disrupting the specimen. Image-processing algorithms will allow reconstruction of images in three dimensions and other formats. Images may be transmitted between academic institutions for discussion, as is the case with medical images at present. Museum curators are reluctant to disturb bog-body remains because of their fragility. It will still, however, be necessary to move them to medical institutions for these examinations to be carried out. With these techniques, extensive investigations can be undertaken without interfering with the remains.

9.
Tissue samples and tests

Máire Delaney

A range of tests were carried out on tissue from the surviving human remains from Tumbeagh. There were, however, three main constraints on the number and type of investigations undertaken. Firstly, a very small amount of any particular tissue was available: either there was not enough available for the tests, or the taking of sufficient material would have significantly altered the appearance of the remains. Secondly, certain tests, such as differential thermal analysis, necessitate comparison with a sample of modern Irish tissue. Such a sample would normally come from a cadaver donated to the Anatomy Department. The legal situation and the sensitivities of the relatives dictate that all remains must be re-interred after use. Thus the taking of samples that would be destroyed without prior consent was not feasible at the time that the study was conducted. Thirdly, there were the familiar financial constraints.

A range of tests that included the potential for examination of all tissues present and accessible—skin, bone, tendon and adipocere—were considered. These tests had mostly been applied to other bog-body material and included analysis for DNA, light microscopy, scanning electron microscopy (SEM) and the analysis of adipocere. For reasons outlined below, these tests were not carried out; instead, tissue analysis focused on dating and trace-metal analysis. To ensure reliability of the results, samples were taken before the remains were freeze-dried. To date, there is no inform-ation about how this process might affect future investigations. In addition, attempts to establish the pH of the human remains and the surrounding peat were made.

Assessing DNA was not part of the original plan as it is well recognised that DNA breaks down in acid conditions, and attempts to isolate it have failed (M.A. Hughes and D.S Jones 1986). For example, Spigelman *et al.* (1995) describe their difficulties in isolating faecal *Escherichia coli* DNA from material relating to Lindow Man. Osinga *et al.* (1992) describe a number of failed attempts to isolate DNA from bog bodies.

Light microscopy (histology) studies of tissue from bog bodies such as Kayhausen Boy (Schübel 1999), Lindow Man (Pyatt *et al.* 1995) and Worsley Man (Garland 1995) have shown that little musculo-skeletal detail, except that of bone, survived satisfactorily. This is because the acid environment of the bog disrupts cell membranes, of both the cell wall and the internal cellular structures. This applies to most pathogenic organisms, as well as to tissues that they may invade. As it did not appear that any new, useful information could be gained by this process, light microscopy was not carried out on samples from Tumbeagh.

SEM produces images of much greater magnification than can be obtained with a light microscope. In the case of Lindow Man (Stead et al. [1986]) SEM indicated that the fingernails were smooth in comparison with those of Meenybraddan Woman. Fingernails did not survive at Tumbeagh, but toenails did; however, toenails are subjected to different stresses and would not be comparable. Although they may indicate the wearing of shoes, there is a lack of comparative material as toenails from a shoe-wearing individual who lived in c. AD 1500 are not available.

Loose adipocere was present in tiny crumbs or in compact masses that delineated parts of the foot (see Chapter 7). Fatty-acid analysis of adipocere from Meenybraddan Woman had been performed by Dr William King of the State Laboratory (Delaney and Ó Floinn 1995), with additional analysis by Evershed (1992). In the case of Tumbeagh it was considered unnecessary to do this analysis as it would have involved the destruction of material that was almost intact and that delineated an anatomical area where the skin was missing, that is, the foot.

Swabs and samples of peat and any mould growth observed were taken but were not analysed. Preservation and patterns of mould growth are discussed in Chapter 10.

Tests conducted

Dating

Dating was an obvious and compelling reason to take samples. The original sample sent for dating was a loose rib found on the field surface, which was found to have insufficient collagen and could not be dated. It was clear that another sample would have to come from some part of the body that had remained immersed in the bog. In the absence of hair, bone is the preferred tissue to sample (W.A.B. van der Sanden, pers. comm.). However, bone from Tumbeagh was generally very thin, decalcified and light. Compact bone, such as the shaft of a long bone, is preferable, but the removal of sufficient bone for conventional dating would have significantly altered the appearance of the remains. The fragments of bone that were not easily visible were of trabecular or spongy bone, and their removal might have damaged the tissues around them. Consequently, skin was the tissue chosen for dating (van der Sanden and van der Plicht, Chapter 6; Table 6).

Trace-metal analysis

The significance of the presence of various trace metals in bog bodies is as yet unclear. In the case of Lindow Man an attempt was made to ascertain whether pigment existed on the skin (Pyatt et al. 1995); the results were equivocal. However, very little of this type of investigation has been carried out on bog bodies, and more information will lead to more insight.

As all of the available bone from the Tumbeagh body had been submitted for radiocarbon dating, only skin and tendon were analysed for trace elements. The skin came from the upper outer aspect of the right leg, just above the knee, close to the flap that had been exposed on the bog surface. The peat that had covered it had been disturbed and replaced during field excavation. The tendon was from an area that had been covered by intact peat but that was bare of skin. The analysis was carried out at

The bog body from Tumbeagh

Sample	Al	Si	P	S	Cl	K	Ca	Fe	Cu	Zn
Skin	8.01	5.94	2.02	43.39	5.12	4.75	20.37	4.73	0.78	1.28
Tendon	1.60	1.40	2.32	31.77	3.49	2.01	24.41	16.61	2.11	1.53

Table 14: Trace-element composition (%) of samples of skin and tendon derived from the Tumbeagh remains.

Sample				Order of concentration					
Skin	S	Ca	Al	Si	Cl	K	Fe	P	Zn	Cu
Tendon	S	Ca	Fe	Cl	P	Cu	K	Al	Zn	Si

Table 15: Trace elements in the Tumbeagh remains in descending order of concentration.

the State Laboratory, Abbotstown, Co. Dublin, by Dr Conor Murphy using X-ray fluorescence spectroscopy on an Oxford Instruments ED 1000 instrument (Tables 14, 15). This technique is valuable in archaeological work as it yields semi-quantitative values for the principal metals present with minimal sample preparation. It is, however, insensitive to the lighter elements, and carbon, hydrogen, oxygen and nitrogen, which are undoubtedly present in the sample, are not detected (C. Murphy, pers. comm.).

The samples were tested for ten trace elements: aluminium (Al), silicon (Si), phosphorous (P), sulphur (S), chlorine (Cl), potassium (K), calcium (Ca), iron (Fe), copper (Cu) and zinc (Zn) (Table 14).

Although there are obvious differences between the values from the skin and the tendon, it is difficult to assess the significance of these. In future analysis, comparison with modern samples would be very helpful.

Although silicon and calcium are the most abundant trace elements in both the skin and the tendon, the profile changes for the other elements (Table 15). Aluminium is the third most abundant trace element in the skin but the eighth most abundant in the tendon. Silicon, which is the fourth most abundant in the skin, is the least abundant in the tendon. Copper, the least abundant in the skin, is sixth most abundant in the tendon. Iron is the third most abundant in the tendon but the seventh in the skin.

The other trace elements, though in different orders, are not as greatly removed from one another in abundance; for instance, the apparent distance in rank of abundance between the concentrations of phosphorous in skin and tendon is misleading as there is only 0.3% between them. This is less than the difference in concentrations of chlorine (1.63%), at fourth (tendon) and fifth (skin) in rank of abundance. This implies that not only must the different composition of the tissues be taken into account but also the differences in the chemical reactions of their components should be considered.

Lindow II and Lindow III were also analysed for trace elements using electron probe X-ray microanalysis (Connolly *et al.* [1986]). The elements listed above were analysed. Other elements tested for in Lindow that were not tested for in the Tumbeagh sample were magnesium, manganese, nickel and titanium. These elements are not included in the tables below. In the case of Lindow, modern samples were used for comparison, but it is unclear what type of modern tissue was used (Pyatt *et al.* 1995). This is discussed further below.

Tissue samples and tests

Body	Sample	Al	Si	P	S	Cl	K	Ca	Fe	Cu	Zn
Tumbeagh	Skin	8.01	5.94	2.02	43.39	5.12	4.75	20.37	4.73	0.78	1.28
Lindow II	Skin	5.8	5.0	6.0	55.4	14.7	0.7	7.9	1.1	0.8	—
Lindow III	Skin	7.7	7.8	—	45.2	13.7	1.5	17.3	3.5	0.8	—

Table 16: Trace-element composition (%) of samples of skin derived from the Tumbeagh remains, Lindow II and Lindow III.

Body	Order of concentration								
Tumbeagh	S	Ca	Al	Si	Cl	K	Fe	P	Zn	Cu
Lindow II	S	Cl	Ca	P	Al	Si	Fe	Cu	K	—
Lindow III	S	Ca	Cl	Si	Al	Fe	K	Cu	—	—

Table 17: Trace elements in skin samples from the Tumbeagh remains, Lindow II and Lindow III in descending order of concentration.

Comparison of the trace-element composition of the skin samples from the Lindow and Tumbeagh bodies has produced some similarities but also some clear differences (Table 16). The greatest concordance between the three samples is in copper, where the differences are minimal (0.02%). Zinc is present in the Tumbeagh sample in small quantities and absent in both of the Lindow samples. Sulphur has the highest concentration in all samples. Aluminium is similar in Tumbeagh and Lindow III; silicon is similar in Tumbeagh and Lindow II. Phosphorous is present in low amounts in both Tumbeagh and Lindow II but absent in Lindow III. Chlorine and potassium are similar in both of the Lindow samples, but in the Tumbeagh sample potassium is noticeably higher. Calcium is high in both the Tumbeagh sample and Lindow III but notably lower in Lindow II. The percentage of iron in the Tumbeagh sample and Lindow III is close, but it is much reduced in Lindow II.

The ranks of concentration for the three samples are given in Table 17. It can be seen that Lindow III is closer in trace-element composition to Tumbeagh than Lindow II is. Identifying reasons for this is difficult, particularly as Lindow II and III are prehistoric and near to each other geographically, coming from the same bog, while Tumbeagh is medieval and from another country. Both Lindow Moss and Tumbeagh Bog are raised bogs, and the human remains come from acid *Sphagnum* peat. In addition, both the Tumbeagh body and Lindow III were severely damaged by mechanical peat harvesting, which may have affected the element composition in a similar way. Interpretation of the results is made difficult by the fact that the parts of the remains of Lindow II and III that were sampled, and their state of preservation, are not specified

Trace-metal analysis was carried out on the hair of Meenybraddan Woman in 1994 by Dr Conor Murphy using XRF. The Meenybraddan bog body was found in blanket bog in County Donegal (Delaney and Ó Floinn 1995). The sample of hair from Meenybraddan was compared with three modern samples (Table 18).

Sample origin	S	Ca	K	Fe	Cu	Zn
Meenybraddan	80.81	16.09	0.71	1.02	0.79	1.20
Modern sample 1	69.46	29.57	0.43	—	—	0.42
Modern sample 2	90.12	6.63	2.35	0.18	—	0.65
Modern sample 3	96.15	2.17	0.96	—	0.17	0.48

Table 18: Concentrations of trace metals in the hair of Meenybraddan Woman and modern samples.

As in the skin and tendon samples from Tumbeagh, sulphur is by far the most abundant trace element in both the bog body and the modern hair. It is followed by calcium in all samples. The most noticeable feature is the varying levels of the trace elements analysed and the relative inconsistency of potassium, iron, copper and zinc. In two modern samples (1 and 3) iron does not appear; it is most abundant in the bog body. In two modern samples (1 and 2) copper does not appear; again, it is most abundant in the bog body. The other element that is most abundant in the bog body is zinc. Aluminium, silicon and phosphorous were not tested for.

Hair from Lindow II was compared with modern hair by Shortall ([1986]) using X-ray energy-dispersive microprobe analysis. As in the case of the Meenybraddan and modern hair samples from Ireland, the sulphur content of the ancient and the modern hair samples from Lindow was high. Aluminium seems to be the next most abundant element, roughly equal in the two samples. Silicon and phosphorous are slightly higher in the modern sample. Calcium appears to be as abundant as aluminium in the modern sample and very much lower in the bog-body sample. The number of modern samples used is not stated.

It can be seen from comparison with Meenybraddan and modern hair that the concentration of calcium in the Tumbeagh body is the second highest of the five samples. One might expect it to be lower, given that the Tumbeagh body lay in the bog longer than the body from Meenybraddan. It may, however, reflect a difference in the calcium concentration in the surrounding peat.

That decalcification occurs in the bog is well demonstrated by the analysis of bone. Shortall ([1986]) draws attention to the fact that the trace-element concentrations in the bone of Lindow II reflect the trace-element concentrations of the surrounding peat and raises the possibility of replacement of the original trace elements by those from the surrounding environment. It is interesting that, although calcium is the commonest element in modern bone, sulphur is by far the commonest in Lindow II bone and is also the commonest element in the Lindow peat sample. The significance of this for hair is obscured by the fact that sulphur is the commonest element in both modern and bog-body hair.

A brief description of trace-metal analysis carried out on Worsley Man in England by energy-dispersive electron probe analysis (Garland 1995) showed the presence of sodium, chlorine, silicon and lead in the skin. Sodium was not tested for in either Meenybraddan or Lindow, but chlorine was tested for in Lindow (Table 16). The interesting thing about this report on Worsley Man is that sulphur, the main component in both Meenybraddan and Lindow, is not mentioned. The principal peaks for Worsley hair were for chlorine, calcium and sulphur. Again, as far as there is any overlap (given that chlorine was not tested for in Meenybraddan), this accords with findings from Meenybraddan and modern Irish hair.

Discussion

The few investigations carried out to date illustrate the variability and unpredictability of trace-element concentrations in organic tissues immersed in bog and the difficulties surrounding their interpretation. The single constant is the high concentration of sulphur in all bog-body samples. T. Walsh and T.A. Barry (1958) showed that the mineral composition of three Irish bogs differed with depth. Two of the bogs were blanket bogs; one, in Glenties, Co. Donegal, included the area in which Meenybraddan lay. Most of it had been worked by hand over the centuries. Sodium, potassium and phosphorous concentrations did not alter much with depth and were relatively low. Iron levels started low and increased steadily with depth. This phenomenon was observed for other metals such as nickel, copper and lead. Calcium started at a level of concentration second to that of magnesium. Its concentration peaked at *c.* 2m deep, where it greatly outstripped the other elements tested; then it fell to its original level at *c.* 4m deep, the maximum depth of the sample.

The raised bog in Kilmacshane, Co. Galway, showed that at 2m deep calcium reached a far greater peak, but it was absent from lower layers. Iron, though low to begin with, increased erratically with depth. The other metals mentioned above decreased within the first 1m and then stayed more or less steady in concentration through the depths sampled. Unfortunately, sulphur was not tested for in this survey; nor were aluminium, silicon, chlorine or zinc.

This study did not take into account the horizontal variations in bog chemistry. The differences between hummocks and hollows and standing water were not measured, and the content of various horizons was not considered. The measurement was of concentrations at particular depths only. For these reasons, the application of the information gained is of limited value. Many bog bodies were buried in pools or very wet boggy areas that initially and subsequently may have influenced the chemistry between the body and the environment. The subsequent movement of elements, ions and molecules within the bog must also be taken into account. Leaching of minerals out of tissues and the possible replacement of some elements by others cannot be ignored.

For example, the alteration of the proteins as described by Painter (1995) illustrates how the chemical composition of proteins changes in the bog environment. There is also the question of differences between the trace-metal concentrations in the living tissues of modern and of ancient individuals. Modern urban dwellers are exposed to pollutants, such as lead from fuel exhaust, that would not have been present in the ancient environment. Similarly, chemicals used extensively in the farming community for pest and weed control and for animal husbandry are of recent introduction. From our present state of knowledge, it would seem unwise to speculate on the significance of the concentrations of trace elements in various tissues until more extensive work has been done in this area.

Estimation of pH

Sphagnum peat is very acidic, remaining so even when drained. One of the characteristics of peat chemistry is that acid is constantly produced by the *Sphagnum* moss. It is also produced by the anaerobic partial breakdown of organic material trapped lower down in the bog. T. Walsh and T.A. Barry (1958) tested three bogs for pH at different depths, one a raised bog at Cloncreen, Co. Offaly, where the pH recorded ranged from 4.3 to 4.6. The minimum pH (the most acidic part) was found to occur at a depth of 0.50–1.50m below the present surface. In the case of Cloncreen Bog the lowest pH (4.3) occurred between 1.00m and 1.50m below the surface. Despite the fact that the acid produced in the bog quickly reacts with air and becomes less acidic, the first 0.20m had a pH of 4.5, which was low enough to discourage many of the chemical processes involved in putrefaction. This surface depth still contained significant amounts of oxygen (Doyle and Dowding 1990). From this it can be seen that the constant activity of the *Sphagnum* mosses maintains a high acid level even at the surface. It should be noted that many Irish bogs, Tumbeagh being one, are even more acidic than quoted above (Hammond 1981). Acidic conditions discourage putrefaction and are conducive to the preservation of soft tissues (see Chapter 10).

We attempted to establish the pH of the human remains and the peat in which they lay in order to examine further the relationship between *Sphagnum* and preservation. Testing of the pH did not take place on-site; rather, it was decided to take an initial pH reading in the laboratory and another reading after the excavation had finished, using a WTW model P4 multimeter. If any deterioration was observed during the period of excavation in the laboratory, this regimen would be reassessed.

When the block was unwrapped on 26 April 1999, Mark Kavanagh of the Ecological Services Unit, TCD, measured the pH of the peat: two readings showed a pH in the region of 3.8. The readings were broadly indicative of a low pH, but there were concerns that they were not wholly accurate as the pH was taken from peat in solid form rather than in solution. In view of the drawbacks of using the conventional pH meter, it was considered that the use of pH papers for subsequent readings would be acceptable, provided that it was borne in mind that they also would give an approximate reading. The papers measure the pH of the moisture adhering to the surface of a structure rather than the substance of the structure itself.

The remains were inspected again by Máire Delaney and Claire Murphy, of the Department of Anatomy, TCD, in May 2002 with a view to assessing the pH at that time. They were still covered in peat that had been thoroughly wetted with deionised water and wrapped in black plastic. They had been inspected on a few occasions by the staff of the conservation laboratory, but there had been minimal disturbance. In this position the remains lay with the underside uppermost.

The black plastic was removed from the block. Drops of moisture adhered to its underside. The peat was moist on the surface and throughout. Initially, the condensation droplets on the underside of the plastic sheeting were tested. Then five sites on the peat block were selected: on the north, south, east and west ends and approximately in the middle. The surface of the peat at these locations was tested, then the peat at *c.* 20mm deep, followed by the peat at *c.* 50mm deep. Because the peat was lumpy, the depths were approximate and dependent on the consistency of the peat at that point. Finally, the moisture on the surface of the human remains themselves was tested.

The parts tested were the right leg, just above the knee; the left calf; the right foot; and the left foot. The remains were not fully exposed. A small area of the skin was uncovered, and the paper was pressed down on this area. Thus an exact location was not established except in the area of the feet, which had been covered by <20mm of peat. Their appearance, however, was unaltered from the time when they had been covered after excavation.

The pH was taken using Whatman pH indicator papers, which detect a range of pH values, with a different colour corresponding to each value. In the middle is a blank (white) square, and, when applied to a substance, this changes colour to correspond to a specific value in the pH scale. Four ranges of pH were available and these overlapped slightly. The first paper used measured pH in the range 1.8–3.8, the second 3.8–5.5, the third 5.2–6.8, and the fourth 6.0–8.1. The control was deionised water from the conservation laboratory of the National Museum of Ireland.

The pH papers were pressed onto the damp surface until they were saturated. Three readings were taken of each pH range, and an average of the readings was used. The results were disappointing. Deionised water and the water adhering to the plastic cover gave reasonably unambiguous readings: pH of 6.00 and *c.* 5.00 respectively. Papers applied to the peat surface and the surface of the remains gave a different picture. Initially, the colour change was in most cases in the direction of a low pH. However, in a short time the indicator window stained more then one colour, giving a pH reading of differing ranges. In some cases the indicator window streaked colours across the range of the pH spectrum, therefore not giving a coherent or accurate reading.

The initial readings indicated that the surface of the peat had a pH of 4.0–5.0, and readings taken during the original laboratory excavation seemed to indicate a pH of 3.8. This was interesting as the peat was not compacted and air could circulate through most of it: loose peat subject to air circulation might be expected to have a more regular or even pH throughout. When the papers were reinspected the next day, the colours had altered and, allowing for the difficulty in interpretation, the pH now indicated seemed to have risen. It was decided to do the experiment again.

In September 2002 a second set of readings was taken. The strips were mounted and photographed on the spot. Again, the water results were easier to read and consistent: the water adherent to the cover had a pH of 5.5–6.00. The readings for peat and moisture adhering to the skin were, however, as imprecise and difficult to read as previously (Table 19), that is, the colours streaked after the initial readings.

Test area	pH
pH upper surface peat	4.7–5.9
pH deeper peat	4.9–5.9
pH of moisture on skin	5.5–5.9

Table 19: pH readings from peat and moisture adhering to the surface of the skin.

It is not clear whether the initial readings were taken too soon and the final colour that had been observed the next day was correct or the initial intervention caused a rise in the pH that was recorded on the second attempt at measuring it. Although the initial results are believed to be a true reflection of the ability of *Sphagnum* to keep pH in the bog low, thus acting as a preservative, the experimental methods used failed to prove this. It is clear, however, that pH papers are an unsatisfactory and unreliable method of measuring the pH of bog bodies.

10.
Preservation

Máire Delaney

Preservation of organic material in *Sphagnum* bogs has traditionally been attributed to its acidic, anaerobic and waterlogged nature. Painter (1995) gives a comprehensive overview of the preservative properties of bog and indicates that the process is much more complicated than previously thought. He postulates that a polysaccharide, which he calls sphagnan, causes a tanning effect. This renders certain organic materials resistant to subsequent decay, even when taken out of the bog environment. This is accompanied by the Malliard reaction, which produces a dark, coffee colour (Painter 1991).

Doyle and Dowding (1990) demonstrated the decay rate of cotton strips of pure α-cellulose in Mongan Bog, Co. Offaly. They examined hummocks, lawns, pools and hollows and established that the highest decay rates were in the surface 0.10m of hummocks and lawns. Pools and hollows were more variable but overall had lower decay rates. These varied with temperature and therefore with season, the least decay taking place in winter. Interestingly, in one year of the two-year study (1985) the decay rate in pools in summer was at its highest at a depth of 0.15–0.20m, higher than in other habitats. Above and below this depth the decay rates were lower than in the other habitats. The relative climatic conditions of that year are not discussed. Temperature fluctuations were also interesting. *Calluna* shaded the surface of the hummocks in summer, so the surface was cooler than at other sites. Not surprisingly, the temperature at 0.50m was more stable than the surface temperature and in fact was higher in all habitats in winter than that of the surface 0.10m. In the Mongan Bog study, the most important factor affecting the decay rate was the presence of oxygen. In anoxic zones the decay slowed down considerably. The depth in centimetres above the anoxic zone averaged 32mm. Although the area in which the Tumbeagh body lay was not technically a hollow, it had many of the characteristics of one, such as extreme wetness, particularly in the area of the feet (Casparie and Reilly, Chapters 13 and 14). It may be that bodies buried in a 'hollow habitat' would not need to be submerged as deeply in the bog as bodies buried in other habitats in order to survive.

Bog bodies in 'a remarkable state of preservation' (O'Kelly 1829) have been recorded in Ireland since at least the seventeenth century (Ó Floinn 1995a). We know

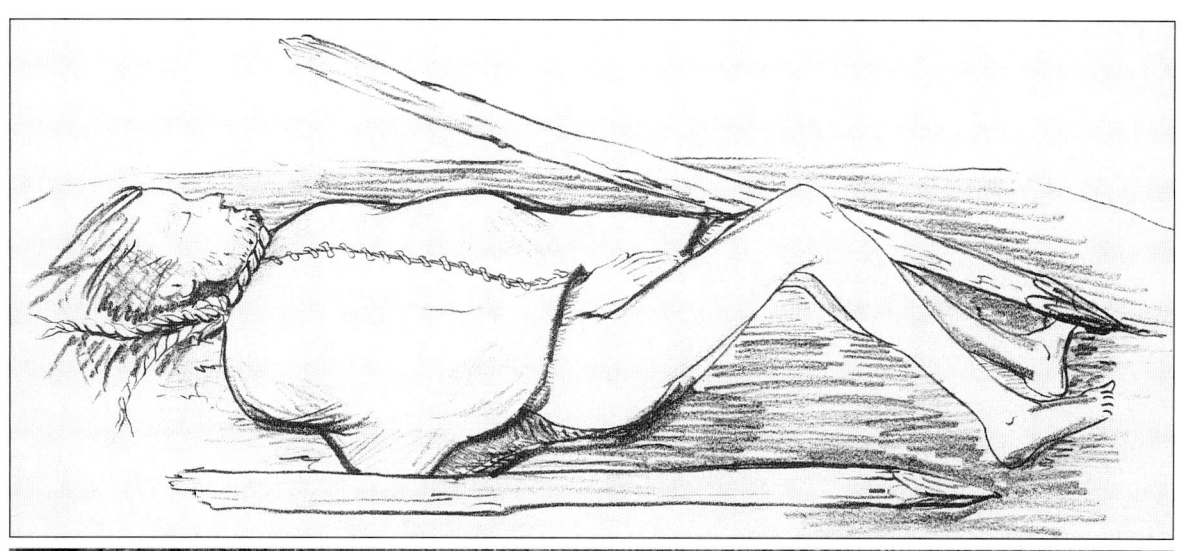

Pl. 41:
The body of Gallagh Man as it survives today. It had been allowed to air dry in the past (photo: NMI). A reconstruction drawing shows how the body, wrapped in a leather cape and probably weighed down by poles, lay in the bog.

that the chemical processes in a *Sphagnum* bog decalcify bone (Connolly *et al.* [1986]; Painter 1995). They also preserve the gross appearance of collagenous structures, such as skin and tendon, and of keratinous structures, such as skin, nails and hair, and do not inhibit the formation of adipocere.

The phenomenon for which bog bodies are famous and that leads to their existence today is their resistance to autolysis—bacterial and fungal decay and insect infestation—both while immersed in the bog and after the material has dried out. The Tumbeagh discovery was due to the sharp-eyed recognition of the difference in appearance between the dried-out skin and the more common, poorly humified bog vegetation. The skin was typical of dried, bog-preserved skin. It was hard—but not brittle—dark brown and dull.

This appearance is well demonstrated by Gallagh Man (Pl. 41), currently on display in the National Museum of Ireland. His original appearance was described thus:

> his teeth are all perfect, as are [*sic*] his hair (which is of a dark brown colour). His lips, tongue, ears, fingers and his skin and flesh are perfectly hard and dry like tanned leather. His beard is quite observable, and seems like a fortnight's growth (O'Kelly 1829).

The subsequent deterioration is described as he is uncovered repeatedly:

> It is only a fortnight or three weeks since I had him taken up last…his skin has become dingy and discoloured, the hair too is loosened from his head and the features somewhat defaced, but in every other respect, he is as before, and even the most fleshy parts, and those which would be expected soonest to waste, are perfectly sound and firm (*ibid.*).

His present appearance is wizened, dry and hairless. There is some warping of the bones; the right femur in particular shows localised warping of the bone.

Another example of the changes brought about by natural drying is the Weerdinge find. A photograph of the find, which consisted of two men buried side by side, that was taken shortly after their discovery demonstrates straight, parallel legs. Warping of the bones on drying led to their present, crossed appearance, on which so many false conclusions were based (van der Sanden 1990). Another Dutch body, from Exloërmond, shows similar post-drying bowing of the legs, leading to their crossing (van der Sanden 1990). Meenybraddan Woman was frozen three days after her discovery. Subsequent defrosting and freezing resulted in visible deterioration of the remains (Delaney and Ó Floinn 1995). The skin altered slightly in colour and texture, becoming a little paler and dull. Her remains were never allowed to dry out, however, and, although the surface texture of the bone altered slightly, no further distortion occurred.

The state of preservation of the Tumbeagh remains when they emerged from the bog is indicated by the detailed anatomical description in Chapter 7. As has been noted previously, muscle tissue seemed to have disappeared. This was borne out by imaging (Chapter 8). The absence of muscle tissue may be explained by the greater blood supply to muscle than to tendon or skin. This probably plays a part in the disappearance of muscle by supplying oxygen to the tissue for longer and sustaining aerobic chemical reactions leading to the breakdown of the tissue.

The bone from Tumbeagh was dark brown and decalcified. The sections of the shafts of the long bones exposed were bendable, and in many areas the bone was very thin. Tissue interpreted as articular hyaline cartilage was also brown but not as darkly pigmented as the bone (Pls 18–20). Other fragments of human bone were found and are described in Chapter 7. These were presumed to have come from this body, as evidence of more than one individual was not recovered. These fragments had been redeposited on the surface of the find field, in the adjacent field and in the stockpile (Chapter 3). They were dry, dusty, dark brown, hard and very light. They were of a rougher texture than other bone from bog bodies, even those that had dried after exhumation (M. Delaney, unpublished data). One fragment of rib submitted for radiocarbon dating was found to contain an insignificant amount of collagen and was unusable. There was no reason to suspect that the other fragments were of significantly different composition. It has generally been thought that the fraction of bone that survives in the bog is the collagenous and other organic parts. The composition of these randomly found bones has not as yet been assessed. However, it is interesting that recognisable fragments remain after decalcification in bog water and the action of aerobic decay above ground afterwards. Repeated wetting and drying and exposure to air may have leached the sphagnan and other preservatives from this bone, leading to the decay of the organic matter but the retention of the small amounts of inorganic material left after bog immersion.

The tendon and skin from Tumbeagh were remarkably light in colour. Painter (1995) states that a 'very dark, coffee colour is so characteristic of tanning by sphagnan that one could confidently assert that any body of a different colour must have been preserved in some other way'. However, we know that the body from Tumbeagh has lain for some hundreds of years undisturbed. Tanning of the collagen in these tissues by sphagnan or other peat processes must have proceeded without the Malliard reaction producing the dark pigments.

Adipocere is fat that has been altered by hydrolysis in moist, anaerobic conditions. It is pale cream in colour, with the consistency of Cheshire cheese, and is often present in bog bodies. In the case of the Tumbeagh body it was preserved in the knee region and in the foot, but there seems to be very little in the subcutaneous tissues preserved. There is more fatty tissue in the hollow just behind the knee, the popliteal fossa, than beneath the skin of the parts of the lower leg present. Fatty tissue is present with fibrous tissue on the heel and outer, weight-bearing aspect of the right foot. There is generally not a great deal of fat in the foot. Thus the adipocere found reflects the anatomical distribution of fat. Painter (1995) has described the extrusion of fat from skin on tanning. This may explain small deposits of adipocere around some of the tarsal bones. The absence of adipocere in the other tissues present may represent the absence of fat in the subcutaneous tissue in life.

In other bog bodies, such as Meenybraddan Woman (Delaney and Ó Floinn 1995) and Huldermose Woman (Brothwell 1996), adipocere was observed deep to the skin only and not on the outer surface. In Lindow Man (Stead et al. [1986]) and Gallagh Man (M. Delaney, unpublished data), where adipocere was not found subcutaneously, imaging has shown the presence of central nervous tissue, most notably the brain. There is a large amount of fat in the central nervous system, and adipocere formation would explain the presence of remains of the tissue. The absence of adipocere peripherally may be due to the absence of significant amounts of subcutaneous fat or to the decay of the fatty tissue before the formation of adipocere. The depth of the central nervous structures within the bodies in these cases may have given rise to circumstances more suitable to the formation of adipocere.

No hair was observed on the surviving remains from Tumbeagh, but a few of the toenails were present. These were a dirty mid-brown colour and softer in consistency than fresh nail (Pl. 17). As with other bog bodies, the structures were relatively durable and not particularly fragile. Delicacy of handling was more important for the protection of the relationships between the loose and unconnected parts of the find than for the protection of the individual structures.

During the laboratory excavation, close observation was paid to any deterioration in the quality of preservation. With the exception of the minor changes outlined in

Chapter 4, deterioration was not noted on subsequent occasions when the block was uncovered. There had been no shrinkage and no colour change. The fragment of skin originally exposed in the bog remained as it was: slightly shrunken, dark in colour and stiff despite constant wetting and covering with peat. It seemed to have been the part most vulnerable to mould growth. Once the remains were uncovered from the peat in which they were embedded, they could not have been said to be anaerobic. We know from swabs taken during the excavation of Lindow Man that micro-organisms are present in peat, albeit in small numbers (Ridgway *et al.* [1986]). Nevertheless, growth took place only transiently or on areas not in contact with the peat.

The greatest threat to the remains in general seemed to be from drying out. Drying and deterioration seemed to extend from the area of skin that had dried in the field. Again, the progress of the drying was counteracted by keeping the remains wet within peat taken from the site where they were found, and no serious extension of the deterioration resulted.

Overall, the preservation of the partial bog body from Tumbeagh is in keeping with what is known of the preservation of other bog bodies. Conditions, however, were somewhat different, as demonstrated by the failure of the Malliard reaction to occur. Work on the Tumbeagh remains has also demonstrated that bog bodies can remain stable over a few years, if kept wet and covered in peat taken from the findspot, without the state of preservation being adversely altered.

III.
WIDENING THE VIEW

The bog body from Tumbeagh

The person found in Tumbeagh was alone in a wet, inhospitable, boggy tract of land flanked on the west by low-lying dry land on the east by more than 2km of bog that millennia before had claimed the former basin and enclosed outcrops of higher ground within it. This was the world in which the teenager ended up: cut off from the local population, their relatives, perhaps, the land they may have worked and the church they may have attended. But what was this world like? Tumbeagh itself is a townland of just over 228ha, seemingly indistinguishable from its neighbouring townlands, which comprise bog and farmland. No major monuments are known, and there is no record of events of major significance. In the following chapters, records from history, archaeology, peat, pollen and insects are used to provide a stronger sense of the area's past. Each treatment is wider than the later medieval time frame in which the Tumbeagh youth once lived. The timelines vary as each particular record has its own chronology, although these are connected and overlapping because of the body in the bog. We start by looking at the bog as it is today, using this as a springboard into the history of the wider Lemanaghan area in which Tumbeagh lies. The focus is initially broad and then zooms in on north-west County Offaly to view more closely kingdom, parish, bogland and upland (Bermingham, Chapters 11 and 12). Then we move into the bog itself, getting to know its hydrology, its features and its dynamism (Casparie and Reilly, Chapters 13 and 14). Finally, the pollen that fell on the bog shows us the character of the nearby upland and the role that humans had in shaping it (Weir, Chapter 15).

11.
The bog at Tumbeagh

Nóra Bermingham

Location

Tumbeagh is both a townland name and a bog name, the latter derived from the former. Situated in west County Offaly, it lies north of the Ferbane–Clara road but is best entered from a minor link road that clips the northern extent of the Lemanaghan Group of bogs (Fig. 2). Tumbeagh Bog covers an area of 130ha on the north-western edge of the 1200ha Lemanaghan Group (Pl. 1). An old road known as Connor's Road bisects Tumbeagh. This route, rather advantageously, occupies the line of a subsurface gravel ridge, reflecting earlier and natural landscape divisions. The road/ridge extends in an arc between the upland to the west and a dryland island farm, known as Broder's Island, in the east. Before relatively recent agricultural improvements, this island was composed of two smaller islands, and it lies almost at the heart of the Lemanaghan Group, surrounded in all directions by more than 1km of bog. It is hardly surprising, then, that trackways of varying date have been found radiating from it (Fig. 2). East of here the bogs of Castletown and Killaghintober stretch to pastureland that covers gently rising spurs of esker.

To the south, Tumbeagh opens into a greater expanse of peat known as Lemanaghan Bog. Since the mid-1950s a Bord na Móna narrow-gauge railway, used to transport peat to the power station at Ferbane, has divided the two areas of bog. Lemanaghan Bog is the largest open area of bog in the group and sits squarely above a dryland island of the same name. The island interrupts the bog, forcing it to extend southward in two spurs known as Curraghalassa and Derrynagun. Beyond these, there was callow that formed a lowland wet zone between the bog and the River Brosna, into which the bogs drained.

Early industrial surveys

Detailed surveys of the extent and nature of a bog were completed by Bord na Móna to assess its suitability for exploitation. The surveys covered bog classification, peat depth and peat quality (in terms of future use as fuel or moss) and included recommendations for future exploitation. Survey results took the form of peat stratigraphical tables, cross-sections, and contour and extent plans (Fig. 15). Today these records are housed in the Peat Energy Division in Boora, Co. Offaly. From a topographical point of view, the records provide comprehensive pre-drainage and pre-exploitation data on a landscape that has since been hugely altered.

In 1945 Robert Dubsky made a report to the then Turf Development Board on the results of a survey of the Lemanaghan group of bogs. He described Lemanaghan as an expansive basin bog, the floor of which was almost entirely blue clay, with the occasional occurrence of marl. The average bog depth was 22 feet (*c.* 6.7m), with depths of up to 39 feet (*c.* 11.8m) in places. Highly decomposed, lake-formed *Phragmites* peats covered the basin floor for up to 5 feet (*c.* 1.5m), and these in turn were overlain by horizons of 'Older' and 'Younger' *Sphagnum* peats. More than twenty years after this initial survey, Bord na Móna returned to the Tumbeagh area to carry out further survey. To some extent Dubsky's initial findings were repeated. Sections through Tumbeagh showed its domed upper surface and basin-shaped floor punctuated by peaks and troughs, with peat depths (before drainage) of 6m and more.

Fig. 15: Longitudinal cross-sections through Tumbeagh showing the sub-peat topography and the depth of peat before drainage. This Bord na Móna survey dates from the mid-1940s. Dr. = drain; F.B. = face bank; CL = level crossing; B.L. = baseline.

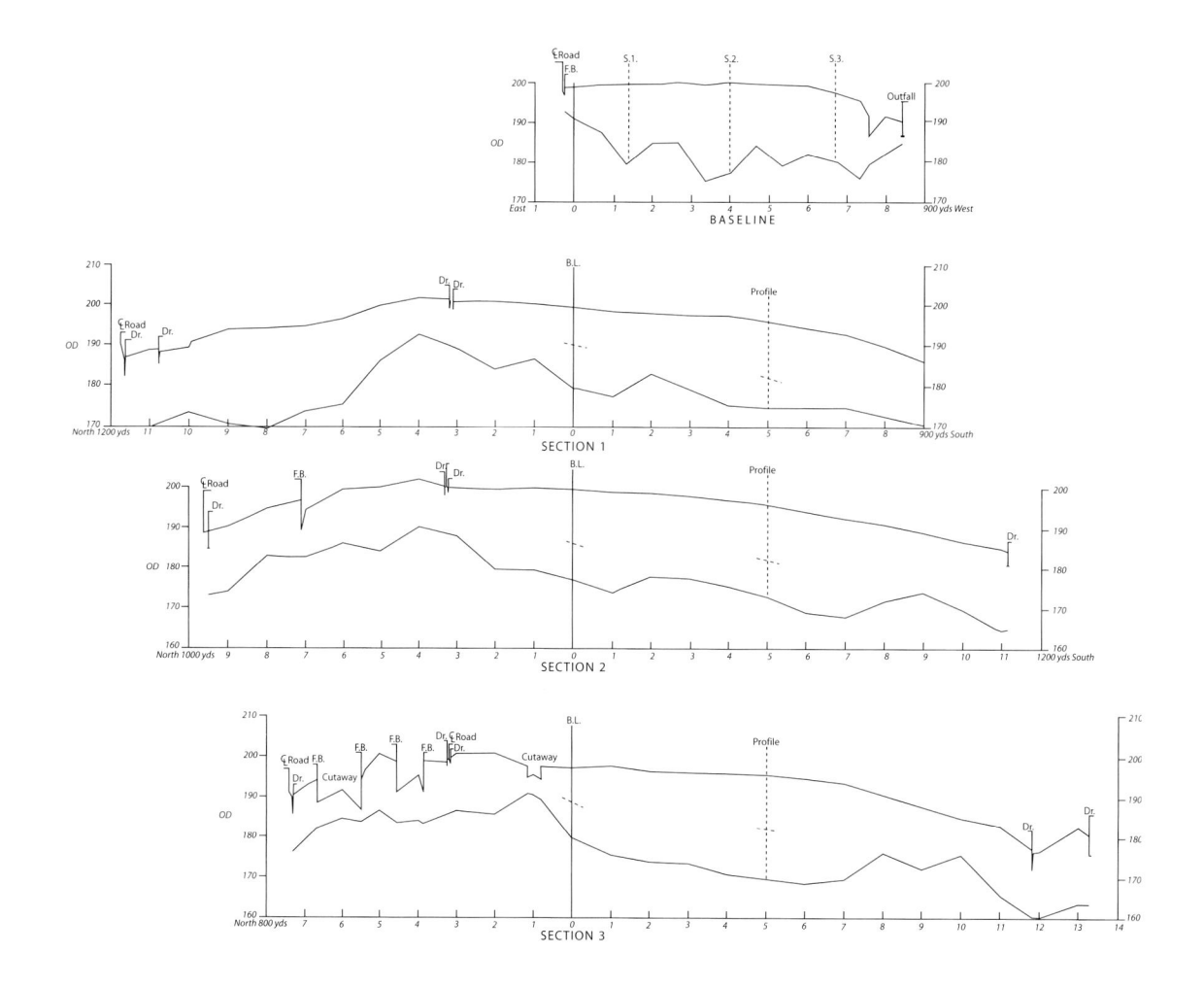

It had formed in the greater Lemanaghan basin on either side of an east–west-running gravel ridge (Connor's Road), which had had a direct influence on its development (Casparie, Chapter 13).

Production history of Tumbeagh

Tumbeagh was first drained in the mid-1980s. The drains run the length of the bog and are oriented approximately north–south. The bog is remembered locally as being particularly wet, especially in its westernmost parts. By the 1980s, mechanised cutting of drains was the norm. Before the manufacture of custom-made ditching machinery, all drains were cut by hand. Eventually the bog spade was replaced by the disc-ditcher. At Tumbeagh, however, attempts to use a mechanical ditcher had failed: the area was too wet, and machinery was repeatedly mired in the bog. Consequently, in certain parts of the bog the drains were cut by hand (M. Guinan, pers. comm.).

Bord na Móna applies a standard layout to bogs subject to milling. Drainage takes place via a network of parallel open drains, *c.* 1m wide, 1m deep and 15m apart (Pl. 1). The strip of bog between the drains is called a field. These are domed in cross-section to facilitate drainage. The highest point is the field centre. Once the initial drainage is in place, it takes 7–8 years for the bog surface to drain sufficiently to allow peat extraction to begin. The bog surface is levelled and cleared of its skin or surface vegetation. Extraction is by milling. An average annual peat harvest removes a depth of 0.10–0.12m of peat from each field under production in that year. Milling began in Tumbeagh in the early 1990s. By 1998, when the bog body was found, 0.30–1.0m of drained, compressed peat had been extracted from the bog.

Archaeological survey of the bog

The first archaeological survey of Tumbeagh took place in 1997. Before this, no archaeological sites were known from the bog. Survey involved inspection of drain faces and field surfaces at 30m intervals. Archaeological sites were identified in the southern and middle parts of the bog, and it was here that follow-up investigations concentrated in 1997 (Fig. 2). Excavations in the area in 1999 revealed short brushwood trackways, one of which dates to *c.* 171 cal. BC (OCarroll 1999). In 1998 the survey returned to Tumbeagh and found the pattern of site distribution to have altered little, with one exception: close to the northern end of the bog the remains of the bog body were found.

Why was the discovery not made when the bog was first surveyed? A variety of factors influence the discovery of sites and finds in bogs. Milling results in a cover of loose peat on the field surface. Depending on the stage of the milling, peat cover can range from light to heavy. Generally it is heavier in the field centre than at the edges. The recutting of drains can result in heavier peat cover on the field surface, thus obscuring the field centre. In 1997 the peat cover may have been sufficiently heavy to obscure the flap of skin identified. The weather too can play a part in the identification of sites. Heavy rainfall reduces visibility and can make the bog surface difficult to negotiate. The first survey of Tumbeagh, in 1997, took place in a downpour; during the second survey, in September 1998, the sun shone. Survey methods may also have played a part. The 1998 survey used an interval of 15m rather than 30m, which may have led to the discovery. There is also a human factor: in this case the degree of experience of the archaeologist involved played a significant part in the discovery of the bog body, given the limited exposure of the find. A less experienced archaeologist may not have spotted the difference in colour and texture of the flap of skin against a saturated, brown background. There is perhaps no single reason that the discovery was made in 1998 and not 1997. Clearly, however, in the space of a year, conditions had altered sufficiently to allow the discovery.

12.
Tumbeagh and Lemanaghan: an archaeological and historical perspective

Nóra Bermingham

Ireland and controlling forces

Ireland in *c.* AD 1100 was a mass of territorial divisions, with the major divisions being the provincial kingdoms of Leinster, Munster, Ulster, Connacht and Mide (Smyth 1982). Each was made up of sub-kingdoms, the controlling dynasties of which swore allegiance to the chief dynastic family of the province. Allegiances frequently changed, and recurrent political and territorial disputes between rival Gaelic dynasties at small-kingdom and provincial-kingdom level were commonplace. The extent of a kingdom was frequently determined by geography. Rivers, mountains, bogs and woodland acted as barriers to expansion and shielded Gaelic kingdoms from rival dynasties, as well as invading foreign armies (Lennon 1994). This was the case in the area of County Offaly in which Tumbeagh lies.

With the arrival of the Anglo-Normans in the twelfth century, however, things began to change significantly. The Anglo-Normans extended the rule and influence of the English Crown over the island, with varying degrees of success. The succeeding centuries saw changes in urban and rural settlement patterns, as well as economic and agricultural practices (Barry 1987). A new administrative system was imposed in which landlords ran the countryside, where they could. English influence over the island expanded and contracted, dictated by internal, international and natural pressures (Richter 1988; Lennon 1994).

During the fourteenth and fifteenth centuries there was a fusion of the Anglo-Norman, or by this time Anglo-Irish, and Gaelic social systems, with the earls at the forefront of this merger. England was concerned with matters closer to home (Scotland) and on the Continent (France). Disasters such as the Great European Famine of 1315–18 and the Black Death in 1348–50 also contributed to a reduced interest in Ireland. Increasingly, landlords were absent, and there was a lessening of direct rule over the island. Power was returning to the Gaelic lords, and the claims of the Anglo-Irish were consolidated in earldoms. Throughout the fifteenth century the earls were the main vehicle of English representation and administration in Ireland beyond the Pale. By the end of the fifteenth century, England's lordship extended over the Pale, east Munster, urban centres and their hinterlands, and dispersed locations in Connacht and Ulster.

In the mid-sixteenth century the Tudor Crown was concerned with the expansion and protection of its territorial borders. As a result, it initiated a series of state-funded plantations in the eastern halves of counties Laois and Offaly and in parts of counties Limerick, Waterford, Kerry and Cork—within the former earldom of Desmond—as well as in County Antrim and north County Down. The success of the plantations varied greatly, as they were the objects of frequent attacks by Gaelic lords and Old English landholders. By the end of the sixteenth century, rebellion, headed by Hugh O'Neill, had gripped the country, but a stronger English force resulted in his defeat and the eventual departure to France of surviving earls in 1607. This opened the way for further plantations, and in 1620 west County Offaly, along with the extreme west of County Westmeath and parts of Longford and Leitrim, received Jacobean settlers and/or saw the redistribution of land to those loyal to the Crown. The vigour with which the plantations were made was too much for the remnant native political system. It had continued to function, evolve and adapt alongside that of the Anglo-Normans and the earls until well into the seventeenth century, when it was finally replaced over the entire island.

A Gaelic kingdom

Tumbeagh lies in the parish of Lemanaghan, forming part of the barony of Garrycastle (Figs 16, 17). Defined in the late sixteenth century, Garrycastle corresponded to the territory or sub-kingdom of Delbhna Eathra (Delvin), in the extreme west of the province/kingdom of Mide, which was under the dominion of the Southern Uí Néill (Cox 1973; Duffy 1997). Delbhna Eathra/Delvin is known to have existed from the early ninth century, when reference is made to raids on the territory by the neighbouring kingdom of Munster (Annals of the Four Masters (AFM), 823, 831, O'Donovan 1851). By the eleventh century the principal dynasty was the Mac Coghlans, who then dominated from the mid-thirteenth to the mid-seventeenth century.

The western frontier of Delvin was marked by the River Shannon, tributaries of which, the Brosna and the Blackwater, ran through the north-west part of the territory. To the south and east its border ran through the Boora Bogs and across a series of low gravel hills that provided north–south access between Munster, Mide and Leinster.

Framed to the north by the hills of the Eiscir Riada, or Great Esker, an important routeway between Dublin and the Shannon at Clonmacnoise (Sheehan 1993; Tubridy 1998), Delvin, or Mac Coghlan country as it was also known, was described by Matthew de Renzi in 1617 as 'infenced with bogges, woods, water and mountains, that is in a manner of a bullwarck of it selfe, and wherein there is but twoo open passages in pases of woods and bogs on either side' (MacCuarta 1987, 136).

But Delvin was not without good land. A description of the area, then known as the barony of Garrycastle, in the Civil Survey of 1654–6 refers to its soil as being 'good and fitt both for tillage and grazinge of cattle, it is well watered with rivers, brookes and streames...very convenient for the inhabitants, and afford some eeles, pickarells, troutes and salmon' (Simington 1961, 36). It would not be unreasonable to assume that this record is also applicable to the preceding centuries (Weir, Chapter 15).

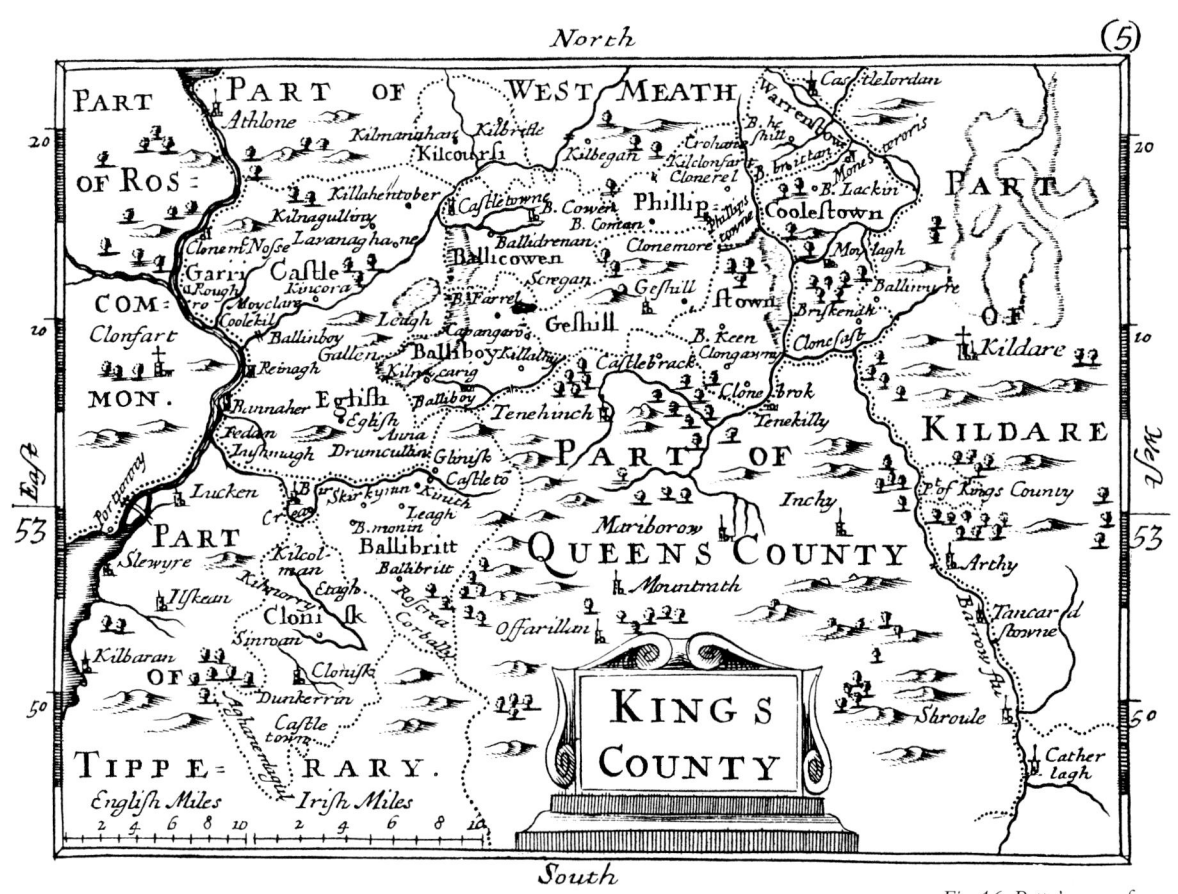

Tumbeagh and Lemanaghan: an archaeological and historical perspective

Fig. 16: Petty's map of King's County, as County Offaly used to be known, c. 1685; Lemanaghan is spelt Lavanaghane (Petty and Lamb 1969).

Fig. 17: Extract from Petty's map (1685) of the barony of Garrycastle (Garriecastle) showing the extent of bogs in the Lemanaghan area, spelt Lismanaghan/Limanaghan (Petty and Lamb 1969).

Much of the territory, however, was raised bog (Smyth 1982, pl. 24), a terrain neither the Anglo-Normans nor succeeding English armies entered happily. Indeed, de Renzy comments on how the bogs had always afforded the Mac Coghlans and their herds protection from attacking neighbouring lordships (MacCuarta 1987). By the time that de Renzy took up residence in Delvin in the early seventeenth century, there were still no English living in the territory (Loeber 1980).

In the early 1260s the English succeeded in subjugating Delvin but were driven out in 1264 by Art O Melaghin, then king of Mide, who established native lords in Delvin—including the Mac Coghlans—who were loyal to him. The dominance of the Mac Coghlans in Delvin was tested on many occasions between the thirteenth and the sixteenth century (Cox 1973; 1974; B. Ryan 1994). It is recorded that in 1551, under the programme of 'Surrender and Regrant' enacted by Parliament in 1541, the then lord, Art Mac Coghlan, submitted to the Crown, resulting in Delvin becoming a tributary to the king (AFM 1552, O'Donovan 1851). This process appears to have been repeated in 1582, when John Mac Coghlan surrendered and was subsequently knighted (P. Walsh 1960). Delvin and the surrounding territories of Fir Ceall and Ely O Carroll country, which lay to the south, were incorporated into King's County in the early seventeenth century. By the end of the seventeenth century many of the native lords had fled to the Continent, and ownership of their property had been transferred to English Protestants (Loeber 1980). Among them were those named Hamilton, Jones, Smyth, Strongman, Harford and Warburton, some of the 158 English residing in Garrycastle who were recorded in the census of Ireland in 1659. This survey recorded the total population of the barony as 1118, of which 960 were Irish, including the families of Coghlan, Horan, Rigny, Larkin and Madden (Pender 1939).

From personalities to monuments

That the Mac Coghlans were for many centuries lords of Delvin is reflected in the survival of many of their castles, albeit that they survive today as ruinous sixteenth/seventeenth-century structures or have been incorporated in later buildings. Ringing the Lemanaghan bogs are a series of castles known to have been Mac Coghlan strongholds in the late sixteenth and the early seventeenth century—Ballycumber, Kilcolgan More, Coole, Kilnagarnagh—as well as the tower-house just north of the church at Lemanaghan (Fig. 17; Pl. 42). The last is known to have been the property of the duke of Buckingham in 1641, and a now lost sheela-na-gig was once incorporated in the structure (O'Brien and Sweetman 1997). There are other castle sites at Bellair/Ballyard and Rashinagh and a fortified house at Castlearmstrong. All of these, dating from the mid-seventeenth century, are later than those built and owned by the Mac Coghlans.

It is now known where the Mac Coghlans lived before the late sixteenth century. Their longevity in Delvin has resulted in a seemingly impoverished native medieval archaeological record over much of the territory, particularly when compared with those areas either settled or under the influence of the English. This characteristic is by no means exclusive to Delvin. The difficulty of identifying native settlement and other, contemporaneous sites, apart from ecclesiastical centres, in Gaelic-dominated

Pl. 42:
The Lemanaghan
tower-house as it was
in 1937 (photo:
DoEHLG).

parts of medieval Ireland has been highlighted by several authors, most recently Kieran O'Conor (1998; Barry 1987).

For those who did not live in Anglo-Irish towns, villages and tower-houses, it has been suggested that some ringforts, the most common settlement form in the preceding Early Christian period, and crannogs may have continued in use up to the seventeenth century (Fredengren 2003). There are fifteen ringforts on the uplands to the north and west of the Lemanaghan bogs, although none has been investigated or dated. On the same uplands, to the north and west, there are fourteen enclosures of unknown date and function (O'Brien and Sweetman 1997). Some of these may date from the medieval period, but without investigation it cannot be said whether any were native medieval habitation sites.

Pl. 43: The church at Lemanaghan with its walls revealed after the removal of vegetation in 2002/3 (photo: Nóra Bermingham).

In striving to identify the presence of the local medieval/later medieval population in the Lemanaghan area, we have to look to its bogs and to an ecclesiastical complex situated almost at the heart of the Lemanaghan bogs. On the largest dryland island in the Lemanaghan bog complex is a monastic centre (Pl. 43) that, though still a functioning church in AD 1200, has origins in the mid-seventh century AD. The first abbot, after whom the site takes its name, was St Manchán, whose death from an epidemic was recorded in AD 665 (Reynolds 1929; Gwynn and Hadcock 1988). Although no standing remains of the early church survive, a series of graveslabs, their motifs reputedly derivative of the Clonmacnoise school (Crawford 1911), and a bullaun stone point to the Early Christian existence of the site. Close by, *c.* 350m to the east of the present church, is a rectangular enclosure inside of which is a small oratory of seventh-century date, known as St Mella's Cell, which was built by St Manchán for his mother, St Mella. A flagstone road runs between the oratory and the church. The present, ruinous, stone-built church is an amalgamation of Romanesque and fifteenth-century architecture (Fitzpatrick and O'Brien 1998) and was home to one of Ireland's finest twelfth-century shrines, that of St Manchán. This shrine, which still houses a number of human bones, purportedly those of its namesake, is a silver and gold gabled-tomb-shaped reliquary (Ó Floinn 1994). Another fine example of religious metalwork was retrieved from the bog immediately north of Lemanaghan. Fragments of a bronze crozier with silver inlay panels were found in 1977 and 1991 (M. Ryan 1991). This crozier dates to the eleventh century and, like St Manchán's shrine, reflects the financial well-being and perhaps the religious and political importance of the monastic settlement at Lemanaghan in local and regional terms.

Since the Church was established in Ireland, there have always been strong economic, political, and religious bonds between it and those who held power, be they Anglo-Norman or Gaelic. Church foundations required lay patrons, and in Delvin the Mac Coghlans were patrons to many of the churches, including Lemanaghan. In 1426 Lemanaghan had become a parochial church (Joseph 1930), the parish priest, or vicar, of which in 1531 was Murtough, son of Conor Mac Coghlan (AFM 1403, O'Donovan 1851). Murtough or his predecessor may have overseen the alterations to a window in the church on which is a hood-moulding with a carving of a dragon over which stands a small figure that appears to be cowing the beast; this has been dated to the early sixteenth century on stylistic grounds (Newman Johnson 1987). Much later, in his will, the lord John Mac Coghlan included Lemanaghan in a series of bequests to the churches of Delvin in 1590. These churches included Clonmacnoise, Reynagh, Gallen, Ferbane and Tisaran.

With the decline and eventual replacement of the Mac Coghlans as lords of Delvin and the campaign of religious conversion instigated by the English, Lemanaghan, like many other churches in Delvin, diminished in importance. After more than 500 years, the church fell into ruin, its late seventeenth-century vicar choosing to preach from a private house rather than the crumbling temple (Ellison 1975).

Raised-bog records of a local population

Over a decade, archaeological surveys of Irish raised bogs have resulted in the identification of more than 2000 sites. Bogs, as rich archaeological repositories, are well demonstrated in the Lemanaghan Group, where around 750 sites are known (Fig. 2; IAWU 1997a). This figure is particularly astounding when compared with the significantly smaller number of sites known from the surrounding dry land. This may, however, just be a question of visibility. In the open, cut bog, large numbers of sites of all periods can be identified in one season of survey, giving the initial impression perhaps of constant and intense activity in the bog. With dating, a better picture of the frequency of site construction and by implication the level of human activity in the bog can be established. Dates so far returned from a series of archaeological projects in Lemanaghan allow individual sites or groups of sites to be extricated from the mass and to be looked at in relation to specific chronological periods.

In Tumbeagh itself IAWU surveys have identified 97 archaeological sites: 31 toghers, 66 deposits of worked and unworked wood, and two finds—the bog body and a textile fragment. Of the toghers, twelve have been dated, with ten returning prehistoric dates and two dating from the medieval period. Lying less than 200m north and east of the findspot of the bog body (immediately north of Connor's Road) is a brushwood and roundwood togher (IAWU catalogue code: OF-TBH 0078) dating to c. cal. AD 1217–1407 (690±70 BP, Beta-118036). This site was traced for 30m and is the nearest medieval structure to the bog body, albeit clearly of earlier origin. Just over 1km to the south of the bog body lies a 20m-long togher constructed

The bog body from Tumbeagh

Pl. 44: An excavation cutting dating to 1996 exposed the multi-phased nature of this roadway in the Lemanaghan bogs; the final construction phase is represented by flagstones (photo: Nóra Bermingham).

of layers of brushwood secured with pegs (IAWU catalogue code: OF-KNY 0007). Birch, hazel, ash and cherry feature among the species represented. This site, dated to cal. AD 1410–1633 (420±50 BP, Beta-118038), is more or less contemporary with the bog body, which has been dated to *c*. AD 1500.

Elsewhere in the Lemanaghan complex, prehistoric structures more than 2000–3000 years old are known; indeed, almost every bog in the group has produced at least one prehistoric site (IAWU 1998; OCarroll and Whitaker 1999). The early historic period is also well represented, perhaps most intriguingly by the lowest level of a multi-period togher clearly constructed to provide access to and from the dryland island on which the monastic settlement of St Manchán was situated.

Dendrochronological dates for the site show long-lived usage and repeated construction: AD 653±9, AD 1158±9 and AD 1212 (OCarroll 1997, 94). The site was surveyed again in 2001, as part of the writer's PhD research on the development of the Lemanaghan group of bogs. At its south-western end, flags are visible in a perimeter drain that disconnects the bog from reclaimed pastureland now fringing the dryland island. The north-eastern end of the road was situated in the high bog at the edge of the worked area and was traced into the grass fields, where its flagstone upper surface was visible. An additional 200m can be added to its recorded length of 750m. It seems likely that the road extends beneath the modern Ferbane–Clara road and into fields of gorse and scrub on the other side, its landfall obscured by recent sediment and heavy vegetation. From single-plank walkway to corduroy road to limestone-flagged surface (Pl. 44), the life of this roadway appears to have kept pace with that of the monastery. It is not unknown, though uncommon, for a routeway in an extensive bogland tract to be reused and rebuilt over many centuries: the togher of flagstone, wood and boulder clay excavated by Breen (1988) in Bloomhill Bog, also in County Offaly, has returned a date range similar to that of the roadway in Lemanaghan. Clearly, while other sites were permitted to fall out of use, most probably because they were enveloped by continually growing bog, significance greater than necessity alone, perhaps induced by religion, economics or politics, was attached to some.

In Castletown Bog, immediately to the north-east of Lemanaghan Island, a single-plank walkway returned a dendrochronological date of AD 665±9, with additional dates of AD 667±9 and AD 684±9 (Bermingham 1997a). The site again cuts through a narrow stretch of bog, providing a very direct connection between the northern uplands and Lemanaghan. Together, this site and the multi-period togher connect the monastery to the Eiscir Riada, the east–west midland routeway between Clonmacnoise and Dublin. The use of the Castletown site, however, was not prolonged. It may have been built as an attraction, an easy means of getting future converts to visit the new monastery, which, once established, reverted in places to going around the bog rather than through it. The togher may even have been built to carry grieving congregants when the first abbot, St Manchán, died in AD 665.

Along with the toghers referred to above, which serviced Lemanaghan Island on its north-eastern side, there are others reflective of medieval activity in and around the Lemanaghan group of bogs. Immediately to the west of Lemanaghan Island is a multi-phased togher of oak planks, roundwoods, gravel and flags with a single date of AD 1219±9 (IAWU 1997a; 1997b). The site runs roughly parallel to the modern Ferbane– Clara road. South of this, in Curraghalassa Bog, a sixteenth-century leather shoe was recovered from the top of a 1m-deep archaeological horizon, the lower levels of which have returned dates from the Iron Age and the seventh century AD (IAWU 1997a; 1997b). Farther into Lemanaghan Bog is Broder's Island. On its north-eastern side, in Killaghintober Bog, a site yielded a date range of cal. AD 1292–1399; and to the south-east, in Castletown Bog, a cluster of narrow, linear brushwood tracks with lengths of 8–31m returned a series of dates with a similar range to those of the Tumbeagh bog body. These sites were built sometime between the mid-fifteenth and the mid-seventeenth century AD (E. OCarroll, pers. comm.). That a number of similarly constructed and similarly dated structures occur close to one another suggests a shared origin and function. Such structures did not serve to cross the bog but rather to provide access to a specific location in the bog. It may be that this part of the bog held or offered access to a particular resource, such as rushes or even peat for fuel. Perhaps butter or cheeses were stored in this part of the bog. Whatever the reason for the multiplicity of sites, their proximity to Broder's Island, within 100m, suggests that the associated activity may have sprung from settlement on the island or at least use of the island by local inhabitants.

On the western side of the Lemanaghan Group is a stretch of bog known as Corhill. Here in 1997 a hoard of twenty silver coins was found, scattered over the milled field surface of the bog, one of the few hoards known to have been retrieved from a bog (Halpin 1984). The coins fall within the period AD 1279–1301 and were minted during the reign of Edward I; all but one were minted in London, with Waterford being the origin of the other (IAWU 1997a; 1997b). The combination of London and Waterford coinage indicates access to money at a time when the Irish economy was bankrupt and virtually coinless by the late 1330s: by this time neither the Dublin nor the Waterford mint was issuing coins, despite earlier reforms by Edward I that allowed only pennies to be issued from the Irish mints (Flanagan 1992). Given the troubled state of the Irish economy, it seems that a native origin for the coins is unlikely. In the mid-thirteenth century it is recorded that the English succeeded in taking Delvin but only for a few years (see above). The coins, which could have been lost or hidden, may reflect attempts at subjugation of the area. Alternatively, a merchant may have lost the coins, perhaps when trading with the Mac Coghlans or their church at Lemanaghan and other churches dotted along the tangential ribbons of the Eiscir Riada. Whatever their origin, the coins illustrate an unmistakably human presence in the Lemanaghan bogs and the surrounding dry land at around the turn of the fourteenth century. A few centuries later, artefacts retrieved from the same bog reinforce this illustration: lost or discarded items include two seventeenth-century leather shoes and a lathe-turned ash bowl (IAWU 1997a; 1997b).

It is evident that people have lived and operated in and around Tumbeagh and Lemanaghan for many centuries. It is clear that, in the medieval period, access that necessitated site construction was generally not intensive, with the exception of those long-lived sites that were revisited, repaired and replaced from generation to generation. It is within this setting of human occupation of the low-lying eskers and the evolving bog that the body of the teenager from Tumbeagh must be viewed.

13.
Tumbeagh Bog, Co. Offaly, an extremely wet landscape: 7500 years of peat growth reconstructed

Wil A. Casparie

Introduction

This chapter presents the peat growth and development of the area of Tumbeagh Bog where the human remains known as the Tumbeagh bog body were discovered. The remains were found on 17 September 1998 by archaeologist Cathy Moore when surveying the bog. The study is mainly based on a gross peat stratigraphical survey of the area conducted simultaneously with the field excavation of the bog body. The palynological analysis (Weir, Chapter 15) and coleopteran analysis (Reilly, Chapter 14) were also part of the research programme. The combined investigations were arranged in order to study the palaeoenvironmental conditions in which the body of the young person was preserved.

The archaeological survey of the bogs of County Offaly by the Irish Archaeological Wetland Unit, conducted from 1993 to 1997 (McDermott 2001), revealed large numbers of trackways, platforms and related finds, indicating the accessibility of these wet soils in prehistoric and historical times. In some peatland areas, however, the presence of trackways was not demonstrated, suggesting the impossibility of passing the soft bog surface in earlier times. It was assumed that this was not a consequence of the method of survey but that it could be attributed to the former bog surface being too wet or too dangerous for the construction of trackways. The bogs of Lemanaghan, near the River Brosna in north-west County Offaly, are an example of this (Fig. 2). Tumbeagh Bog, as part of the Lemanaghan bogs, is characterised by the remarkable absence of trackways.

The main aims of the peat stratigraphical survey were:

(1) to describe the overall conditions of peat growth, necessary for understanding the development of the area in which the body remains were found and where trackways are absent; this will allow reconstruction of the main lines of hydrological, vegetational and spatial development of this area of Tumbeagh Bog;

(2) to analyse in as much detail as possible the peat sequence at the location of the find, in order to reconstruct the environmental conditions of the bog in the window of time in which the body became deposited in the bog; the results

The bog body from Tumbeagh

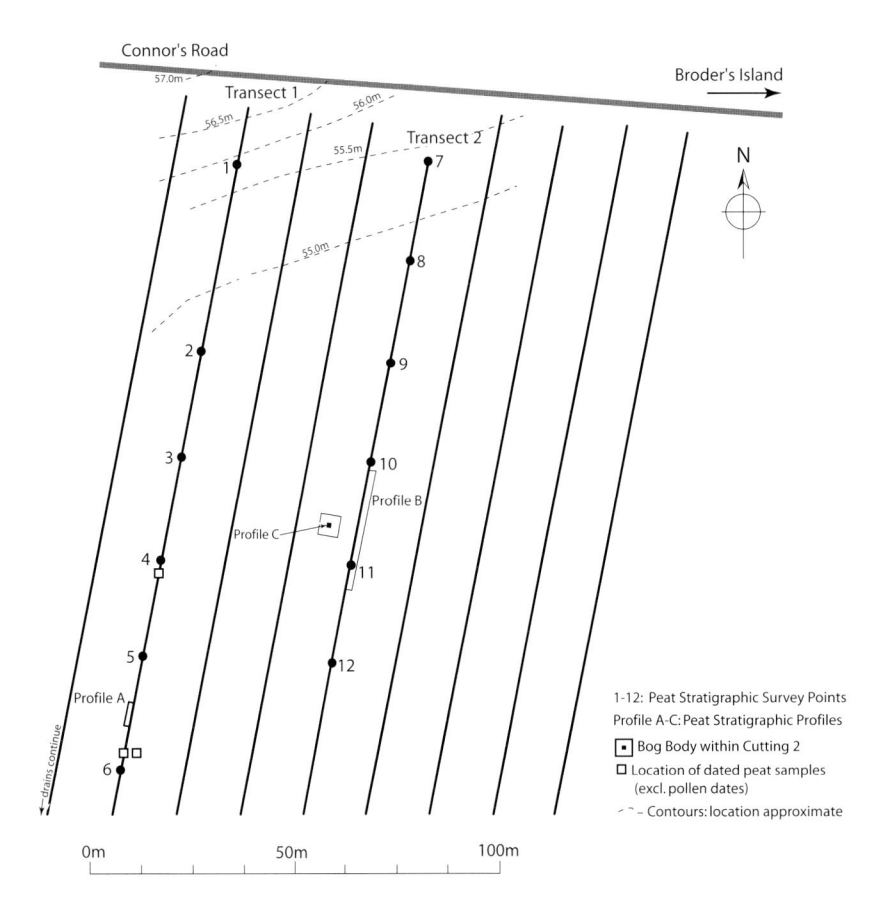

Fig. 18: Location of Transects 1 and 2, peat stratigraphic survey points and peat stratigraphic profiles A–C.

should allow a better understanding of the circumstances behind the death of the person and the location in the peat of the body.

During the survey it became clear that before the raised-bog growth in this area a large bog lake had developed. The lake catastrophically discharged a few times, affecting the local hydrology and thus the succeeding raised-bog growth and conditions of access to the bog. For this reason, the peat stratigraphical survey focused greatly on the development of this lake, the related discharge events and the accessibility of the bog surface in general, especially for the period to which the bog body has been dated. The findspot can be described as gully fill inside the former shore area of the huge bog lake, which had drained centuries before but which considerably influenced the later, raised-bog development.

Tumbeagh Bog had already been drained and milled by Bord na Móna for peat extraction for 8–10 years; the upper, compacted 0.30m peat had been removed. The survey included the study of the peat sequence in all of the drain faces in a large area surrounding the findspot; the recording of two peat faces near the findspot and of specific features on the truncated bog surface; and a detailed study of the peat accumulation in three profiles (Fig. 18). All peat-type identifications were made in the field, and each peat type is defined below. A series of cross-sections (vertical exaggeration x25) have been produced in which the original bog-surface elevations have been reconstructed (Figs 29–34).

Peat types and their characteristics

Peat symbols (Figs 19–24, 29–34)

The numbers refer to the symbol numbers of the legends to Figs 20–24 (Fig. 19) and 29–34.

1. Poorly humified *Sphagnum* peat, indicating oligotrophic, very humid and acidic conditions. The most likely primary peat formers were the large-leaved moss species *Sphagnum papillosum* and *S. imbricatum*; *S. magellanicum* may also have been present.
2. Moderately humified *Sphagnum* peat, representing a combination of higher-humified hummock peat with poorer-humified hollow peat. The environment is characterised by oligotrophic and acidic conditions, with somewhat drier hummocks and wet hollows.
3. Highly humified *Sphagnum* peat, mostly grown in oligotrophic, humid and rather acidic conditions.
4. Poorly humified *Sphagnum cuspidatum* (water moss) peat, indicating the fill of shallow pools and hollows with open water in oligotrophic and acidic conditions.
5. *Scheuchzeria palustris* (rannock rush) remains, indicating slowly flowing, shallow open water, mostly in a somewhat mesotrophic or minerotrophic and rather acidic environment.
6. *Calluna* (heather, ling) remains. These were recorded only when abundant and/or present as a layer, mostly indicating rather dry or locally desiccated situations.
7. *Eriophorum vaginatum* (hare's tail grass) remains, indicating a fluctuating bog water-table and relatively dry conditions.
8. Poorly humified Hypnaceae peat (brown-moss peat), representing a number of moss species and vascular species, characteristic of systems of water flow in a soak or seepage environment with clear, non-acidic water. *Drepanocladus*, *Hypnum*, *Calliergon* and *Scorpidium* mosses belong to the Hypnaceae family.
9. Highly humified Hypnaceae peat. The highly decomposed state of the deposit suggests that it results from peat accumulation in a soak or seepage environment.
10. Grey, laminated gyttja (lake-bottom sediment), representing the bottom fill of a long-standing lake, mostly rich in algae remains. Mineral particles (sand, clay, silt) are absent. This is the main deposit of Phase 1 of the bog lake. The suggested depth of water is 0.5–1.0m. The microtopography of the deposit indicates that substantial and repeated fluctuations in the water depth occurred, sometimes giving way to the sedimentation of pure algae gyttja.
11. Grey to dark grey, laminated gyttja, locally brownish and pool-fill-like, indicating shallower water depth. This is the main deposit of Phase 2 of the bog lake; the water depth was at most *c.* 0.5m. The brownish colour can be attributed to the increasing influence of raised-bog peat deposits (decaying peat, dissolved peat particles or humic colloids) on the water chemistry, perhaps caused by the expansion of peat-forming vegetation on stretches of the lake bottom during low water levels.
12. Fen peat, mostly rich in sedges (*Carex* spp) and reed (*Phragmites australis*) remains and in many locations with abundant remains of bog bean (*Menyanthes trifoliata*). The wood content is remarkably low. This minerotrophic peat grows in a

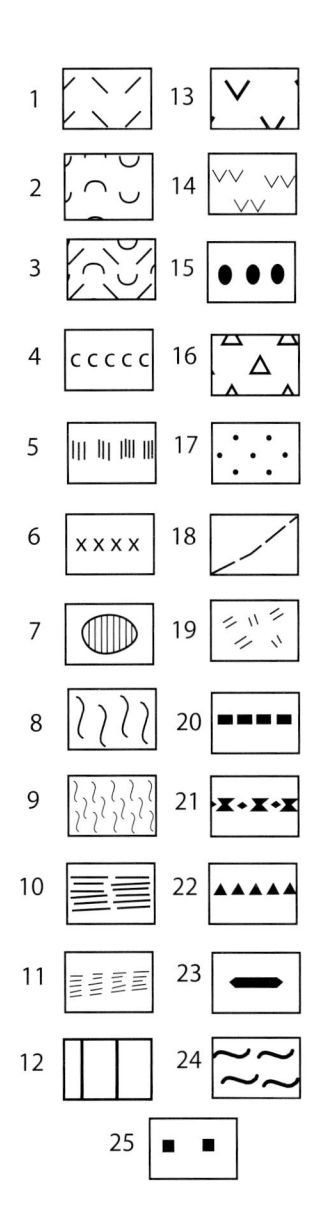

Fig. 19: The peat types distinguished at Tumbeagh. Legend to Figs 20–24, 29–34.

The bog body from Tumbeagh

groundwater environment under very wet conditions. The occurrence of shallow pools with open water during its development is likely.

13. Wood-rich peat and wood layers, the bog-marginal forest of mostly alder (*Alnus*) trees, surrounding the ridge of the subsoil.
14. Wood-rich peat deposit with mainly willow (*Salix*) wood remains; shore area of the lake, Phase 1a.
15. Pine (*Pinus*) stumps in the basal fen-peat deposits, indicating a submerged forest, most likely of Boreal age.
16. Mineral subsoil, lacustrine clay, most probably indicating a glacial lake fill.
17. Subsoil unknown or not specified, probably lacustrine clay.
18. Mineral subsoil was not reached; assumed top of the mineral subsoil/base of bog.
19. Decayed Hypnaceae peat, probably redeposited.
20. Dark to black layer of highly decayed peat; very likely an old soil or temporary bottom of (erosion) gully; somewhat eroded and oxidised.
21. A heavily cracked, black and nearly amorphous organic layer, most likely the eroded and oxidised top of the gyttja, indicating a significant drop of the water-table of the lake and exposure of the lake bottom to the air.
22. Oxidised and eroded top of desiccated gyttja; south bank of the erosion gully.
23. Level and location of the bog body in the peat profiles.
24. Assumed water-table of the bog lakes, Phases 1 and 2.
25. Survey points of the peat stratigraphical survey of October 1998.

Ash-content analysis and results

During the excavation, peat samples were taken from six locations to establish their ash content (Table 20; Fig. 18). To an extent, this provides insight into the water chemistry, as the samples concern well-defined peat types (methods: ISO 1170–1).

The samples of *Sphagnum* peat (A2) and Hypnaceae peat (A4) have low ash-content values. These indicate an oligotrophic water supply and can be expected for ombrotrophic (A2) or nearly ombrotrophic (A4) peat types. The values for the fen-peat samples (A1 and A3) indicate a minerotrophic origin for the water supply, although the mineral content of the groundwater was relatively low (mesotrophic).

Sample no.	Peat type	Location	Level (m OD)	% ash content
A1	Fen peat	Profile C	55.20–55.50	0.2
A2	Poorly humified Sphagnum peat	Profile C	56.00–56.50	0.1
A3	Fen peat	Transect 2, between Points 11 and 12	55.20–55.50	0.2
A4	Hypnaceae peat	Profile C	55.62–55.75	0.1
A5	Gyttja	Lake Phase 1, Transect 2, Point 8	56.40–56.70	0.2
A6	Gyttja	Lake Phase 2, Transect 2, Point 8	56.80–56.95	0.4

Table 20: Percentage ash content of peat samples from Tumbeagh.

The ash content of the gyttja of Phase 1 of the bog lake (A5) indicates that the lake developed in environmental conditions with the same mesotrophic water chemistry as occurred during fen-peat growth. Different water sources, therefore, did not play a role in the drowning of the fen-peat surface; it was probably increased water supply and compaction of the fen peat that caused the shift from fen to Phase 1 of the lake.

The significantly higher value for the ash content of the gyttja of Phase 2 of the bog lake (A6) can likely be attributed to the influx of oxidised and decayed peaty material from the nearby shore area in very shallow water, as recorded during the field survey (Peat Type 11). The emptying of Phase 1 of the bog lake would have induced a considerable increase in biological activity, including the decay and rotting of vegetation of the drained soil, redeposited peat and shore area (eutrophication). With the development of Phase 2 of the lake, particles of these rotting products must have been precipitated in the shore area of Phase 2. For this reason the water of Phase 2 was probably not as clear as Phase 1, at least in the shore area. In addition, it is possible that deforestation and increased pressure of habitation on the upland near this bog caused the precipitation of aerosols with somewhat higher dust content than previously, or even air pollution, resulting in a larger supply of minerals to the peat-growing vegetation and the bog lake.

Dating the bog development

Radiocarbon dates for important features in Tumbeagh Bog are available (Table 7). Throughout this chapter the ages of the features discussed are given as average values cal. BC and cal. AD, here indicated with ≈. Following Weir (Chapter 15), it can be stated that the dates are actually plus or minus 100 years or more.

Samples for dating the bog body (van der Sanden and van der Plicht, Chapter 6)

(1) Peat; GrA-14393: 765 ± 35 BP, cal. AD 1215–1290, ≈ AD 1250
Profile C, 0–0.02m; Fig. 24; 56.56–56.58m OD
This is the somewhat firmer peat of the base of a hollow or pool, directly beneath the feet of the body. The hollow was filled with algae-rich *cuspidatum* peat, indicating an original depth of *c.* 0.10m. It is likely that this sample pre-dates the bog surface and the human remains by more than two centuries.

(2) Wood; GrA-15314: 545 ± 45 BP, cal. AD 1305–1440, ≈ AD 1370
Profile C, 0.02–0.05m; Fig. 24; 56.55–56.58m OD
The difference in time between the skin and the bone may indicate that the wood cannot be directly associated with the body, although the ranges of these dates do overlap (see p. 55).

(3) Skin; GrA-15627: 430 ± 60 BP, cal. AD 1405–1635, ≈ AD 1500
Profile C, 0–0.06m; Fig. 24; 56.54–56.60m OD
A date for the bog body in the late fifteenth century AD is possible. In this chapter the date AD 1500 will be used for both the body and the bog surface.

Samples for dating Profile C (Weir, Chapter 15)

(4) Peat; UB-4694: 1642±43 BP, cal. AD 260–543, ≈ AD 410
Profile C, 0.29–0.32m; Fig. 24; 56.28–56.31m OD

(5) Peat; UB-4693: 1928±44 BP, 35 cal. BC–cal. AD 142, ≈ AD 73
Profile C, 0.60–0.63m; Fig. 24; 55.98–56.01m OD

(6) Peat; UB-4692: 2390±44 BP, 760–392 cal. BC, ≈ 407 BC
Profile C, 0.84–0.89m; Fig. 24; 55.78–55.83m OD

Samples for dating the peat sequence

(7) Peat; UCD-01110: 1595±50 BP, cal. AD 344–598, ≈ AD 430
Transect 1; Fig. 20, at 20m; 56.40m OD
Top of Phase 2 of the bog lake.

(8) Peat; UCD-01109: 1800±60 BP, cal. AD 77–391, ≈ AD 240
Transect 1; Fig. 20, at 20m; 56.21–56.18m OD
Top of Phase 1 of the bog lake.

(9) Peat; UCD-01108: 2540±60 BP, 815–411 cal. BC, ≈ 779 BC
Transect 1; Fig. 20, at 60m; 55.97–56.00m OD
Top of fen peat overgrown by raised-bog peat; shore area of the bog lake. This date is used to indicate the extension of the bog lake over the raised-bog shore area in Transect 1.

(10) Peat; Wk-12086: 5417±90 BP, 6400–5950 cal. BP, ≈ 4300 BC
Transect 1; Fig. 20, at 25m; 53.45–53.50m OD (estimated; not levelled).
Base of fen peat, indicating a certain stage in the increasing groundwater-table.

Dating of archaeological activities in the Lemanaghan area
Dated sites in the Lemanaghan bogs (McDermott 2001) illustrate important aspects of the hydrological development of the bog with regard to the accessibility of the area in relation to the bog lake. This is discussed below (p. 134, Fig. 25). It is sufficient to note here that there are two notable clusters of trackway dates: 960–900 BC and AD 550–700. The bog lake and its eroding bog bursts can be placed between these date clusters. It is probable, therefore, that the bog lake and the accessibility of the bog are closely related, and this is discussed below.

The peat faces: stratigraphy and environmental implications

Transect 1 (Fig. 20) and Profile A (Fig. 21)
In Transect 1 the level of the subsoil (blue clay) was established at Survey Points 1 and 5 and the bog road only; its deepest point is probably *c.* 53.20m OD. Fen-peat growth

began *c.* 4700–4600 BC. The mineral ridge to the north is clearly apparent. The stratigraphy inside the fen-peat deposits was not established; peat accumulation most probably occurred under very wet conditions. During a period of fen-peat growth, the adjacent mineral ridge had been surrounded by a bog-marginal forest, which consisted mainly of *Alnus* (alder) trees. This stretch of forest can be dated to *c.* 2400–2200 BC. Part of the fen peat is covered by gyttja of the Phase 1 lake, suggesting the inundation of large parts of this deposit (Phase 1a) before raised-bog growth had begun. Based on the 0.3m lower level of the transition from fen peat to gyttja in Survey Point 6 compared with Survey Point 4, it is likely that the bog lake was already in existence by 900–950 BC. A subsequent rise of the lake water-table resulted in the expansion of the lake and the inundation and drowning of the raised-bog peat growing along its northern shore area (Phase 1b). This event may have occurred *c.* 700 BC after the fen had become inundated (after 780 BC, that is, the top of the fen and the beginning of a century of raised-bog growth to *c.* 680 BC).

The grey gyttja of the first phase is almost 0.5m thick. Its deposition appears to have been uninterrupted. The northern shore area, just north of Survey Point 2, seems to have been defined by the mineral ridge below Connor's Road to the north. The gyttja of Phase 1 is covered by moderately humified *Sphagnum* peat, mostly replaced peat. This indicates the emptying of the lake, dated to AD 240, and the occurrence of drier conditions. Profile A (Fig. 21) demonstrates that this discharge was followed by the desiccation and oxidation of the drained lake bottom and a short period of peat growth before the area was inundated again (Phase 2 of the bog lake), probably within a few decades. Survey Point 6 shows a remarkably thick layer of intercalated peat between the two phases of gyttja sedimentation. When the second phase of the bog lake was developing at this location, raised-bog growth could survive the continuing rise of the lake water-table for a while. The thicker peat accumulation at Survey Point 6 belongs to a stretch of peat 0.2–0.4m higher, measuring *c.* 30m by 40m (Fig. 21). This stretch of peat was not affected by the erosion when Phase 1 of the bog lake drained, and its growth probably lasted for a few decades.

There is an abrupt shift from the Phase 2 gyttja to the overlying, moderately humified *Sphagnum* peat, which occurred *c.* AD 430. There is a change to a hummock–hollow system, with many flooded hollows, in which *Sphagnum cuspidatum* peat could grow. This means that the second phase of the lake was emptied by large-scale and very probably catastrophic discharge, in the form of a bog burst, as many erosion features can be identified over wide areas at this level. The two gullies, at 29m and 56m (Fig. 20), are products of this erosion.

The northern lakeshore area of Phase 2 was similar in location to that of Phase 1b, implying that the two phases had a similar water-table. Despite the lack of data on landfall levels of the lake deposits, some tentative remarks concerning original water-tables can be made. If we assume that the modern shrinkage of the fen peat in this location (Survey Points 4–6; Survey Points 1–3 are not suitable for this approach) is *c.* 0.5m, the base of the lake, before expanding over the raised-bog peat, lay at 56.20–56.40m OD. The original thickness of the gyttja deposit can be estimated to be 0.85m. The water-table of the lake during its first phase increased to *c.* 57.50m OD at least, perhaps to *c.* 58.00m OD at the maximum. The water-table during the second phase of the lake must have been at around the same level.

The bog body from Tumbeagh

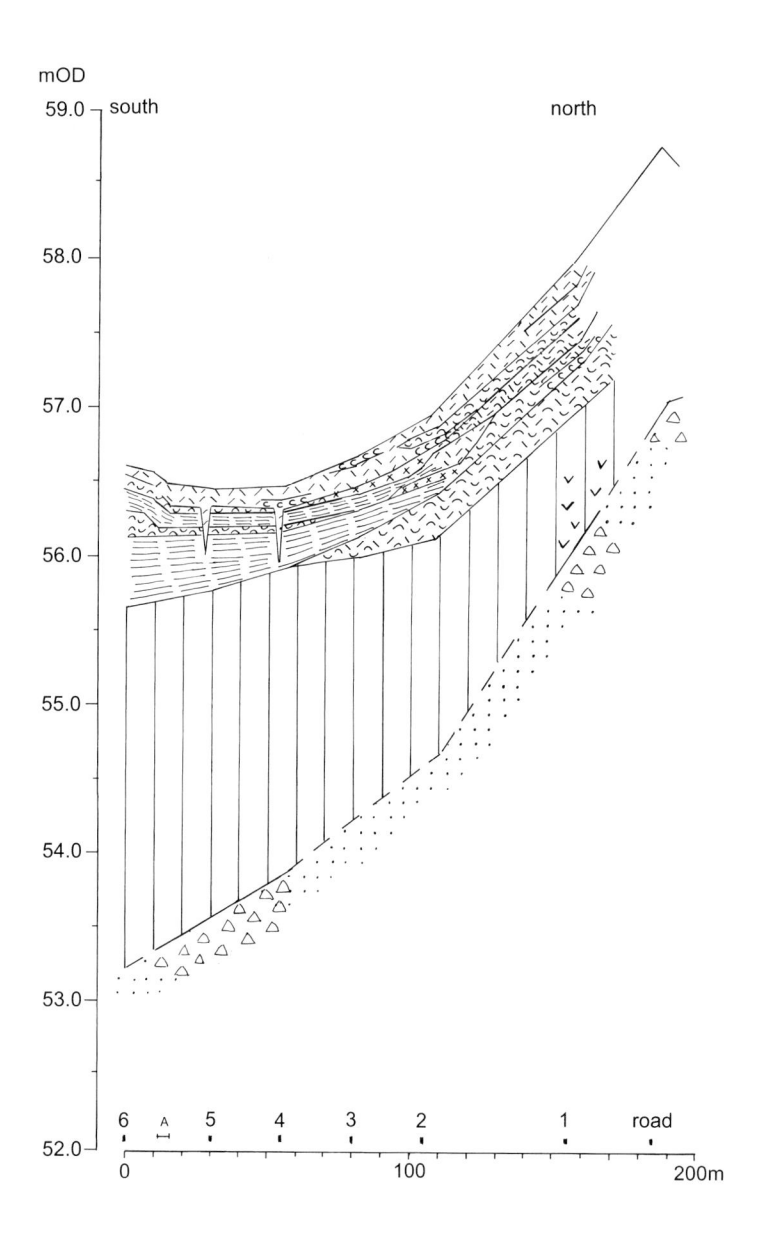

Fig. 20:
Peat face, Transect 1.
Vertical exaggeration x50.
The stratigraphy is
explained in the text.
Profile A is situated
between 11m and 14m.

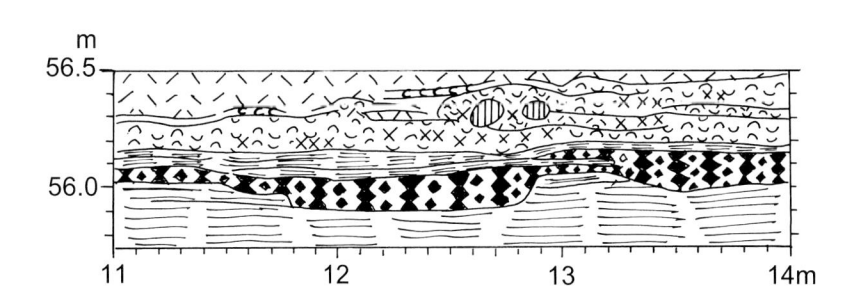

Fig. 21:
Profile A, Transect 1.

126

The hummock–hollow system, overgrowing the drained lake bottom after the second phase of the lake (AD 430), is characterised by many pools with open water, indicative of wet conditions. This deposit is indicated in Fig. 20 as moderately humified *Sphagnum* peat. It is overgrown by poorly humified *Sphagnum* peat in which hummock–hollow systems are difficult to distinguish. The transition between the two peat types is rather sharp, suggesting that the end of the moderately humified peat growth indicates an environmental shift or change. Most likely the discharge function of the two gullies (at 29m and 56m) decreased considerably and was succeeded by the fill of poorly humified *Sphagnum* peat. This can be dated to *c.* AD 800 (see below, Profile B, the gully). Erosion features could not be recorded in relation to the discharge, which occurred between AD 430 and AD 800.

The upper layer of poorly humified *Sphagnum* peat looks rather uniform in composition, indicating good water supply. This continued to at least *c.* AD 1500, the date for the bog body.

Transect 2 (Fig. 22) and Profile B (Fig. 23)
The deepest point in the fen is at *c.* 52.20m OD (Survey Point 12) and is underlain by mineral subsoil, consisting of lacustrine clay. Before fen-peat growth, dated at this location to *c.* 5800 BC, a pine (*Pinus*) forest with mature trees (K. Molloy, pers. comm.) covered the low-lying area. This is the last phase of the Boreal pine forest. The initial flooding of the area took place *c.* 6000 BC. The fen peat deposits, *c.* 3.5m thick, have the same characteristics as described for Transect 1. The fen-peat growth had taken place in extremely wet conditions. Bordering the mineral ridge, a bog-marginal forest had developed for some time, likely from *c.* 2400–2200 BC on (Survey Point 7, *c.* 55.40–56.00m OD).

The well-laminated and bright grey gyttja of the first phase of the bog lake is more affected by erosion here than in Transect 1 (see below). Near Survey Point 8, at 115–120m, a real algae-gyttja layer, 0.04m thick and extending over *c.* 3m, was visible in the lake-bottom sediment.

The transition from fen peat to gyttja at 10–60m was rather vague, indicating the gradually rising water-table, which resulted in the eventual drowning of the fen in which reed and bog bean had played dominant roles. At Survey Point 10 the level is 55.48m OD, *c.* 0.20m lower than in Transect 1. This marks the beginning of the bog lake at *c.* 950 BC (see above).

The continuing rise of the lake water-table caused expansion of the lake in a northward direction, thus inundating large stretches of the *Salix* (willow) carr vegetation that bordered the bog lake. This is the same event as the expansion over the raised-bog deposits in Transect 1 (Fig. 20) at *c.* 60m, dated to 700 BC (the top of the fen peat was dated to 780 BC). The maximum expansion of the northern shore area of the lake can be observed at 115–125m, at about Survey Point 8, where the top level of the deposit lies at *c.* 56.70m OD. Phase 1 of the bog lake can be divided into two Phases: 1a, between 950 BC and 700 BC, and 1b, from *c.* 700 BC to AD 240 (see above, Transect 1 and Profile A).

The laminated structure of the gyttja demonstrates that fluctuations in the water-table took place during the first phase of the lake, but there are no indications that the lake bottom became exposed to air. The heather-rich layer that intercalated in this

The bog body from Tumbeagh

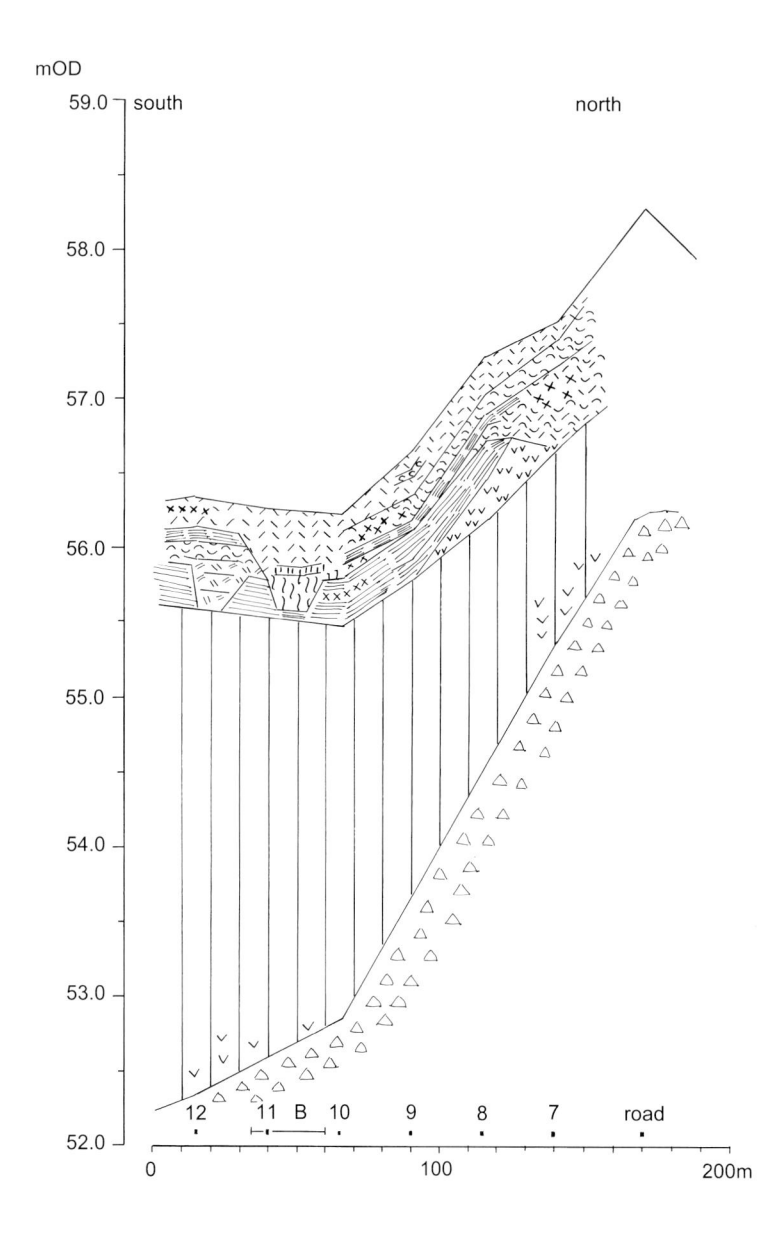

Fig. 22: Peat face, Transect 2. Vertical exaggeration x50. The stratigraphy is explained in the text. Profile B (the gully) is situated between 34m and 60m.

gyttja at Survey Point 10, at *c.* 55.70m OD, may represent redeposited peat. Water movement before AD 240 may have moved this layer from a higher level (OD); it was not a floating vegetation mat that eventually became sedimented at the lake bottom.

At Survey Point 12, at 12–30m, the laminated gyttja deposit of Phase 1 is interrupted by a deposit of very loose peat, identified as the fill of an erosion gully. Obviously, the emptying of the first phase of the bog lake was associated with remarkable erosion—the bog burst—dated to AD 240. Another interruption of the gyttja deposit is present, at 30–70m, in the form of a large gully. The erosion that caused this feature can be dated to AD 430 (end of Phase 2). The relevant stratigraphy of the gully is illustrated in Profile B (Fig. 23) and discussed below.

Unlike the Phase 1 gyttja deposit in Transect 1 (Fig. 20), decaying, oxidising or cracking phenomena (see Profile A, Fig. 21) are absent in the top of the lower stretches of the Phase 1 gyttja of Transect 2, at 0–100m. This suggests that the drop in water-table after the drainage of Phase 1 of the lake (AD 240) can be averaged between the top of the gyttja deposit in Transect 1 (in the central area of the lake recorded at 56.40m OD) and in Transect 2, between 0m and 90m (in the central area at 55.90m OD). If we convert the levels of the drained peats to the reconstructed levels (see below), we can assume that the original lake water-table lay between 57.50m and 58.00m OD and the dropped water-table probably between 56.50m and 56.70m OD. This equates to the top of the Phase 1 gyttja in the central part of the drained lake and indicates a drop in the water-table of over 1m. This significant drop is reflected in the peat stratigraphy. The highest gyttja deposits of Phase 1 in Transect 2 (Fig. 22) above *c.* 56.70m OD (Survey Point 8 and surroundings) occur locally as a darker (drier) layer, somewhat affected by oxidation. This suggests aeration for a while. Reconstruction of the original levels suggests that this occurred at *c.* 57.30m OD, shortly after AD 240. During the eroding bog burst, the water-table sank to a much lower level, to at least below the base of the gully of this bog burst, originally at *c.* 56.00m OD. Although direct data are lacking, a level between 55.00m and 55.50m OD can be assumed, occurring probably quite far away to the east or south of Transect 2. At a number of spots, the Phase 1 gyttja is covered with a rather thin layer of replaced peat. The presence of peat-growing vegetation in this layer (Survey Point 12, between 0m and 30m), while not ascertained, cannot be excluded.

Phase 2 of the lake resulted in the deposition of gyttja, which had in its northern stretches (between 100m and 150m) more or less the character of pool-fill mud, indicating minimal water depth. The northern shore area of Phase 2 of the lake is at about the same location as that of Phase 1b (Fig. 22, between 110m and 120m), suggesting that both phases had about the same water-table, probably up to between 57.50m and 58.00m OD (see above). In Transect 2 the gyttja of Phase 2 is covered with raised-bog peat. It indicates a pronounced hummock-and-hollow system, with the hummocks rather dry (highly humified *Sphagnum* peat) and the hollows wet or even flooded. Poorly humified *Sphagnum cuspidatum* peat occurs as fill in many of these hollows. The transition from the gyttja of Phase 2 to this raised-bog peat deposit is rather sharp, indicating a sudden shift in environmental conditions, when the bog burst and subsequent drainage of the lake, dated to AD 430, resulted in the sharp decline in the lake water-table. This event involved much erosion and is discussed below (Profile B, Fig. 23).

The hummock-and-hollow system (Fig. 22, indicated as moderately humified *Sphagnum* peat), which covers the gyttja of Phase 2 of the bog lake, is overgrown by poorly humified *Sphagnum* peat, in which hardly any spatial structure, such as hummocks and hollows, or more humified inclusions occur. This can be dated to *c.* AD 800, when the gully lost its discharge function (see below). In the poorly humified peat, *Sphagnum cuspidatum* layers, when present, are only small. This suggests the abrupt ending of the well-pronounced hummock-and-hollow system. It gives way to the development of an extreme oligotrophic and very acidic bog surface, suitable for the luxuriant growth of poorly humified *Sphagnum* peat. This poorly humified peat is the uppermost deposit in Tumbeagh Bog, identified during the field survey and continuing up to at least AD 1500, perhaps to the nineteenth or twentieth century.

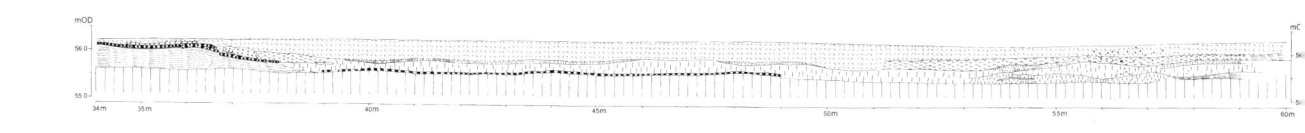

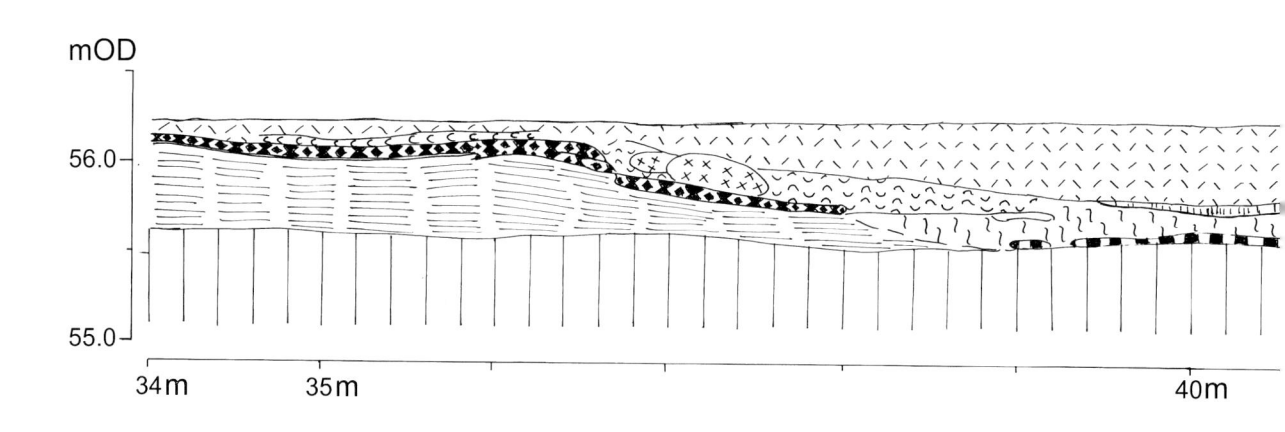

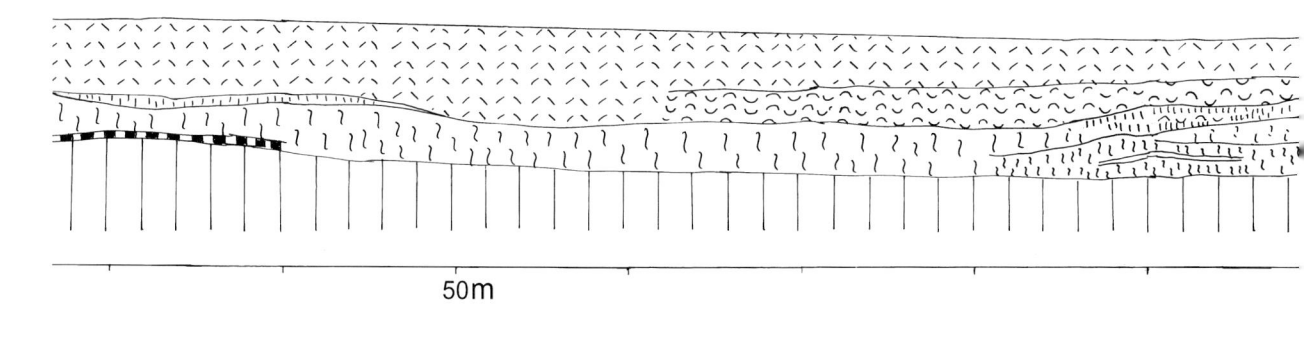

Profile B: the gully (Fig. 23)

As mentioned above, in Transect 2 the gyttja of Phase 1 is missing between 38m and 60m. This interruption represents an erosion gully whose course is depicted in Fig. 26. The sediment has been washed away by intensive erosion, which formed the gully. In Fig. 23 this stretch of peat face is illustrated in more detail. Here the gully can be distinguished with a clear south bank, having a highly eroded top between *c.* 35m and 37m, and a shallow north slope at 54–60m. In this gully the gyttja deposit of Phase 2 is also lacking, indicating large-scale erosion after Phase 2 of the bog lake, thus dated to AD 430. Most of the eroded gully bottom became occupied with moss species of the family Hypnaceae (brown mosses; not further identified), indicating that the gully functioned as a soak in a mesotrophic but not acidic environment. At 39–49m, this gully may have functioned for a considerable time, probably to *c.* AD 800, the very dark to black layer at its base being the old gully bottom or soil.

Between *c.* 51m and 59m the Hypnaceae peat is overgrown by moderately

Fig. 23:
Profile B, between
34m and 60m in
Transect 2.

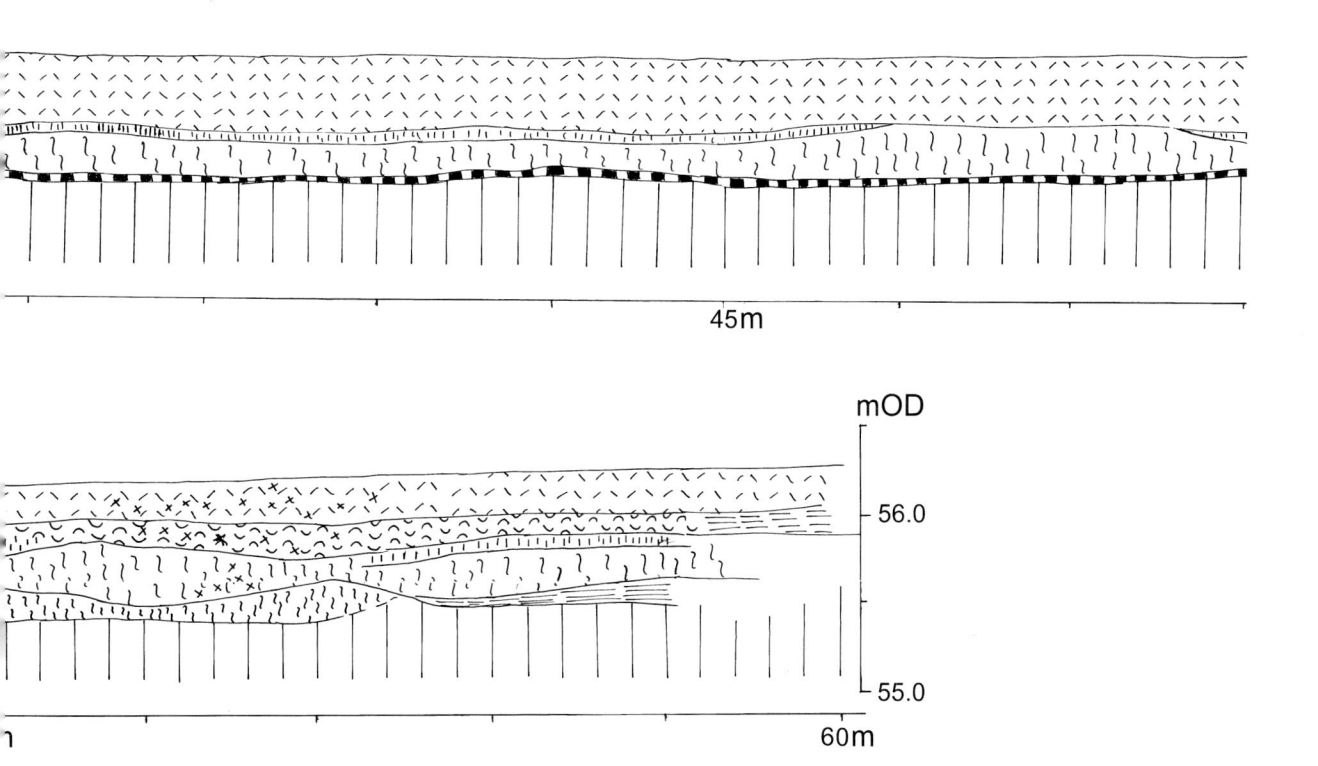

humified *Sphagnum* peat, because of the expansion of this type of peat over the gyttja of Phase 2 of the (emptied) bog lake. Between 39m and 50m the Hypnaceae peat deposit is covered with a thin layer of *Scheuchzeria palustris* peat, pointing to increasing wetness and increasing acidity of the surrounding area of bog, discharging via this gully. Eventually the environmental conditions became extremely oligotrophic, very acidic and sufficiently wet for the optimal growth of poorly humified *Sphagnum* peat. This marks the change in function of the gully from discharge system to pool-like water accumulation. This deposit, which reached more than 0.60m thick and in which hardly any spatial structures occur (see below, Profile C), represents rather consistent hydrological conditions over centuries, from *c.* AD 800. Serious decline of the water supply, giving way to drier conditions (more humified peat) or long-lasting flooding (characterised by thick layers of *cuspidatum* peat), did not take place. This type of bog surface must have been extremely difficult to gain access to, given the high water content of such peat.

In the poorly humified *Sphagnum* peat of Profile B, as in the entire Transects 1 and 2 and in Profile C, no erosion gullies have been recorded. This indicates that the water supply did not result in the development of strongly eroding water currents.

Profile C (Fig. 24)
This profile represents the sequence of the peat block extracted for laboratory excavation. Profile C is situated in the erosion gully (Fig. 18), *c.* 5m west of point 45m of Profile B (Fig. 23). The higher level of the top of Profile C (*c.* 56.60m OD) in relation to the top of Profile B (*c.* 56.25m OD) can be attributed to the cambered surface of the Bord na Móna field. The detailed archaeological investigation of the peat block and the available dates allow clear observations to be made regarding the fill of the gully between AD 430 and AD 1500, including the hydrological conditions of the bog surface at the time of the deposition of the body. This will be discussed in more detail below.

Profile C resembles the stratigraphy of Profile B at 45m (Figs 23, 24), apart from the top. The fen peat, up to 55.60m OD, is covered with the dark to black layer of highly decayed peat, the base of the erosion gully of AD 430, at the same level as Profile B. The level with remains of *Scheuchzeria palustris* (rannock rush) at the top of the Hypnaceae peat, at *c.* 55.90m OD, was not as clear as that in Profile B and as Fig. 24 suggests. This level dates to *c.* AD 800, representing the base of the fill of the gully following the much-reduced discharge function of the gully. Given this evidence, the peat samples, dated to 407 BC, AD 73 and AD 410, represent replaced peat blocks, redeposited in the gully in AD 430. There is some weak palynological evidence for this (Weir, Chapter 15).

Poorly humified *Sphagnum* peat, present at this location from 55.90m to 56.60m OD, accumulated between the replaced peat blocks in the gully. *Sphagnum* peat growth continued most likely up to the nineteenth and twentieth centuries AD (the modern drainage) uninterrupted by the deposited bog body. Increasing acidity and ombrotrophy of this gully fill occurred. Although all of the peats are poorly humified, some small gradations in colour and humification were recorded and are presented in Fig. 24.

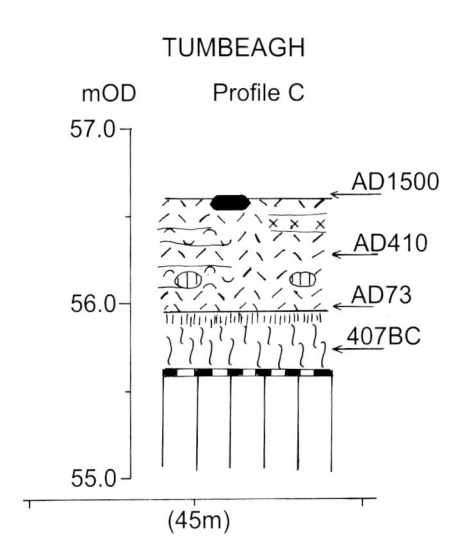

Fig. 24: Profile C, from the peat block in which the human remains were isolated; 5m west of Profile B at 45m. The relevant dates have been added to the column.

At 56.10m OD the presence of a few small tussocks of *Eriophorum vaginatum* may indicate less humid conditions for a short while. The occurrence of some small remains of *Calluna* at 56.45m OD demonstrates the temporary presence of one or more specimens of ling or a related genus rather than the extension of hummock vegetation.

Though not indicated in the peat profile, a number of thin, poorly humified and probably small *cuspidatum* layers that were rich in algae remains (Diatomeae) were scattered through the entire peat deposit. Nóra Bermingham (pers. comm.) documented such a layer directly under the left leg of the bog body (Fig. 14). These pool-like features, existing in general for at least decades or perhaps over a century, indicate continuing wet conditions during the raised-bog growth. The absence of erosion gullies in this peat deposit, and thus the absence of heavy water currents, has already been mentioned. This very soft peat, originally *c.* 1.20m thick, must have been extremely difficult to gain access to. The date AD 1255 indicates the existence of a pool from the second half of the thirteenth century AD probably up to the sixteenth century.

The main lines of the hydrological development

In *c.* 4300 BC the bog water-table lay at *c.* 53.50m OD (Fig. 20, Survey Point 5). In the Tumbeagh region the rise of the groundwater-table (Fig. 22, Survey Point 12), began much earlier, probably *c.* 6000–5800 BC. The water-table increased in such a way that fen-peat-growing vegetation became established from that time; the earlier pine forest became overgrown, and within two centuries the forest was drowned and covered with fen peat, rich in reed. Most likely this is an aspect of the regional rise of the post-glacial groundwater-table from *c.* 8000–7000 BC, originating in the lowest parts of the Lemanaghan area, near Derrynagun and Curraghalassa bogs and the River Brosna, *c.* 5km south-south-east of Tumbeagh.

Fen-peat growth continued until *c.* 950 BC, most likely with fluctuations in the rise, but without distinguishable drops, in the water-table, except *c.* 1000–950 BC. From *c.* 2400 BC the forest covering the mineral ridge to the north of the study area (Connor's Road), with its level at *c.* 56.50m OD, became gradually overgrown. Around 950 BC the fen-peat surface was at *c.* 56.30m OD. Thus, the water-table rose *c.* 2.80m (from 53.50m to 56.30m OD) in less than 3400 years (between 4300 BC and 950 BC), an accumulation rate of *c.* 8.36cm per 100 years. This is an impressive tempo and much more than in Derryville Bog, Co. Tipperary, where a fen-peat accumulation rate of 6.38cm per 100 years has been suggested (Casparie and Gowen 2001, 98). If we extrapolate from the growth rate of 8.36cm per 100 years to the lowest level of fen peat (Fig. 22, Survey Point 12: 52.20m), peat growth began in Tumbeagh probably between 6000 BC and 5800 BC.

The first occurrence of raised-bog growth (Fig. 20, Survey Point 3) can be dated to shortly after 780 BC, when the fen-peat surface just outside the bog lake, Phase 1a, became overgrown. In nearby bogs, such as Kilnagarnagh, the transition to raised-bog growth began much earlier, as can be concluded from the dates of wooden trackways built on raised-bog surfaces. In Tumbeagh the oak walkway dated to 1509±9 BC (Q-9291) lies *c.* 800m to the north of the location of the bog body. Most likely, raised-bog growth began here *c.* 2000–1800 BC. Climatic conditions for raised-bog growth were already favourable in Ireland from *c.* 6400 on (P.D.M. Hughes 2003).

The development of the bog lake (Phase 1a), represented by open-water accumulation on the bog surface, may have begun *c.* 950 BC (see above). Further support for this suggestion is provided by the chronology of trackways constructed in the surrounding peatlands. In Tumbeagh Bog and nearby Killaghintober Bog a series of trackways has been dendrochronologically dated to 960–940 BC (Fig. 25). This is interpreted as an attempt to withstand increasing wetness on the bog surface in the northern stretches of the Lemanaghan area, which failed within one or two decades. From *c.* 920 BC it was impossible to gain access to large parts of the Lemanaghan bogs, as the lack of trackways until *c.* AD 560 (Fig. 25) indicates. A small number of tracks dated to 960–940 BC display important erosion features (C. McDermott, pers. comm.), implying heavy erosion *c.* 950 BC or shortly afterwards.

Given the rate of fen-peat accumulation and the possibility of increasing wetness reflected in changes in trackway construction, two possibilities for the establishment of the bog lake (Phase 1a) can be proposed:

(1) a rising bog water-table, by well over 8.36cm per 100 years (i.e. the growth rate for the fen peat);
(2) a steep drop in the bog water-table around or just before 950 BC that resulted in compaction of the drained fen-peat deposits to a bowl-shaped surface and subsequent flooding of the lower-lying parts of the bog surface.

There is no evidence for the first possibility, but the second possibility can be supported.

(a) The ash content of both the fen peat and the gyttja deposit of this Phase 1 indicates that fen-peat growth and the lake fill developed under similar, mesotrophic conditions. The lake had no rooted or floating aquatic plant species. The sedimented algae indicate clear-water conditions.
(b) Although the fen peat surface is recorded in a drained and thus compacted situation (Figs 20, 21), an original bowl-shaped surface is likely.
(c) The coleopteran information of the fen peat (Reilly, Chapter 14) suggests for Column B1, Sample 9, a significant drop in the bog water-table, most likely caused by discharge from the basin to the south. Reilly dates this sample to *c.* 1000 BC.

These arguments provide good evidence for a bog burst dated to *c.* 1000 BC that resulted in the establishment of a bowl-shaped fen surface and continuing open-water accumulations, that is, Phase 1a of the bog lake.

The assumption of McDermott (2001) that the dramatic increase in construction of these tracks between *c.* 1100 BC and 900 BC can be attributed to drier climatic conditions, and as a consequence to drier bogs in relation to Baillie's 'narrowest ring event' of 1159 BC, is highly unlikely. In Tumbeagh the onset of the large bog lake occurred in exactly this window of time (1000–900 BC). Furthermore, the absence of trackways preceding 1600 BC in this area is very probably related to the fen-peat

Fig. 25 (opposite): Dated archaeological sites in County Offaly (provided by the IAWU), with the dates of the bog lake and associated discharge events added.

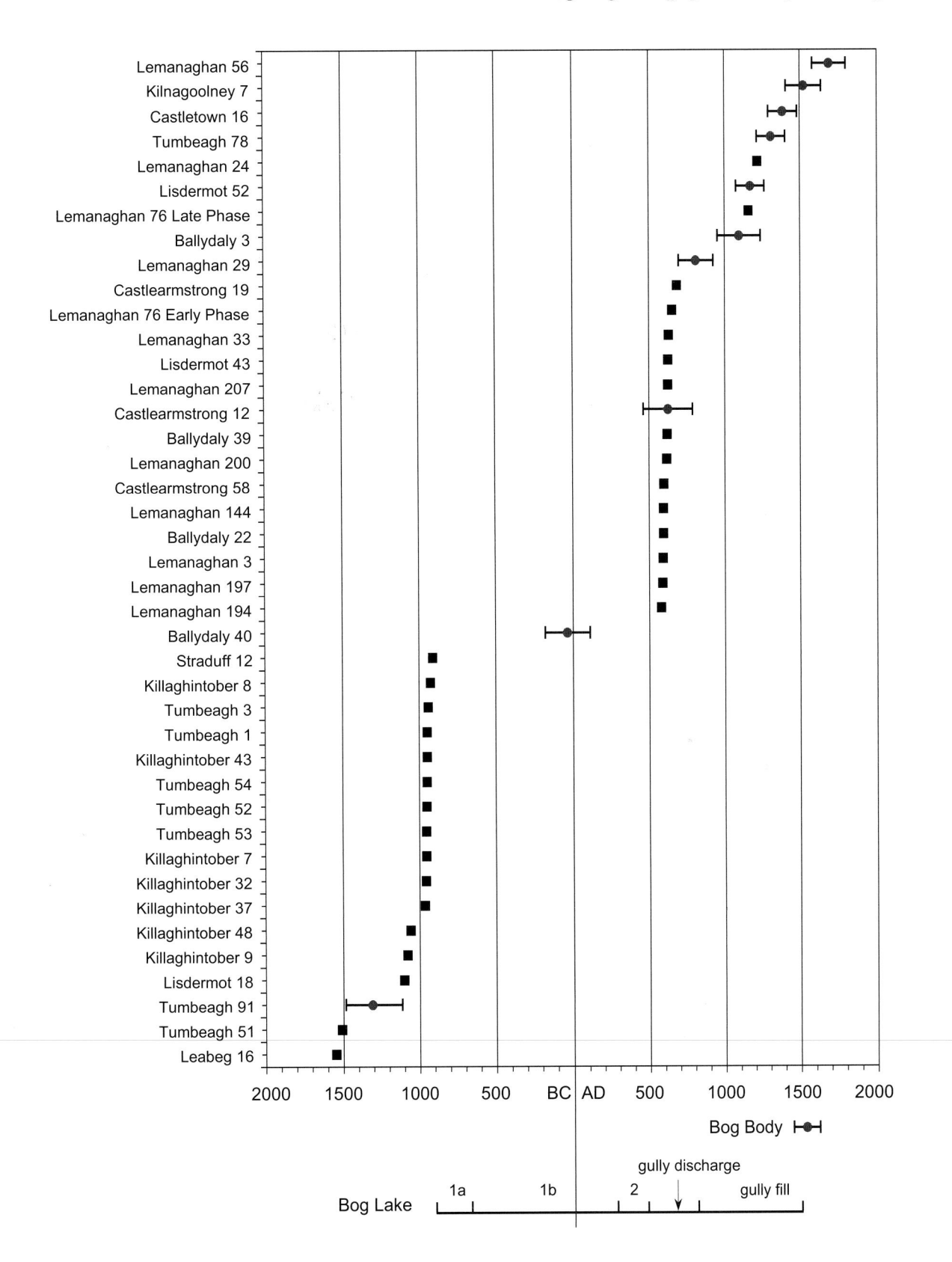

Tumbeagh Bog, Co. Offaly, an extremely wet landscape

growth at that time. It was impossible to gain access to the fen surface as it was too wet.

In *c.* 700 BC the bog lake expanded over the shore areas of raised-bog peat and *Salix* carr, probably as a result of a rise in the water-table; this is Phase 1b. The presence of the sedimented algae gyttja and the low value for the ash content referred to above show that the lake contained clear water, without aquatic plant species rooting in the lake bottom. The water depth was most likely 0.5–1.0m. Phase 1b continued to *c.* AD 240, when the lake drained in a southern or south-eastern direction to the River Brosna, causing a bog burst. It is likely that the weakest bank of the lake collapsed. This happened far outside the study area, where a sharp drop in water level to *c.* 55.00m OD may have initiated the bog burst (Transect 2 and Profile B). It can be assumed that just before this catastrophe the lake water-table was 57.50–58.00m OD, indicating a fall in water-table of 2.5–3.0m. The level of the partially recovered water-table shortly after AD 240 is estimated to have been 56.50–56.70m OD (Transect 2 and Profile B), *c.* 1m lower than before the bog burst.

Very soon after the water-table lowered, the drainage system became blocked and the water-table recovered to 57.50–58.00m OD, enabling Phase 2 of the lake to develop. Around AD 430 the lake became drained again, by a huge, catastrophic bog burst, indicated by the large erosion gully visible in Transect 2 (Fig. 23). Based on the sedimented brownish peat-like algae gyttja and the remarkable high ash content of Phase 2, the water depth was less than in Phase 1, most likely 0.2–0.5m at the most. The lesser depth can be explained by the increasing level of the lake bottom owing to the sedimentation of algae. After the drainage of AD 430, the gully retained its drainage function for centuries, indicating a pause in the rise of the bog water-table. The run-off system was replaced by renewed peat growth, that is, the infill of the gully with poorly humified *Sphagnum* peat, indicating a rising bog water-table. The transition level is marked in Fig. 23 by the *Scheuchzeria* layer at 55.80m OD. This transition happened between AD 650 and AD 900, perhaps *c.* AD 800. With regard to the regional run-off of the water surplus of Tumbeagh Bog to the River Brosna, two main routes can be considered.

(1) The discharge occurred most likely via Derrynagun Bog, east of Lemanaghan Island (Fig. 2). Here the single-plank footpath, Lemanaghan 76 (Early Phase), dated to AD 653±9 (Q-9281), is present. In the following centuries it was extended to a very heavy multi-phase togher of wood, boulders, sand and flagstone (Lemanaghan 76, Repair and Late Phase) (McDermott 2001; OCarroll 2001), in use until at least the fourteenth century. This heavy construction must have blocked the discharge in Lemanaghan to some degree and may have resulted in a rise of the regional bog water-table, which after some time also affected the water-table in Tumbeagh Bog. A date of *c.* AD 800 is therefore not impossible.

(2) The discharge flow reached—running in southern direction, via Curraghalassa Bog (Fig. 2)—the River Brosna. Curraghalassa Bog developed under moderately wet conditions; it shows a high density of lightly constructed archaeological sites and, in the middle of the bog, a mineral outcrop. To the west of this outcrop or island the mineral subsoil is deep lying (McDermott 2001). No hydrological obstacles seem to be present, so there is no archaeological or peat stratigraphical evidence that the run-off was blocked in this bog in the eighth or ninth century.

The changing hydrology of the Lemanaghan bogs is reflected in the occurrence of a large number of lightly constructed trackways, dated to between AD 570 and AD 690, in Curraghalassa Bog, *c.* 4km to the south of Tumbeagh Bog (Figs 2, 25). When the drainage gully changed function to a water-saturated depression with poorly humified *Sphagnum* peat growth, the entire Tumbeagh Bog surface became increasingly wetter, enabling continuing poorly humified peat growth and a rising bog water-table until at least AD 1500, and possibly even up to the nineteenth or twentieth century. There are no indications of an interruption in this rise in the window of time that the body came to lie in the bog (*c.* AD 1500).

Reconstruction of the original bog surface levels

In order to understand the peat growth in Tumbeagh Bog, reconstruction of the original bog surface levels is of great importance. In general it is accepted that bog surface and bog water-table are closely related and share the same elevation. In the case of Tumbeagh Bog the apparent occurrence of the bog lake indicates that the bog water-table considerably exceeded the bog surface.

Based on a series of dated steps in the elevation of the bog surface, a model of the rise of both the bog surface and the lake water-table (between 1000 BC and AD 800) has been constructed as a curve (Fig. 26). It illustrates the wet development of Tumbeagh Bog and the irregularities in the water-table since *c.* AD 240/430.

The solid line of Fig. 26 indicates the estimated rise of the bog surface. The broken lines (before 4300 BC and after AD 1500) represent the extrapolated parts of the rise of the bog surface. The dotted line indicates the water-table of the bog lake between 1000 BC and AD 800, including the steep drops. Both curves represent the development near the location of the bog body but just outside the gullies. The rise of the bog surface inside the large gully is represented by a line of rectangles (AD 430–1500). The level of the base of both gullies (AD 240 and AD 430) is indicated in the steep drops of the bog water-table.

This model shows two conspicuous characteristics, apart from the 'normal' regional rise of the groundwater-table from 6000 BC to 1000 BC: the increasing rise of the water-table since *c.* 1000 BC; and the irregular course of the curves since *c.* AD 430. Both can be attributed to regional or local conditions rather than to climatic oscillations; however, the latter may have played a role in the background. The development since AD 430 can be regarded as the effect of the unstable hydrological regime of the area.

At least four major drops in the bog water-table caused the compacted peat deposits recorded in the peat stratigraphical survey (Figs 20–24, 26):

(1) the significant drop in water-table in the fen basin caused by discharge to the south, as stated by Reilly (Chapter 14); this event is likely to have occurred *c.* 1000 BC;
(2) the emptying of the bog lake Phase 1, dated to AD 240;
(3) the emptying of the bog lake Phase 2, dated to AD 430;
(4) the modern drainage of the bog before peat extraction by Bord na Móna, in the late twentieth century.

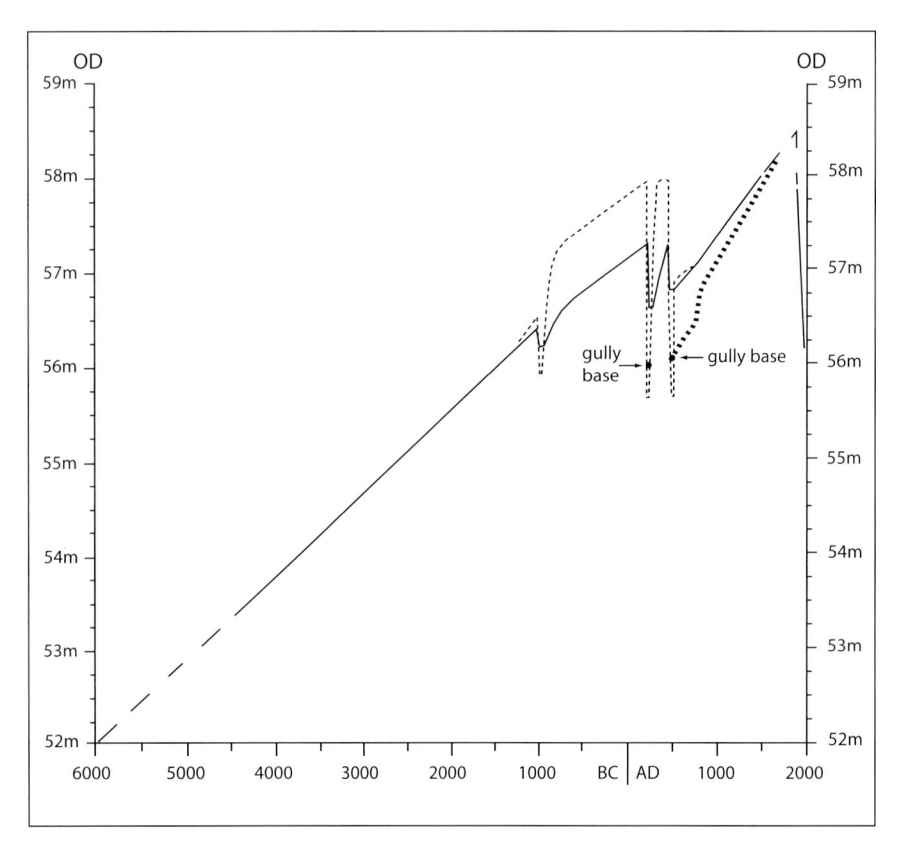

Fig. 26:
Time–depth model of the rise of the bog surface and the bog lake water.

In addition, a large number of less prominent fluctuations must have influenced the steady rise of the bog water-table to a lesser degree. Furthermore, the field survey may have missed a number of important drops in the bog water-table, as these events may not have left identifiable peat stratigraphical traces. In any case the four major drops mentioned above can be evaluated to reconstruct the original bog surfaces during peat growth with a reasonable degree of accuracy.

Fen peat, surface up to 950 BC
The mineral ridge at a level of 56.30m OD (Fig. 22, Transect 2, Survey Point: bog road) was overgrown by peat by 950 BC, indicating a fen-peat surface of *c.* 56.50m OD at the most. Owing to the assumed drop in bog water-table dated to *c.* 1000 BC, this level dropped by *c.* 0.2m to *c.* 56.30m OD, giving way to a very shallow bowl-shaped surface of the fen. The shrinkage of the fen peat did not result in the development of dry peat types near Connor's Road. Nevertheless, drier conditions in the vegetation were present (Reilly, Chapter 14, Column B1, Sample 9). Thus, the drop in bog water-table was not deep, and it recovered in a short time, perhaps within a couple of decades. The original fen-peat thickness was *c.* 4.20m at Survey Point 12. The growth rate of the upper 2.80m of this deposit (Survey Point 5) between 4300 BC and 950 BC has been estimated to be 8.36cm per 100 years (see above). It is assumed that fen-peat growth preceding 4300 BC occurred under the same conditions, that is, with a rising water-table. The modern fen-peat top below the gyttja is at *c.* 55.50–55.70m OD. The compaction at Survey Point 12 can be estimated to be 20 per cent.

The bog lake, lake bottom and water-table, both phases
The highest levels in the compacted peat faces where gyttja of Phase 1 is documented are 56.50m OD (Survey Point 2, Fig. 20) and 56.75m (Survey Point 8, Fig. 22). The water-table of Phase 1 (in fact, Phase 1b) must have been higher than 57.25m OD, probably between 57.50m and 58.00m OD. For Phase 2 the highest occurrence of the compacted gyttja is at 57.00m OD (Survey Point 8, Fig. 22). Therefore in Phase 2 the lake water-table must have been higher than 57.30m OD. These estimates are, however, based on compacted peats. Originally the elevation of the lake bottom and lake surface must have been higher. This is addressed in more detail below.

Remarkably, in both phases (Phase 1b and Phase 2) the shore area was at about the same location (Fig. 20, Survey Point 2, and Fig. 22, Survey Point 8). This suggests that the stretch of bog where Connor's Road is situated functioned as the northern margin of the lake and that in both phases the maximum water-table was at the same level. The peat deposits on the ridge did not become inundated. This suggests a maximum lake water-table below 58.50m OD.

Gyttja, Phase 1, up to AD 240
The maximum thickness is *c.* 0.40–0.45m (Fig. 20, Survey Points 5 and 6). If we assume compression of 50 per cent, the original thickness of the sediment can be averaged at 0.85m, deposited at 56.50–57.35m OD. The water depth above the gyttja must have been at least 0.50m. If we accept this as the actual depth, the water-table of the bog lake rose to *c.* 58.00m OD just before AD 240.

Gyttja, Phase 2, up to AD 430
The emptying of Phase 1 caused a considerable collapse of the lake bottom. Based on the two peat faces, the top level of the gyttja of Phase 1 (Fig. 20, Survey Points 4–6 at 56.15m OD) was probably *c.* 56.50m OD, increasing to just over 57.00m OD (Fig. 22, Survey Point 7, in compacted form documented at 56.80m OD). This indicates a bowl-shaped lake bottom. The water depth in the centre of the lake was *c.* 0.50–0.70m, greater than in the shore area, where a depth of 0.30m is likely. Phase 2 produced a gyttja deposit of 0.10–0.14m in compacted form. If we assume compaction of *c.* 50 per cent, its original thickness was *c.* 0.25m, deposited at a level from 56.50m up to 56.75m OD in the central zone and between 57.10m and 57.35m OD in the shore area. If we take here a water depth of 0.30m, the bog water-table can be estimated to be 57.65m OD or higher. As the highest gyttja level of Phase 2 exceeded that of Phase 1 by *c.* 0.20m (Fig. 22, Survey Point 7), the maximum lake water-table at the end of Phase 2 must have been the same as in Phase 1, probably *c.* 58.00m OD.

The fill of the gully: poorly humified peats, up to AD 1500
The bog burst of AD 430 caused a significant drop in the bog water-table and thus a lowering of the bog surface, at least in the gully itself. In Profile C (Fig. 24), where the gully base is documented at 55.60m OD, it is clear that, in an uncompacted situation, this base was above 56.00m OD. Based on the assumptions made for the top of the fen peat (see above), the gully base must have been at *c.* 56.20m OD at least. The *Scheuchzeria* layer at 55.95m in the compacted profile, in fact the base of the

poorly humified *Sphagnum* peat development, occurred originally at a level of 56.40–56.50m OD. This level is assumed to date to *c.* AD 800.

The poorly humified *Sphagnum* peat deposit, on the top of which the human remains were found at a level of 56.55–56.60m OD, can be dated to between AD 800 and AD 1500. It now has a thickness of 0.65m. It accumulated as very loose peat under quite wet conditions, indicating a rising bog surface and probably an increase of 15cm per 100 years in the bog water-table. This suggests that the deposit had an original thickness of *c.* 1.0m. The bog surface in the gully at the time that the body was deposited can thus be estimated to be *c.* 57.60m OD, somewhat lower than the bog surface outside the gully. The difference in height did not exceed 0.40m; in the wet seasons and after rainy periods it was less, perhaps *c.* 0.20–0.30m. This is the normal relief of a living raised-bog surface. This gully zone would have been barely visible in the surface relief from about AD 1250. The peat inside the gully was much softer because of its higher water content. In addition, the peat in the gully lacked the somewhat firmer substrate of the underlying gyttja deposits (providing more resistance when walking) present outside the gully (see below). The combination of the two characteristics suggests that this gully zone was quite treacherous.

Poorly humified Sphagnum peat outside the gully, up to AD 1500
Between AD 430 and AD 800 the elevation of the bog surface increased moderately because the area drained into the gully (Fig. 27). The accumulation of about 0.20–0.30m of fresh peat raised the bog surface to a level of *c.* 57.00m OD. From AD 800 to at least AD 1500 the accumulation of peat increased considerably. This happened under wetter conditions than before, as the *Scheuchzeria* and *cuspidatum* fields on Fig. 28 indicate. This bog surface occurred at a level of *c.* 58.00m OD. The presence of the somewhat compacted gyttja deposits at *c.* 1m below the bog surface meant that gaining access to this bog surface was difficult but not as dangerous as inside the gully zone.

The growth of Tumbeagh Bog

The bog development is depicted in six steps in the Figs 29–34; in every figure only the relevant peat symbols are indicated.

6000 BC to 700 BC: fen peat and bog lake, Phase 1a (Fig. 29)
From *c.* 6000 BC water supply to the Tumbeagh basin, with its subsoil of lacustrine clay, increased, thus drowning the Boreal pine forest already present for some centuries at levels up to 52.20–52.50m OD. Most likely around 5800 BC, continuing rise of the groundwater-table created wet spots suitable for the establishment of fen-peat growing vegetation. By 4300 BC the surface of the fen vegetation occurred at a level of *c.* 53.50m OD. This vegetation would mostly have been sedges, reed, bog bean and rushes. From the initiation of the fen, water supply and fen-peat accumulation continued apparently uninterrupted for thousands of years to *c.* 1000–950 BC, causing a steady rise of the bog water-table of over 4m, to 56.40m OD, at an average of 8.36cm per 100 years (Fig. 29). Large areas of the Lemanaghan basin, of which the

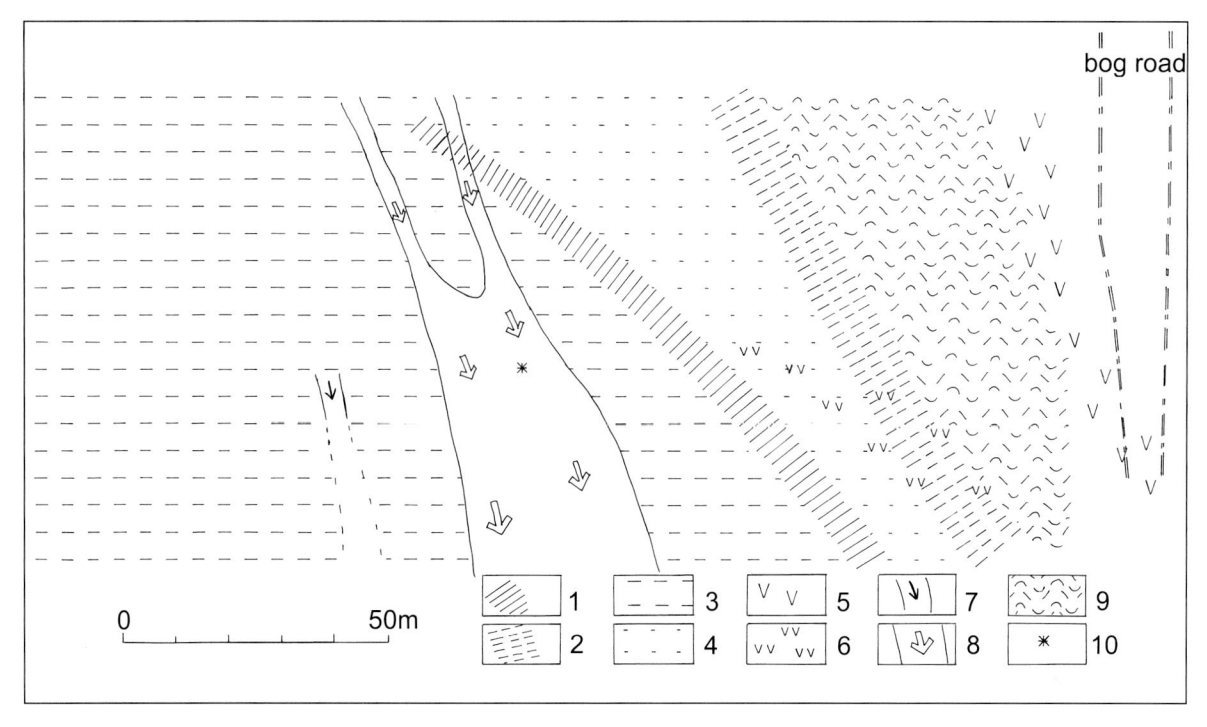

Fig. 27: Image of the bog surface between AD 430 and AD 800.
1: shore area of the bog lake (Phase 1a, up to 700 BC) on the fen-peat surface; 2: shore area during the maximum extension of Phase 1b (700 BC–AD 240) and Phase 2 (AD 240–430) of the lake; 3: extension of the gyttja layer over the fen peat (Phase 1a); 4: extension of the gyttja layer of both Phase 1a and Phase 2 over the raised-bog peat area; 5: wood peat (mostly Alnus wood) in fen peat; 6: deposit of Salix wood peat; 7: erosion gully and flow direction associated with the emptying of Phase 1 of the bog lake (AD 240); 8: erosion gully/discharge channel (the main gully) and flow direction associated with the emptying of Phase 2 of the bog lake (AD 430); 9: raised-bog surface outside the lake; 10: location of the bog body.

Tumbeagh basin is part, became covered with more than 4m of fen peat. The environment was mostly too wet for the establishment of trees on the fen-peat surface; the accumulated peats are remarkably poor in wood remains. Probably, large pools were permanently present on the bog surface, and perhaps some fen peat formed as floating mats in these pools. The low ash content (Table 20, Sample A3) marks the minimal influence of run-off water from the surrounding upland on the water chemistry.

From *c.* 2400–2200 BC the flanks of the mineral ridge below Connor's Road became forested, mostly with *Alnus*. This was drowned when the ridge became overgrown with fen peat, perhaps between 1200 BC and 800 BC. In the meantime in the peatlands surrounding Tumbeagh Bog, such as Killaghintober and Kilnagarnagh, environmental conditions of the bog surface shifted to oligotrophy and acidity, in such a way that raised-bog growth established itself here from *c.* 2000–1800 BC. In the central part of the Lemanaghan complex, fen-peat growth most likely continued for a much longer period.

Around 1000 BC a fall in the fen surface by a maximum of 0.20–0.30m occurred, probably as a result of a sudden, short-term but significant drop in the bog water-table, as the coleopteran analyses indicate (Reilly, Chapter 14, Column B1, Sample 9). This initiated the establishment of a bowl-shaped fen surface. Around 950 BC the

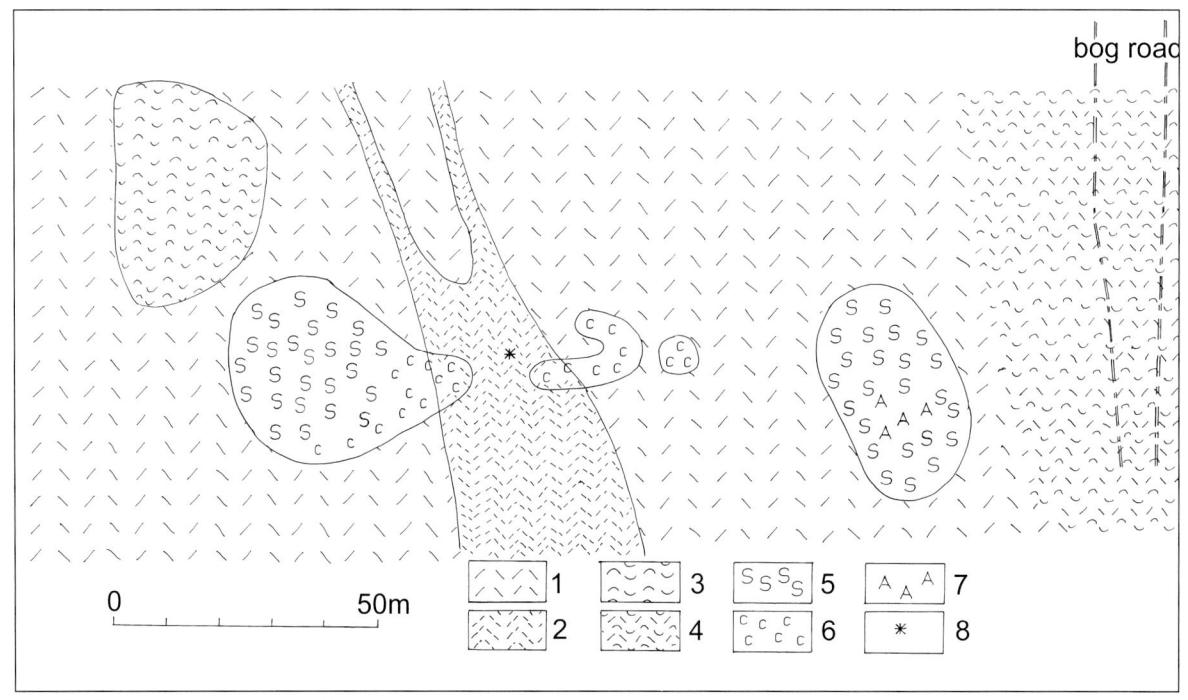

Fig. 28: The bog surface c. AD 1500.
1: raised-bog surface, mainly poorly humified peat; 2: peat deposits in erosion gully/discharge channel, mainly poorly humified Sphagnum*; 3: a higher area of raised-bog peat, probably moderately humified* Sphagnum*; 4: raised-bog surface, mainly highly humified* Sphagnum *peat (area of Connor's Road); 5: fields with* Scheuchzeria palustris *vegetation; 6:* Sphagnum cuspidatum *fields; 7:* Alnus *scrubs on the bog surface; 8: location of bog body.*

recovered and abundant water supply increased further, causing inundation of large stretches of the bowl-shaped fen-peat surface. This led to the existence of a bog lake that covered the lower places in the fenland at that time. Floating algae lived in the open water, eventually resulting in the sedimentation of algae gyttja. This is Phase 1a of the lake. On the stretches of the fenland that were not yet inundated, environmental conditions developed in an oligotrophic and acidic direction, leading to the establishment of ombrotrophic vegetation such as highly humified *Sphagnum* peat. Willow scrub also developed, indicating that somewhat mineralised and less acidic conditions bordering the bog lake.

The increasing wetness of the bog surface was not a local phenomenon. This can be concluded from the dated trackways (Fig. 25), especially from the period from 900 BC on, within which there is only one dated track: Ballydaly 40. It can be assumed that wetness increased remarkably in the entire Lemanaghan area.

The rise of the bog lake water-table continued at a steady pace, so that in *c.* 700 BC the lake expanded, flooding the former shore area with *Sphagnum* peat growth and *Salix* carr. These vegetation types occurred near the low mineral ridge, Connor's Road, the top of which lay at *c.* 56.50m OD and was covered with fen peat. Its summit, however, was barely, if at all, higher than the lake water-table. The bog lake Phase 1a most probably developed in the lee of this ridge. Between 950 BC and 700 BC the lake water-table rose *c.* 0.30–0.40m: this is the beginning of Phase 1b.

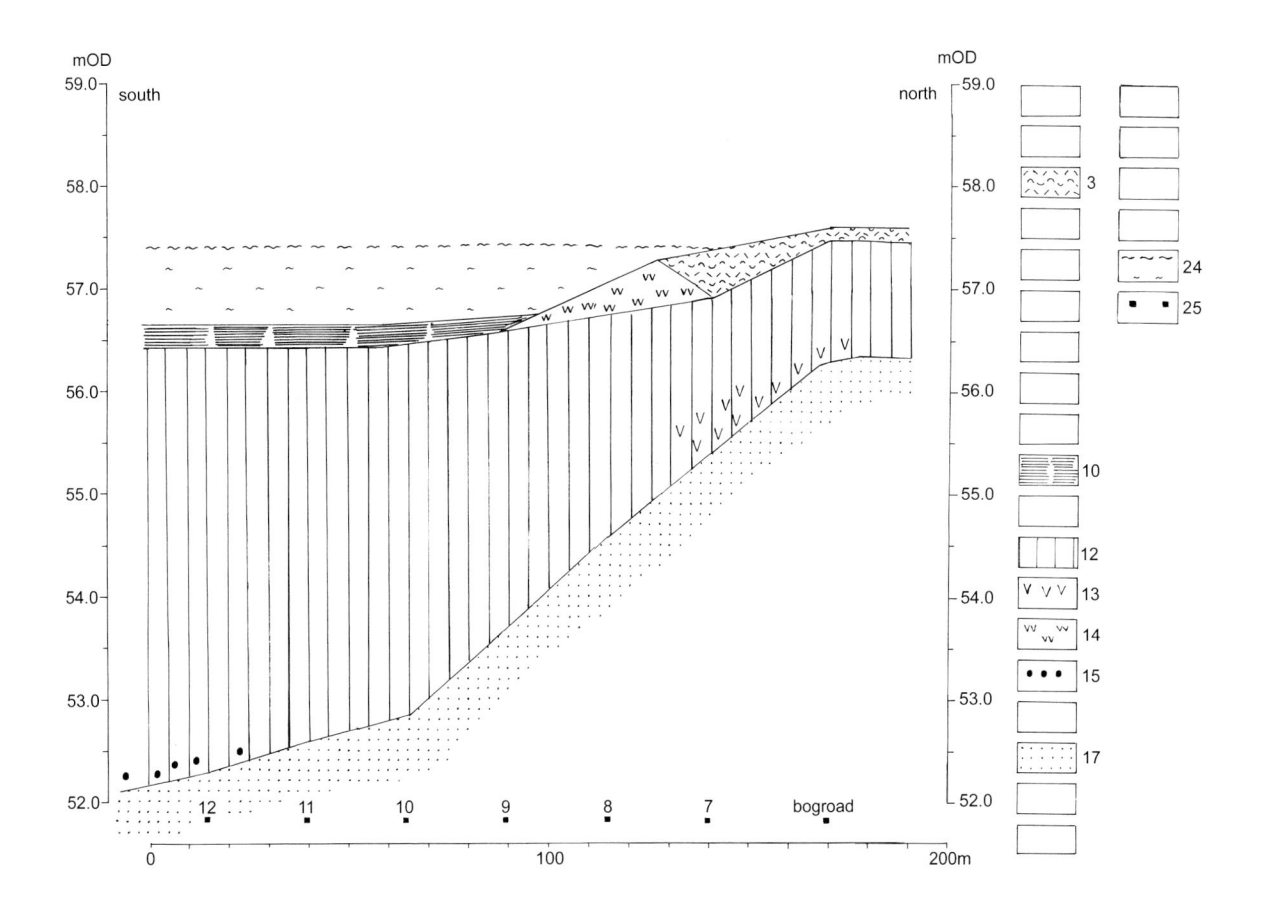

Fig. 29:
Development of
Tumbeagh Bog
between 6000 BC
and 700 BC.

The northern shore area for both Phase 1b and Phase 2 did not extend over the ridge, although their highest level exceeds the level of the ridge by *c.* 0.50m (Fig. 22, Transect 2, between Survey Points 7 and 8). This shows that the Phase 1a lake developed only after shrinkage of the fen-peat surface, after the significant drop in the water-table dated to *c.* 1000 BC. In 700 BC the peat deposits overlying the ridge probably had a thickness of *c.* 1.30m.

700 BC to AD 240: bog lake, Phase 1b (Fig. 30)
From *c.* 700 BC the increased water supply that resulted in the growth of the bog lake in size and depth must have been considerable, for fen-peat growth stopped totally in the flooded areas. Even the establishment of marshy and aquatic plant species failed to occur. Only large amounts of floating algae (Diatomeae) lived in the lake. It can be assumed that the water depth was soon more than 0.5m, perhaps 1m. The lake bottom was at a level of *c.* 56.50m OD. The water-table of the bog lake increased in a short period from *c.* 56.80m OD to *c.* 57.20m OD. This rise represents the beginning of Phase 1b: the growth from isolated flooded pools to the lake, with one large, serried water surface. This occurred within three centuries, between 950 BC and 700 BC.

The water in the lake must have been clear, its surface free of floating aquatic plant species; plants rooting in the lake bottom were also absent. The grey gyttja represents

143

The bog body from Tumbeagh

Fig. 30: Development of Tumbeagh Bog up to AD 240.

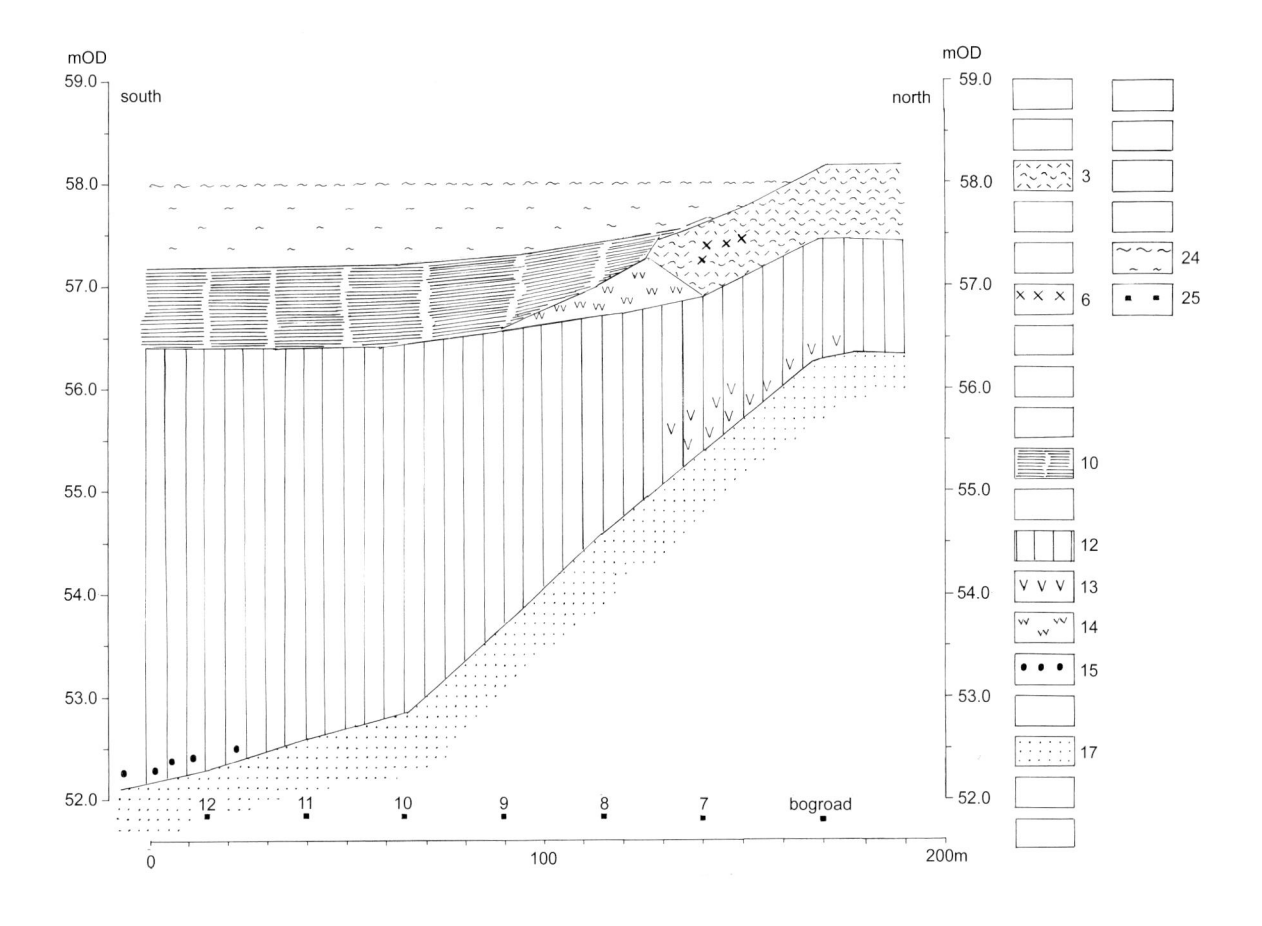

the sedimented remains of floating algae vegetation that lived in the water. Its bright grey colour indicates that peaty remains did not reach this area of the bog lake. Thus, the water supply did not derive from the surrounding bog complexes of Kilnagarnagh, Killaghintober or Castletown. This is confirmed by the low ash content (Table 20) and by the coleopteran analyses (Reilly, Chapter 14). Mineral particles in the form of sand, silt or loam were not identified in the sediment, implying that the mineral upland cannot be regarded as the main water source. Most of the water supply can therefore be attributed to direct rainfall, stored in the Lemanaghan basin, of which Tumbeagh Bog is one of the outer parts. This means that there was minimal discharge and explains the rather mesotrophic conditions of the lake environment. The apparently not very acidic character of this water accumulation is remarkable.

The lamination of the gyttja of both Phase 1a and Phase 1b, referred to above, takes the form of alternate bright grey and grey layers, each in general up to 5mm thick, including the less frequent occurrence of a thin, dark grey layer. This reflects fluctuations in water chemistry and in the water-table. Significant drops in the latter, causing desiccation and aeration of the bottom, did not occur. All of these observations indicate that the depth of water was more than 0.5m, perhaps 1m or somewhat more, as has previously been indicated.

Once in existence, the lake, Phase 1b, increased considerably in size in a short period of time. As Fig. 27 shows, the northern shoreline shifted in the study area *c.* 30m to the north-west. The western lake margin, occurring *c.* 100m to the west, shifted over the same distance. The nearby mineral ridge (Connor's Road) was fully overgrown by peat but did not become part of the lake itself: it was the northern shore area. To the east the lake may have extended some hundreds of metres, although this margin was not surveyed. To the south the lake extends over at least 200m, but its full extent was not established. It is unclear whether the lake was this size when it first formed (Phase 1a) or it was smaller. It is likely that within three centuries the lake covered most of the area mentioned above.

Where the gyttja sediment has been observed in the Bord na Móna drain faces, its lamination is clear, representing remarkably quiet conditions during the entire period of the rise of the bog water-table between 950 BC and AD 240 (Fig. 30), by at least 12.5cm per 100 years. The lake water-table can be assumed to be at *c.* 58.00m OD (Fig. 30), at least just before the first catastrophic emptying. Eroding water movements generally appear to have been absent, with the exception of the filled gully-like structure in Transect 2, at 10–30m (Fig. 22; see also Fig. 27, symbol 7). The gully can be dated to AD 240. The unclear character of the gully fill hinders explanation of the surveyed feature. Outside the study area, clear erosion structures, interrupting the laminated gyttja sediment, have not been observed.

AD 240 to AD 430: bog lake, Phase 2 (Fig. 31)
The emptying of Phase 1b of the bog lake, dated to AD 240, resulted in the steep drop of the lake water-table of *c.* 1m, from 57.50–58.00m OD to 56.50–56.70m OD. The draining of the lake did not affect the gyttja sediment as recorded in Transect 2 (Fig. 22, top level in compacted form *c.* 55.90m OD). In Transect 1, however, the top of the sediment was significantly affected by desiccation and oxidation (Fig. 20, top level in compacted form *c.* 56.15m OD; see also Fig. 21, symbol 21). The original levels can be estimated to be 56.70m OD and 56.40m OD respectively. This indicates a drop of the bog lake water-table of at least 1m. The gully base of the erosion of Phase 1b is estimated to be at *c.* 56.00m OD (Fig. 31). The drop during the bog burst was much more, perhaps to between 55.00m and 55.50m OD, over 2m. The absence of heavy erosion phenomena in the study area in relation to the steep drop of the water-table of over 2m makes it clear that the centre of the erosion was far away from the study area. At the erosion centre it must have been a tremendous bog burst, caused by the pushing away of the weakest bank of the bog lake in the direction of the River Brosna. The gully indicated in Fig. 27 with symbol 8 does not belong to this catastrophic drainage; this gully originated from the eroding activities dated to AD 430 (see below).

After the emptying of Phase 1b of the bog lake, a humid lake bottom remained, which was perhaps bowl shaped and was largely covered with a thin layer of replaced peat. Renewed peat growth barely occurred. Only the upper stretches of the gyttja Phase 1b were exposed to air and thus were oxidised and considerably decayed (Fig. 21, symbol 21). Very soon this mostly bare bog surface became drowned again, giving way to the rise of the water-table and the deposition of the gyttja of Phase 2 of the lake. Within a relatively short time the channel into which the lake drained became blocked, losing its discharge function, and the (regional) water-table recovered. The probably irregular relief of this surface must have caused a superficial pattern of drier and wetter spots, the latter soon becoming shallow pools with open water. This period dates to one or two decades after AD 240 at the latest. The emptying of Phase 1b can for this reason be viewed as a short-term interruption in the regional rise of the water-table. Most likely, the regional water-table had very soon increased to such a degree that the area of Phase 1 of the bog lake became fully inundated, giving rise to Phase 2 of the bog lake. This recovery can be dated to shortly after AD 240.

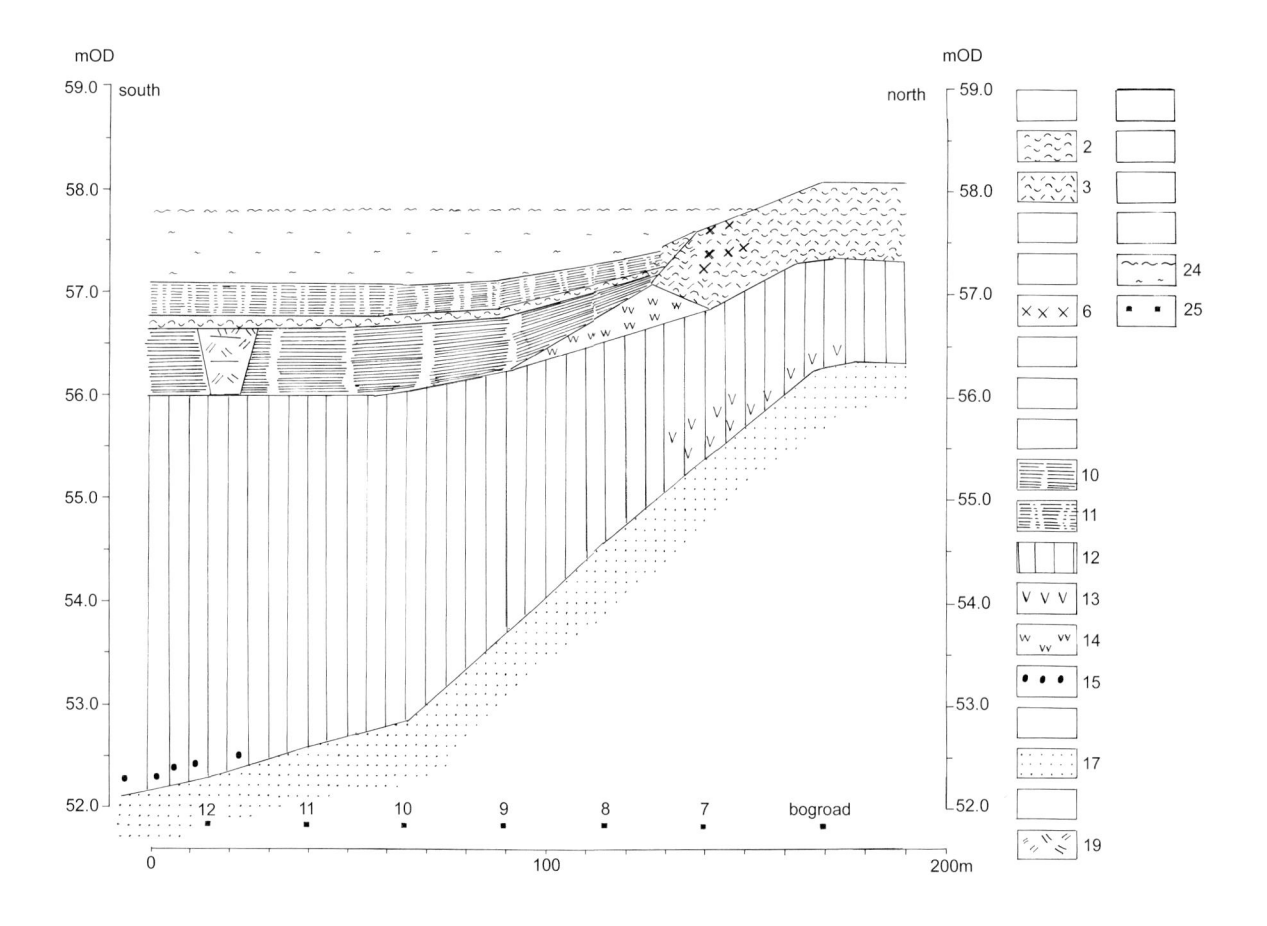

The second phase of the bog lake is recorded in the peat faces as grey to grey/brown gyttja, indicating a lake with a depth of *c.* 0.50m outside the shore area, with open but less clear water than in Phases 1a and 1b. In the centre the lake was probably deeper. Surrounding peat complexes and decaying replaced peat and gyttja blocks influenced the water chemistry by dissolving peaty components as humic acids and peat particles in the water. This is well confirmed by the ash content and the coleopteran analyses. In the shore area, at least, eutrophic conditions occurred. The gyttja deposit, measuring up to 0.25m in uncompacted form, is mostly well laminated; the northern stretches of the deposit (Transect 1, Survey Points 2 and 3; Transect 2, Survey Points 8 and 9) resemble pool-fill deposits: dark brown, nearly amorphous, and undergoing intensive cracking when drying. It can be assumed that the water depth here was only 0.10–0.30m.

As stated above, the northern shore of Phase 2 covers about the same area as in

Fig. 31: Development of Tumbeagh Bog up to AD 430.

Phase 1b (Fig. 27, symbol 2). For this reason, it can be concluded that the maximum level of the water-table was about the same in both phases: 57.50–58.00m OD (Fig. 31), as already discussed. During Phase 2 the lake bottom (base of gyttja, Phase 2) outside the marginal zone increased from *c.* 56.70m OD to 57.50m OD in the shore area in about 190 years, from AD 240 to AD 430. The lake water-table rose from 56.70m OD to over 57.50m OD, perhaps up to 58.00m OD, suggesting an increase of 42cm per 100 years, an astounding value, even for an inundation. In Derryville Bog, Co. Tipperary, during raised-bog growth the bog surface increased by *c.* 13.8cm per 100 years, despite a number of bog bursts (Casparie and Gowen 2001).

AD 430 to AD 800: the huge erosion gully (Fig. 32)
The emptying of the second phase of the lake, dated to AD 430, most probably occurred in the same way as the drainage of Phase 1b: a steep lowering of the water-table and bog-burst-like erosion in the central discharge area. However, the drainage of Phase 2 had a greater eroding impact than that of Phase 1b. This can perhaps partly be attributed to the higher, and thus more erosion-sensitive, lake bottom: *c.* 57.00m OD at the end of Phase 1b (Fig. 30) and *c.* 57.30–57.65m OD at the end of Phase 2 (Fig. 31). However, it cannot be excluded that there was a steeper drop in the water level during the bog burst of Phase 2 than of Phase 1 (a and b), where it averaged over 2m. Perhaps in around AD 430 the water-table fell by up to 3m.

The spatial situation of the erosion phenomena in Transect 1 (Fig. 20), as erosion gullies at 27m and 53m, and in Transect 2 (Fig. 22), the gully between 30m and 70m (depicted in detail in Fig. 23), is presented in Fig. 27 as symbol 8. The large widening at the location where the two gullies unite to form a single gully, *c.* 25m wide, over a distance of less than 40m indicates the very high energy level of the eroding water currents. This suggests that the lake water-table in the central discharge area of this bog burst, situated far from Tumbeagh Bog, has dropped significantly. Again, it must have been the weakest bank of the bog lake that collapsed. After Phase 2 of the bog lake emptied in *c.* AD 430, the water-table did not recover as it had after the emptying of Phase 1 (Fig. 31). The presence of the gully influenced the water-table and the succeeding bog development in this area (see below). The steep south bank, today at 55.70–56.30m OD and heavily affected by erosion, aeration and decay (Fig. 23, between 34m and 38m, symbol 21), represents an erosion level lying at 56.20m OD, at the most, after the break of the underlying gyttja deposit of Phase 1. The northern bank, which is also eroded but gradual sloping (Fig. 23, between 49m and 59m), displays no aeration and decay, but undermining and collapse seem to have occurred. Here, different types of Hypnaceae vegetation established themselves for centuries (up to *c.* AD 800).

The bowl-shaped, irregularly undulating and desiccated lake bottom had undergone significant decay and oxidation, causing the total disappearance of the gyttja deposit at a number of locations, as observed in the peat faces. The surface outside the gully was locally covered with replaced peat remains. It was also the basis for the development of *Sphagnum* growth, but this resulted in only small measure in the accumulation of (moderately humified) peat, at least up to *c.* AD 800. Its remarkably wide pools, filled with poorly humified *Sphagnum cuspidatum* peat, indicate open-water conditions in many places. In the field it was not always possible to

The bog body from Tumbeagh

*Fig. 32:
Development of
Tumbeagh Bog up to
AD 800.*

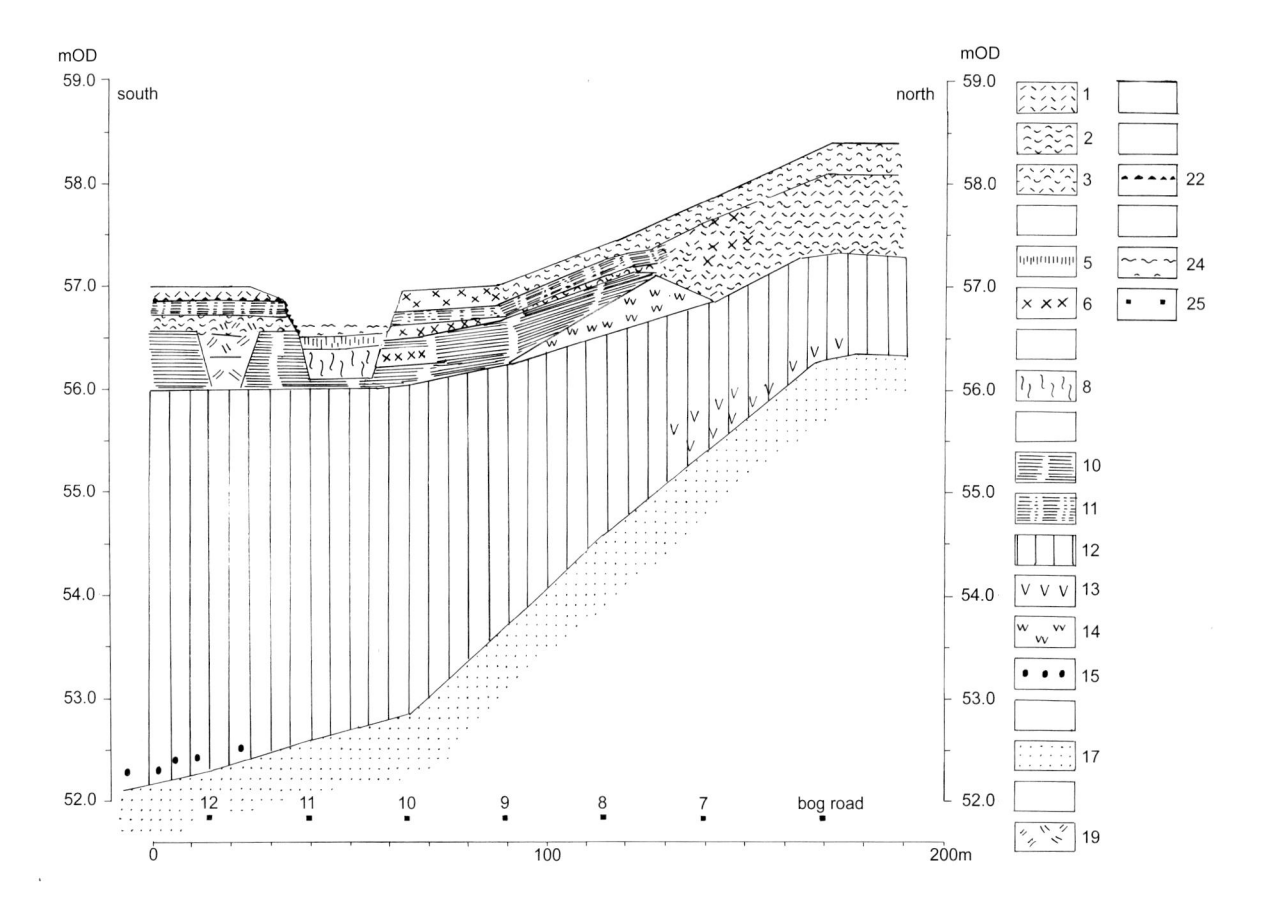

distinguish between the replaced peat and the autochthonous-grown peats. This type of peat growth, resulting in deposits up to 0.20m thick, took place over c. 350–370 years, between AD 430 and AD 800. It is overgrown by poorly humified *Sphagnum* peat, the youngest peat type in the study area. This will be discussed below.

Between AD 430 and AD 800 the main gully in the study area (Fig. 27, symbol 8; Fig. 23, 38–59m, symbols 8, 9 and 20) controlled the discharge of the area in an eastward direction. Its dark-coloured/black bottom level (Fig. 23, 39–49m, symbol 20) represents its function as a discharge channel for a long time. As the radiocarbon dates of the gully fill indicate (dates 4, 5 and 6), blocks of replaced peat and gyttja were deposited on the gully bottom (see above).

The supply of discharge water probably decreased after a while, and the gradually sloping northern bottom of the gully was soon colonised by Hypnaceae, forming highly decomposed brown-moss peat (Fig. 23, 53–57m, symbol 9). Later on, this brown-moss peat deposit and the entire gully base became covered with Hypnaceae, forming poorly humified brown-moss peat (Fig. 23, 49–58m, symbol 8). Eventually, the width of the gully decreased from c. 20m (Fig. 23, 38–58m), to 15m (38–53m), to 11m (38–49m) to c. 6m (40–46m). These developments are not individually dated; they all happened between AD 430 and AD 800. The remaining gully bottom was a suitable base for the growth of very loose, brown-moss Hypnaceae peat. This peat is characteristic of wet soak situations, with some water flow, in a non-acidic environment. Eventually, the remaining discharge channel became overgrown with this type of vegetation (Fig. 23, 38–49m, symbol 8). The entire gully, however, maintained its discharge function. The very loose peat formed by the brown mosses was sufficiently transparent and thus permeable for the non-acidic water flow. The average thickness of the poorly humified Hypnaceae peat deposit in the gully is *c.* 0.20–0.25m (Fig. 23, symbol 8, above symbol 20). It is probable that repeated washing away of parts of the peat in this gully system, caused by temporary increased water flow, took place.

AD 800 to AD 1500: the fill of the erosion gully (Fig. 33)
The Hypnaceae peat deposit in the gully, between 39.50–46.00m and 47.60–50.00m, is overlain by a layer of *Scheuchzeria* peat *c.* 0.10m thick (Fig. 23, gully B, *c.* 55.80m OD, symbol 5). This indicates water that was still flowing slowly, likely somewhat enriched with nutrients but considerably more acidic than the preceding Hypnaceae peat. The date of this layer is estimated to be AD 800; it is also the base of the poorly humified *Sphagnum* peat deposits filling most of the gully. The increasingly acidic environment, implied by the change in conditions, probably enabled the spread of rannock rush over the Hypnaceae peat. This shift shows a rather sharp transition to the poorly humified peat; in Profile C (Fig. 24) this layer could be distinguished at *c.* 55.60m OD. The poorly humified *Sphagnum* peat represents the upper peat deposit in the study area and extends to the south and east but not over the old bog road. In the direction of the western upland, it extends to at least 100m outside the study area. In general the deposit is characterised as grown under wet conditions. These were caused by a (moderate) change in water chemistry and especially by the increased water supply. The gully seemed to have lost its drainage function and transformed into a pool or pond with water that was more or less stagnant, in which luxuriant large-leaved *Sphagnum* peat growth occurred. Perhaps it functioned in this way as the centre of expanding poorly humified *Sphagnum* peat growth over the surrounding bog surface from *c.* AD 800 up to at least AD 1500.

The poorly humified Hypnaceae peat on the gradually sloping northern bank of the gully (Fig. 23) is covered by moderately humified *Sphagnum* peat between 51m and 59m. This may indicate the inwash of peat remains, originating from the higher ground now occupied by the bog road (Fig. 27).

The poorly humified *Sphagnum* peat fill of the main gully has a remarkably homogeneous stratigraphy. Moderately humified peat, indicating hummocks, was not recorded, nor were large layers of *Sphagnum cuspidatum* peat. In the depiction of Profile C (Fig. 24) a few stratigraphical details within the peat type 'poorly humified' have been expressed. As has been discussed above, the details relate to minimal fluctuations in the humidity of the peat and small occurrences of *Sphagnum cuspidatum* peat. The entire deposit gave the impression of an even hydrology with an abundant water supply and without large fluctuations to dry conditions. Long-lasting inundations or drowning of the peat-growing vegetation did not occur. Perhaps existing discharge activity in the base of the gully (via the loose Hypnaceae peat deposit) prevented drowning of the presumably somewhat lower peat-growing zone. Without doubt the small differences in level on the bog surface were hardly visible, and the peat fill was water saturated and soft and thus difficult or impossible to pass. This was the case also for a large portion of

The bog body from Tumbeagh

*Fig. 33:
Development of
Tumbeagh Bog up to
AD 1500.*

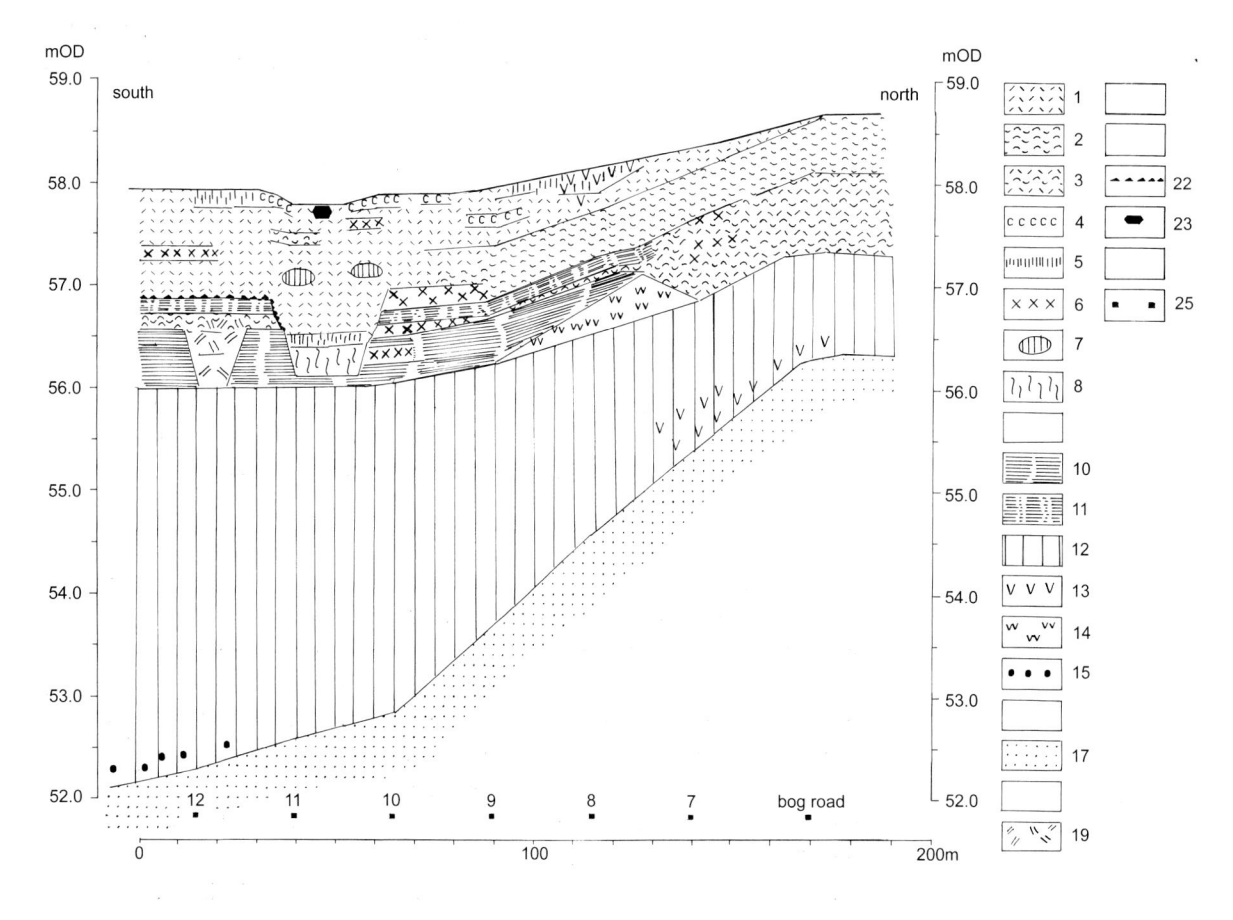

the bog surface outside the gully (Fig. 28). As far as could be established, the gully did not function as an open water channel after AD 800, nor was it covered with a mat of floating vegetation like a quagmire. The characteristics of the bog surface at AD 1500, the date for the bog body, will be discussed in more detail below.

1998: the modern situation (Fig. 34)

The upper deposits of poorly humified *Sphagnum* peat have nearly disappeared, owing to the milling activities of Bord na Móna. Only in the gully has a good portion of the poorly humified deposit been preserved, up to *c.* 0.60–0.68m (Figs 23, 24, symbol 1). At the top of this deposit the remains of the bog body were found at a level of 56.58–56.62m OD. Based on the documented peat faces (Figs 20–24), the large-leaved, poorly humified *Sphagnum* peat growth commenced outside the gully at around the same time as inside the gully (AD 800) or only shortly afterwards. In the northern part of the bog, that is, Connor's Road, highly humified *Sphagnum* peat accumulation continued. This location, with its more compacted peat, can be viewed as a more solid and thus passable zone within Tumbeagh Bog. It also indicates that drops in the bog water-table may have occurred more frequently than could be documented in the field survey. It is likely that attempts at bog reclamation after the sixteenth/seventeenth century resulted in a series of drops in the water-table. With more recent drainage

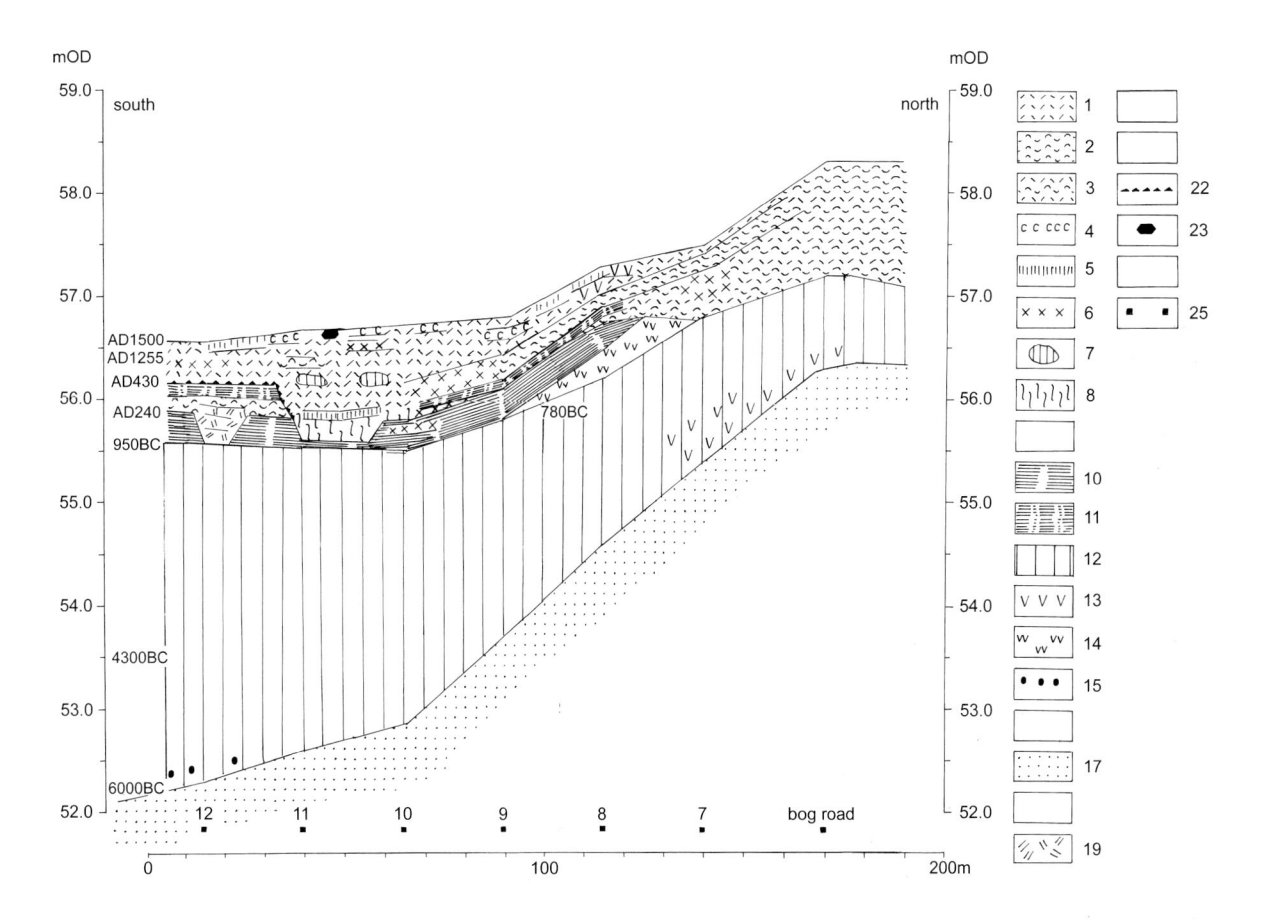

Fig. 34:
The drained deposits of Tumbeagh as surveyed in 1998, with relevant ^{14}C dates added.

works by Bord na Móna, the peat deposits in 1998 were significantly compacted (Fig. 34). The relevant dates for the bog development have been added to Fig. 34.

The raised-bog surface and access

Spatial and hydroecological aspects c. AD 1500
A reconstruction of the bog surface in c. AD 1500 is depicted in Fig. 28. The stretch of bog with highly humified peat (symbol 4) that includes the old bog road to the north of the gully was the best location to enter the bog, but it is unknown how far this zone continued eastward to Broder's Island (Fig. 2). Elsewhere the poorly humified bog surface of Fig. 28 (symbol 1) surrounding the gully (symbol 2) must have been difficult to pass, especially where the hollows, which would have been barely visible, occurred. The somewhat higher island of moderately humified peat (symbol 3) must have been reasonably stable underfoot, in summer for example, but this elevation was surrounded by an inundated zone, c. 2–5m wide (not indicated in Fig. 28), which would have been nearly impossible to pass.

The gully, filled with poorly humified *Sphagnum*, had lost its discharge function by AD 800, and by AD 1500 it was no longer the most well-drained zone in this part

151

of the bog. However, although pitfalls such as unstable vegetation mats over permanent water accumulations or very loose, over-saturated floating peat deposits, appear to have been absent, the gully fill was wet and soft, offering little resistance to walking in comparison to adjacent deposits. Outside the gully the compacted gyttja deposits provided some resistance to walking on the bog surface. Here, the poorly humified *Sphagnum* peat was *c.* 1m thick; in the gully, where the firmer base was absent, it was *c.* 1.5m. Very soft, poorly humified *Sphagnum* peat in the gully would have provided less resistance when walked on and thus could be compressed more easily and to a deeper level. This makes the entire gully the most problematic west–east line on which to cross the bog surface.

On the bog surface, vegetation types that indicate specific hydrological conditions (Fig. 28) reflect the unstable hydrological regime modelled in Fig. 26. The *Scheuchzeria* fields (Fig. 28, symbol 5) represent wet conditions. The zone with *Sphagnum cuspidatum* peat (symbol 6) *c.* 0.10m thick, bordering the southern *Scheuchzeria* field, can be regarded as the wet margin of this field. The northern *Scheuchzeria* field, surrounding a patch of *Alnus* scrubs (symbol 7), represents an area with greater fluctuations in the bog water-table, which is normal near the margins of raised bogs. Under drier conditions *Alnus* can germinate and maintain itself for a rather long period of time, until wetter conditions develop. Frequently, inundations occur surrounding such clumps near the bog margin. Additional enrichment with nutrients (very common near bog margins) creates favourable habitats for the development of *Scheuchzeria* fields. In general such fields are more difficult to pass than the *Sphagnum*-dominated vegetation, as the growing spots resemble shallow pools with open water and the vegetation can reach up to 0.20–0.30m in height. This makes walking very difficult. It can be assumed that this wet situation existed in Tumbeagh for a century or perhaps longer.

The *Sphagnum cuspidatum* fields (symbol 6) between the *Scheuchzeria* fields (symbol 5) indicate shallow hollow fills, surrounding vague hummocks. The original water depth was only 10cm at the most. At both sides of the gully, the *Scheuchzeria* and *cuspidatum* fields represent an extremely wet north–south zone, based on the micro-relief of the bog surface. The bog body was situated at exactly the point where this wet north–south zone crosses the west–east gully, with its very soft peat fill (Fig. 28). Most likely it was the wettest spot in the area. The findspot itself supports this generally wet situation. Where the feet lay, there was a pool fill of *Sphagnum cuspidatum* peat with algae, and near the knees was a concentration of roots of a monocotyledonous species, perhaps *Rhynchospora alba*, white beak-sedge (N. Bermingham and M. Delaney, pers. comm.). The *cuspidatum* peat and algae indicate the presence of a shallow pool, containing open water for most of the year, in which poorly humified *Sphagnum cuspidatum* peat developed and algae could live; the white beak-sedge is also indicative of wet conditions.

The absence of trackways
The archaeological and environmental field survey of the bogs of County Offaly by the IAWU revealed large numbers of wooden trackways and platforms, as well as a few stone-built trackways (McDermott 2001), in nearly all of the raised bogs surveyed (Fig. 2). Remarkably, in the area where the bog body was found, trackways are absent.

During the two phases of the bog lake (between 950 BC and AD 430) the entire Lemanaghan area was totally impassable (see also Fig. 25). It can also be argued that, a number of centuries after the emptying of Phase 2 of the bog lake, the very irregular bog surface and the presence of a number of treacherous gullies in this region continued to act as major obstacles to access for the prehistoric and early historic settlers surrounding Tumbeagh Bog. Probably only after the lake sediments became covered with a relief-smoothing peat cover, from *c.* AD 560 on, did it become technically possible to build trackways to pass through the Lemanaghan bogs, at least in Castletown and Curraghalassa bogs. It appears unlikely that this occurred in the area of Tumbeagh Bog, criss-crossed by soak gullies and wet zones, where the bog body was found.

Increasing climatic wetness
It has been shown that the bog surface at the location of the body was in a wet and thus soft condition, with a low carrying capacity. Indications of local or temporary drier circumstances are not evident. However, there are indications that drier peats had developed at an earlier time. The peat layer dated to AD 1255 can be viewed as a drier intercalation that marks the base of the *cuspidatum*- and algae-filled hollow or pool lying below the feet of the bog body; it is possible that this developed during the 'Climatic Optimum', *c.* twelfth/thirteenth century AD. It can also be assumed that the bog surface outside the gully developed in wet conditions, giving rise to the establishment of the *Scheuchzeria* and *cuspidatum* fields on the bog surface (Fig. 28, symbols 5 and 6) that still existed in *c.* AD 1500. This zone was most likely in existence for one or two centuries before the incorporation of the body in the bog. In wet seasons, marked by increasing rainfall and lower average temperatures, the poorly humified *Sphagnum* peat fill of the gully acted as a water-saturated deposit. This may have occurred during the climatic deterioration known as the 'Little Ice Age', to which period the body (*c.* AD 1500) and the surface on which it lay (*c.* AD 1255) have been dated. The onset of the 'Little Ice Age' deterioration is dated to *c.* AD 1215; a second and a third wet shift are dated as starting in AD 1464 and AD 1601 (Mautouy *et al.* 2002). It can be assumed that raised-bog growth continued after AD 1500, perhaps into the nineteenth or twentieth century.

Concluding remarks

Conditions on the bog surface, as reconstructed here, have implications for the interpretation of the bog body from Tumbeagh. The implications are considered later in this volume, after the presentation of the multiple lines of evidence (see Chapter 18). Clearly the environment played a pivotal role in the arrival and immersion of the body in the bog. In a wider archaeological sense, the absence of trackways from Tumbeagh illustrates the large impact of environmental conditions—in this case the bog lake and its aftermath—on historical activity. In terms of the bog lake, this chapter has provided a first glance of this peculiar type of landscape development, quite different from the raised bogs such as the Mountdillon Bogs, Co. Longford (Raftery 1996), and Derryville Bog, Co. Tipperary (Casparie 1999; Casparie and Gowen 2001), and until now only studied in Clara Bog, 10km east of Tumbeagh (Schouten 2002). Here the raised-bog landscape of Tumbeagh, its disagreeable and dreary character has been revealed.

Acknowledgements

For much information concerning the bog body, for delivering the results of the laboratory excavation, and for good discussions concerning many aspects of the find and the bog, the author is greatly indebted to the members of the Tumbeagh Bog Body Project: Dr Nóra Bermingham (formerly IAWU; now University of Hull, UK), Ms Eileen Reilly (Margaret Gowen and Co. Ltd), Dr David Weir (Queen's University Belfast) and the late Dr Máire Delaney (Department of Anatomy, Trinity College Dublin). Thanks are also due to Professor Barry Raftery (Department of Archaeology, University College Dublin), Mr Conor McDermott (IAWU), Ms Jane Whitaker (formerly IAWU; now Archaeological Development Services Ltd), Ms Cathy Moore (IAWU), who found the bog body, Mr Donal Wynne (Bord na Móna, Tullamore), Mr Tom O'Donnell (Bord na Móna, Tullamore/Dublin) and Dr Karen Molloy (Department of Botany, National University of Ireland, Galway). Without their information, help and advice, it would be questionable that this chapter could have been drawn up in the way it is presented here. Many thanks go to them all.

14.
The beetles, the body and the bog

Eileen Reilly

Introduction

The discovery of a bog body at Tumbeagh Bog, Lemanaghan, Co. Offaly, afforded a rare opportunity to examine well-preserved human remains and the environment in which they were found. Samples for insect remains and pollen were taken from close to the body. A column of insect samples from a peat section face near the body was taken, after consultation with Dr Wil Casparie, in order to provide close correlation between environmental proxies. Insects are useful environmental indicators. The habitat-specific nature of many species of beetles (Coleoptera), in particular, can help to determine the environmental conditions pertaining at the time of their deposition. From the results outlined below, it is clear that their real value to this study lies in their ability to provide a detailed picture of environmental change up to and including the time of deposition of the body.

Sampling strategy

A column of samples was taken from the eastern drain face of the field in which the body was found (B1, Table 21 and Fig. 3). A depth of 1.04m of peat was sampled in this column. Peat identifications were made in the field by Dr Wil Casparie (Casparie, Chapter 13). The stratigraphy here contrasted with the stratigraphy in the immediate environs of the body, and this contrast was considered important in understanding the wider environmental context of the body.

Samples were taken from peat in contact with the body under laboratory conditions. The body had been severely damaged by the milling machines, and very little intact flesh and bone survived. In particular, the head and torso were missing, so it was not possible to examine stomach contents or hair. However, it was hoped that a clear picture of the environmental conditions in which the body was deposited would come from an analysis of the samples around it. This would be correlated with the peat stratigraphical information to provide a more detailed picture. Initially,

The bog body from Tumbeagh

twenty samples were taken from the peat in contact with the body. However, these were subsequently amalgamated into ten samples: four above the body and six below (Table 22).

Sample no.	Description (top to bottom)	Level (top) (m OD)
1	Poorly humified sphagnum peat	57.02
2	Laminated peat and mud, Lake Phase 2	56.92
3	Drier phase, *Calluna* peat	56.81
4	Laminated peat and muds, Lake Phase 1;	56.75
5	*16cm in total, divided into two samples*	56.67
6	Very wet peat, with wood and some ericaceous inclusions	56.59
7	Fen peat (remains of carr woodland visible);	56.53
8	*56cm in total, divided into five samples*	56.41
9		56.29
10		56.18
11		56.07
Bottom of column (mineral soil not reached): 55.97m OD		

Table 21: Column samples.

Amalgamated sample no.	General location	Description
1	Samples from directly over the human remains	From bones at the highest level
2		Skin of left leg
		Bone of left shin
		Top of left tibia; also bottom of bone
		Top of left leg
3		Skin of right leg
		Right leg, north end, adipocere
4		Right foot (upper)
5	Samples from under the human remains	North-east, not in direct contact, left knee
		In direct contact, under knee region, left knee
6		Mid-east, not in direct contact, left shin
		Mid-east, in direct contact, left shin
7		South-east, not in direct contact, left foot
		South-east, in direct contact, left foot
8		North-west, not in direct contact, right knee
		North-west, In dIrect contact, right knee
9		Mid-west, not in direct contact, right shin
		Mid-west, in direct contact, right shin
10		South-west, not in direct contact, right foot
		South-west, in direct contact, right foot

Table 22: Bog-body samples.

Methodology

The samples were processed in the Zoology Department of the National University of Ireland, Dublin, using the paraffin flotation method outlined by Kenward *et al.* (1980) and modified by Kenward *et al.* (1986). The resultant flots were sorted in industrial methylated spirit, and all insect remains were extracted onto damp filter paper. All invertebrate remains, except mites, were recorded quantitatively, and the minimum number of individuals (MNI) was estimated on the basis of counts of fragments present. However, only beetles were examined in detail for this study. All specimens were identified as far as possible using the Gorham and Girling Collections housed in the University of Birmingham, a variety of identification keys and the writer's own collection of identified insect remains.

Species lists were drawn up for both sets of samples (Appendix 2, Tables 1, 2). These tables also contain ecological data and data on present-day occurrence in Ireland of each species or genus, where available. The habitats were grouped into refined ecological ranges, and assemblage statistics were produced (Tables 23, 24), as illustrated in Figs 35 and 36.

Overall, the numbers in each sample from Column B1 were quite good (Table 23). However, the samples did not contain the kinds of numbers needed for detailed statistical analysis (for different methodologies, see Kenward 1978). The index of diversity—a measure of species richness (Fisher's α, Fisher *et al.* 1943)—for each sample with an MNI of twenty or more was calculated, and a graph was produced (Fig. 37). Rank-order tables were also drawn up, and a graph of selected samples is

Sample no. (Column B1)	1	2	3	4	5	6	7	8	9	10	11
Sample size (litres)	2	2	2.5	2	2	3	2	2.5	2	2	3
No. of individuals (MNI)	11	53	27	58	38	77	66	62	44	84	24
No. of taxa (minimum)	10	26	15	30	24	31	28	27	27	32	17
Index of diversity (Fisher's α)	n/a	21	15	26	30	20	19	19	32	19	29r
Refined ecological ranges (MNI)											
General aquatic	3	2	0	6	7	8	8	5	0	4	1
Flowing water	0	1	0	0	0	5	7	0	0	0	0
Base-rich water	0	4	2	5	2	7	4	14	2	11	4
Vegetation-rich pools	0	2	1	2	0	21	17	8	2	11	2
Acid water	0	0	0	0	2	5	3	3	2	6	0
Foul	0	0	0	0	0	0	0	0	0	1	0
General wetland	2	13	6	10	7	5	14	12	15	19	5
Sedge-dominated bog	1	4	3	4	0	3	4	2	6	9	3
Reed beds	1	0	0	0	1	7	1	2	1	3	1
Calluna-dominated bog	0	10	8	3	0	5	1	2	0	3	1
Hygrophilous terrestrial	1	4	3	13	7	4	3	7	4	3	4
Decaying vegetation	2	10	3	12	11	6	4	5	9	12	3
Woodland and deadwood	1	3	1	3	1	1	0	2	3	2	0

Table 23: Assemblage statistics for Column B1 samples.

The bog body from Tumbeagh

Sample no.	1	2	3	4	5	6	7	8	9	10
Sample size (litres)	1	1	1	1	2	2	2	1.5	1.5	1.5
No. of individuals (MNI)	31	28	35	19	12	43	35	11	19	21
No. of taxa (minimum)	12	12	15	8	5	7	8	7	12	11
Index of diversity (Fisher's α)	8	9	11	n/a	n/a	11	3	n/a	n/a	10
Refined ecological ranges (MNI)										
General aquatic	1	1	4	1	0	2	2	0	1	4
Flowing water	1	0	0	0	0	0	1	0	0	0
Base-rich water	0	1	1	0	2	2	2	1	2	0
Vegetation-rich pools	18	19	19	12	3	19	16	2	3	9
Acid water	1	0	0	1	0	0	2	0	1	0
Foul	0	0	0	0	0	0	1	0	0	0
General wetland	1	1	2	3	0	3	2	1	3	6
Sedge-dominated bog	3	2	4	0	6	6	4	3	5	2
Reed beds	0	0	0	0	0	0	0	3	1	0
Calluna-dominated bog	0	0	0	0	0	3	1	0	1	0
Hygrophilous terrestrial	1	0	3	0	1	3	1	0	2	0
Decaying vegetation	4	4	1	1	0	4	3	1	0	0
Woodland and deadwood	1	0	1	1	0	1	0	0	0	0

Table 24: Assemblage statistics for amalgamated bog-body samples.

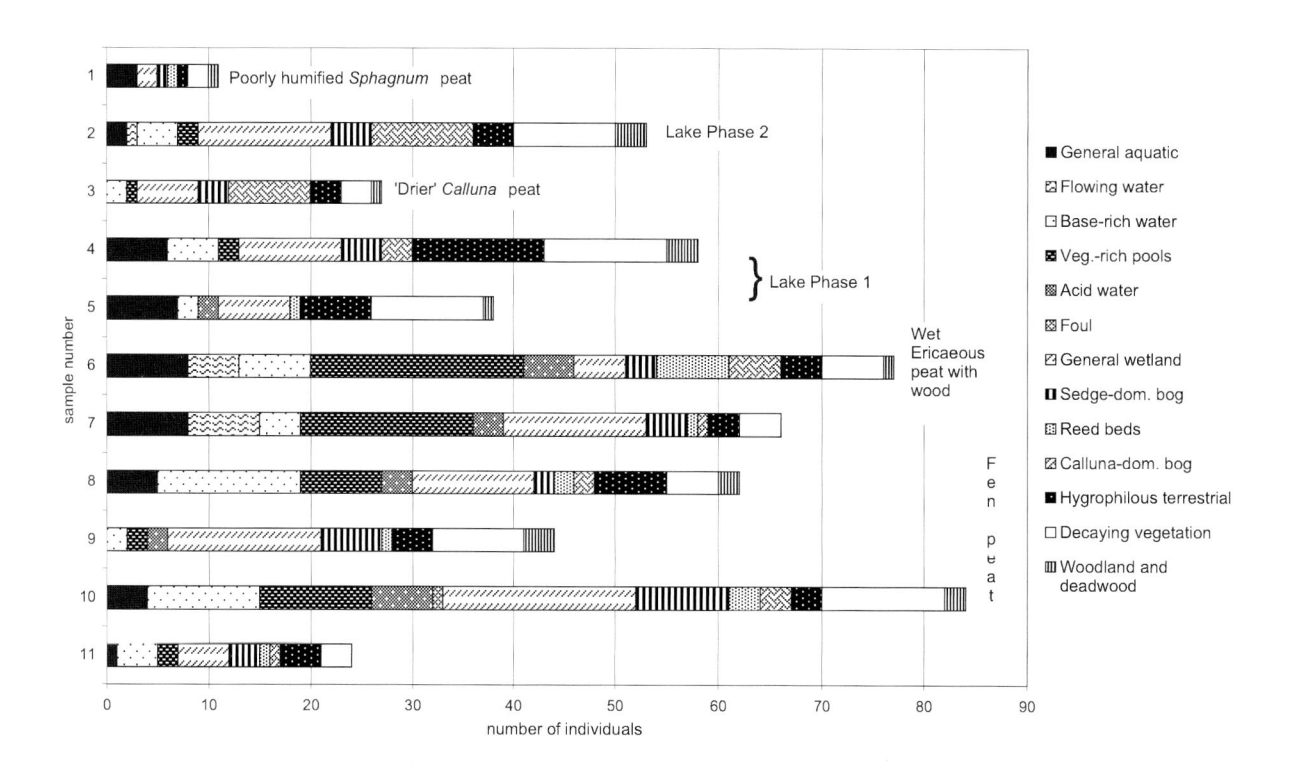

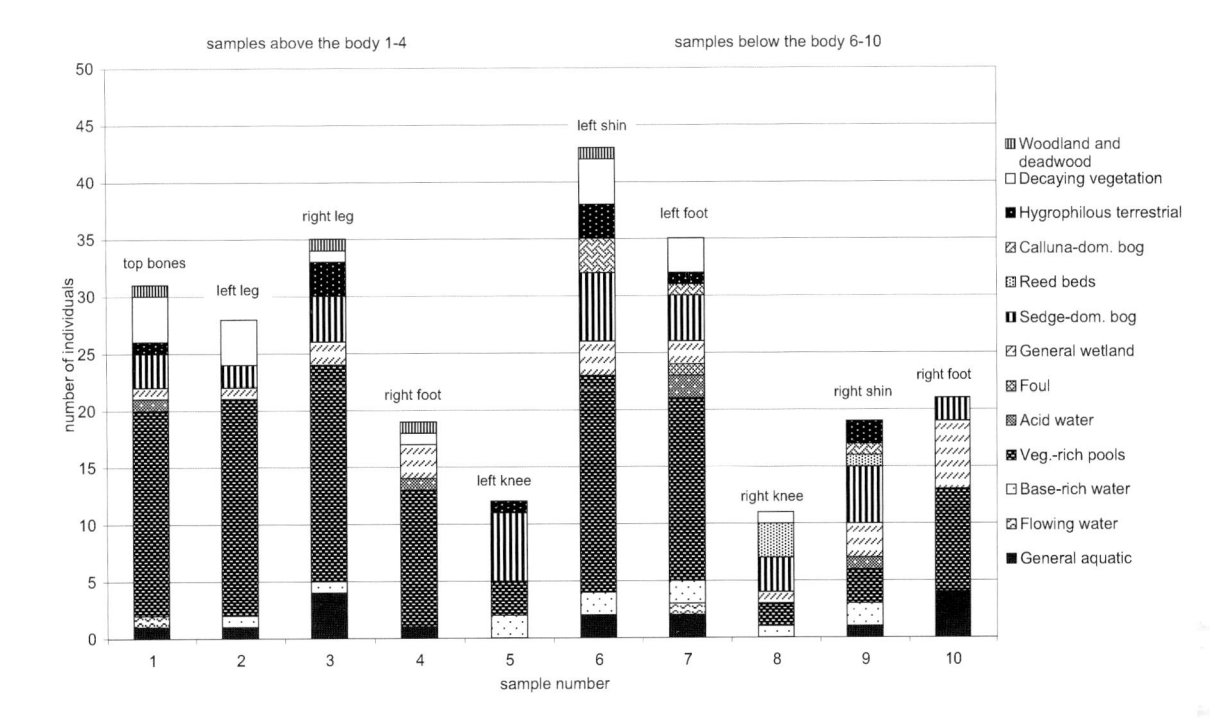

Fig. 36 (above): Refined habitat data for samples around the bog body, Tumbeagh, Co. Offaly.

shown in Fig. 38 to illustrate particular differences between phases of bog development.

The numbers from each sample around the body were quite low, and in many cases the index of diversity could not be calculated (Table 24). However, where it could be, it showed remarkable uniformity, and this is extremely important when analysing the environmental implications.

Analysis

Column B1 samples

Introduction
An analysis of the column is presented below. The sequence runs from bottom to top in chronological order. Three absolute dates anchor three phases in the sequence: the top of the fen peat, the top of Lake Phase 1 and the top of Lake Phase 2. Some approximate dating is also given, according to Casparie's analysis of peat accumulation rates. This sequence of samples was taken from between peat Survey Points 7 and 8, Transect 2 (Fig. 22), between 55.97m and 57.02m OD.

Samples 11 to 7: fen formation and development
The bottom five samples of this section were taken from fen peat (55.97–56.53m

Fig. 35 (left): Refined habitat data for Column B1 samples, Tumbeagh Bog, Co. Offaly.

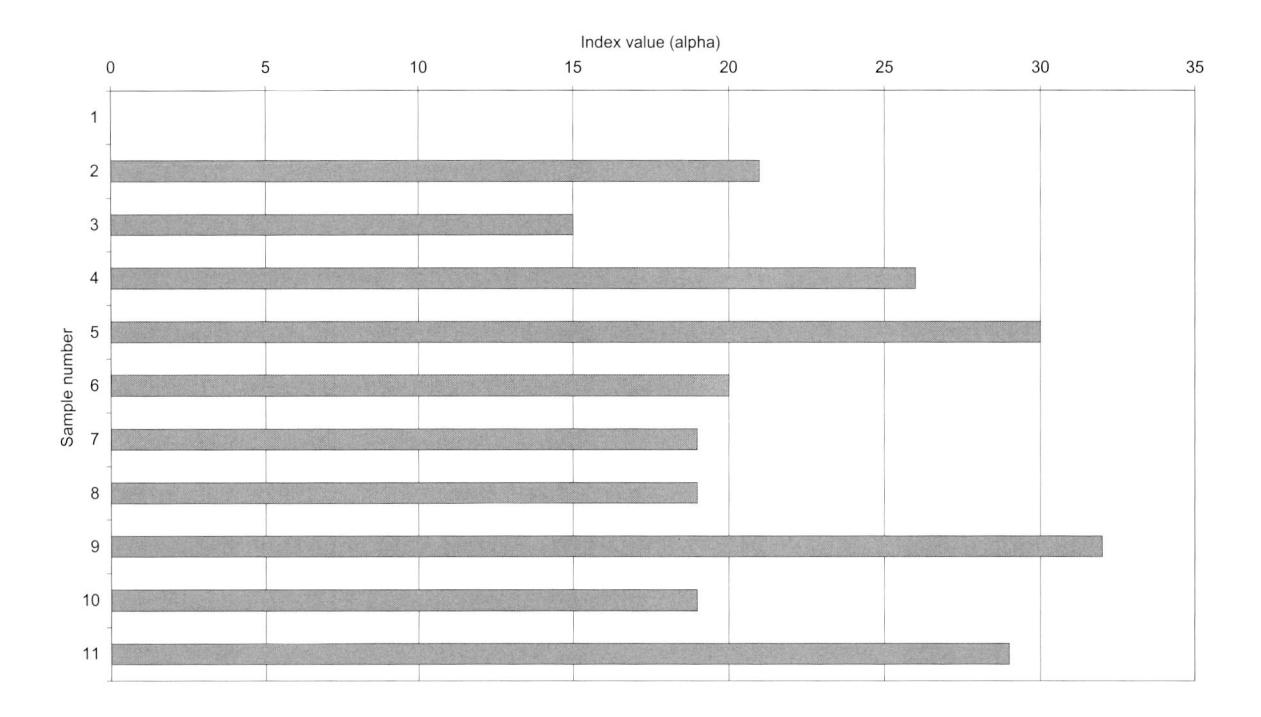

Fig. 37: Index of diversity for all samples from Column B1.

OD). Mineral subsoil was not reached in this location, as there was approximately a further 1.5m of fen peat before the subsoil. The fen peat showed relatively little stratigraphical variation from bottom to top, with Sample 9 (*c.* 56.29m OD) being the notable exception. However, subtle changes were noted throughout this period of fen-peat development, as represented by differences in the beetle assemblages. Fen-peat growth is thought to have ended by *c.* 779 cal. BC (UCD-01108).

At the bottom of the sequence (Sample 11) the insect fauna reflect a freshwater environment (Fig. 35). The water beetle *Agabus biguttatus/guttatus* is found in base-rich water. Other fen or freshwater pool species, such as *Chaetarthria seminulum* and *Graptodytes flavipes*, occur. There are also a number of wetland plant-feeders, including the genus *Bagous*, which could not be identified to species. This genus occurs throughout this entire sequence and is clearly endemic in Tumbeagh. However, almost all species of this genus are considered to be extremely rare, endangered or extinct in Britain and Ireland owing to shrinkage of their natural habitats, so its finding in such consistent numbers at all periods here is quite important (Hyman and Parsons 1992). *Plateumaris sericea*, also recovered at this level, is specifically associated with sedges, iris and great reed-mace. No specific indicators of woodland occur. A small but consistent number of what are know as 'hygrophilous terrestrial' species occur. These are species that otherwise occur on dry land but have a preference for moisture. They can, therefore, occur along riverbanks, in wet meadows, beside lakes or fens and in temporary water. The presence of these species indicates the proximity of upland to the fen edge at the time.

The second sample (Sample 10) from this sequence shows a big increase in the

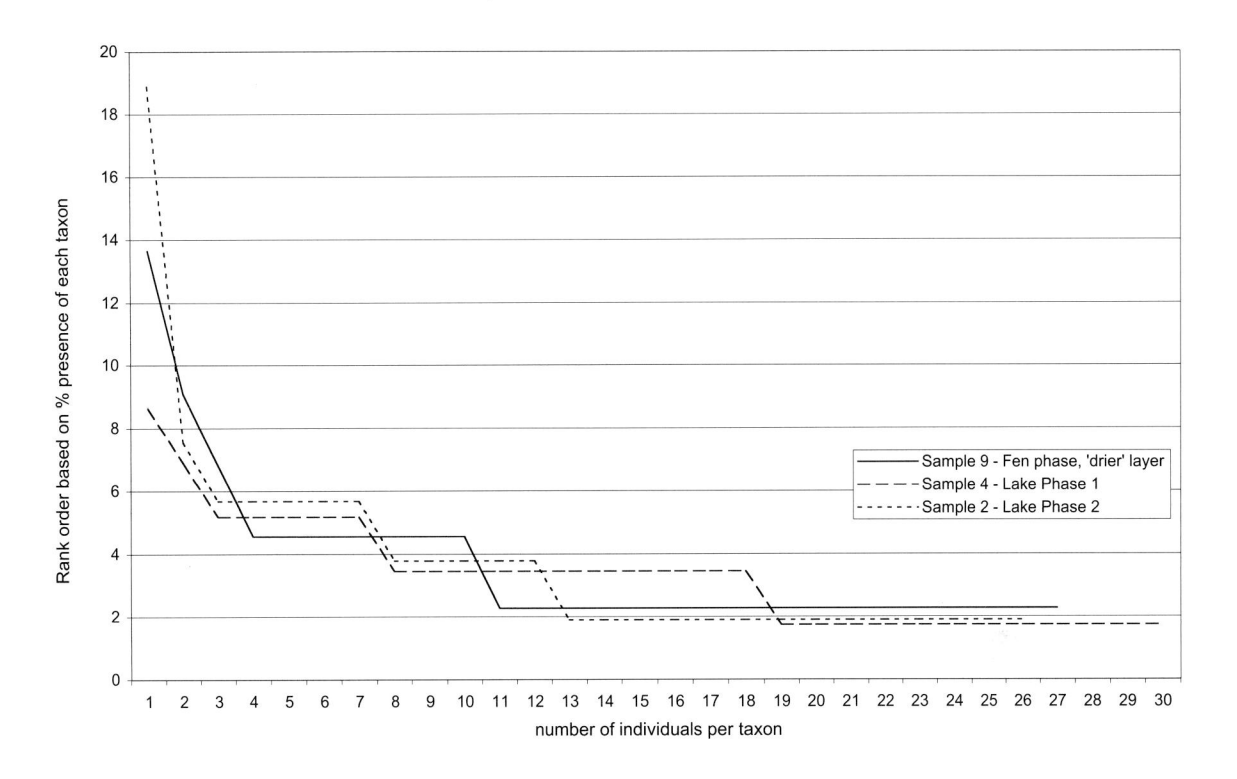

Fig. 38: Rank-order graph for selected samples from Tumbeagh Bog, Co. Offaly.

numbers of beetles recovered (Fig. 35). This is probably due to development or expansion of the fen in a northward direction. A large number of vegetated pool species occur, including *Enochrus* spp, although the underlying base-rich nature of the water here is still clearly indicated by the presence of a consistent number of *Chaetarthria seminulum* and *Agabus bigutatus/guttatus*. There is some evidence of acidification beginning or occurring in isolated locations, perhaps smaller, stagnant pools, with the presence of *Hydroporus ferrugineus* and *H. obscurus*. A large number of *Cyphon* spp also occur, along with *Bagous* sp. and other wetland plant indicators. Sedges, iris and reed-mace are indicated by the presence of *Plateumaris sericea* and *P. discolor*; the latter may also indicate the presence of *Sphagnum*, possibly in stagnant pools. Throughout the fen development phase and the first lake phase there is also a consistent presence of the plant-feeding genus *Phyllotreta* (could not be identified to species). Again, members of this genus are usually found in upland areas but have a preference for moisture, and their host plants include various cruciferes in grasslands and riverside and woodland locations (Bullock 1993). There is some evidence of woodland in the vicinity here too, as the ground beetle *Pterostichus oblongopunctatus* is a forest-floor species and *Rhynchaenus* sp. is a leaf miner of various deciduous tree species. The close proximity of upland to this part of the fen is reflected in these species and other 'terrestrial' species.

The next level in the fen (Sample 9) is indicated by a sharp drop in the number of aquatic species. This may reflect a drop in water-level in the fen basin caused by climatic change or discharge from the basin to the south. The change is quite dramatic. Most notably, species with a preference for base-rich water drop considerably compared with the phase before or after, and a small number of acid-preferring species, such as *Hydroporus nigrita*, occur. It is possible that the stagnation of localised ponds occurred with a drop in the water-table and a low input of nutrient-rich water. The occurrence of decaying-vegetation species (over 20 per cent of all individuals) indicates that humification was taking place, but there are also large numbers of wetland plant indicators such as *Plateumaris discolor* and *Bagous* spp. Some woodland indicators, such as *Rhynchaenus* sp., are present. Together, this may indicate that the water-table dropped sufficiently to allow the growth of some trees and the decay of vegetation. However, the presence of reeds and sedges indicates that there was still some open water nearby. The index of diversity for this sample is higher than for all other fen-level samples, reflecting the slightly 'drier' nature of the layer and the ability for biological decay to set in (Fig. 37). It is not possible to date this event accurately, but an approximate date of 1000 BC is probable, based on the known date for the end of fen-peat development (≈780 BC) and an approximation of peat accumulation rates (Casparie, Chapter 13).

Sample 8 sees a return to more normal fen conditions, in particular a big increase in species preferring base- or nutrient-rich water such as *Chaetarthria seminulum* (Fig. 35). Various *Enochrus* species and plant indicators such as *Bagous* indicate the presence of open, vegetation-rich pools. There are also a number of interesting inclusions of upland, albeit moisture-preferring, species; such as *Phyllopertha horticola*, *Phyllotreta* sp. and *Calathus fuscipes*, a ground beetle often associated with cultivated ground and woodland margins (Lindroth 1974). All of these species may be casualties from the nearby upland or bog-marginal woodland and may indicate some run-off from that direction at this time. Other indirect indicators of woodland include *Rhizophagus bipustulatus*, found under the bark of various trees, and *Rhynchaenus* sp. It may be that small areas of carr woodland occurred in this area, as indicated in the phase below it (Sample 9), although roots and other wood fragments occurred fairly infrequently in these samples. Casparie noted the development of wood-rich peat in this location at this level, but in general the samples do not reflect a woodland environment in the immediate locality.

The last sample of this true fen phase is Sample 7. The first notable change is the presence of a species, *Ochthebius minimus*, indicating flowing or slow-moving water (Fig. 35). This is carried on into the phase above the fen (Sample 6) and may be related to the gradual development of the first phase of the bog lake. The number of species preferring base-rich water also drops quite dramatically, and there is an increase in species indicating vegetated pools, such as a number of species of the genus *Enochrus*. Also present are a number of acid-preferring species, such as *Agabus affinis* and *Hydroporus obscurus*. These various habitats occurring together are understandable in the context of an extension of the water body in which the fen is developing and an active fen edge with mature vegetation and some level of stagnation. The location only slightly to the south of the main discharge channel for the developing bog lake would explain the presence of moving-water species. The number of decaying-vegetation species is low, and no woodland indicators are present. The dominance of these last two samples by a single taxon—*Chaetarthria seminulum* in Sample 8 and *Ochthebius minimus* in Sample 7—means they have much lower indices of diversity than the previous fen phases (Fig. 37).

Sample 6: wet peat with ericaceous and wood inclusions
The next phase of bog development in this location relates primarily to the inundation of the area by the bog lake. The top of this level in this location is at 56.59m OD, and it is relatively short-lived, only 0.07m thick. The sample is dominated by aquatic species indicating a variety of hydrological conditions (Fig. 35). This phase is similar to Sample 10, during the fen development phase, but, unlike in that period, the presence of water largely 'drowns out' the presence of other ecological niches. In particular, there is a dramatic drop in the number of wetland plant indicators. It is clear that the 'fen-edge' environment as indicated in the previous samples is overtaken by a true aquatic environment. The fen edge has in effect shifted north, and the gradually developing lake is now the dominant habitat. However, there are two anomalous elements in this picture: firstly, the presence of a small but significant number of heather weevil *Micrelus ericae*; and, secondly, the presence of wood fragments and the pine-associated species *Dromius quadrimaculatus*. It is possible that *M. ericae* relates to an area of hummock–hollow development elsewhere in the basin that has been drowned by the rising water-table. The presence of *D. quadrimaculatus* is also unlikely to be the result of pine trees growing in the immediate vicinity but is probably an indication of woodland on the margins of the fen; however, as noted above, there may have been a small area of woodland growing in this part of the fen that was subsequently drowned by the rising water-table. This species has a preference for pine, but its presence on other tree species is not unknown (Lindroth 1974; Alexander 1994). It is quite common today owing to widespread planting of conifers in commercial forestry. This peat layer is quite thin and is eventually succeeded by the lake muds, gradually deposited to form a distinct layer.

Samples 5 and 4: Lake Phase 1
As noted above, the beginnings of the development of a lake in this part of Tumbeagh Bog are thought to date to shortly after the fen-peat development stage ended, *c.* 779 cal. BC (UCD-01108). The increased wetness in the sampling location is clear from Sample 7. However, it is clear that this is still a minerotrophic or mesotrophic environment and that ombrotrophic conditions have not developed (Casparie, Chapter 13). The layer is 0.16m thick and under normal rates of peat accumulation may represent a period of up to 200 years. However, the difference in age between the top of the fen peat and the top of Sample 4 (cal. AD 240: UCD-01109) is almost 500 years. Even allowing for the 0.07m of Sample 6 representing 100 years, this indicates that either lake-sediment accumulation took place over a prolonged period of time or a great deal of desiccation, decomposition and probable erosion of this layer occcurred.

The most striking thing about Samples 5 and 4 is that they clearly represent organic-rich sediment and not an aquatic-dominated peat layer, as can be seen during the fen development phase (Fig. 35). The most obvious difference is the huge drop in true aquatic species and the large increase in both decaying-vegetation species and hygrophilous terrestrial species. The index of diversity from Sample 5 is second only to Sample 9, during the fen development phase, indicating the similarities in environmental conditions pertaining at the two periods (Fig. 37). In effect, the insect death assemblages reflect both the active deposition of sediment during the lake phase and the aftermath of the emptying of the basin when the drop in water-table resulted in the drying out and partial decomposition of the gyttja layer. Sample 5 probably better reflects the deposition period, and Sample 4 probably better represents the post-lake phase. The main difference between the two layers is the smaller number of terrestrial species present in the upper part of the gyttja layer (i.e. Sample 4). As noted by Casparie (Chapter 13), the discharge of water from the lake led to drying out and subsequent partial desiccation of the gyttja, allowing some trees to colonise and drier peat types to grow. Some ericaceous remains were noted in the peat stratigraphy at this time at various locations along this section (Casparie, Chapter 13). It is clear that *Calluna* was growing on the surface of the drier gyttja layer at this location, as *Micrelus ericae* is recovered and various dryland plant-feeders such as *Chatocnema concinna*, *Apion* sp. and *Phyllotreta* sp. are also present. Both layers also have a small number of woodland-associated species, including *Rhynchaenus* sp., *Dromius quadrimaculatus* and *Agathedium* sp. These may be related to the recolonisation of part of the lakebed by trees. The lake phase appeared to last for a considerable time before the catastrophic event that resulted in the emptying of the basin. The top of the phase has been dated to cal. AD 238 (UCD-01110). However, this includes the period after it was emptied and the subsequent decomposition of the gyttja layer; it does not date the actual event that emptied the basin. This is assumed by Casparie to be a bog burst, which drained the bog to the south or south-east, toward the River Brosna, and lowered the water-table by up to 1m.

Sample 3: drier *Calluna* peat phase
The end of Phase 1 of the lake and the subsequent emptying caused a drying out of the lake sediments. This compacted layer allowed the growth of drier peat types, and this is very clearly reflected in the insect assemblage of Sample 3 (Fig. 35). This layer effectively represents the entire period of 'drier' peat growth, probably not a very long period of time, given the subsequent dates for Phase 2 of the lake. The assemblage contains a low percentage of true aquatics, and those present mainly indicate small pools of standing water: *Chaetarthria seminulum* and *Graptodytes bilineatus*. The presence of growing *Sphagnum* and other wetland plants is indicated by *Bagous* spp, *Cyphon* spp and *Plateumaris discolor*. However, the presence of *Calluna* is indisputably indicated by a large number of *Micrelus ericae*, representing 30 per cent of the individuals present (Appendix 2, Table 1). A drop in the index of diversity is also noted here owing to the dominance of one taxon (Fig. 37).

Sample 2: Lake Phase 2
Quite soon after the events described above, the discharge channel became blocked again and the beginning of a second lake phase is identified. Another gyttja layer represents this, and there are marked similarities between the insect death assemblages of Samples 4/5 and Sample 2. The layer here, however, is much thinner, and

differences between the deposition phase and the post-emptying phase of the lake are more difficult to distinguish. There is a slightly higher number of freshwater/base-rich water aquatic species, including *Hydroporus rufifrons*, a species not on the current Irish list of Coleoptera (Anderson *et al.* 1997) and considered highly vulnerable in Britain (Hyman and Parsons 1992). Its habitat preference is temporary marsh in oxbow lakes or deep, vegetated ponds and pools (Shirt 1987). *Graptodytes granularis* is found in stagnant pools in fens, and the presence of this and other water beetles reinforces the picture of stagnant, vegetated water. This is probably related to the active deposition period. A number of ground beetles are present, which may reflect the post-emptying phase when the surface of the gyttja layer was temporarily dried out. In addition, a sizeable part of the assemblage is composed of decaying-vegetation species, and there are also some woodland indicators. The most notable feature of the assemblage is, again, the high number of *Micrelus ericae*, the heather weevil. This may indicate one of two things: the drowning of the earlier, *Calluna*-rich peat by the lake or the subsequent drying of the gyttja layer and regrowth of *Calluna*. *Calluna* is noted on the surface of the second gyttja layer in a number of locations in this section (Casparie, Chapter 13), so either scenario is possible. Unfortunately, the need for large samples for the processing of insect remains in effect masks any possibility of being able to distinguish when *M. ericae* was deposited. Although the index of diversity for this lake phase is higher than for the *Calluna* phase (Sample 3), it does not reach the same level as the first lake phase (Fig. 37). This would appear to be primarily a product of the duration of the second lake phase, the end of which is dated to cal. AD 430 (UCD-01110) and seems to have been due to a catastrophic emptying of the lake basin that caused huge erosion gullies (Casparie, Chapter 13).

Sample 1: poorly humified *Sphagnum* peat
The final sample, at the top of this sequence, is taken from poorly humified *Sphagnum* peat. It represents the peat that grew after the emptying of Phase 2 of the lake, after cal. AD 430 (UCD-01110). In other parts of this section, a clear transition from moderately humified *Sphagnum* peat to poorly humified *Sphagnum* peat is distinguished (Casparie, Chapter 13). However, it is possible that this sample came from a hollow in the hummock–hollow system that developed. It should be noted that the top sequence—the bog surface—was not sampled in order to avoid contamination. The beetle assemblage indicates poorly humified *Sphagnum*, as there is a marked drop in the overall numbers recovered (the index of diversity could not be calculated, for example). This is due to the nutrient-poor nature of such peats and the transition to true ombrotrophic conditions. Although some species present are aquatics and wetland plant-feeders, most of the assemblage is from very mixed origins.

Samples from the bog body

Introduction
As noted above, samples were taken from around the remains of the bog body in the laboratory. As far as was practicable, the samples were taken from peat in close contact

with the body. The human remains were not stained very dark brown, as is often observed of bog bodies, but were light brown, indicating deposition in poorly humified *Sphagnum* peat (Bermingham and Delaney, Chapter 4). The peat stratigraphy analysis has identified the presence of a discharge system where the body was located. This channel, from earliest times, filled with soft, poorly humified *Sphagnum* peat and is the location of the two discharge events that emptied Phases 1 and 2 of the lake. Its presence has had a profound influence on the development of the bog in this location.

The peat below the body has been dated to cal. AD 1215–90 (GrA-14393), but the body itself is dated to cal. AD 1405–1635 (GrA-15627) (van der Sanden and van der Plicht, Chapter 6). The discrepancy in dates is most likely due to the displacement of younger peat owing to the weight of the body as it sank (see Discussion, below).

The insect assemblages from the samples around the body differ from each other in subtle ways but, overall, confirm this picture of very wet pool peat. The assemblages are discussed as follows: those below the body, around the left leg; those below the body, around the right leg; those above the body, around the right leg; and those around the left leg and upper bones. This is because the body appeared to be deposited on its left side, and some subtle differences in preservation of the skin were noted from the right leg, situated *c.* 5cm higher (Bermingham and Delaney, Chapter 4).

Samples 5, 6 and 7: below the body, left leg

The assemblages are dominated by the genus *Enochrus*, except the sample taken from around the knee (Sample 5) (Fig. 36). These water beetles mainly prefer well-vegetated pools, tending toward stagnation. The main reason for the poor numbers of insects recovered from the sample around the knee appears to be that the peat had dried out. This is probably a direct result of the effects of milling and does not reflect a dry period contemporary with the deposition of the body. The fact that the peat in the discharge channel was subject to flow is indicated in species found more commonly in base-rich environments and flowing water, but the numbers are very small, and clearly the overwhelming environmental context is poorly humified *Sphagnum* peat. The plant-feeding species—*Plateumaris sericea* and *P. discolor*—indicate *Eriophorum*, sedges and *Sphagnum*; a small number of *Micrelus ericae* are also present, possibly reflecting drier, more humified hummocks near the discharge channel. Other species typical of raised-bog environments, such as the ground beetle *Pterostichus minor*, are also present. One interesting inclusion is the dung beetle *Aphodius* sp., but this is almost certainly just a casualty from the nearby upland. Although a graph has not been produced, the index of diversity for Sample 6 (the shin) and Sample 7 (the foot) were calculated, and both show low values (Appendix 2, Table 2). However, the sample from around the foot is particularly low, and this may reflect the pool of poorly humified *Sphagnum cuspidatum* peat identified around the feet of the body, which was entirely dominated by the genus *Enochrus* (Casparie, Chapter 13).

Samples 8, 9 and 10: below the body, right leg

As noted above, the right leg lay above the left leg, and the skin of the right foot, in particular, appeared to be less well preserved. The pool of *Sphagnum cuspidatum* peat around the feet is certainly confirmed by the insect assemblage (Sample 10), which contains many pool aquatic species and plant-feeders that occur in *Sphagnum*. One interesting inclusion here is the ground beetle *Cymindis vaporariorum*. This species is considered quite rare today, and there are only three recorded findings of the species in Ireland, all before 1970 (Luff 1998). It is generally considered to prefer drier moorland and upland bogs but has been found in association with *Sphagnum* (Eyre *et al.* 1998) and so may also occur in raised bog. However, this is the first time that it has been recovered from a wetland archaeological context in Ireland. In Britain and the rest of Europe it has generally been found in late glacial or very early Holocene contexts (Coope 1968; Lemdahl 1988). Elsewhere, around the rest of the leg and knee, the number of pool species drops off, but the assemblage still indicates the presence of *Sphagnum* and possibly also *Eriophorum* (Fig. 36). Reeds or possibly sedges are indicated by the species *Chatocnema subcoerulea*. It is perhaps unlikely that stands of reeds were present in the channel, unless there was some flow or input of mineral-rich water. It is more likely that this species is associated in this location with *Eriophorum* or other sedges. Some upland indicators are also present, including *Chatocnema concinna*. In general, the number of individuals from each of these samples was low, and the index of diversity could be calculated only for the foot sample; it was unsurprisingly low, reflecting the dominance of one particular taxon (Appendix 2, Table 2).

Samples 1 and 2: above the body, left leg
The two samples from above the left leg and tibia in this location are very similar in that they are dominated by the genus *Enochrus*. One identifiable species of this genus, *Enochrus testaceus*, is generally found in richly vegetated pools occupied by *Sphagnum* but is not considered to be particularly tolerant of acid (Balfour-Browne 1958). This is a very interesting aspect of all of the samples from around the bog body, because, although the gully was dominated by poorly humified *Sphagnum* peat, the samples are not dominated by acid-tolerant taxa. Indeed, from all ten samples only three truly acid-tolerant species occur. This may be because there was, to some degree, a constant throughput of water in the discharge channel and the surface water never acidified to any great extent. One possible running-water species, *Hydroporus marginatus*, is found in the sample from around the top bones. This may also indicate some movement at the surface of the bog, perhaps at certain times of the year after heavy rainfall. The indices of diversity for both samples are very low, reflecting the dominance of *Enochrus* (Appendix 2, Table 2).

Samples 3 and 4: above the body, right leg
The peat above the right leg was again dominated by *Enochrus*. The sample from above the foot contained fewer individuals, but this may simply be due to poorer preservation, as noted earlier. The rest of the assemblage is dominated by plant-feeding species that occur in *Sphagnum* and *Eriophorum*. Both samples contained a very small number of species that are associated with decaying vegetation and woodland. The ground beetle *Nebria brevicollis* is found in forest floors and, along with *Agathedium* sp., which is found under bark, may indicate some woodland

nearby. Alder was noted in contemporaneous levels north of the discharge channel (Casparie, Chapter 13). *Cercyon* sp. is a genus normally found in decaying vegetation and other foul habitats and is not generally associated with wetlands. *Anotylus nitildulus* is a decomposer of vegetation but is also found commonly in carrion (Larsson and Gígja 1959). It is interesting that the only place where taxa possibly associated with decaying flesh are found is above the right foot. It is thought that this foot may have been exposed for a longer period in antiquity than the rest of the body (see Chapter 7).

Discussion

The finding of the body in Tumbeagh Bog has provided an important opportunity to examine in detail the environmental history of the bog in this location. The discharge channel above which the body came to lie in the late fifteenth/early sixteenth century drives the dynamics of this particular bog. The absence of trackways noted during the survey of the bog by the Irish Archaeological Wetland Unit pointed to particular phenomena affecting this area from earliest times (Casparie, Chapter 13). From an examination of the peat, insects and pollen, a more complete picture can be drawn of the development of the bog up to the time of the death of the person in Tumbeagh.

The analysis of insect remains has provided useful and corroborative evidence for the peat stratigraphical analysis. Insects tend to complement peat stratigraphical analysis, as the samples relate specifically to the stratigraphy of peat growth rather than arbitrary sampling intervals through peat layers. Large layers, however, by necessity are divided into more manageable sample sizes, as in the case of the fen peat. This has afforded an opportunity to observe some changes during the development of the fen, most clearly illustrated in the change from Sample 10 to 9 to 8. Here, the early stages of fen development were illustrated by the increased diversity of the taxa owing to the minerotrophic conditions pertaining, but also the possibility that the basin discharged earlier, as seen in Sample 9. Figure 38 illustrates the rank-order curve for three samples from Column B1: Sample 9, Sample 4 (upper layer of lake Phase 1) and Sample 2 (top of Lake Phase 2). All three show remarkably similar curves, with dominance by one or two key taxa but with a large diversity leading to a gradually flattened profile. All three also have quite high indices of diversity, as noted already, which indicate a complex range of ecological niches present during each phase. As noted by Casparie, the emptying of Phase 1 of the bog lake (and, to a lesser extent, Phase 2) would have induced a considerable increase in biological activity, including the decay and rotting of vegetation of the drained soil and shore area. This is clearly reflected in the insect assemblages from these two phases.

Casparie (Chapter 13) also noted that an increased water supply was the most likely cause of a shift from fenland to Phase 1 of the lake. This is also reflected in the assemblage from Sample 6, which shows an increase in true aquatic species and an overall drop in taxa of other ecological ranges (Fig. 35). This is a gradual shift, however, as the increase began slowly from the ending of the possible 'drier' phase during fen development (Sample 9).

The post-lake phases differ from one another as a result of additional environmental factors. The *Calluna*-dominated peats that grew after the emptying of Phase 1 of the lake developed as a direct result of the presence of the dry gyttja layer. However, this short phase, which was followed by the development of Phase 2 of the lake, indicated an overall shift in either the water-table or the climate, giving rise to true oligotrophic conditions. Again, the insect assemblages reflect this development of oligotrophic peats, in terms of a drop both in diversity and in numbers.

There is a gap in the story from the peat examined at the top of the column (*c.* AD 500) and the peat under the body (*c.* AD 1250), owing to the unavailability of peat from the intervening time period. The column of samples taken from the field edge was most likely truncated as a consequence of the milling process, which often sees peat at the field edges more truncated than the centres to aid drainage. The 'young' date for the peat below the body, some three hundred years earlier than the proposed date for the body itself (*c.* AD 1500), is most likely due to the displacement of peat as the body sank. Although the discharge function of this gully had probably lessened or ceased by the time that the body was deposited, it continued to be a very wet lawn of poorly humified *Sphagnum* and the date discrepancy would appear to reflect this. These discrepancies ruled out the possibility of looking at samples from the discharge channel. This gap, however, has been addressed within the peat stratigraphic analysis in other parts of the section and by extrapolation based on surviving sections of younger peat farther away (Casparie, Chapter 13).

The samples from the body confirm the presence of the channel, the overwhelming presence of water and *Sphagnum*, and the likelihood that the body was submerged relatively quickly. The only sample that produced any insect evidence of possible post-mortem decay in antiquity was from the top of the right foot. This foot was possibly exposed for slightly longer than the rest of the body. However, it is not possible to say whether the taxa found were directly associated with the body. Larger numbers would be needed to conclude this.

Few bog bodies in their environmental and landscape context have been studied in such a complete way in Ireland, in Britain or on the Continent. Samples were taken from around Lindow II (known as 'Lindow Man') and Lindow III for environmental analysis, but this analysis concentrated on the immediate body environs and the contents of the stomach (Dinnin and Skidmore 1995). It is interesting that no carrion beetles or flies were found in association with these bodies, and the conclusion was that they were buried or submerged quickly. It is clear from the limited findings from the Tumbeagh bog body that a similar conclusion can be reached. However, in this case the overall environmental context of the findspot can be better understood owing to the examination of the wider landscape using a number of overlapping and integrated proxies. It is certainly hoped that this study can provide a framework for future research into other bog bodies that may be found.

Acknowledgements

The writer acknowledges the assistance of the following people in preparing this paper: Dr Nóra Bermingham, Department of Geography, University of Hull; the late Dr Máire Delaney, Department of Anatomy, Trinity College Dublin; Dr Wil

Casparie; Mr Rolly Read, National Museum of Ireland; Ms Jane Whitaker, Archaeological Development Services Ltd; Mr Eric Callaghan, Department of Zoology, University College Dublin; Dr David Smith, Department of Ancient History and Archaeology, University of Birmingham; and Dr Michael Phillips, Margaret Gowen and Co. Ltd.

15.
Trees, crops and bog plants

David Weir

Methods

Pollen analysis
Under the advice of Dr Karen Molloy (National University of Ireland, Galway), a large monolith of peat was cut from the block of peat on which the body lay (Fig. 8). The monolith was closely wrapped in polythene and stored under a variety of conditions, mostly in cold storage in the National Museum of Ireland. The monolith was sampled for pollen analysis in August 2001; the length of time in storage, however, made changes in stratigraphy difficult to discern clearly, and so no detailed stratigraphical record was made. The monolith was cleaned, and pollen samples were taken at contiguous 5mm intervals using a scalpel.

Samples for pollen analysis were prepared using standard techniques (Moore *et al.* 1991), including sieving at 105μm and 10μm, boiling in hydrofluoric acid, acetolysis and a second sieving at 10μm, to remove all fine particulate matter. The samples were dehydrated in an alcohol series, stained with safranine and mounted in silicone fluid for counting.

Palynological analysis was conducted using a Leitz Ortholux microscope at x625 magnification, with x984 or x1563 with phase contrast used for critical identifications. A minimum of 300 identified pollen grains and fern spores were counted in each sample, with most samples counted to a minimum of 400. Pollen identification was aided by standard keys (for example, Moore *et al.* 1991) and by pollen reference material. No attempt was made to separate pollen of *Corylus avellana* (hazel) and *Myrica gale* (bog myrtle), which were recorded under a single category of *Corylus*-type pollen. Cereal-type pollen is defined as having a minimum length of 37μm and an annulus diameter of over 8μm, but this may also include some wild grass species (Beug 1961). Charcoal particles were counted as they were encountered during pollen analysis (Patterson *et al.* 1987) and expressed as a percentage of the pollen sum. Pollen diagrams have been drawn using TILIA and TILIA.GRAPH (Grimm 1991–3); plant taxonomy follows Kent (1992). The pollen diagram is divided into a series of Local Pollen Assemblage Zones (LPAZ) and sub-zones, which were determined by visual examination, aided by constrained, incremental sum-of-squares (CONISS) analysis (Grimm 1987).

Radiocarbon dating

Samples were selected for radiocarbon dating on the basis of stratigraphical changes in the peat, based on Dr Wil Casparie's analysis of the profile. Slices of 30–50mm width were cut from the monolith and submitted to the Radiocarbon Research Laboratory in the Palaeoecology Centre, Queen's University Belfast. The top of the peat profile had already been dated, by a sample submitted to the laboratory at Groningen. This has been included in the construction of a time–depth curve (Fig. 39), which has been drawn (by TILIA.GRAPH) using the 2-standard deviation age of the samples, in cal. BP. The age of events such as LPAZ boundaries is estimated from this but is simply given in the text as the mid-point of the curve, expressed as cal. AD/BC. These dates are therefore actually plus or minus 100 years or more. The results of the radiocarbon dating are given in Table 25.

Sample depth (cm)	Laboratory no.	^{14}C BP (1σ)	Calibrated age (2σ)	δ^{13}C (‰)
0–2	GrA-14393	765±35	1215–1290 AD	–24.23
29–32	UB-4694	1642±43	260–543 AD	–26.937
60–63	UB-4693	1928±44	35 BC–142 AD	–26.611
84–89	UB-4692	2390±44	760–392 BC	–27.413

Table 25: Radiocarbon dates from peat samples, used in the construction of the time-depth curve (Fig. 38). Samples were submitted to Groningen and the Palaeoecology Centre, Queen's University Belfast.

Results
The pollen diagram (Fig. 40) can be divided into two main pollen assemblage zones, the lower of which is further divided into two sub-zones, and the upper into three sub-zones. The main features of these zones and sub-zones are given in Table 26, and the following narrative discusses the development of the local environment and the evidence of human activity in the period covered by the diagram.

*Some comments on hazel (*Corylus avellana*)*
The pollen diagram is largely composed of pollen of tree or shrubs, with hazel or bog myrtle by far the dominant type. It is possible that at least some of the pollen in this *Corylus*-type category derives from bog myrtle, which is recorded as currently growing in County Offaly (Perring and Walters 1990). It is, however, more likely to be a species of the lagg of a raised bog rather than growing on deeper peat (White and Doyle 1982; Rodwell 1992). Thus it is more likely that the majority of the *Corylus*-type pollen represented in the diagram is from hazel, which is likely to be

Trees, crops and bog plants

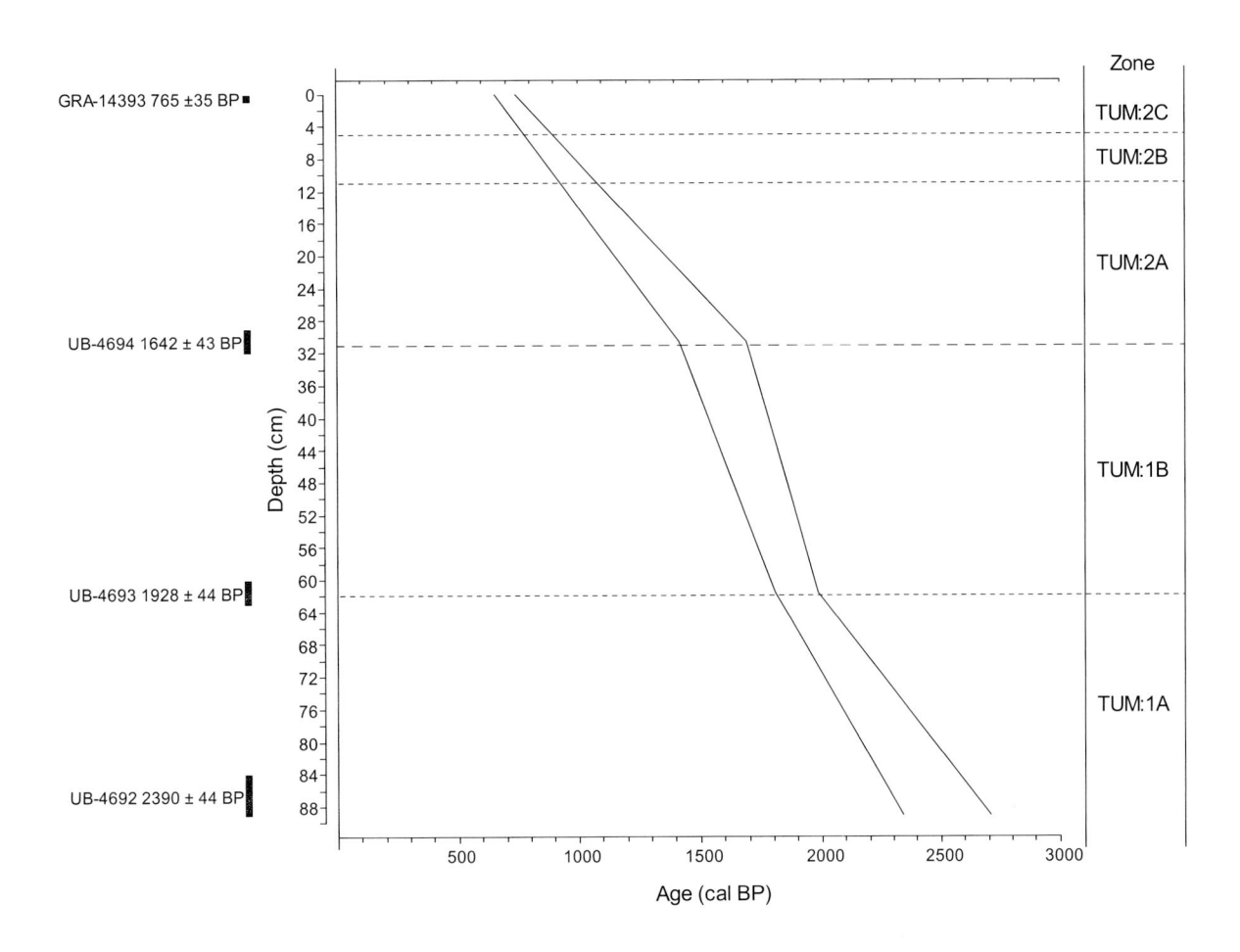

Fig. 39:
Pollen time–depth curve from Tumbeagh Bog, Co. Offaly.

much better dispersed by wind. In the following discussion it is therefore assumed that most of this pollen type represents hazel.

As hazel pollen is prolifically produced and widely dispersed by wind, it is generally held to be over-represented in pollen diagrams (Andersen 1970), with other species, such as ash (*Fraxinus excelsior*), oak (*Quercus* sp.) and elm (*Ulmus* sp.), less well represented. Thus most of the other tree and shrub species may have constituted a larger portion of the woodland than their values in the pollen diagram suggest. Hazel, however, appears to be a major woodland component in most Irish pollen diagrams (Mitchell 1976) and may have been the most common tree or shrub species. As hazel is generally a quick-growing species of woodland edges, in pollen diagrams from the prehistoric phase it often increases during periods of woodland clearance, presumably as the creation of clearings created more woodland-edge habitat. As agriculture intensified from the Early Christian period to the medieval period (or earlier on sites with particularly good agricultural soils, such as Loughnashade (Navan Fort), Co. Armagh (Weir 1997)), hazel decreased in value during clearance phases. This is presumably due to greater pressure on land, with less being allowed to revert to hazel scrub; but hazel was also a valuable building material and would have been intensively coppiced, which may also have reduced its flowering capacity.

173

The bog body from Tumbeagh

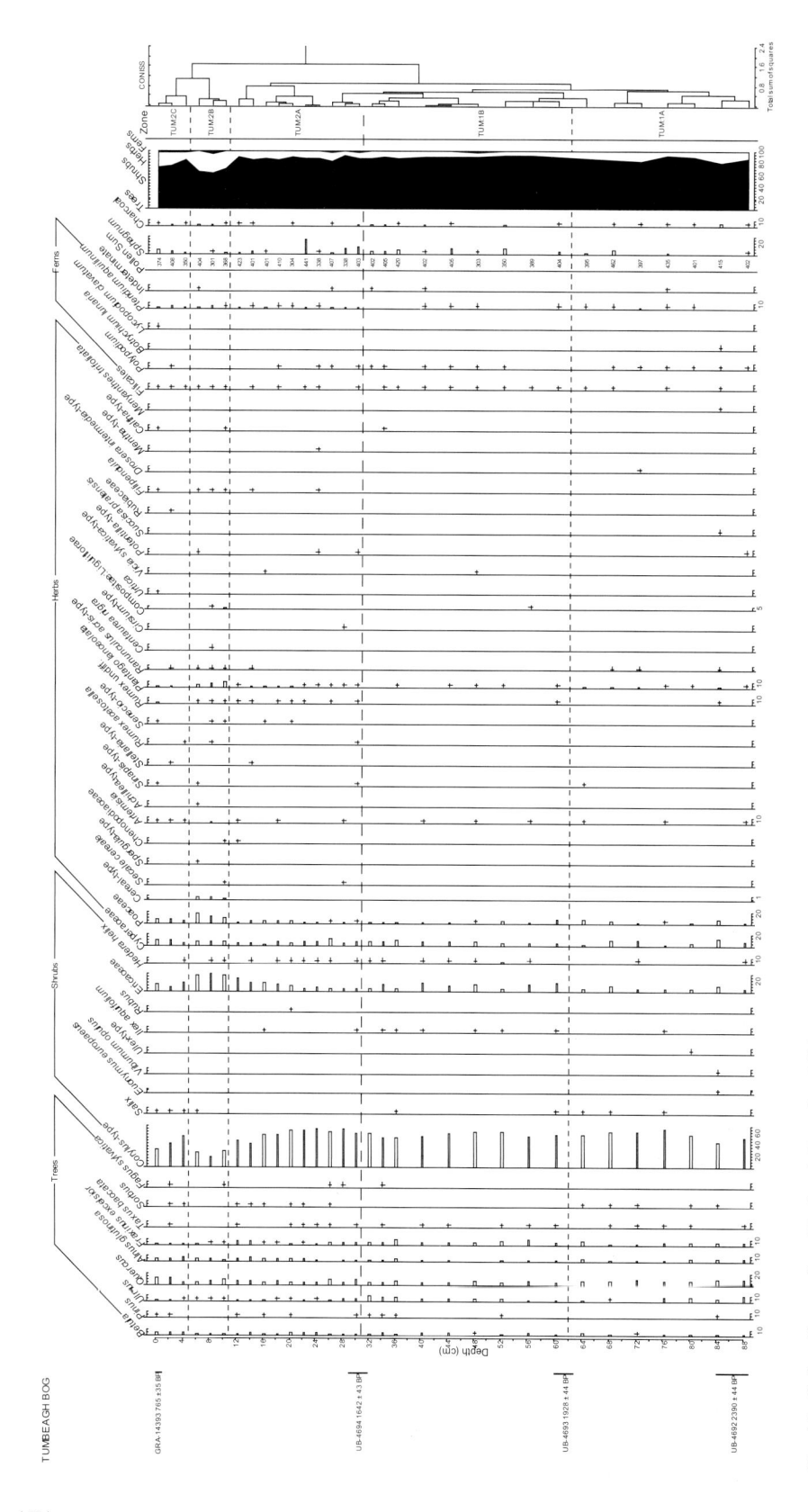

Fig. 40: Pollen diagram from Tumbeagh Bog, Co. Offaly.

Late Bronze Age to Early Iron Age (TUM:1a)

In the earliest period in the pollen diagram, TUM:1a, we see some evidence of human activity throughout, with ribwort plantain (*Plantago lanceolata*) present in all samples, and at over 1 per cent in the upper part of the sub-zone. Grass (Poaceae) and sedges (Cyperaceae) also show evidence of human activity, with peaks in the lower and upper parts of the sub-zone, suggesting two phases of slightly more pronounced activity, separated by a short period of lessened activity. The lower period of activity is not strongly evidenced in the tree and shrub values, but above 76cm there is a pronounced reduction in elm and ash values and a slight reduction in hazel. This is interesting, as elm and ash tend to favour soils that are well suited to agriculture (that is, free-draining and circum-neutral soils). Thus they are usually the tree species that, along with hazel, show the most obvious response to evidence of human agricultural activity, at least until the later medieval period. Much has been written about the Neolithic elm decline (Groenman-van Waateringe 1983; Molloy and O'Connell 1987), but little attention has been given to the fact that most Irish pollen diagrams show multiple elm declines (Weir 1993; 1995), all of which relate to an increase of agricultural activity, with phases of reduced agricultural activity resulting in the regeneration of elm and ash. During the latter part of the first millennium AD this cycle tends to come to an end, or is at least reduced in extent, owing to the increase in population and the intensification of agriculture, and around the same time elm in particular seems to become quite scarce in the landscape (Mitchell 1976). This pattern is followed to a large extent at Tumbeagh, and thus by the top of TUM:1a both elm and ash increase in value, as agricultural activity is reduced and woodland regeneration begins.

The evidence of agricultural activity in TUM:1a is of relatively small-scale, or low-intensity, pastoral activity, with no firm evidence of any arable agriculture. This is in keeping with the general evidence for this period, which gives very little indication of arable activity, either from pollen results (Weir 1995) or from charred plant material (Monk 1985/6). The preceding period, at *c.* 1000 BC, has evidence of considerable arable activity, with finds of large-scale charred cereal assemblages—for example, Haughey's Fort, Co. Armagh (Weir 1993), and Killymoon, Co. Tyrone (D. Hurl, pers. comm.)—and pollen evidence—for example, Loughnashade, Co. Armagh (Weir 1993; 1995), Essexford Lough, Co. Louth (Weir 1995), and Killymaddy and Weir's Lough, Co. Tyrone (Hirons 1984). The reasons for the apparent reduction in arable activity are unclear, but it may be due to either a cultural change or a climatic change that was less favourable to cereal cultivation. As mentioned above, two peaks in agricultural activity are represented: a lesser one, at *c.* 460 BC, and a slightly more pronounced one, at *c.* 280–60 BC.

Evidence of the development of the raised bog is difficult to decipher from the pollen diagram. Part of the problem is the lack of specific identification of certain key pollen types, particularly grasses and sedges. Sedges are often thought of as wetland species, but there are several that inhabit grassland and woodland. Grassland, in particular, before agricultural drainage and seeding of grass monocultures became widespread, would have contained a high proportion of sedges. Thus it is impossible to be sure what habitat the sedges in a pollen diagram represent, although there is a peak in sedge pollen at 68–72cm, which is likely to correspond to the layer of

Table 26: Summary description of the local pollen assemblage zones (LPAZ) in the Tumbeagh Bog pollen diagram.

LPAZ	Depth (cm)	Age	Main characteristics	Human activity
TUM:1a	88–62	c. 610 BC	*Corylus*-type–*Quercus*–*Ulmus*–Cyperaceae–(*Plantago lanceolata*) Arboreal pollen totals 80–90%. *Corylus*-type dips to c. 40% at 84cm but is mostly 55-60%; *Quercus* is at 8–10%; *Ulmus* is c. 10% between 88cm and 76cm (with a drop to 4% at 84cm) but falls to <1% at 68cm and then increases to 2% at 64cm; *Fraxinus* is c. 4%, falling to 1.5% at 68cm but rising to 7% at 64cm; *Betula* is 1.5–3%; *Alnus* is c. 6% between 88cm and 80cm, falling to 2–4% in the upper levels; pollen of *Taxus* and *Sorbus*-type is present in a number of levels. Ericaceae pollen (virtually all *Calluna vulgaris*) is 5–10% throughout the sub-zone, with slight peaks at 84cm and 68cm; Cyperaceae also has peaks at these levels, of 12% and 10% respectively. Other bog or wetland species include the only occurrences in the diagram of *Menyanthes trifoliata* (at 84cm), *Drosera* (at 72cm) and *Succisa* (at 84cm). *Sphagnum* spores increase above 80cm, mostly at 1–2% but with a peak of 8% at 68cm. Poaceae also has two peaks, of 12% at 84cm and 7.5% at 64cm, falling to <1% at 76cm. Relatively few weed species are present, these being mostly weeds of grassland; *Plantago lanceolata* is present in all levels, with a peak of 1.7% at 84cm and another of 1–3% between 72cm and 64cm; *Artemisia*, *Ranunculus acris*, *Sinapis*-type and *Rumex* are present in some levels. *Pteridium* is also present in most levels, generally at <1%. Charcoal is present in most levels, generally at low values of <1%, except at 84cm, where it is 4%.	There is evidence for low-level disturbance throughout the zone but with two peaks of activity, around 84cm and between 72cm and 64cm, with some woodland regeneration between these peaks. There is no cereal-type pollen present, and the disturbance weeds are largely indicative of grassland, suggesting that land use was largely pastoral.
TUM:1b	62–31	c. AD 50	*Corylus*-type–*Ulmus*–*Fraxinus*–Ericaceae–Cyperaceae Arboreal pollen is 86–92%. *Corylus*-type again dominates, at 50–60%; *Quercus* is 4–6%; *Ulmus* increases from TUM:1a, rising from 3.5% to 9% across the sub-zone: *Fraxinus* initially increases to 9% but falls to 4–5% by 48cm; *Betula* and *Alnus* are both around 2%; *Taxus* and *Ilex* are present in most levels, but *Sorbus*-type is absent. Ericaceae increases in this sub-zone, generally being >10%, but falling to c. 6% in the upper levels; Cyperaceae increases across the sub-zone, from 4.5% to 9–10%. Other bog or wetland species are represented only by a single occurrence of *Caltha*-type at 34cm. *Sphagnum* spores demonstrate a high variability between samples, absent or at <1% in alternate levels below 36cm with peaks of 10% in the other levels. Above 36cm, representation is more consistent, 5–8% in all levels. Poaceae is initially at 6%, falls to <1% by 48cm, and increases slightly to 2% between 40cm and 32cm; Cereal-type pollen is present in only one level, at 56cm. Weed species are at lower levels than in TUM:1a, with *Plantago lanceolata* at <1%, and present only in about half of the levels; *Artemisia* is also present at <1% in some levels; *Rumex* and Compositae:Liguliflorae both have single occurrences; *Pteridium* occurs in less than half of the levels, at <1%. Charcoal occurrence is sporadic, with a single peak of 2.5% at 52cm, but above 40cm it is consistently at c. 2%, peaking at 3% in TUM:2a at 30cm.	Human activity seems to be at a lower level than in TUM:1a, with reduced levels of grass pollen and weeds of disturbance. A single occurrence of cereal-type pollen does not point to any significant arable activity. Conversely, there is evidence of woodland regeneration, most notably in the increase of *Ulmus* and *Fraxinus* pollen.

Trees, crops and bog plants

Table 26 (contd): Summary description of the local pollen assemblage zones (LPAZ) in the Tumbeagh Bog pollen diagram.

LPAZ	Depth (cm)	Age	Main characteristics	Human activity
TUM:2a	31–11	c. AD 400	*Corylus*-type–Ericaceae–Cyperaceae–*Plantago lanceolata* Tree and shrub pollen remain fairly constant at 85–90%, but the major change is a decrease in *Corylus*-type, from 65% to 40–45% across the sub-zone. *Quercus* remains at c. 5–6%; *Alnus* initially dips to c. 2% and then increases to 6–7%; *Betula* is c. 3%; *Ulmus* initially declines to <1% in the middle levels and then increases to 2–3% in the upper levels; *Fraxinus* displays a similar pattern, dipping to <1% and then increasing to 6–7.5%; *Taxus* and *Sorbus*-type are present in most levels, and *Fagus* occurs in two levels; *Ilex* is present only in two levels. Ericaceae initially remains at c. 5% but above 20cm increases steadily to 22%; Cyperaceae initially increases to 13% at 26cm and then decreases to 4–5% by 12cm; other wetland species present include two occurrences of *Filipendula* and a single occurrence of *Mentha*-type pollen; *Potentilla*-type pollen could also represent a wetland species, such as *P. palustris*. *Sphagnum* spores initially have a slight peak of 10–12% and then decrease to 2–5%, with the exception of a peak of c. 20% at 20cm. There are signs of increased human activity across the sub-zone, with Poaceae pollen increasing from <1% to 5.5% at 16cm, with a slight decrease to 2.5% at 12cm; *Plantago lanceolata* also increases, being present between 30cm and 22cm at <1% and then increasing to 3% at 16cm, before dropping to <1% by 12cm. Cereal pollen is present in two levels, and a wider range of disturbance weeds are present; some such as Chenopodiaceae, *Sinapis*-type, *Stellaria*-type and *Senecio*-type are possibly indicative of arable conditions, and others such as *Rumex*, *Cirsium* and *Ranunculus acris*-type are indicative of pasture. There is also a marked increase of *Pteridium*, which is present in every level, with maximum values of c. 2%. Despite the signs of increased human activity, charcoal is only sporadically present, at <1%.	There is evidence for an increase in human disturbance, rather gradually at first, but with a main episode between 20cm and 14cm. This seems to be largely for pasture, but there is some suggestion of arable agriculture. There is some suggestion of woodland regeneration in the upper two levels, with *Ulmus* and *Fraxinus* both recovering.
TUM:2b	11–5	c. AD 1000	Ericaceae–*Corylus*-type–Poaceae–*Plantago lanceolata*–(Cereal-type) Total arboreal pollen drops to 61% at 8cm, but, as Ericaceae pollen peaks at 30%, this represents a rather open landscape. *Ulmus* is <1% in all samples; *Fraxinus* <1% in the lower two levels, rising to 1.5% at 6cm; *Corylus*-type pollen falls to 17.5% at 8cm, its lowest level in the diagram; *Quercus* falls to 3% at 6cm. The peak in Ericaceae is not accompanied by a marked increase in other bog or wetland species; Cyperaceae increases slightly to 9%; *Filipendula* is present in all levels; single grains of *Caltha* and *Potentilla*-type occur. *Sphagnum* spores drop to <1% at 8cm and are otherwise c. 2% Evidence of agricultural activity is strongest in this sub-zone. Poaceae peaks at 16%, the highest level for the diagram; cereal-type pollen is 0.5–0.75%, and a single grain of *Secale cereale* occurs. Weeds that might be indicative of arable agriculture also occur, including *Spergula*, Chenopodiaceae, *Achillea*-type and *Sinapis*-type. Other weeds, which might indicate pasture, also increase, including *Plantago lanceolata* at 5–9%, *Rumex* and *Ranunculus acris*-type; most of these species can also occur in arable habitats. *Pteridium* has its maximum value of 5% at 8cm. Charcoal rises to 2.5%, but this is not markedly high, given the evidence for agricultural activity.	This is the most pronounced period of activity in the diagram, with grasses and other indicators of disturbance reaching their maximum. Cereal-type pollen (most of it almost certainly from cereals) also has a small but significant peak, indicating the presence of some level of arable agriculture. It is not clear whether the peak of ericaceous pollen relates to human activity, colonising cleared areas of poor soil, perhaps; or it might represent drying out of the bog surface and a resultant increase in *Calluna vulgaris*.

Table 26 (contd): Summary description of the local pollen assemblage zones (LPAZ) in the Tumbeagh Bog pollen diagram.

LPAZ	Depth (cm)	Age	Main characteristics	Human activity
TUM:2c	5–0	*c.* AD 1250	*Corylus*-type–*Quercus*–Ericaceae–Cyperaceae–*Alnus* Arboreal pollen increases again, quite sharply to 84% at 4cm, dropping to 72% at 0cm. Initially, *Corylus*-type increases to 51%, dropping to 30% at 0cm; *Ulmus* and *Fraxinus* increase to 3% by 0cm; *Quercus* increases to 12%, *Alnus* to 7% and *Betula* to 6%; *Salix* is present in all samples. Ericaceae pollen drops to 7.5% at 2cm, rising to 11% by 0cm; Cyperaceae increases slightly to 10%; Rubiaceae, *Filipendula* and *Caltha*-type are present, and the occurrence of *Lycopodium clavatum* is at 0cm. *Sphagnum* increases to 8% by 0cm. There appears to be a reduction in agricultural activity, with Poaceae falling to 4% initially and then increasing to 6%; a range of disturbance weeds, such as *Artemisia*, *Sinapis*-type, *Stellaria*-type and *Rumex*, occur; Cereal-type pollen is present in two levels, and *Plantago lanceolata* is 3% in the upper two levels. *Pteridium* is *c.* 3%, while charcoal is mostly <1%.	There appears to be quite rapid woodland regeneration, initially mostly of *Corylus*-type, followed by most other woodland trees. Some level of agricultural activity is maintained, including some possible arable agriculture, and by the top of this sub-zone agricultural activity may be increasing again.

rannock rush (*Scheuchzeria palustris*) evident in the stratigraphy. A single pollen grain of bog bean (*Menyanthes trifoliata*), its only occurrence in the pollen diagram, was found at 84cm. This is a plant of bog pools, or at least very wet areas, and sundew (*Drosera intermedia*-type at 72cm) also tends to be found in wetter areas of acidic bogs. This suggests that quite wet conditions existed at this stage, probably with some open pools.

Early Iron Age (TUM:1b)

This is a fairly prolonged period of quite stable woodland, with evidence of little agricultural impact. The woodland regeneration begins in the previous sub-zone, at *c.* 60 BC, which is a widespread feature in Irish pollen diagrams at this time. Mitchell (1976) referred to it as a 'lull in agriculture'. The reasons for this 'lull' are not entirely clear, particularly if it represents a decline in overall population or if it is a shift in agricultural economy toward a more woodland-subsistence-based economy (Weir 1995; Raftery 1995). The extent of the change is not as marked in the Tumbeagh pollen diagram as it is in others from more pollen-sensitive sites, on better agricultural soils, such as Littleton Bog, Co. Tipperary (Mitchell 1965), Loughnashade (Weir 1993; 1997) and Essexford Lough (Weir 1995). The time of the changes however, appears to match those at other sites, such as Loughnashade, very closely. Caution has to be exercised here, however, as the margin of error on radiocarbon dates is such that these events may not be as synchronous as they first appear, and some important sites, such as Loughnashade, are not yet fully independently dated by radiocarbon. Indeed, when one notes that in this diagram the duration of this period could be 120–570 years at 2-sigma standard deviations, this point is reinforced. More attention deserves to be paid to elucidating the chronology of these changes, but it appears likely that they will prove to be largely synchronous, at least across large regional areas.

This is not to say that there is no evidence of agriculture across this period, but it is rather sparse. The presence of ribwort plantain, which is wind pollinated, is usually a very good indicator of agricultural disturbance, but in this sub-zone it is present in only five of nine samples, and at less than 1 per cent. There are few other weeds of disturbance: a few occurrences of mugwort (*Artemisia*), and single occurrences of dock (*Rumex*) and dandelion-type (Compositae: Liguliflorae). A single cereal-type pollen grain occurred at 56cm, but this type can include wild grasses, such as *Glyceria*, and, in the absence of much other evidence of agriculture at this level, it is most likely to belong to this group. Grass values are also low, despite the fact that it would be expected on the surface of a raised bog, even in the absence of agriculture, and the grasses and sedges in this zone are likely to represent mainly species growing on the bog itself.

The stratigraphy indicates the development of *Sphagnum* at *c.* 0.65–0.68m, and from this level upward there seems to be a higher representation of *Sphagnum* spores, especially in this sub-zone. The presence of these seems to be highly erratic between samples in the lower part of the sub-zone, but they are continuously present toward the top of the sub-zone. Heather values are also higher than in the previous sub-zone, which suggests somewhat drier conditions than in TUM:1a. Sedge pollen is also at fairly high levels, particularly toward the top of the sub-zone. Given that there is little evidence of agricultural activity, the pollen presumably derives from species growing on the raised bog, such as cotton grasses (*Eriophorum* spp).

Early Christian period (TUM:2a)
The beginning of this zone, with evidence of an increase in agricultural activity, dates to AD 260–543, with a mid-point of *c.* AD 400. This is similar to the evidence from some sites, such as that emerging from recent work at Navan Fort and Loughnashade, Co. Armagh (Weir 1993; in prep.). Again, there is a fairly wide age spread from standard radiocarbon dates for this intensification of agriculture, which may range from the first to the sixth century AD, and more work needs to be done to determine whether this is a single event, synchronous over a wide area, or a number of separate events. At Tumbeagh there appears to be a fairly gradual intensification of agriculture, with ribwort plantain occurring in every sample, grasses increasing slightly and a wider range of disturbance weeds appearing (see Table 26). This again appears to indicate largely pastoral agriculture, although a single grain of rye (*Secale cereale*) occurs at 28cm, suggesting that there was some arable agriculture. Agricultural activity in this period peaks at 20–14cm (*c.* AD 740–910), with grasses and ribwort plantain having slight peaks, suggesting predominantly pastoral agriculture. To some extent this evidence is in contrast with that from some sites in the east of Ireland, for example Essexford Lough and Whiterath Bog, Co. Louth (Weir 1995), and Loughnashade, Co. Armagh (Weir 1993; 1997; in prep.). In these sites the intensification in agricultural activity is much more marked, with a major level of cereal cultivation. The sites are, however, small lake basins, which are more effective at trapping pollen from poorly dispersed species, such as cereals, than a large raised bog such as Tumbeagh, and they are also situated in areas with very good agricultural soils. There may, therefore, be a somewhat higher level of arable agriculture in the landscape surrounding Tumbeagh Bog, which is not detected in this diagram.

The changes in woodland composition follow the pattern discussed above, with elm and ash both decreasing to insignificant levels during the main agricultural period in the middle of the zone and hazel increasing in value during the beginning of the period. There is a reduction in agricultural intensity toward the top of the zone, and it is interesting that elm and ash values increase to some extent, as grass and ribwort plantain decrease.

In the lower part of this sub-zone, *Sphagnum* spores and sedge pollen are at a similar level to the top of TUM:1b. From *c.* 20cm upward, heather increases and sedge pollen and *Sphagnum* spores decrease, suggesting that the surface of the bog may have dried out somewhat. These changes are discussed below. Of interest also is the occurrence of meadowsweet (*Filipendula ulmaria*) and mint-type (*Mentha*-type), which are not raised-bog species but may have grown in more nutrient-rich wet areas around the edge of the bog.

Early Christian period (TUM:2b)
The episode of woodland regeneration at the top of the previous sub-zone is rather slight, and there is a marked increase in agricultural activity in this sub-zone. The peak in grasses and ribwort plantain, along with a range of other disturbance weeds (see Table 26), suggests that the agriculture is largely pastoral. Cereal-type pollen, however, is present in all samples, at 0.5–0.75 per cent, and a single grain of rye has been distinguished. The size and morphology of the grains suggest that they are all cereal pollen, and the occurrence of the peak of this pollen type in the most intense phase of agriculture in the diagram supports this. As discussed above, cereal pollen may be under-represented in a pollen diagram from a raised bog, and arable agriculture was quite probably of more importance in the overall agricultural economy at this time than the relatively low pollen representation would suggest.

This is also the period of the lowest woodland cover, with all woodland species being reduced in value, especially hazel. In part, this is an artefact of the increase in heather (Ericaceae) pollen, which has steadily increased from 20cm in TUM:2a but has a very marked peak in this sub-zone, which mirrors the dip in hazel values. To some extent this problem is due to the calculation of pollen values as percentages, which makes all of the values relative to each other, and a real increase in one species can cause decreases in others. The decrease in hazel may therefore be exaggerated, but the increase in heather pollen (nearly all *Calluna vulgaris* or ling) is quite marked. It may represent colonisation of areas of poor, acidic soil after woodland clearance; ling often occurs in areas of poor pasture (Grime *et al.* 1988). The increase of bracken (*Pteridium aquilinum*) spores in this zone may also indicate areas of acidic grassland. Heather pollen, however, tends to be rather localised in its distribution (it is partly insect pollinated); and its increase is perhaps more likely to be due to drying of the bog surface sufficient to allow more widespread colonisation by ling, or at least development of tussocks of grasses etc., which develop areas above the general water-table and which ling can then colonise. Remains of *Calluna* were found at around this level in the stratigraphical investigation (see Casparie, Chapter 13), but the stratigraphy does not seem to suggest a general drying-out phase at this period. It is therefore more likely that a more pronounced hummock-and-hollow system developed than the stratigraphy alone suggests.

Medieval period (TUM:2c)

If the presence of heather pollen indicates the development of a hummock-and-hollow pattern on the bog surface, such a pattern ends in this sub-zone, and the bog surface may have become generally wetter. There is also a decrease in signs of agricultural activity, which returns to a level and type similar to that in the middle of TUM:2a. That the changes in heather values largely mirror the changes in agriculture suggests some direct or indirect linkage. It may be direct, in that heather is colonising areas of poor pasture. Or it may be indirect: for example, if it represents a period of drier conditions (perhaps due to a drier climatic episode), people may have been taking advantage of these conditions and expanding agriculture onto the drier fringes of the bog. Heather would have been present as a lower shrub layer in fairly open woodland; if the woodland were cleared, the heather would have expanded rapidly and dispersion of its pollen would have been aided.

Unfortunately, the peat between the top of the monolith and the period during which the body was deposited has been removed by milling, so there is a gap in the pollen record of perhaps 300 years. The core was taken from the field surface and from as close to the human remains as possible, but the camber of the field has resulted in this gap in the sequence. There is little point in making too many guesses about what the vegetation was like at this time, but it seems unlikely that woodland regeneration would have continued to any great extent. Although elm, oak and ash continue to increase toward the top of the diagram, this is not very pronounced, and hazel decreases again quite markedly. Grasses, ribwort plantain and docks increase, and a wide range of disturbance weeds still occur (see Table 26). The most likely scenario is that the fringes of the bog became wetter, and agricultural activity may have moved away from it but continued farther away and is not therefore registering as well in the pollen diagram. This trend is unlikely to have continued into the sixteenth century, and intensification of agriculture may well have occurred, probably to a more intense level than evidenced in TUM:2b. This is, however, speculation.

Conclusions

Although it is unfortunate that the truncation of the peat does not allow the pollen diagram to cover the period of deposition of the bog body, the diagram provides a record of environmental and agricultural change over a period of *c.* 1800 years. Late Bronze Age/Early Iron Age agriculture was largely pastoral and not very intense. After a lull, accompanied by woodland regeneration, there was an expansion of agriculture in the Early Christian period. Initially, this also seems to have been largely pastoral, but the most intense period of agriculture evident, *c.* AD 1000–1180, included some arable cultivation. After this, there was a reduction in agricultural intensity, with some woodland regeneration. The level of agriculture is, however, at no point particularly intense, and it occurs in an environment apparently dominated by woodland, particularly hazel scrub. Changes in tree species, particularly elm and ash, follow the pattern of agricultural activity very closely.

The evidence from the pollen diagram for the development of the raised bog can be difficult to interpret but generally follows the pattern described by the stratigraphy. The exception appears to be the increase in heather in TUM:2a/b, which seems to indicate drier conditions than those suggested by the stratigraphy.

IV.

PARALLELS, THOUGHTS AND POSSIBLE ANSWERS

16.
Irish and European parallels

Nóra Bermingham

Ireland's bog bodies

The medieval date of the Tumbeagh find places it well outside the prehistoric period traditionally associated with such finds. While prehistoric finds serve to illustrate that bogs have always been places where bodies have been deposited, the emphasis here is on discoveries dating to within the last one thousand years. By virtue of the records and finds that survive, parallels date mostly to its latter half.

Ireland is well represented in the catalogue of European bog-body finds, with current estimates of 130 individual bog bodies (*c.* 115 instances) of varying date and description (Fig. 41). Resulting in particular from the research of Dieck (1965), Briggs and Turner ([1986]) and Ó Floinn (Appendix 1; 1995a), Irish bog-body discoveries dating from the late eighteenth century are known (Table 27).

In the late 1700s three finds were made, and since then a relatively steady number of complete and partial bodies, single and multiple burials, and adult and child corpses have been chanced upon. Increased use of peat in domestic and commercial contexts led to greater numbers of finds being made in the succeeding centuries.

Ó Floinn (Appendix 1; 1995a) lists 45 nineteenth-century and 62 twentieth-century bog-body finds, which works out at one discovery per 1.6 years. The interval of discovery was by no means regular. Before the recent finds made in 2003 and 2005, the peak in Irish bog-body discoveries was in the 1950s, when fifteen finds were made as more bogs were opened up to industrial extraction. Improvements in technology

Period	Number of discoveries
18th century	3
19th century	45
20th century	62
21st century (–2005)	5

Table 27: Number of bog body finds made in Ireland since the eighteenth century. Data compiled from Ó Floinn (Appendix 1; 1995a). The twenty-first-century finds are derived from D. Wynne (pers. comm.), the Irish Independent *(16 May 2003) and I. Mulhall, NMI (pers. comm.).*

The bog body from Tumbeagh

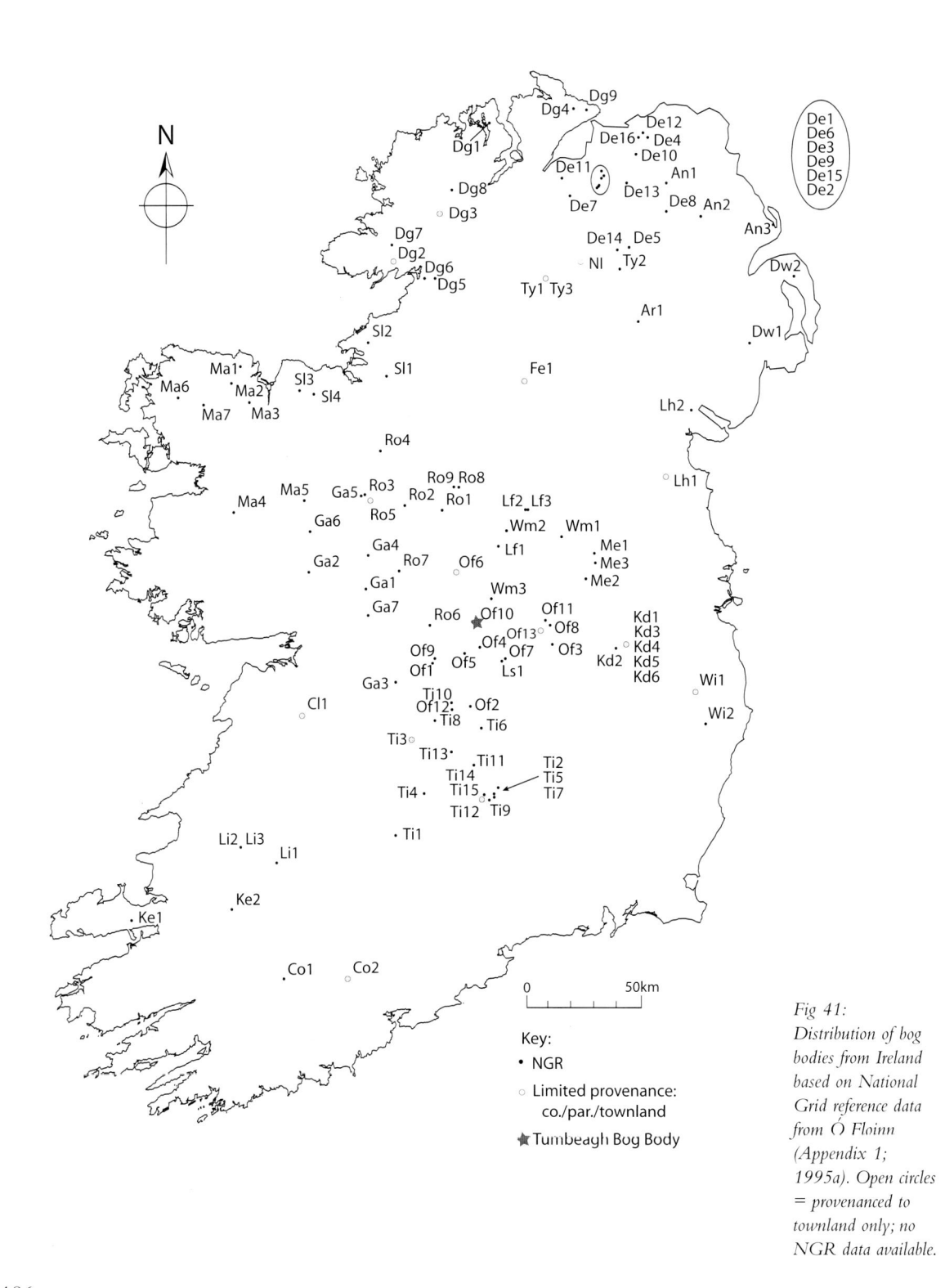

Fig 41:
Distribution of bog bodies from Ireland based on National Grid reference data from Ó Floinn (Appendix 1; 1995a). Open circles = provenanced to townland only; no NGR data available.

and the greater use of machinery in bogs has seen this figure decrease rapidly, with only eight finds in the 1960s, seven in the 1970s, two in the 1980s and one in the 1990s. The decrease in the number of bodies found is mirrored in the reduced rate of finds retrieved from bogs (Ó Floinn 1988). In general, the machinery used to extract peat today places the operator high above the level of the bog, removing probing eyes and sensitive hands from the bog surface. This suggests that future bog-body finds may be made only by archaeologists carrying out survey or excavation in peatlands already under production or being developed for other purposes.

Peat cutting, however, remains a significant means of discovery. The unearthing of two new bodies in early 2003 and three new finds in 2005 shows that chance discoveries continue to occur (Me3, Of11, Of 13, Ro8, Ro9, Appendix 1). In March 2003 a male torso with head was found in peat in Ballivor Bog, Co. Meath (D. Wynne, pers. comm.). This body was spotted on a sorting screen by Bord na Móna operatives after it had been removed in a block of peat extracted using a mechanical digger. In early May Mr Kevin Barry was digging a drain in Clonerl, Co. Offaly; he gave the following account to journalists: 'I was digging in the bog when I saw what looked like an animal's leg. Then I saw nails and a hand. When I turned it over, I saw another hand attached to an arm…It was in the digger's bucket before I saw it was a torso with no head. I was terrified when I realised what it was. It had obviously been there for some time as it looked very old' (*Irish Independent*, 16 May 2003).

The overwhelming popular image of bog bodies is one of murky rituals and distressing ends spanning the Iron Age of north-west Europe. This singular image is remarkable in its longevity and perpetuity. Yet, although Mesolithic, Neolithic, Bronze Age, Roman, early medieval, post-medieval and modern bodies have all been found, the chronological and cultural links between these are not considered in the same way as those made between the Iron Age bodies. Briggs addressed this issue extensively in 1995, but popular consideration of other interpretations has yet to take place.

Ó Floinn (1995b) proposed 18 prehistoric or early medieval instances and 32 late medieval or modern occurrences in Ireland through a combination of radiocarbon dating, finds and clothing associations, descriptions contemporary with the discovery, and local knowledge regarding the identity of the bodies. This suggested that, of the then total of 89 cases, the majority of Irish bog bodies were medieval or later, although the age of a considerable number (39) remained undetermined *(ibid.)*. Ó Floinn's recent work (Appendix 1) appears to reinforce this picture, with six of the new records belonging to the later grouping while twelve may be considered of unknown date and none is clearly prehistoric. The two finds made in 2003 (Me3 and Of11, Ó Floinn, Appendix 1) are, at the time of writing, undated. Experience with Tumbeagh has shown that it is perhaps easy to make erroneous assumptions about the date of a find based on initial observations. The two finds made in 2003, however, may have compelling evidence in support of an earlier date. Preliminary reports suggest that each lay more than 1–1.5m deep in the bog. Each was apparently naked; and, in the case of the body from Clonerl, the decapitation and the severing of the torso from the lower body indicate elaborate treatment before immersion in the peat, a feature well known among prehistoric cases (Brothwell *et al.* 1990; van der Sanden 1996; Fischer 1998).

The bog body from Tumbeagh

It is perhaps not surprising, then, that the Tumbeagh find falls into the later category of bodies. The relatively late date for the Tumbeagh find means that drawing comparisons with those of an earlier, prehistoric date is not relevant. Suffice to say that Ireland is not without prehistoric examples. The best-known case is Gallagh Man from County Galway, whose Iron Age date, cut throat and naked form (but for a deerskin cape) (Pl. 41) make him best viewed as part of the tradition that resulted in the burial of bodies in bogs in Denmark, Holland and England.

Bordering the late prehistoric and the early medieval period is the body of a young adult, possibly male, from Derrydooan Middle, Co. Westmeath, which dates to cal. AD 648–874 (Brindley and Lanting 1995). Chronologically, the next is Tumbeagh, with its date of *c.* AD 1500, narrowing the gap between the Derrydooan Middle body and the sixteenth-, seventeenth-, eighteenth- and nineteenth-century bodies from the rest of Ireland. In his original gazetteer Ó Floinn (1995a) lists twenty occurrences from counties Derry, Donegal, Armagh, Antrim, Tyrone and Down, seven from counties Mayo, Sligo, Cork, and only five from the midland bogs of counties Tipperary, Kildare, Louth and Offaly. Thus, while the interment of bodies in bogs in the later and the post-medieval period occurs, it does so with less frequency in the midland raised bogs than in other areas. This pattern is little changed by the addition of the gazetteer entries published in this book (Appendix 1).

All of the bog-body finds referred to above, with the exception of Tumbeagh, have been made by chance, either thrown up by mechanical peat extraction or uncovered in hand-won areas of turf. Although the Tumbeagh find is the first set of Irish remains removed from the bog by archaeologists and the only one subject to a laboratory excavation, its investigation follows on from earlier work carried out in Ireland and Britain on another Irish body: Meenybraddan Woman (Pl. 45).

It can happen that a discovery in one country triggers fresh research/ investigations in another. The discovery of Lindow Man not only rekindled interest in bog bodies in Britain but also acted as a catalyst for bog-body research in Ireland. Closely linked with the Lindow investigations is the resurrection of an Irish bog body from cold storage. Meenybraddan Woman, pulled from a truncated peat bed in County Donegal in 1978 (Pl. 45), is the most comprehensively studied Irish bog body, subject to scientific examination involving autopsy, dental studies, endoscopy examinations, and CT and X-ray imaging (Delaney and Ó Floinn 1995). The body, that of an adult female, was found wrapped in a woollen cloak secured by a woollen thong. Stylistically, the cloak suggests a late sixteenth- to late seventeenth-century date. Those involved in the study readily accept the cloak as a more accurate reflection of the date than the much earlier, and possibly contaminated, radiocarbon date of 730 ± 90 BP, with a mean age in the thirteenth century AD. The reason for the woman's death is not known—the autopsy did not identify a cause of death—but her burial in a bog, beyond the churchyard, has evoked suggestions of suicide or murder.

Ireland's bog-body finds vary considerably chronologically. They are also widely distributed over the island and have been recovered from both raised bogs and blanket bogs, although known prehistoric examples have been found only in the former. There is also great variation in the type of remains retrieved: in County Offaly, before the Tumbeagh discovery, two skeletons, one body, part of a skull with skin, and a single femur were known (Ó Floinn 1995a). Just as in Europe, suggestions about how

Pl. 45: The body of Meenybraddan Woman after conservation (photo: NMI).

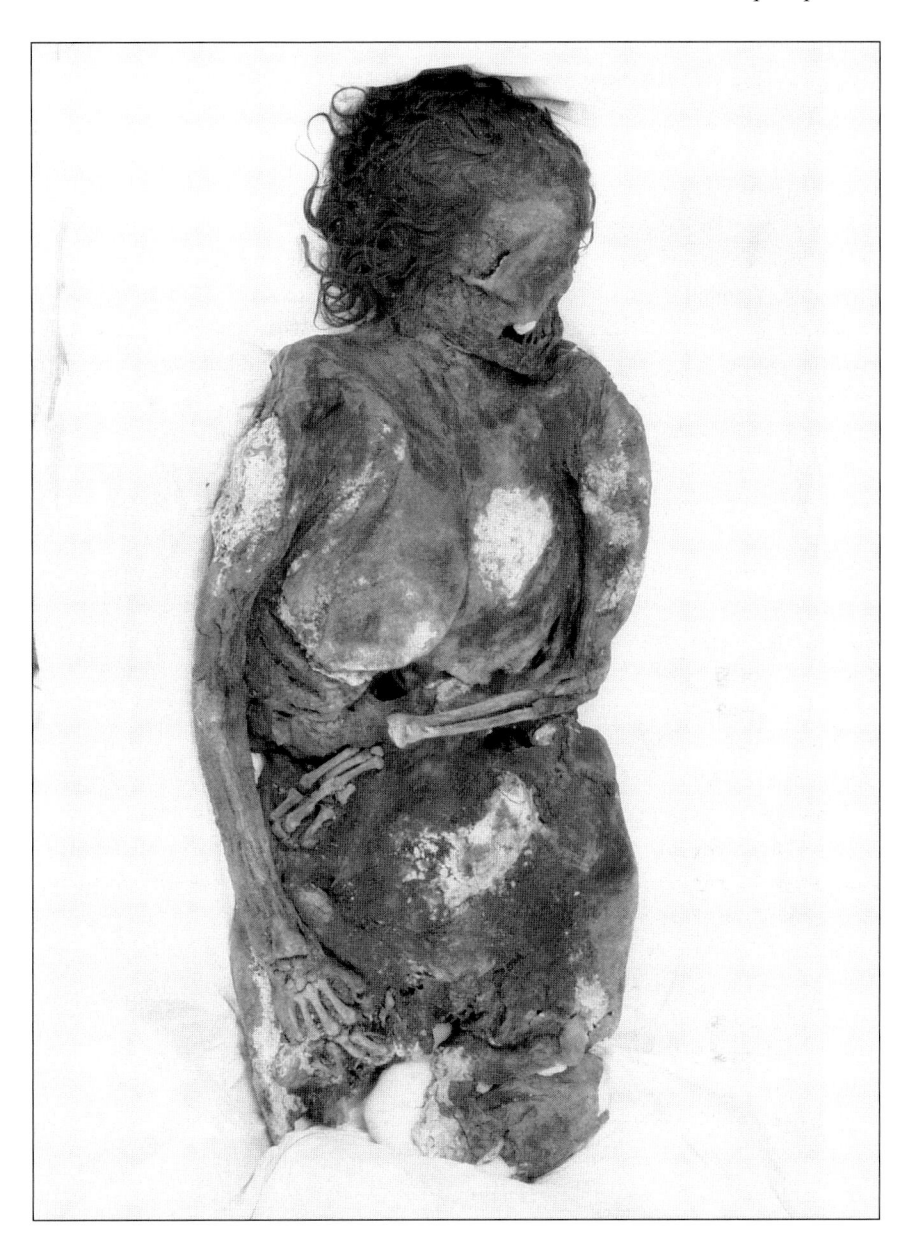

human remains arrived in bogs in Ireland vary and have included murder—ritual or otherwise—suicide and accidental death. This is discussed in greater detail below. One may accept, however, that common to all finds, regardless of date, is the fact that burial—intentional or otherwise—in the bog did not form part of the everyday funerary practice. In medieval Ireland and later, burial was regulated, with interment in a grave within a churchyard being the norm (see Chapter 17).

European comparison

European contemporaries of the Tumbeagh find are not common. Of the 56 bodies from the Netherlands, 46 may pre-date the medieval period, suggesting that only ten

The bog body from Tumbeagh

are medieval or post-medieval. Four of these bodies are preserved and are considered 'to be either victims of murder and violent attacks or "normally" buried bodies' (van der Sanden 1996, 164). From Germany, where Dieck (1965) lists more than 900 bodies, few of the surviving ones have been dated. In Lower Saxony three bodies have returned medieval dates, two of AD 800–1200 and one, a boot-covered foot from Hunteberg, of the thirteenth to fourteenth century. From Schleswig-Holstein, four of the ten bodies, or parts of bodies, still extant yielded prehistoric radiocarbon dates (Dieck 1965). Although the surviving population with which medieval comparisons might be found is small, the recent dating of an old find from Lower Saxony has produced a relatively contemporaneous parallel.

In 1996 some hair of Kreepen Man, a bog body recovered from Lower Saxony in 1903 and later destroyed in World War II, was rediscovered by Wijnand van der Sanden in a museum in Elisabethfehn, Germany. Kreepen Man was young; his body was naked; and he lay on his back, with twig-bound hands and feet (Fig. 42). Stones found next to him may have been used to weigh the body down. This bog body has elements in common with prehistoric ones: nudity, isolation and pre-burial treatment of the corpse—in this case binding and efforts made to ensure its long-term interment in the bog. Yet radiocarbon dating of the hair has shown Kreepen Man to have lived in the fifteenth, sixteenth or early seventeenth century (390±60 BP) (van der Sanden 2000). This body provides the closest European parallel to the Tumbeagh find.

England, Wales and Scotland have yielded 130 finds from raised bogs, fens, intertidal peats and upland blanket bog. The late seventeenth-century bodies of a man and a woman, who had lost their way on an upland blanket bog in winter, were discovered at Hope, in Derbyshire, England (Turner 1995a; 1995b). In Wales, coffin burials from the seventh to ninth century AD are the latest known finds. In contrast,

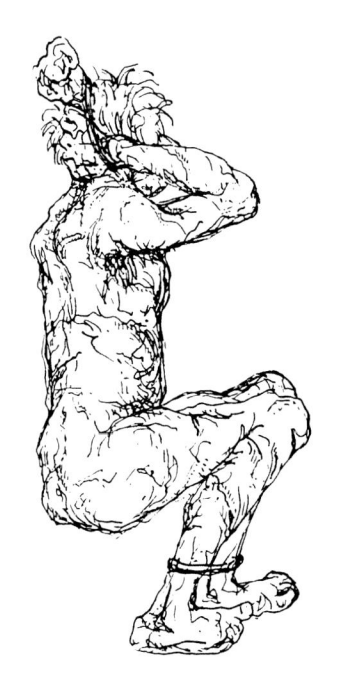

Fig. 42: A reconstruction drawing by Hahne of medieval Kreepen Man, whose body was discovered in 1903. (Taken from van der Sanden (1996, 89) from an original drawing in the Institut für Denkmalpflege, Hannover).

there is 'no certain evidence of any prehistoric bog bodies' from Scotland (*ibid.*), with all 37 finds thought likely to date from the medieval or post-medieval period. All of the Scottish finds are from upland bogs, with none from raised bogs.

Some of the Scottish finds, though somewhat later in date, have parallels with the Tumbeagh find. A relatively young individual from Dava Moor, Morayshire, was found with a birch stick laid over its woollen-clad body (Briggs and Turner [1986]). Its sixteenth-century or, more likely, seventeenth-century date has a rough contemporary in Caithness, where the body of a male teenager was discovered, its upper body wrapped in a woollen jacket and its lower body seemingly naked. The only other find was a rope of twisted heather that lay along the length of the body (*ibid.*). Another male, from Lanarkshire, was found extended on his back with his head to the west. Overlying the body were five silver birch poles set *c.* 6ft (*c.* 1.8m) apart and all parallel with the body. The wood may have been used to carry the body into the bog. The date of this case is a matter of divided opinion. One clothing expert suggests a date of *c.* 1680, but another places the find in the late eighteenth/early nineteenth century (Briggs and Turner [1986]).

17.
A summary of explanations for the occurrence of bog bodies

Nóra Bermingham

> *...spectacular survival is prone to encourage spectacular explanations*
> *(Turner 1999, 232).*

Turner's phrase neatly sums up the tendency to instil in bog-body finds strange and often macabre reasons for their occurrence. Here we look briefly at the array of explanations cited for the presence of bodies in bogs, from the earliest examples to the youngest group of discoveries.

The idea that bog bodies represent a special or untoward occurrence has been circulating since 1780, when Lady Moira recovered the remnants of clothing removed from the skeleton found in Drumkeeragh Bog (van der Sanden 1996). The association of the bog body with ritual practices—in Lady Moira's view, druidic ceremonies—developed over time into a single explanation of human sacrifice or ritual execution, perhaps hitting an interpretative crescendo in the 1980s with the discovery of Lindow (Stead *et al.* [1986]).

This was not, however, the only interpretation on offer. As more bodies were found and interest grew, other explanations were suggested, most of which did not stray from the idea of intentional but irregular burial. The buried bodies were thought to have been social outcasts, law-breakers or possibly murder victims, whom society wished to preclude from burial alongside more law-abiding elements and those less likely to return from the grave. The occasional author allowed for accidental death, but generally an unknown other party (or parties) was considered to have been behind the burials (see Table 28).

By the mid-1900s some researchers called for individual assessment of each occurrence, rather than the application of a single theory of origin, and opposed the view that bog bodies were a geographically and chronologically linked phenomenon (Hayen and Dieck in van der Sanden 1996), arguing instead that their widespread distribution and broad chronological span favoured multiple explanations.

The application of radiocarbon dating since the 1950s and more recently to earlier finds (van der Sanden 2000) has allowed clearer chronological and consequently cultural and social distinctions to be made within the European bog-body population. The earliest bog bodies date from the Mesolithic and are thought to lack any suggestion of human sacrifice. Judgement is reserved on the reasons behind Neolithic occurrences in watery places. The nature of the evidence in the Neolithic is somewhat different from later occurrences as it comprises skeletal material, such as

Table 28: Reasons cited for the presence of bodies in bogs (not period specific).

Irregular burial as a reaction to some impropriety or socially unacceptable deed committed while living, such as adultery, homosexuality or birth of children outside marriage
Isolated immersion in the bog to protect the living from contagious disease
Burial beyond consecrated ground for victims of suicide
Religious/ritual event aimed at appeasing pagan gods
Superstition and the belief in restless spirits that otherwise could return to haunt the living
Accidental death resulting from getting lost
Burial following a fatal assault such as murder or robbery

skeletal remains of bodies originally lain in open water or lake bottoms, similar to the Stoneyisland burial from Galway (Shea 1931) or the skeletons of two children from Tysmosen in Zealand, Denmark (Bennike 1999).

Considerably later are those bodies dating from the Late Bronze Age to the middle of the first millennium AD. Isolated, mutilated and naked bodies may represent votive offerings or severely punished individuals devoid of ritual associations (Brothwell 1986). Superstition is also thought to have guided these bodies into the bog: relatives anxious about the dead finding peace or fearful of the dead returning to haunt them may have chosen the desolate bog burial-ground. The German archaeologist Struve (1967) regarded the Late Iron Age bog body Dätgen Man as an expression of superstition: a *Wiedergänger*—someone whose body and spirit could not be housed in the local cemetery for fear of a restless and vengeful return. In direct opposition to such views are those of Briggs (1995), who favours less religious, ritualistic or superstitious interpretations, emphasising instead the fact that bogs are dangerous and inhospitable places, easy to become lost in and, once entered, voluntarily or not, difficult to exit. Briggs also questions our ability to distinguish between injuries inflicted through ritual and those resulting from assault, and even between those received before and after burial.

Lastly, there are medieval and later finds. With the advent of Christianity, a shift in religious and cultural views of peatlands—from venerated landscapes to godless territories (van der Sanden 1996)—meant that later interments had less attachment to custom. Rather, they were irregular, orchestrated less by design than by circumstances or opportunity. The story cited at the beginning of this book provides just one example of where punishment involved not only death but also burial in a place worthy of traitors and bad soldiers (O'Grady 1893). The idea of a person losing their way in a bog, being buried there as a result of suicide or perhaps hidden after a fatal robbery is more readily applied to the later finds, particularly given the lack of evidence of elaborate treatment before burial. In Scotland most bog bodies are considered to be post-medieval. They are perhaps 'easily explained as inhumations following accidental death from cold, shipwreck and other causes, with at least one murder' (Turner 1999, 232). Later finds are not, however, devoid of sensational explanations. Interpretations evocative of older, pagan traditions have been applied to later bodies, as bogs were still regarded with superstition and wariness. Irish folklore includes references to the will o' the wisp, or water sheerie, a malevolent bog sprite that lured people into the bog only for them to die (Feehan and O'Donovan 1996). Superstitions recorded in German folklore, such as that suggested by Struve (1967), above, have recently been put forward as an explanation for the burial of late medieval Kreepen Man (Fig. 42) (van der Sanden 2000).

18.
Assessing the evidence: the Tumbeagh body and its interpretation

Nóra Bermingham, Máire Delaney, Wil A. Casparie and Eileen Reilly

One of the main objectives of the Tumbeagh Bog Body Project has been to establish how the body came to lie in the bog. This question is central to the interpretation of all bog-body finds, as there are only two ways that this can happen: either a person walked onto the bog and for some reason died there, or they were brought onto the bog, alive or dead, by another party. Addressing this issue depends on the quality of available evidence. Some bodies, in particular prehistoric examples, display dramatic evidence of deliberate deposition in the form of slashed throats, stab wounds and other forms of mutilation (van der Sanden 1996). There are also less horrific but perhaps no less tragic instances known, some of which date to the medieval period. For example, the body of Meenybraddan Woman was wrapped in a woollen mantle and inserted in the blanketed mountainside, although the cause of her death is unknown (Delaney and Ó Floinn 1995). There are cases where bog bodies are remembered locally as persons who, having taken their own lives, could not be buried in consecrated ground and so were interred in a bog (Ó Floinn 1995a). Bogs are, however, well known for being dangerous places in which it is easy to become lost. Late seventeenth-century records tell of a couple from Derbyshire, England, who became trapped on a bog in a winter storm. Their bodies were found five months later and immediately buried, only to be dug up nearly 30 years later as a matter of curiosity (Briggs and Turner [1986]). Unlike the examples cited above, the interpretation of the Tumbeagh find does not lie in historical accounts or in clear signs of ante- or post-mortem treatment of the body itself (e.g., Brothwell *et al.* 1990; Briggs 1995). However, the Tumbeagh find is distinguished from earlier bog-body finds by having had detailed modern field and laboratory excavations, as well as a comprehensive palaeoenvironmental study of the findspot, which allow the question of deliberate burial or accidental death to be addressed. In this chapter, what the human remains reveal about the position of the body in the bog is first considered, followed by the palaeoenvironmental reconstruction of the bog in which the body was preserved and, lastly, the implications of the collection of wood found with the body.

The position of the body in the bog

At the time of this young person's death, the main rite of burial was Christian (Fry 1999). Acceptable places for burial were clearly defined and well understood within the community. Interment was in a grave in consecrated ground, normally hallowed ground set aside for the purpose of burial, that is, a cemetery. Graves were of sufficient depth to prevent scavenger disturbance. Ideally, bodies were placed in a supine extended position, oriented east–west, with the head to the west and the feet to the east. Other places were known to be suitable for burial of the unbaptised or the miscreant. *Cillíní*, unofficial burial-grounds for the deposition of children, were often found outside the walls of graveyards or in ringforts. The children buried in *cillíní* were not always infants, and occasionally adults were buried there. The bodies of drowned sailors were traditionally buried in unconsecrated ground, as were those of suicides, murder victims and adulterers. Places suitable for irregular burials of a semi-formal nature often had liminal connotations, such as no-man's land and the area between two townlands. These areas often included boggy land. As implied by the number of bodies known, bog was considered a suitable place for irregular burial. Unworked bog was relatively deserted. It often divided areas of useful land; it is soft, and objects can be concealed. It does not escape scavengers, however, and birds and foxes can move about on its surface.

The position of a body that has been deliberately interred may differ from the natural position that a body would assume at rest or if left unmoved after death. In repose, the body takes up a position of flexion, which is especially noticeable if it is lying on its side. This means that the head is slightly bent forward and the arms are close to the sides and bent at the elbows, with fingers curved slightly inward; the lower limbs are bent slightly forward at the hip, and the knees and ankles are slightly bent. This is due to the greater influence of the muscles that perform these movements. Thus the flexed position, though part of a recognised rite, also represents the natural position of the body in repose. Bodies recovered in a flexed position may represent ritual interment, casual interment or unattended death. In general, supine extended bodies are more likely to be deliberately placed. It is possible for bodies to fall into a supine and extended position, but the limbs are usually somewhat splayed.

The excavated remains of the Tumbeagh body consist of a right and a left leg lying on their left sides, with the knees at a higher level that the feet. The upper parts of the body must have lain higher still, either originally or because of drainage by Bord na Móna. This indicates that the body lay on its left side. It is possible that the upper body lay on its front, but in this case we would expect the right leg to have lain in front of the left leg, not behind. A body recovered in the flexed position from a medieval context implies an irregular burial. If the body were deposited after death, it would assume the flexed position if it were moved and laid on its side without constraint before rigor mortis set in. If the arms were not in the flexed position or if the upper body were twisted upward, intervention would have to be taken into account. If the upper body were face down, it may indicate that the body had fallen from an original position of lying on its side.

There is little consistency in the position of bodies buried in bogs (Table 29). The position of the Tumbeagh legs tells us that the body had not been laid in a supine

Assessing the evidence: the Tumbeagh body and its interpretation

Code	Townland and county	Date	Type of burial	Other details
Co1	Moanflugh, Co. Cork	17th century AD	Body placed on its back at full length overlain by sticks and a large stone	Body reputed to be of Denis Looney, who had committed suicide 200 years earlier
De2	Flanders, Co. Derry	?	Body stretched at full length; head severed from body	Body may be that of a Derry drover who fell victim to robbers
De11	Ballygroll, Co. Derry	?	Presumable supine extended position	Body of a child wrapped in paper in a coffin
Dg7	Meenybraddan, Co. Donegal	16th/17th century AD	Appears to have been buried in a supine extended position, but orientation is not recorded	
Ke2	Kilquane, Co. Kerry	?	Extended	Naked except for a piece of woollen cloth covering the upper body to the waist
Me2	Kilwarden, Co. Meath	?	Body extended east–west with head to the west; hands crossed over head and bound; left leg broken	
Of2	Ballyrickard Beg, Co. Offaly	?	Extended supine position, with head to the east	
Ro4	Derrymaquirk, Co. Roscommon	2420±70 yrs BP	Extended supine position, oriented east–west with head to the west	Placed in a dug grave with a wooden block at head and stone over pelvis
Sl3	Tawnamore, Co. Sligo	17th century AD	Supine on birch twigs with head to south-south-east and feet to north-north-west	Fully clothed
Sl4	Trasgarve, Co. Sligo	?	Two skeletons; both supine, one above the other; oriented east–west with head to the west	
Ti4	Gortmahonoge, Co. Tipperary	Late 16th/early 17th century AD	Extended, oriented east–west with head to the west	In a woollen suit
Ty2	Kildress, Co. Tyrone	Post-medieval or modern	Body crouched	Appears to have been murdered; head split with spade

Table 29: Some of the positions in which Irish bog bodies lay (not period specific). Data extracted from Ó Floinn (1995a).

extended position nor been oriented east–west. It also shows that the legs could not have lain inside a coffin. The positions extrapolated for the body (Chapter 3) may be consistent with death from exposure, drowning or burial.

Dressed or undressed?

No remains of clothing or coverings of any sort were found in association with the Tumbeagh body. This may be due either to a lack of preservation or to the fact that the body was naked or partly naked when it came to rest in the bog. Raised bogs preserve some fabrics and not others. Linen does not survive well, but clothes of wool or leather may be preserved. If clothing of this composition had been present, we might expect to have found some ragged remnant, particularly as loose bones and

197

torn skin were recovered from adjacent fields. Arguably, however, such evidence may have escaped detection by inclusion in earlier peat harvests. Alternatively, the body may have been originally naked. A body devoid of clothing or a covering is more likely to have been placed in the bog: the possibility of a naked person having walked onto the bog is perhaps remote. The bodies of a teenage boy from Caithness and Kreepen Man provide parallels in an otherwise clothed later medieval catalogue (see Chapter 16). Although the bare legs of the Tumbeagh body and the existence of broadly contemporaneous parallels may hint at the nakedness of the body, the evidence can be regarded as inconclusive. Limited preservation has played a part, but it is also easy to picture how someone might choose to travel barefoot over a bog, given that bogs can be soft and wet.

The human remains and the contemporaneous bog conditions

The body from Tumbeagh is that of a young woman or man of around 18 years of age. We cannot really know who this person was or where she/he came from. Tumbeagh lay in the barony of Garrycastle, in the former territory of Delvin, an area somewhat politically insulated from the wider midlands. Its boggy terrain assisted the Gaelic lords the Mac Coghlans—who dominated locally from the thirteenth to the seventeenth century—to retain these lands. Economically, mixed agriculture, fishing and hunting were significant, and well-positioned churches such as Lemanaghan were long-lived under Mac Coghlan patronage. Trade, marriage, politics and religion necessitated movement across the territory. Thus both locals and travellers had reason to be in the area, and the body may have been that of a local or someone passing through. Given the make-up of the contemporaneous population, she/he was presumably white, but otherwise her/his identity and origin are unknown.

The body is incomplete: only the lower legs have been preserved. Milling has clearly taken its toll on the extent to which the body has survived. The possibility of decomposition before submergence in the bog cannot be ruled out. It may be that different parts of the body were subject to different decay and preservational forces. The slightly better-preserved left leg and the identification of two beetle taxa that may be associated with rotting vegetation and carrion (Reilly, Chapter 14), from peat lying immediately above the right foot, hint at this possibility. Hence the body may have been only partly subject to good preservation, which might occur in a body lying on a wet, raised-bog surface rather than a buried or covered body. Nonetheless, the quality of preservation of the surviving remains (Delaney, Chapter 7) implies the rapid assimilation of at least part of the body into the anaerobic zone of the growing bog (Reilly, Chapter 14; Buckland 1995). The skin of the lower legs, though tanned, is soft but intact; hair follicles are easily discerned, and on the heel pad of the left foot the individual footprint is clearly visible. Growth striations are visible to the naked eye on the toenails, which in the peat looked like fragments of hazelnut shells. For this level of preservation to occur, a body has to be buried, pushed or able to sink into the peat with little possibility of its resurfacing. At Lindow Moss in Cheshire, England, where the body of Lindow Man was deliberately deposited, Buckland (1995, 50) suggests that '[in] cold weather in particular, a human body deliberately pushed down...would be unlikely to break the surface again, as the processes of decay, which would normally liberate gases to buoy up the corpse, would be inhibited by the low temperatures'. This may also be applicable to a body that sank in a soft, wet part of a bog. The Tumbeagh remains were light brown in colour, and this, along with the quality of preservation, suggests that there was a water surplus at the location and that it was not 'hot summer'. The water must have been rather cold. In this instance the bright colour reflects preservation in an environment of poorly humified *Sphagnum* peat, within a relatively short period, under wet and very acidic conditions.

At Tumbeagh there is no evidence that a grave or pit had been dug, implying that the bog surface was soft enough to allow a body either to sink quickly or to be forced below the surface. A similar situation prevailed at Lindow, where the bog surface was soft enough to have caused a person to sink up to their knees. Here, the body lay in a pool, and the strata showed no signs of having been disturbed by digging or trampling. The pool itself was shallow, 0.10–0.20m deep, and filled with *Sphagnum cuspidatum*. Two explanations for the absence of broken strata have been suggested. Barber ([1986]; 1995) suggested that *S. cuspidatum* was peeled back and replaced once the body had been inserted and that it would not have been possible to detect such an occurrence in the peat stratigraphy record. Buckland (1995) proposed that the body was pushed into the peat and that any related stratigraphical interruptions were obscured owing to compression from overlying and adjoining peat deposits. At Tumbeagh there is no evidence for mats of *S. cuspidatum* that could have been replaced after the sinking of a body, nor can compression account for the unbroken stratigraphy. It has been estimated that, before milling, *c.* 0.30m of drained peat sealed the body, and this would not allow disturbed strata to be obscured.

The peat survey implies that in the early sixteenth century Tumbeagh Bog was soft underfoot and shallow pools lingered on the bog surface (Casparie, Chapter 13). This part of the bog was wetter and more unstable, seasonally and year round, than areas 100m to the north or south. Many centuries earlier, a large bog lake had occupied much of the area. Two major phases in its existence have been identified, along with a discharge corridor or gully soak through which it emptied into the greater Lemanaghan Bog. The findspot of the body lies at the intersection of this east–west soak and a north–south *Scheuchzeria–cuspidatum* zone (Fig. 28, symbols 4, 5/6). This soak had an abundance of water, allowing, over time, the rapid accumulation of poorly humified *Sphagnum* peat. This provided for a soft bog surface, and the contemporaneous adjacent surface was one of shallow hollows and vague hummocks flanked by rush fields (Fig. 28). During the laboratory excavation, examination of the surface on which the legs lay identified a small, shallow pool and a layer of pool algae—*Sphagnum cuspidatum*—in the area of the feet, suggesting a constant presence of water (Fig. 13). Near the knees, monocotyledon remains (possibly *Rhynchospora alba*) were recorded, a further indication of wet conditions on the bog surface.

This picture of a wet, *Sphagnum*-dominated bog surface with richly vegetated pools is enhanced by the coleopteran evidence extracted from peat lying immediately below and above the legs (Reilly, Chapter 14). Here, the bog was home to water beetles and plant-feeders that inhabited *Sphagnum* mosses, sedge and adjacent *Eriophorum* tussocks. The feet lay in a pool, the shins and knees on its margins, where

Eriophorum and sedge were growing. Clearly, then, the carrying capacity of this part of the bog was weak, the soft gully fill easily giving way under pressure. The weight of the body may have compressed the soft and water-saturated bog surface, probably by *c.* 0.20–0.30m, a feasible estimate based on observations of heavy wooden and stone-built trackways in Irish raised bogs such as Corlea Bog, Derryoghil Bog (Raftery 1996) and Derryville Bog (Gowen 1999; Casparie 1999; 2001; Casparie and Gowen 2001; Casparie and Stevens 2001). Given the wet conditions, most of the body may have sunk below the bog water-table within a few hours. This may also explain the slightly better preservation of the left leg, which lay deeper in the peat than the right leg, and the absence of either carrion beetles or flies.

Both the conditions on the bog and the quality of preservation of the surviving human remains suggest that access to the part of Tumbeagh in which the body lay was highly problematic, even, at least in periods of greatest wetness, impossible, although conditions were not such that immediate drowning was a major danger. On entering this bog, a pedestrian would have sunk with every step, perhaps up to 0.10m, enough warning to tread carefully or return to safer soil. Undoubtedly, this part of the bog was recognised locally as inhospitable: the absence of earlier or contemporaneous archaeological sites is perhaps a reflection of a long-lived policy of avoidance (Casparie, Chapter 13). Few would voluntarily venture into the area, and it is easy to picture how a person might have become trapped in such an environment, particularly in poor weather. Treacherous situations mostly arise only after or during poor weather, with lengthy periods of solid rainfall, and during fog. The body lay south of a higher, drier route through the bog, now known as Connor's Road (Figs 2, 3). This links the western upland and a prominent ridge of mineral soil, Broder's Island, a clearly visible dry point in the otherwise treeless bog. Situated about halfway between these areas of higher ground was the bog body. It is estimated that walking between these points, a distance of *c.* 1.5km, under 'normal' bog conditions, i.e. on a less wet or unstable surface, would take about one hour and that the treeless nature of the bog surface guaranteed that any pedestrian would have been visible from the higher ground to the east and west. It seems likely that the body of a person who became trapped and died on the bog would have been noticed from the surrounding uplands, but the presence of the body suggests that it escaped both the attention of people and animals and other decay in a very short time. This can best be explained by the minimal carrying capacity of the soft bog surface, which ensured rapid assimilation of the body into the bog and/or which may have prevented a trapped person from being rescued.

The palaeoenvironmental reconstruction of conditions in Tumbeagh suggest that this part of the bog was dangerous and inaccessible. Hence, the bog body may represent an individual who strayed from Connor's Road, became trapped and eventually died on the bog. She/he may have died of exposure or drowned, shallow pools were present, as shown by the peat survey (Casparie, Chapter 13) and the position of the legs within a pool. This is most likely to have occurred during periods of higher rainfall, such as between October and March, when the bog water-table was highest. Although this is perhaps the worst time of year to enter a bog, there may be evidence to suggest that the body came to lie in the bog sometime between the autumn and the spring. Wood found beside the human remains had been cut in the autumn, at the end of the growing season (Chapter 4). If the wood and the body are contemporaneous, then the teenager may have died in late autumn or not long after. The implications of the presence of the wood from Tumbeagh are considered below.

Sticks of contention

The wooden remains from Tumbeagh consist of a few short hazel rods, a hazel withy, a birch pole and three stakes of birch. Their close proximity to the human remains suggests that they are part of the material culture of this bog-body find, and the radiocarbon date returned for one of the stakes indicates that the wood and the body may be considered to be contemporaneous. The relationship between the wood and the body, however, is not straightforward, as limited preservation has impinged on its integrity.

The withy lay *c.* 1m from the feet. It may have been displaced: nearby were crumbs of body fat and toe bones, demonstrating the displacement of other material to the south of the feet. The withy itself was crushed rather than torn; its light construction would hardly have survived being pulled or torn by the peat-cutting machinery. In the context of bodies and bogs, the withy has few Irish or European medieval parallels. The only other recorded Irish instance is prehistoric: Gallagh Man, discovered in 1821, was found to have a withy of hazel sally rods around his neck that may have played a role in his demise (Ó Floinn 1995b). Another prehistoric body, Windeby Man from Germany, was found with a hazel branch around his neck (van der Sanden 1996). Elsewhere, a late medieval body from Caithness in Scotland was accompanied by a twisted heather rope (see Chapter 16). The recent dating of Kreepen Man to the fifteenth/sixteenth century AD indicates a medieval event involving the binding of the hands and feet with twigs: a bound body may have been easier to carry onto the bog. Although a parallel exists, there is no direct evidence from Tumbeagh to suggest that the feet were bound. No fragments or splinters of hazel were retrieved from around the feet, nor were there any obvious binding marks or impressions on the surviving skin. Perhaps the wood found on the site was carried onto the bog in a faggot bound by the withy, which was subsequently dropped on the bog once the wood had been used. Four stakes associated with the body of a man from Clongownagh, Co. Kildare, had been bound with a loop of twisted twigs (Delaney *et al.* 1999). This find, though considerably earlier than Tumbeagh, shows the possibility of using a withy in this manner.

The birch pole extended northward from the knee region (Figs 7, 8); it lay horizontally, with a shredded upper surface and an intact underside retaining bark. Initially, it was thought that, for the roundwood to have survived where the body had not, the wood must have lain under the body and been shielded from the milling machines. The manner in which the body probably lay, however, either on its left side or in a somewhat more flexed position along a north-north-west/south-south-east line, makes this unlikely (Chapter 2). It is also not certain whether the position occupied by the pole was that in which it had been deposited. Machine damage or compression from overlying peat may have caused it to roll into another position. Poles used as a means of weighing bodies down, are a feature from other bog-body finds (van der Sanden 1996), but at Tumbeagh not enough of the corpse has survived, and the pole itself was incomplete, so the exact relationship between it and the bog body remains uncertain.

The arrangement of the wood found beside the knees looks like a deliberate setting (Fig. 12). The longest brushwood, with its chisel-pointed tip, appears to have been driven into the bog, with the shortest, lighter stake pushed in with it. The third piece lay at a shallower angle. In the earliest stages of the laboratory excavation this arrangement, in particular the manner in which the third stake lay beneath the lower thigh region, was taken to represent a light structure on which the body had been lain (Bermingham and Delaney 2000). Instances of bodies lying on top of wood are rare, and none is known from an Irish context. The skeleton of a woman lying on 'a platform of logs' (Turner [1986], 121) was found in fenland peats in the parish of Methwold, Norfolk, in 1967. The find dates from the Early Bronze Age, and it has been suggested that it may reflect a previously unrecognised form of burial practice (*ibid.*). At Bunsoh, Germany, in 1890 a body was discovered that was described as resting on a bed of twigs with small stakes at the head and feet, and posts on top of the body. The arrangement of wood is thought to have formed a burial chamber in which the body was placed (van der Sanden 1996). The Bunsoh find, however, represents an early entry in the broader bog-body catalogue and may be best interpreted cautiously.

As the laboratory excavation progressed, it became clear that machinery and the compaction of the peat had damaged the stakes and resulted in breaks. Recent damage was found on the lower end of stake 98E452:5:8, which had been rotated where it lay without being lifted out of place, similar to the epiphysis of the left femur of the body, which, though inverted and separated from the rest of the bone, occupied its correct anatomical position. The stakes, then, could have lain in such a way as to pin the legs down in the bog. The effectiveness of this, however, is open to question, as the soft bog surface might suggest that longer and more stakes would have been required to secure a body in the peat.

Generally, where wood is associated with bog bodies, it lay either above or beside the body. Only in a minority of cases was a body found staked in the bog. There are late post-medieval instances where wood was used in this way. In Scotland, birch sticks had been placed over bodies in Dava Moor and Lanarkshire (see Chapter 16). Irish instances, both prehistoric and later, are also known. A possible suicide burial in Mounflugh, Co. Cork, was found with nine or ten upright stakes around the body (Ó Floinn 1995a). The burial was thought by locals to date to the mid-seventeenth century. Possible prehistoric instances include Gallagh Man and some less well-known finds such as a skeleton from Drumcroon, Co. Derry, alongside which a single pole was found. Two ash stakes are held in the National Museum of Ireland that were originally associated with a body, possibly of a woman, from Newhill, Co. Tipperary, which lay 2.4m deep in the peat. One of the stakes was almost 0.5m long, with a cut but blunt-pointed end. The Derry and Tipperary finds have not been dated, but Ó Floinn (1995b) suggests a prehistoric date for them on the basis of the depth of overlying peat and the fact that each was naked.

The above discussion has shown that wood is commonly found in association with bog bodies and that there are parallels, some more convincing than others, for the use of wood in fixing a body in a bog. At Tumbeagh almost all of the pieces of wood show signs of having been worked, that is, humanly altered. In general, this implies that human agency was responsible for their deposition, although this need not have been the case, as stray finds of worked and unworked wood are commonly recovered from bogs (e.g., Moloney *et al.* 1995; Raftery 1996). Increased rainfall resulting in inundation of the bog surface can result in the random deposition of wood on the bog surface. At Tumbeagh the wood and the body share the same findspot, and, given their possible contemporancity, the wooden remains can be said to form part of the material culture of the find. The wood, however, need not have had a pinning function but may represent a bundle carried by the youth onto the bog.

Conclusion

In common with many other bog bodies, few definite statements can be made about the body from Tumbeagh. We know that the remains represent an individual who died in *c.* AD 1500 at around 18 years of age. How this person died and the reason for her/his presence in the bog are unknown. The evidence regarding whether the body was naked or was pinned down in the bog is inconclusive, and there is no evidence of deliberate burial in the form of a grave or pit. In contrast, the palaeoenvironmental reconstruction provides compelling evidence of a hazardous and dangerous bog environment that precluded deliberate access. The bog surface itself was perhaps not dangerous enough to explain this death but in the event of straying from the road, perhaps during poor weather conditions, could have caused the person to become trapped. Death as a result of exposure or even drowning after some time remain distinct possibilities.

19.
'Sure it's only a pair of legs': some concluding remarks

Nóra Bermingham and Máire Delaney

This project began to take shape on 17 September 1998. The discovery of the remains late that afternoon set many actions in motion that have found in this publication an outlet for expression; ten days in the field have led to a period of investigation spanning five years. The Tumbeagh find is the first Irish bog body to be found by an archaeologist. The project is the first of its kind undertaken in Ireland and the most recent in Europe since 1984. The project is among the most comprehensively studied sets of human remains and sites from a bog. It represents the first opportunity in Ireland to ensure that the human remains left the bog only when everything else had been recorded, surveyed, photographed, drawn and sampled.

And yet many have said: 'sure it's only a pair of legs'. Why has all this fuss been made about a pair of legs, an incomplete pair at that? With extensive tracts of bog surviving in Ireland, new bog-body discoveries will be made at some point; the discoveries of bodies in 2003 and 2005 are a reminder of this potential. Over the last 20 years in Ireland there has been an increased archaeological presence on the midland raised bogs, leading to huge increases in the numbers of trackways and artefacts found (Raftery 1996; Bermingham 1997b). We have shown how the discoveries at Lindow had a knock-on effect on the study of Irish bog bodies (Chapter 16), with Delaney and Ó Floinn (1995) undertaking the first comprehensive investigations into an Irish bog body. The discovery of the Tumbeagh remains was really just a matter of time, and it signalled the necessity of identifying the existence of expertise in Ireland appropriate to this and to future finds. The Tumbeagh Project was regarded as a benchmark, in which the investigation would be not only into the find itself but also into the resources, experience and possibilities for the study of bog bodies in Ireland. Mindful of a longer European history of bog-body research, we endeavoured to place this project within this broader framework, and as a result the project has benefited greatly from the interest and contributions of international researchers, as well as the goodwill and support of external agencies and individuals.

Archaeological mitigation in Ireland is primarily funded by developers; sites are rescued via paper and digital records and the careful collection of sequences and artefacts. There are, of course, occasions where a discovery may also require the input of state resources. Bog bodies are such finds, offering rare opportunities for research and extending our archaeological knowledge of the person, place and period in question. The Tumbeagh Project has attempted to achieve a balance between the demands of a rescue situation and the research requirements demanded by the find itself. This was not always easy, not least because of financial constraints. However, although the balance between rescue and research archaeology can be difficult to achieve, the cooperative approach taken by the funding agencies represents a significant move forward in research into bog bodies and bogs in Ireland.

It is important to acknowledge that the Tumbeagh Project has had its own limitations, largely dictated by the limited preservation of the body; for example, we lacked internal organs, from which we might find out what the person had last eaten. In the area of testing, there was no need for microscopic analysis of fingernails as none were found. Each new bog body will have its own set of archaeological and forensic requirements, dictated by the extent to which the body is preserved and the circumstances of its discovery. The Tumbeagh find was limited to the lower legs, with skin, toenails, bone and body fat all present. We now know that these elements are more robust than hitherto believed, if a strict maintenance programme is adhered to. But what of a bog body with hair? Will hair react adversely to repeated exposure and packing in peat?

These issues should be kept in mind in the study of future finds. Already, between 2003 and 2005, the Irish midlands seems to be going through a 'bog-body bonanza'. The 2003 finds were made within weeks of one another (see Chapter 16), as were the later, 2005 finds, although little information is currently available about these discoveries. All are safely housed within peat blocks in refrigerated storage in the National Museum of Ireland, Collins Barracks. The treatment of the Tumbeagh remains has shown that immediate conservation is not necessary once adequate precautions are taken. It also shows that a body can be maintained, at least in the short term, until a sound strategy has been formulated and adequate resources are in place.

Arising from the discovery of the Tumbeagh body is new evidence of long-term environmental development that has implications beyond the snapshot of time to which the bog body belongs. Archaeological sites jostle for space in parts of the Lemanaghan Group of bogs, but until this project there was little investigation into the wider dynamics of the mire system and how the bog influenced the lives and actions of the people operating within its environs. We have seen the fen develop and be replaced by a bog lake that burst, reformed and burst again. The area was so wet at times that people avoided it or, unlike elsewhere in Lemanaghan, left no trace of their presence. Eventually, the raised bog took over—a changing landscape that called for frequent renegotiation on the part of the local population. We know that the resting place of the teenage girl or boy was a difficult, unstable and dangerous landscape best entered under advisement or not at all. The lack of scavenger insects on the legs shows that the body passed quickly into its peaty residence. Elsewhere in the bog complex, trackways dating from the second millennium BC to the later medieval period show that people resorted to construction in order to pass more easily through the bog. These trackways were the products of local populations who inhabited the esker ridges fringing the bog where woodland was cleared to make way for pasture and pasture gave way to woodland.

We have also seen that new discoveries continue to be a real prospect. New finds should benefit from immediate and appropriate archaeological responses of the kind applied at Tumbeagh. Bog bodies are, of course, not confined to raised bogs. Meenybraddan Woman was found in an upland blanket bog in County Donegal, and these areas are subject to development at a variety of scales, for example peat cutting, wind farms and electricity pylons, as well as turbary. Despite recent events, bog-body finds are not common, but accidental discoveries are likely to be repeated. This can result in the premature removal of a body from the bog, as was the case at Clonerl, Co. Offaly. Bodies can also be unwittingly cut from a bog by a machine operator, as the case from Ballivor Bog demonstrates (see Chapter 16; Me3, Appendix 1). The finders of these bodies, however, responded quickly and in this way ensured that further damage to or exposure of the bodies was prevented.

This pair of legs from an area of west County Offaly in the shadow of the Eiscir Riada, the monastic town of Clonmacnoise and the church of St Manchán has led to the advancement of established areas of investigation in the study of bogs and bog bodies in Ireland. Though by no means exhausting or utilising all of the areas of investigation possible, the Tumbeagh remains have been subjected to experimental and innovative approaches that have bettered our knowledge of the treatment and investigation of bog bodies and, within Ireland, provided a modern foundation for further study.

References

Alexander, K.N.A. 1994 *An annotated checklist of British lignicolous and saproxylic invertebrates*. Cirencester.

Andersen, S.T. 1970 The relative pollen productivity of North European trees, and correction factors for tree pollen spectra. *Danmarks Geologiske Undersogelse* 96, 1–99.

Anderson, R., Nash, R. and O'Connor, J. 1997 Irish Coleoptera: a revised and annotated list. *Irish Naturalists' Journal*, special entomological supplement.

Balfour-Browne, F. 1958 *British water beetles, III*. London.

Barber, K. [1986] Peat macrofossil analyses as indicators of the bog palaeoenvironment and climatic change. In I.M. Stead, J.B. Bourke and D. Brothwell (eds), *Lindow Man: the body in the bog*, 86–9. London.

Barber, K.E. 1995 Peat stratigraphy and the Lindow bog body: a reconsideration of the evidence. In R.C. Turner and R.G. Scaife (eds), *Bog bodies: new discoveries and new perspectives*, 50–1. London.

Barry, T.B. 1987 *The archaeology of medieval Ireland*. London.

Bennike, P. 1999 The Early Neolithic Danish bog finds: a strange group of people! In B. Coles, J. Coles and M. Schou Jørgensen (eds), *Bog bodies, sacred sites and wetland archaeology*, 27–32. Wetland Archaeology Research Project Occasional Paper 12. Exeter.

Bermingham, N. 1997a 96E150, Castlearmstrong, Cornafurrish, Lemanaghan. In I. Bennett (ed.), *Excavations 1996: summary accounts of archaeological investigations in Ireland*, 93. Bray.

Bermingham, N. 1997b The current position of the Irish Archaeological Wetland Unit. *NewsWarp* 21, 7–9.

Bermingham, N. and Delaney, M. 2000 The Tumbeagh bog body. *Institute of Field Archaeologists: yearbook and directory of members*, 40–2. Macclesfield.

Beug, H.-J. 1961 *Leitfaden der Pollenbestimmung für Mitteleuropa und angrezende Gebiete*. Stuttgart.

Bourke, J.B. [1986] The medical investigation of Lindow Man. In I.M. Stead, J.B. Bourke and D. Brothwell (eds), *Lindow Man: the body in the bog*, 46–51. London.

Breen, T. 1988 Excavation of a roadway at Bloomhill Bog, Co. Offaly. *Proceedings of the Royal Irish Academy* 88C, 321–39.

Briggs, C.S. 1995 Did they fall or were they pushed? Some unresolved questions about bog bodies. In R.C. Turner and R.G. Scaife (eds), *Bog bodies: new discoveries and new perspectives*, 168–82. London.

Briggs, C.S. and Turner, R. [1986] The bog burials of Britain and Ireland. In I.M. Stead, J.B. Bourke and D. Brothwell (eds), *Lindow Man: the body in the bog*, 144–61. London.

Brindley, A.L. and Lanting, J.N. 1995 Irish bog bodies: the radiocarbon dates. In R.C. Turner and R.G. Scaife (eds), *Bog bodies: new discoveries and new perspectives*, 133–6. London.

Brothwell, D. 1986 *The bog man and the archaeology of people*. London.

Brothwell, D. 1996 Recent research on the Lindow bodies in the context of five years of world studies. In R.C. Turner and R.G. Scaife (eds), *Bog bodies: new discoveries and new perspectives*, 100–4. London.

Brothwell, D. and Bourke, J.B. 1995 The human remains from Lindow Moss, 1987–8. In R.C. Turner and R.G. Scaife (eds), *Bog bodies: new discoveries and new perspectives*, 52–8. London.

Brothwell, D., Liversage, D. and Gottlieb, B. 1990 Radiographic and forensic aspects of the female Huldremose body. *Journal of Danish Archaeology* **9**, 157–78.

Buckland, P.C. 1995 Peat stratigraphy and the age of the Lindow bodies. In R.C. Turner and R.G. Scaife (eds), *Bog bodies: new discoveries and new perspectives*, 47–50. London.

Bullock, J.A. 1993 Host plants of British beetles: a list of recorded associations. *Amateur Entomologist* **11A**, 1–24.

Caseldine, C.J., Gearey, B.R. and Hatton, J. 2004 Palynological and palaeohydrological investigations at Derryville, Co. Tipperary. Unpublished report for Margaret Gowen and Co. Ltd, Glenageary, Co. Dublin.

Casparie, W.A. 1999 Peat morphology and bog development of Derryville Bog, Co. Tipperary. In M. Gowen (ed.), Final report: Lisheen Archaeological Project, 1996–1997, vol. 1A, 1–173. Unpublished report by M. Gowen and Co. Ltd, Glenageary, Co. Dublin.

Casparie, W.A. 2001 Prehistoric building disasters in Derryville Bog, Ireland: trackways, floodings and erosions. In B. Raftery and J. Hickey (eds), *Recent developments in wetland research*, 115–28. Seandálaíocht Monograph 2/Wetland Archaeology Research Project Occasional Paper 14. Dublin.

Casparie, W.A. and Gowen, M. 2001 Die zahlreichen Moorwege von Derryville Bog, Co. Tipperary, Irland: über die Zusammenhang von Bautechnik und Moorhydrologie. In M. Fansa (ed.), *Moor—eine verlorene Landschaft*, 91–106. Scriftenreihe des Landesmuseum für Natur und Mensch 20. Oldenburg.

Casparie, W.A. and Stevens, P. 2001 Bronze Age stone-built way through an Irish bog: site 'Killoran 18'. In W.H. Metz, B.L. van Beek and H. Steegstra (eds), *Patina: essays presented to Jay Jordan Butler on the occasion of his 80th birthday*, 195–206. Groningen.

Cockburn, A., Cockburn, E. and Reyman, A. (eds) 1998 *Mummies, disease and ancient cultures* (2nd edn). Cambridge.

Connolly, R.C., Evershed, R.P., Embery, G., Stanbury, J.B., Green, D., Beahan, P. and Shortall, J.B. [1986] The chemical composition of some bodily tissues. In I.M.

Stead, J.B. Bourke and D. Brothwell (eds), *Lindow Man: the body in the bog*, 72–6. London.

Coope, G.R. 1968 Fossil beetles collected by James Bennie from late glacial silts at Corstorphine, Edinburgh. *Scottish Journal of Geology* **4**, 339–48.

Cox, L. 1973 The Mac Coghlans of Delvin Eathra. *Irish Genealogist* **4** (6), 534–46.

Cox, L. 1974 The Mac Coghlans of Delvin Eathra. *Irish Genealogist* **5** (1), 21–32.

Crawford, H.S. 1911 The early slabs at Lemanaghan, King's County. *Journal of the Royal Society of Antiquaries of Ireland* **1**, 151–6.

Delaney, M. and Ó Floinn, R. 1995 A bog body from Meenybraddan Bog, County Donegal, Ireland. In R.C. Turner and R.G. Scaife (eds), *Bog bodies: new discoveries and new perspectives*, 123–32. London.

Delaney, M., Ó Floinn, R. and Heckett, E. 1999 Bog body from Clongownagh, Baronstown West, County Kildare, Ireland. In B. Coles, J. Coles and M. Schou Jørgensen (eds), *Bog bodies, sacred sites and wetland archaeology*, 67–8. Wetland Archaeology Research Project Occasional Paper 12. Exeter.

Dieck, A. 1965 *Die europäischen Moorleichenfunde (Hominidenmoorfunde)*. Neumünster.

Dinnin, M.H. and Skidmore, P. 1995 The insect assemblages associated with Lindow III and their environmental implications. In R.C. Turner and R.G. Scaife (eds), *Bog bodies: new discoveries and new perspectives*, 31–8. London.

Doyle, T. and Dowding, P. 1990 Decomposition and aspects of the physical environment in the surface layers of Mongan Bog. In G.J. Doyle (ed.), *Ecology and conservation of Irish peatlands*, 163–71. Dublin.

Duffy, S. (ed.) 1997 *An atlas of Irish history*. Dublin.

Ellam, D. 1984 Wet bone: the potential for freeze drying. In K. Starling and D. Watkinson (eds), *Archaeological bone, antler and ivory*. United Kingdom Institute for Conservation Occasional Paper 5. London.

Ellison, C.C. 1975 Bishop Dopping's visitation book 1682–85. *Ríocht na Midhe* **6** (1), 3–13.

Evershed, R.P. 1992 Chemical composition of a bog body adipocere. *Archaeometry* **34**, 253–65.

Eyre, M.D., Luff, M.L. and Lott, D.A. 1998 Rare and notable beetle species records from Scotland from survey work with pitfall traps, 1992–1996. *Coleopterist* **7**, 81–90.

Feehan, J. and O'Donovan, G. 1996 *The bogs of Ireland*. Dublin.

Fischer, C. 1998 Bog bodies of Denmark and northwestern Europe. In A. Cockburn, E. Cockburn and A. Reyman (eds), *Mummies, disease and ancient cultures* (2nd edn), 237–62. Cambridge.

Fisher, R.A., Corbet, A.S. and Williams, C.B. 1943 The relation between number of species and the number of individuals in a random sample of an animal population. *Journal of Animal Ecology* **12**, 42–58.

FitzPatrick, E. and O'Brien, C. 1998 *The medieval churches of County Offaly*. Dublin.

Flanagan, L. 1992 *A dictionary of Irish archaeology*. Dublin.

Fredengren, C. 2002 *Crannogs: a study of people's interaction with lakes, with particular reference to Lough Gara in the north-west of Ireland*. Bray.

Fry, S. 1999 *Burial in medieval Ireland, 900–1500*. Dublin.

Garland, A.N. 1995 Worsley Man, England. In R.C. Turner and R.G. Scaife (eds), *Bog bodies: new discoveries and new perspectives*, 106–7. London.

Glob, P.V. 1969 *The bog people*. London.

Gowen, M. (ed.) 1999 Final report: Lisheen Archaeological Project, 1996–1997. Unpublished report by M. Gowen and Co. Ltd, Glenageary, Co. Dublin.

Grime, J.P., Hodgson, J.G. and Hunt, R. 1988 *Comparative plant ecology*. London.

Grimm, E.C. 1987 CONISS: a Fortran 77 program for stratigraphically constrained cluster analysis by the method of incremental sum of squares. *Computers and Geosciences* **13**, 13–35.

Grimm, E.C. 1991–3 *TILIA and TILIA-GRAPH*. Springfield, Illinois.

Groenman-van Waateringe, W 1983 The early agricultural utilisation of the Irish landscape: the last word on the elm decline? In T. Reeves-Smyth and F. Hamond (eds), *Landscape archaeology in Ireland*, 217–32. British Archaeological Reports, British Series 116. Oxford.

Gwynn, A. and Hadcock, R.N. 1988 *Medieval religious houses: Ireland*. Dublin.

Halpin, A. 1984 A preliminary survey of archaeological material recovered from peatlands in the Republic of Ireland. Unpublished report, Office of Public Works, Dublin.

Hammond, R. 1981 *The peatlands of Ireland*. Dublin.

Hart, E. 2003 *Haunted ground*. London.

Heaney, S. 1998 *Opened ground: poems 1966–1996*. London.

Hirons, K.R. 1984 Palaeoenvironmental investigations in east Co. Tyrone, Northern Ireland. Unpublished PhD thesis, Queen's University Belfast.

Housley, R.A., Walker, A.J., Otlet, R.L. and Hedges, R.E.M. 1995 Radiocarbon dating of the Lindow III bog body. In R.C. Turner and R.G. Scaife (eds), *Bog bodies: new discoveries and new perspectives*, 39–46. London.

Hughes, M.A. and Jones, D.S. 1986 A body in the bog but no DNA. *Nature* **323**, 208.

Hughes, P.D.M. 2003 Review of the routes to ombrotrophy in raised bogs from Britain and Ireland. In A. Bauerochse and H. Haßmann (eds), *Peatlands: archaeological sites, archives of nature, nature conservation, wise use. Proceedings of the Peatland Conference 2002 in Hannover, Germany*, 188–95. Hannover.

Hyman, P.S. and Parsons, M.S. 1992 *A review of the scarce and threatened Coleoptera of Great Britain, part 1* (rev. edn). Peterborough.

IAWU 1997a Filling in the blanks: an archaeological survey of the Lemanaghan bogs, Co. Offaly. *Archaeology Ireland* **11** (2), 22–5.

IAWU 1997b Surveys of Lemanaghan and Bellair works, Co. Offaly. In I. Bennett (ed.), *Excavations 1996: summary accounts of archaeological investigations in Ireland*, 121–3. Bray.

IAWU 1998 Assessment and mitigation in Lemanaghan: IAWU final report. Unpublished report for Bord na Móna, Newbridge, Co. Kildare.

Joseph, J.J. 1930 Parish names in Ardagh and Clonmacnoise. *Ardagh and Clonmacnoise Archaeological Journal* **2** (8), 47–60.

Kent, D.H. 1992 *List of vascular plants of the British Isles*. London.

Kenward, H.K. 1978 *The analysis of archaeological insect assemblages: a new approach.*

Archaeology of York 19/1. London.

Kenward, H.K., Hall, A.R. and Jones, A.K.G. 1980 A tested set of techniques for the extraction of plant and animal macrofossils from waterlogged archaeological deposits. *Science and Archaeology* **22**, 3–15.

Kenward, H.K., Engleman, C., Robertson, A. and Large, F. 1986 Rapid scanning of urban archaeological deposits for insect remains. *Circaea* **3**, 163–72.

Larsson, S.J. and Gígja, G. 1959 *Coleoptera*. Zoology of Iceland 43A. Copenhagen.

Lemdahl, G. 1988 *Palaeoclimatic and palaeoecological studies based on subfossil insects from the Late Weichselian sediments in southern Sweden*. Lundqua Thesis 22. Lund.

Lennon, C. 1994 *Sixteenth century Ireland: the incomplete conquest*. New Gill History of Ireland 2. Dublin.

Lindroth, C.H. 1974 Coleoptera: Carabidae. *Handbooks for the identification of British insects*, vol. 4, part 2. London.

Lindsey, N.E. [1986] Photogrammetric recording of Lindow Man. In I.M. Stead, J.B. Bourke and D. Brothwell (eds), *Lindow Man: the body in the bog*, 31–7. London.

Loeber, R. 1980 Civilisation through plantation: the projects of Matthew de Renzi. In H. Murtagh (ed.), *Irish midland studies: essays in commemoration of N.W. English*, 121–35. Athlone.

Lucht, W.H. 1987 *Die Käfer Mitteleuropas. Katalog*. Krefeld.

Luff, M.L. 1998 *Provisional atlas of the ground beetles (Coleoptera, Carabidae) of Britain*. Abbots Ripton.

MacCuarta, B. 1987 Mathew de Renzy's letters on Irish affairs 1613–20. *Analecta Hibernica* **34**, 107–82.

McDermott, C. 2001 Trekkers through time: recent archaeological survey results from Co. Offaly, Ireland. In B. Raftery and J. Hickey (eds), *Recent developments in wetland research*, 13–25. Seandálaíocht Monograph 2/Wetland Archaeology Research Project Occasional Paper 14. Dublin.

Mauqoy, D., van Geel, B., Baauw, M. and van der Plicht, J. 2002 Evidence from northwest European bogs shows 'Little Ice Age' climatic change driven by variations in solar activity. *Holocene* **12** (1), 1–6.

Mitchell, G.F. 1965 Littleton Bog, Tipperary: an Irish agricultural record. *Journal of the Royal Society of Antiquaries of Ireland* **95**, 121–32.

Mitchell, G.F. 1976 *The Irish landscape*. London.

Molloy, K. and O'Connell, M. 1987 The nature of the vegetational changes at about 5000 BP with particular reference to the elm decline: fresh evidence from Connemara, western Ireland. *New Phytologist* **106**, 203–20.

Moloney, A., Bermingham, N., Jennings, D., Keane, M., McDermott, C. and OCarroll, E. 1995 *Blackwater survey and excavations: artefact deterioration in peatlands, Lough More, Co, Mayo*. Dublin.

Monk, M.A. 1985/6 Evidence from macroscopic plant remains for crop husbandry in prehistoric and early Ireland. *Journal of Irish Archaeology* **3**, 31–6.

Mook, W.G. and Streurman, H.J. 1983 Physical and chemical aspects of radiocarbon dating. In W.G. Mook and H.T. Waterbolk (eds), *Proceedings of the First International Symposium, ^{14}C and archaeology: Groningen 1981*, 31–55. Strasbourg.

Moore, P.D., Webb, J.A. and Collinson, M.E. 1991 *Pollen analysis* (2nd edn). Oxford. Blackwell.

Newman Johnson, D. 1987 An unusual amphisbaena in Galway City. In E. Rynne (ed.), *Figures from the past: studies on figurative art in Christian Ireland in honour of H.M. Roe*, 233–41. Dún Laoghaire, Co. Dublin.

O'Brien, C. and Sweetman, P.D. 1997 *Archaeological inventory of County Offaly*. Dublin.

OCarroll, E. 1997 96E151, Lemanaghan and Derrynagun. In I. Bennett (ed.), *Excavations 1996: summary accounts of archaeological excavations in Ireland*, 93–4. Bray.

OCarroll, E. 1999 Archaeological excavations in Lemanaghan. *Scéal na Móna* **13** (27), 24–5.

OCarroll, E. 2001 *The archaeology of Lemanaghan: the story of an Irish bog*. Bray.

OCarroll, E. and Whitaker, J. 1999 A trek through time. *Archaeology Ireland* **13** (3), 31–2.

O'Conor, K.D. 1998 *The archaeology of medieval rural settlement*. Discovery Programme Monograph 3. Dublin. Royal Irish Academy.

O'Donovan, J. (ed.) 1851 *Annals of the kingdom of Ireland by the Four Masters, from the earliest period to the year 1616*. Dublin.

Ó Floinn, R. 1988 Irish bog bodies. *Archaeology Ireland* **2** (3), 94–7.

Ó Floinn, R. 1991 A prehistoric bog burial at Baronstown West. *Journal of the Kildare Archaeological Society* **17**, 148–50.

Ó Floinn, R. 1994 *Irish shrines and reliquaries of the Middle Ages*. Dublin.

Ó Floinn, R. 1995a Gazetteer of bog bodies in Ireland. In R.C. Turner and R.G. Scaife (eds), *Bog bodies: new discoveries and new perspectives*, 221–34. London.

Ó Floinn, R. 1995b Recent research into Irish bog bodies. In R.C. Turner and R.G. Scaife (eds), *Bog bodies: new discoveries and new perspectives*, 137–45. London.

O'Grady, S. 1893 *The bog of stars*. Dublin.

O'Kelly, A. 1829 Appendix II, vi–viii. *Proceedings of the Royal Irish Academy*, 65.

Omar, S., McCord, M. and Daniels, V. 1989 The conservation of bog bodies by freeze drying. *Studies in Conservation* **34**, 101–9.

Osinga, J., Buys, C. and van der Sanden, W.A.B. 1992 DNA and the Dutch bog bodies. *Ancient DNA Newsletter* **1** (2), 21–2.

O'Sullivan, A. 1996 Neolithic, Bronze Age and Iron Age woodworking techniques. In B. Raftery, *Trackway excavations in the Mountdillon Bogs, Co. Longford, 1985–1991*. Irish Archaeological Wetland Unit Transactions 3. Dublin.

Painter, T. 1991 Lindow Man, Tollund Man and other peat bodies: the preservative and antimicrobial actions of sphagnan, a reactive glycuronoglycan with tanning and sequestering properties. *Carbohydrate Polymers* **15**, 123–42.

Painter, T. 1995 Chemical and microbiological aspects of the preservation process in *Sphagnum* peat. In R.C. Turner and R.G. Scaife (eds), *Bog bodies: new discoveries and new perspectives*, 88–99. London.

Patterson III, W.A., Edwards K.J. and Maguire, D.J. 1987 Microscopic charcoal as a fossil indicator of fire. *Quaternary Science Reviews* **6**, 3–23.

Pender, S. (ed.) 1939 *A census of Ireland circa 1659*. Dublin.

Petty, W. and Lamb, F.R. 1969 *Hiberniae delineatio, with geographical description of ye kingdom of Ireland*. Shannon. [Facsimile of 1st edn, Dublin, 1685.]

Perring, F.H. and Walters, S.M. 1990 *Atlas of the British flora* (3rd edn). London.

Pyatt, F.B., Beaumont, E.H., Buckland, P.C., Lacy, D., Magilton, J.R. and Storey, D.M.

1995 Mobilisation of elements from the bog bodies of Lindow II and III and some observations on body painting. In R.C. Turner and R.G. Scaife (eds), *Bog bodies: new discoveries and new perspectives*, 62–73. London.

Raftery, B. 1995 Pre- and protohistoric Ireland: problems of continuity and change. *Emania* **13**, 5–9.

Raftery, B. 1996 *Trackway excavations in the Mountdillon Bogs, Co. Longford, 1985–1991*. Irish Archaeological Wetland Unit Transactions 3. Dublin.

Reynolds, Rev. D. 1929 Who was St Manchan? *Journal of the Ardagh and Clonmacnoise Archaeological Society* **1** (3), 65–9.

Reznek, R.H., Hallett, M.G. and Charlesworth, M. [1986] Computed tomography of Lindow Man. In I.M. Stead, J.B. Bourke and D. Brothwell (eds), *Lindow Man: the body in the bog*, 65–71. London.

Richter, M. 1988 *Medieval Ireland: the enduring tradition*. New Gill History of Ireland 1. Dublin.

Ridgway, G.L., Powell, M. and Mirza, N. [1986] The microbiological monitoring of Lindow Man. In I.M. Stead, J.B. Bourke and D. Brothwell (eds), *Lindow Man: the body in the bog*, 21. London.

Robinson, M.A. 1991 The Neolithic and Late Bronze Age insect assemblage. In S. Needham (ed.), *Excavation and salvage at Runnymede Bridge, 1978: a Late Bronze Age waterfront site*, 277–326. London.

Rodwell, J.S. (ed.) 1992 *British plant communities, vol. 2: mires and heaths*. Cambridge.

Roentgen, W.C. 1959 [1895] On a new kind of ray (first report). *Munch Med Wochenschr.* **101**, 1237–9.

Rudenko, S.I. 1970 *The frozen tombs of Siberia*. London.

Ryan, B. 1994 *A land by the river of God: a history of Ferbane parish from earliest times to c. 1900*. Offaly.

Ryan, M. (ed.) 1991 *The illustrated archaeology of Ireland*. Dublin.

Schouten, M.G.C. (ed.) 2002 *Conservation and restoration of raised bogs: geological, hydrological and ecological studies*. Dublin.

Schübel, J. 1999 Histologische Untersuchungen von Präparaten des Jungen von Kayhausen, Weder See noch Land. Moor—eine verlorene Landschaft. *Beiträge zur Austellung Oldenburg*, 73–5. Oldenburg.

Shea, S. 1931 Report on the human skeleton found in Stoney Island Bog, Portumna. *Journal of the Galway Archaeological and Historical Society* **15**, 73–9.

Sheehan, J. 1993 *The eskers of Ireland*. Moate Historical Society Occasional Paper 6. Moate.

Shirt, D.B. (ed.) 1987 *British red data books, 2: insects*. Peterborough.

Shortall, J.B. [1986] Inorganic constituents of bone, hair and finger nail. In I.M. Stead, J.B. Bourke and D. Brothwell (eds), *Lindow Man: the body in the bog*, 74–5. London.

Simington, R.C. 1961 *The Civil Survey, 1652–56, vol. X*, 35–6. Dublin.

Smyth, A. 1982 *Celtic Leinster: towards an historical geography of early Irish civilisation*. Blackrock, Co. Dublin.

Spigelman, M., Fricker, C.R. and Fricker, E.J. 1995 Extracting DNA from Lindow Man's gut contents: modern technology looking for answers from ancient tissue. In R.C. Turner and R.G. Scaife (eds), *Bog bodies: new discoveries and new perspectives*, 59–61. London.

Spindler, K. 2001 *The man in the ice*. London.

Stead, I.M. [1986] Excavation and examination. In I.M. Stead, J.B. Bourke and D. Brothwell (eds), *Lindow Man: the body in the bog*, 14–16. London.

Stead, I.M., Bourke, J.B. and Brothwell, D. (eds) [1986] *Lindow Man: the body in the bog*. London.

Struve, K.W. 1967 Die Moorleiche von Dätgen: ein Diskussionsbeitrag zur Strafopferthese. *Offa* 24, 33–76.

Stuijts, I. 2001 Bronze Age landscape changes in the midlands of Ireland. In W.H. Metz, B.L. van Beek and H. Steegstra (eds), *Patina: essays presented to Jay Jordan Butler on the occasion of his 80th birthday*, 527–37. Groningen.

Stuiver, M. and Pearson, G.W. 1986 High-precision calibration of the radiocarbon time scale, AD 1950–500 BC. *Radiocarbon* 28 (2B), 805–38.

Stuiver, M. and Polach, H.A. 1977 Discussion: Reporting of ^{14}C dating. *Radiocarbon* 19 (3), 355–63.

Stuiver, M. and Reimer, P.J. 1993 Extended ^{14}C database and revised CALIB 3.0 ^{14}C age calibration program. *Radiocarbon* 35 (1), 215–30.

Stuiver, M. and van der Plicht, J. (eds) 1998 INTCAL98 calibration issue. *Radiocarbon* 40 (3), 1041–159.

Tubridy, M. 1998 The prehistoric environment at Clonmacnoise. In H.A. King (ed.), *Clonmacnoise studies, volume 1: seminar papers 1994*, 1–6. Dublin.

Turner, R.C. [1986] Discovery and excavation of the Lindow bodies. In I.M. Stead, J.B. Bourke and D. Brothwell (eds), *Lindow Man: the body in the bog*, 10–13. London.

Turner, R.C. 1995a Gazetteer of bog bodies in the British Isles. In R.C. Turner and R.G. Scaife (eds), *Bog bodies: new discoveries and new perspectives*, 205–20. London.

Turner, R.C. 1995b Recent research into British bog bodies. In R.C. Turner and R.G. Scaife (eds), *Bog bodies: new discoveries and new perspectives*, 108–22. London.

Turner, R.[C.] 1999 Dating the Lindow Moss and other British bog bodies and the problems of assigning their cultural context. In B. Coles, J. Coles and M. Schou Jørgensen (eds), *Bog bodies, sacred sites and wetland archaeology*, 227–34. Wetland Archaeology Research Project Occasional Paper 12. Exeter.

Turner, R.C. and Scaife, R.G. (eds) 1995 *Bog bodies: new discoveries and new perspectives*. London.

van der Plicht, J., van der Sanden, W.A.B., Aerts, A.T. and Streurman, H.J. 2004 Dating bog bodies by ^{14}C-AMS. *Journal of Archaeological Science* 31, 471–91.

van der Sanden, W. 1990 *Mens en Moeras*. Assen.

van der Sanden, W. 1996 *Through nature to eternity: the bog bodies of northwest Europe*. Amsterdam.

van der Sanden, W. 2000 De man van Kreepen: verslag van een zoektocht. In W.H. Metz, B.L. van Beek and H. Steegstra (eds), *Patina: essays presented to Jay Jordan Butler on the occasion of his 80th birthday*, 481–92. Groningen.

Walsh, P. 1960 *Irish chiefs and leaders*, ed. C. O'Lochlainn. Dublin.

Walsh, T. and Barry, T.A. 1958 The chemical composition of some Irish peats. *Proceedings of the Royal Irish Academy* 59B, 305–28.

Webb, D.A., Parnell, J. and Doogue, D. 1996 *An Irish flora*. Dundalk. Dundalgan Press.

Weir, D.A. 1993 An environmental history of the Navan area, Co. Armagh. Unpublished PhD thesis, Queen's University Belfast.

Weir, D.A. 1995 A palynological study of landscape and agricultural development in County Louth from the second millennium BC to the first millennium AD. In *Discovery Programme Reports 2: project results 1993*, 77–126. Dublin.

Weir, D.A. 1997 An outline of vegetational history in the Navan area from Late Mesolithic to medieval times. In C.J. Lynn (ed.), *Excavations at Navan Fort, 1961–71*, 111–17. Northern Ireland Archaeological Monograph 3. Belfast.

White, J. and Doyle, G. 1982 The vegetation of Ireland: a catalogue raisonné. In J. White (ed.), *Studies on Irish vegetation*, 289–368. Dublin.

APPENDIX 1
SUPPLEMENTARY LIST OF IRISH BOG BODIES NOTED SINCE 1995

Raghnall Ó Floinn

The following is intended as a supplementary list of Irish bog bodies noted since the publication the 'Gazetteer of Irish bog bodies' in R.C. Turner and R. Scaife (eds), *Bog bodies: new discoveries and new perspectives* (London, 1995), 221–34. The format used there, in which the entries are given numerically by county, is adopted again here.

The 1995 publication listed 88 sites, representing 100+ individuals. Since then 30 new instances of bog bodies have been reported to the writer, bringing the total to 118 sites, representing 130+ individuals, an increase of 34 per cent. All but six (Me3, Of10, Of11, Ro6, Ro7 and Ro8) of these new reports are 'paper' bodies. Only one (An3) is a multiple burial.

Most of the entries are taken from reports in local newspapers, and I thank in particular Mr Pat Bracken, Clongour, Co. Tipperary, for bringing to my attention twelve of the new reports, ten of these from the pages of the *Nenagh Guardian*, and Ms Isabella Mulhall, Irish Antiquities Division, National Museum of Ireland, for details on the most recent finds.

ANTRIM

An3
Date of discovery: Before 1810
Findspot: 'Lockstown Bog' (Lockstown townland, Larne parish)
County: Antrim
NGR: J430955
Depth: 'near the bottom'
Sex: —
Age: 'young and grown persons'
Preservation: 'skeletons'; one body 'was in a wonderful state of preservation'
Associated artefacts: One body 'was dressed in a frock of tanned leather, buttoned with metal buttons from the chin downwards'
Present location: —
Reference: J. O'Laverty, *An historical account of the diocese of Down and Connor, ancient and modern*, vol. 3 (Dublin, 1884), 120–1

CORK

Co2
Date of discovery: 1834
Findspot: —
County: Cork

NGR: —
Depth: —
Sex: —
Age: —
Preservation: —
Associated artefacts: Covered by stakes
Remarks: —
Present location: —
Reference: *Saunders Newsletter*, 27 July 1834, 3. There is a possibility that this is the same body as Co1 (but the latter was reportedly found in 1838).

DERRY

De 16
Date of discovery: Before 1812
Findspot: 'at Coleraine'
County: Derry
NGR: C8532
Depth: —
Sex: —
Age: —
Preservation: 'corpse'
Associated artefacts: 'clothes and shoes on, together with shoemaker's implements'
Remarks: —
Present location: —
Reference: E. Wakefield, *An account of Ireland, statistical and political* (London 1812), 94

KILDARE

Kd5
Date of discovery: —
Findspot: —
County: Kildare
NGR: —
Depth: —
Sex: —
Age: —
Preservation: bones
Associated artefacts: —
Remarks: —
Present location: Possession of the Clements family, Killadoon, Celbridge, Co. Kildare
Reference: Information from Mr Charlie Clements, Celbridge, Co. Kildare

Kd6
Date of discovery: Before 1806
Findspot: —

County: Kildare
NGR: —
Depth: —
Sex: Male
Age: Adult
Preservation: —
Associated artefacts: Clothing, shoes
Remarks: —
Present location: —
Reference: J. Carr, *Stranger in Ireland* (Dublin, 1806)

LIMERICK

Li2
Date of discovery: 1881
Findspot: 'near Athea'
County: Limerick
NGR: R1335
Depth: —
Sex: Female
Age: 19-22
Preservation: 'remarkable state of preservation'
Associated artefacts: The body was 'enveloped in a dark, loose mantle, with head gear of same material'. A dish of bog oak was found near body, containing shoemaker's implements; the base of dish was inscribed 'in rude Irish characters' with the name 'Maryanne Ca…'. The following Latin inscription was found on one of the objects: 'Johannem cahill, Natus. Deccem. XXI, MDCCXXI. Obit. Atheaiensis, April IX, MDCCC'.
Remarks: Found in 'out of the way locality in a wood adjacent to Athea village'
Present location: —
Reference: *Nenagh Guardian*, 6 July 1881 (information from Mr Pat Bracken)

Li3
Date of discovery: 1879
Findspot: 'near Athea'
County: Limerick
NGR: R1335
Depth: 5ft
Sex: —
Age: —
Preservation: Human skeleton. 'A lock of brown hair, much longer than men usually wear, was found attached to the skull'.
Associated artefacts: —
Remarks: 'Found in a solid bank which…had never been disturbed'
Present location: —
Reference: *Nenagh Guardian*, 24 May 1879 (information from Mr Pat Bracken)

LAOIS

Ls1
Date of discovery: 1881
Findspot: 'Derry Bog, near Clonaslee' (Derry townland, Kilmanman parish)
County: Laois
NGR: N265130
Depth: 2ft
Sex: —
Age: —
Preservation: 'Human remains'
Associated artefacts: Body 'wrapped up in an old blanket'
Remarks: —
Present location: —
Reference: *Nenagh Guardian*, 30 April 1881 (information from Mr Pat Bracken)

MAYO

Ma6
Date of discovery: Before 1954
Findspot: 'near Bangor'
County: Mayo
NGR: F8623
Depth: —
Sex: —
Age: —
Preservation: Skeleton, hair
Associated artefacts: 'Brown garments and big cloak'; pair of leather shoes
Remarks: Reburied in disused graveyard near Bangor
Present location: —
Reference: Irish Antiquities Division file (IA/173/54)

Ma7
Date of discovery: 1905
Findspot: 'near Corick' (Bellacorick)
County: Mayo
NGR: F9720
Depth: 4ft
Sex: Male
Age: 'about 40'
Preservation: Flesh intact; beard and hair, reddish in colour; fingernails over 1in long
Associated artefacts: The body was wrapped 'in a home-spun woollen blanket' and clothed 'in a long coat'. 'A flint stone with two (*recte* tow?) or wadding, was found in an old tobacco pouch on the body'.
Remarks: The body lay extended on its back with the hands across the chest, as if laid out for burial, the head facing the west. The body was medically examined.

Present location: —
Reference: Irish Antiquities Division file (IA/173/54)

MEATH

Me3
Date of discovery: 2003
Findspot: Clonycavan townland, Killaconnigan parish
County: Meath
NGR: N665540
Depth: Unknown; found *ex situ*
Sex: Male
Age: Adult
Preservation: Head, upper torso and upper arms
Associated artefacts: —
Remarks: —
Present location: National Museum of Ireland (2003:84)

OFFALY

Of6
Date of discovery: 1866
Findspot: 'Bog of Kuilawn, near Birr' (Killaun townland, Drumcullen parish)
County: Offaly
NGR: —
Depth: 5ft
Sex: —
Age: —
Preservation: Head and trunk, skin and adipocere; arms missing
Associated artefacts: —
Remarks: body lay 'in a reclining position, the feet and legs higher than the trunk'
Present location: —
Reference: *Tipperary Advocate*, 18 August 1866 (information from Mr Pat Bracken)

Of7
Date of discovery: 1881
Findspot: 'near Killoughey, Queen's County' (Killoughy townland, Killoughy parish)
County: Offaly
NGR: N2814
Depth: —
Sex: Male?
Age: —
Preservation: 'body...in a state of remarkable preservation'; 'Some wound on the head'
Associated artefacts: The body was wrapped 'in an old blanket, which was but little

injured by the turf'
Remarks: The body lay 'in a reclining position, the feet and legs higher than the trunk'
Present location: —
Reference: *Nenagh Guardian*, 4 May 1881 (information from Mr Pat Bracken)

Of8

Date of discovery: 1878
Findspot: 'near Daingean'
County: Offaly
NGR: N4728
Depth: —
Sex: Female?
Age: —
Preservation: Skeleton
Associated artefacts: Body in lidded wooden coffin; knitted woollen stockings on feet, which were tied
Remarks: At the inquest, an old man gave evidence suggesting that the body might have been that of a woman called Bermingham, who had died nearly 70 years previously; she had committed suicide and been denied a Christian burial.
Present location: —
Reference: *Nenagh Guardian*, 21 May 1878 (information from Mr Pat Bracken)

Of9

Date of discovery: *c.* 1922
Findspot: Lusmagh parish
County: Offaly
NGR: M9814
Depth: —
Sex: —
Age: —
Preservation: —
Associated artefacts: —
Remarks: —
Present location: Buried immediately
Reference: Irish Antiquities Division file (IA/102/01) (information from Mr Val Trodd, Banagher, Co. Offaly)

Of10

Date of discovery: 1998
Findspot: Tumbeagh townland, Lemanaghan parish
County: Offaly
NGR: 215622 229398
Depth: —
Sex: —
Age: 16–18 years old

Preservation: Lower limbs below the knee, soft tissue and skeletal remains
Associated artefacts: Pointed stakes, birch pole, hazel withy
Remarks: —
Present location: National Museum of Ireland (98E452)
Reference: This book

Of11
Date of discovery: 2003
Findspot: Oldcroghan townland, Croghan parish
County: Offaly
NGR: N4530
Depth: *c.* 1.7m
Sex: Male
Age: Adult
Preservation: Upper torso, decapitated in antiquity; soft tissue and skeletal remains
Associated artefacts: Braided leather armband with copper-alloy mounts on left arm.
Remarks: The remains are severed at the neck and above the waist. Both arms were pierced in the upper arm, both with remains of twisted withy *in situ*.
Present location: National Museum of Ireland (2003:14)
Reference: Irish Independent, 16 May 2003

Of12
Date of discovery: 1899
Findspot: Kilballyskea townland, Shinrone parish
County: Offaly
NGR: S0392
Depth: 3ft
Sex: Female
Age: Adult?
Preservation: Skeleton
Associated artefacts: Skeleton enshrouded in a hide; wooden goblet placed beside it
Remarks: Find situated on slopes of Knockshigowna Hill beside Killballyskeagh Castle
Present location: Remains re-interred; remains of goblet retained by Head Constable Comerford of Shinrone
Reference: supplement to the *People*, 24 June 1899; copy preserved in the National Archives, file 98/4/1/3 (information from Ms Aideen Ireland, National Archives)

Of13
Date of discovery: 2005
Findspot: Daingean South bog
County: Offaly
NGR: —
Depth: Found *ex situ* on surface of milled peat
Sex: —
Age: Young adult
Preservation: Left patella only

Associated artefacts: —
Remarks: —
Present location: National Museum of Ireland (05E0553)
Reference: Identification by Ms Laureen Buckley; reported by Ms Jane Whitaker

ROSCOMMON

Ro6
Date of discovery: 2000
Findspot: Cappaleitrim townland, Moore parish
County: Roscommon
NGR: M959279
Depth: —
Sex: —
Age: —
Preservation: Single bone, right tibia
Associated artefacts: —
Remarks: Recovered from spoil of Bord na Móna drain
Present location: National Museum of Ireland (2000:70)

Ro7
Date of discovery: 1946
Findspot: Taghboy, Four Roads
County: Roscommon
NGR: M825505
Depth: 2ft
Sex: Male
Age: 40–50 years
Preservation: 'Mummified body' including hair and skin
Associated artefacts: —
Remarks: —
Present location: —
Reference: *Sligo Independent*, 20 April 1946 (information from Mr Martin Timoney, Keash); *Roscommon Champion*, 13 April 1946 (information from Mr Albert Siggins, National Museum of Ireland)

Ro8
Date of discovery: 2005
Findspot: Mountdillon Bog (Derrycashel townland, Lissonuffy parish)
County: Roscommon
NGR: N0482
Depth: —
Sex: —
Age: 25–35
Preservation: Torso and limbs, bone and soft tissue
Associated artefacts: —

Appendix 1

Remarks: Found *ex situ*; body appeared to have been placed in a flexed position
Present location: National Museum of Ireland (2005:3)
Reference: Reported by Ms Jane Whitaker

Ro9
Date of discovery: 2005
Findspot: Mountdillon Bog (Cloonshannagh townland, Bumlin parish)
County: Roscommon
NGR: N0381
Depth: *c.* 1.0m
Sex: Female
Age: —
Preservation: Skeleton, hair, soft tissue
Associated artefacts: Woollen clothing
Remarks: Found *ex situ*, badly disturbed
Present location: National Museum of Ireland (2005:35)
Reference: Reported by Garda Ray Creevin (Longford)

TIPPERARY

Ti10
Date of discovery: 1880
Findspot: Garryclough Bog (Garryclogh townland, Fennor parish)
County: Tipperary
NGR: —
Depth: 4ft
Sex: female
Age: Adult, 'full-grown female'
Preservation: 'wonderfully preserved'
Remarks: Body of a female about 5ft 5in high found lying full length on its back, naked. The inquest found 'a depressed fracture of the frontal bone of the skull…quite sufficient to have caused death'. The radius and ulna of the left forearm were missing. The inquest heard 'that the person was unidentified but the general belief is that the deceased was murdered as far back as 60 years ago, and the body placed where it was, denuded altogether of clothes to prevent identification'.
Present location: Reburied in Buolick cemetery
Reference: *Clonmel Chronicle*, 5 June 1880 (information from Mr Pat Bracken)

Ti11
Date of discovery: 1890
Findspot: Kilcurkee Bog (Kilcurkree townland, Loughmore East parish)
County: Tipperary
NGR: S145695
Depth: 3ft
Sex: Male(?)
Age: Adult

Preservation: Skeleton
Associated artefacts: Naked; large limestone boulder weighing 28lb placed over skull, which was smashed.
Remarks: Reputed to be a murder victim, possibly of a person missing either 3 or 30 years earlier
Present location: Unknown, presumed reburied
Reference: *Nenagh Guardian*, 31 May 1890 (information from Mr Pat Bracken)

Ti12
Date of discovery: 1950s
Findspot: Littleton Bog
County: Tipperary
NGR: S2355
Depth: —
Sex: Female
Age: —
Preservation: 'Head and shoulders with long blond hair'
Associated artefacts: —
Remarks: —
Present location: —
Reference: Irish Antiquities Division file (IA/102/01) (information Mr Val Trodd, Banagher, Co. Offaly)

Ti13
Date of discovery: 1905
Findspot: 'Borrisnafarney, Devil's Bit Mountain' (Borrisnafarney townland, Borrisnafarney parish)
County: Tipperary
NGR: S0575
Depth: 3ft
Sex: Male
Age: 'about 45 years'
Preservation: 'the flesh had rotted away, but the hair on the head was quite unchanged'
Associated artefacts: 'A whip and some twisted sally twigs were also found in the grave'.
Remarks: 'The findspot was at an elevation of 1500'. Examined by a Dr Mitchell of Templemore.
Present location: —
Reference: Irish Antiquities Division file (IA/71/00); *Nenagh Guardian*, 7 June 1905 (information from Mr Pat Bracken)

Ti14
Date of discovery: 1905
Findspot: Noard townland, Twomileborris parish
County: Tipperary

NGR: S2357
Depth: 4ft
Sex: Female
Age: —
Preservation: 'the trunk of a woman's body, on the head skin and hair'
Associated artefacts: 'The body was enshrouded in a ram skin'
Remarks: Local tradition that the body was that of a woman who, with her husband (Ti15 below), had disappeared
Present location: —
Reference: Irish Antiquities Division file (IA/71/00); *Nenagh Guardian*, 17 June 1905 (information from Mr Pat Bracken)

Ti15

Date of discovery: *c.* 1875
Findspot: Noard townland, Twomileborris parish
County: Tipperary
NGR: S2357
Depth: —
Sex: Male
Age: —
Preservation: —
Associated artefacts: —
Remarks: The skeleton of a man, presumed to be the caretaker husband of Ti14 above, had been found 'under similar circumstances' some 30 years earlier than Ti14
Present location: —
Reference: Irish Antiquities Division file (IA/71/00); *Nenagh Guardian*, 7 June 1905 (information from Mr Pat Bracken)

WICKLOW

Wi2

Date of discovery: *c.* 1820
Findspot: 'Killalish Bog' (Killalish Upper/Lower townland, Kilranelagh parish)
County: Wicklow
NGR: S912850
Depth: —
Sex: —
Age: —
Preservation: Skeleton
Associated artefacts: Skin belt, wooden three-pronged fork, 8½ft long
Remarks: —
Present location: —
Reference: W. FitzGerald, 'An ancient wooden three-pronged fork', *Journal of the County Kildare Archaeological Society* **5** (3) (1907), 208–10 (information from Mr Conor McDermott, IAWU)

APPENDIX 2
COLEOPTERAN DATA

Eileen Reilly

Table 1: Insect taxa from Column B1 samples, Tumbeagh Bog, Co. Offaly (see Table 21, p. 156, for sample source). Nomenclature follows Lucht (1987). The key (after Robinson 1991) is as follows: A = aquatic; B = bankside; C = carrion; D = disturbed or bare ground; F = foul (dung); M = marsh (fen/bog); T = terrestrial; V = decaying plant matter; W = woodland. RDB = Red Data Book.

Family/species	1	2	3	4	5	6	7	8	9	10	11	Habitat	Status in Ireland
Carabidae													
Notiophilus substriatus Water.	—	—	—	1	—	—	—	—	—	—	—	BV	Generally common
Calathus fuscipes (Goez.)	—	—	—	—	—	—	—	1	—	—	—	TV	Common
Pterostichus diligens (Sturm.)	—	—	1	—	—	—	—	—	—	—	1	BM	Common
P. minor (Gyll.)	—	3	—	—	—	—	—	—	—	—	—	MB; both wooded and open	Common
P. nigrita (Payk.)	—	—	—	—	—	1	2	—	—	—	—	BMW	Common
P. oblongopunctatus (F.)	—	—	—	—	—	—	—	—	—	1	—	W	Local (RDB UK status: Notable B)
P. strenuus (Panzer)	—	4	—	2	—	1	2	—	1	1	1	BMW	Common
Pterostichus sp.	—	—	1	1	1	—	—	1	1	—	1	Various	Common
Dromius quadrimaculatus (L.)	—	1	—	—	1	1	—	—	—	—	—	W; pine	Common
Dysticidae													
Agabus affinis (Payk.)	—	—	—	—	—	—	1	1	—	—	—	A; acid	Common
A. biguttatus (Ol.)/*guttatus* (Payk.)	—	1	—	—	—	—	—	—	—	5	2	A; base preferring	Occasional/common (RDB UK status: Notable B)
Agabus sp.	—	1	—	—	1	—	—	—	—	1	—	A	Generally common
Hydroporus ferrugineus Steph.	—	—	—	—	—	—	—	—	3	—	—	A; acid preferring, but also pools	Unknown (RDB UK status: Notable B)
H. longicornis Sharp.	—	—	—	—	1	—	—	—	—	—	—	A; springs, bogs	Occasional (RDB UK status: Notable B)
H. longulus Muls.	—	—	—	—	—	—	—	—	1	—	—	A; springs, bogs	Local (RDB UK status: Notable B)
H. melanarius Strm.	—	—	—	—	—	—	1	—	—	—	—	A; bog pools, leaf-rich woodland pools	Common
H. nigrita (F.)	—	—	—	—	—	—	—	—	2	—	—	A; stagnant water, acid preferring	Common
H. obscurus Strm.	—	—	—	—	4	2	2	—	3	—	—	A; acid water, *Sphagnum*	Common
H. planus (F.)	—	—	—	—	1	—	—	—	—	—	—	A; vegetation-rich pools, woodland pools, mineral substrate	Common
H. rufifrons (Mull.)	—	2	—	—	—	—	—	—	—	—	—	A; fens, lakes, river oxbows (moribund UK species)	Unknown (RDB UK status: Vulnerable)
Hydroporus spp	2	1	—	4	1	2	6	2	—	2	1	Various	Generally common
Graptodytes bilineatus (Strm.)	—	—	1	2	—	—	—	—	1	—	—	A; fens, bog pools	Occasional (RDB UK status: Rare)
G. flavipes (Ol.)	—	—	—	—	—	—	—	—	—	—	2	A; pools, temporary water	Unknown (RDB UK status: Vulnerable)
G. granularis (L.)	—	2	—	—	—	—	—	—	—	—	—	A; stagnant pools in bogs, fens	Occasional (RDB UK status: Notable B)
Graptodytes sp.	1	—	—	—	4	2	1	—	—	—	—	Various	Generally rare
Hydraenidae													
Hydraena gracilis Germ.	—	—	—	—	—	2	—	—	—	—	—	A; flowing water	Common
Hydraena sp.	—	—	—	—	—	—	—	1	—	—	—	A	Generally common
Octhebius minimus (F.)	—	—	—	—	—	3	7	—	—	—	—	A; flowing and stagnant water	Common
Ochthebius sp.	—	—	—	—	1	—	—	2	—	1	—	A	Generally local
Limnebius sp.	—	—	—	—	—	—	1	—	—	—	—	A; bog, fens	Generally very local

Table 1 (contd): Insect taxa from Column B1 samples, Tumbeagh Bog, Co. Offaly.

Family/species	1	2	3	4	5	6	7	8	9	10	11	Habitat	Status in Ireland
Hydrophilidae													
Helophorus sp.	—	—	—	—	—	1	—	—	—	—	—	AV	Generally common
Coelostoma orbiculare (F.)	—	—	—	—	1	6	1	2	1	3	1	MV; swamps, decaying vegetation	Common
Cercyon sp.	1	—	—	—	—	—	—	—	—	—	—	VF	Generally common
Megasternum boletophagun (Marsh.)	—	—	—	—	—	1	—	—	—	—	—	VF	Common
Hydrobius fuscipes (L.)	—	1	—	—	—	—	—	—	—	—	—	AV; slow-moving water	Common
Cymbiodyta marginella (F.)	—	—	—	—	—	1	—	—	—	—	—	A; stagnant water and woodland pools	Occasional
Enochrus cf. fuscipennis (Thoms.)	—	—	—	—	2	—	—	—	—	—	—	A; bogs	Occasional
Enochrus spp (at least four species)	—	—	—	—	—	21	15	8	1	11	—	A; pools, detritus ponds etc.	Generally local, occasional or rare
Chaetarthria seminulum (Hbst.)	—	1	2	5	1	6	4	14	1	6	2	A; under detritus, pools, bogs	Rare (RDB UK status: Notable B)
Leiodidae													
Agathidium sp.	—	—	—	1	—	—	—	—	—	—	—	VW	Generally common
Scydmaenidae													
Scydmaenidae gen. et. sp. indet.	—	—	—	—	—	—	—	—	1	—	—	V	Variable status
Ptilidae													
Ptenidium sp.	—	—	—	—	1	—	—	—	—	—	—	V; marshes, woods, associated with ants	Some common; some local
Staphylinidae													
Acidota crenata (F.)	—	2	—	—	—	—	—	—	1	1	—	VTM; hygrophilous	Local
Lesteva heeri Fauv.	—	—	—	—	—	—	—	—	1	—	—	VM	Common
Lathrobium spp	—	5	1	3	1	2	2	4	2	4	2	V; eurytropic	Common
Stenus spp	—	3	1	5	2	—	—	1	1	—	—	TM; hygrophilous	Some very local; some common
Philonthus sp.	—	—	—	1	6	1	1	1	1	—	1	VF	Some common; some very local
Staphilinus sp.	—	—	—	1	—	—	—	—	1	—	—	VF; marshes, woodland	Generally common
Drusilla canaliculata (F.)	—	—	—	1	—	—	1	2	1	—	—	MW; predatory on ants	Common
Aleocharinae gen. et. sp. indet.	1	1	1	3	2	2	—	—	2	3	—	Various habitats	Some local; some common
Pselaphidae													
Bryaxis sp.	—	1	1	3	1	—	1	—	1	1	—	V; reed refuse, moss, under bark	Generally common
Reichenbachia juncorum (Leach)	—	—	—	—	—	—	—	—	1	1	—	V; reed beds, moss, *Sphagnum*	Common
Brachygluta sp.	—	1	—	1	—	—	—	—	—	—	—	MV; various V in wet locations	Generally common
Pselaphus heisei (Hbst.)	—	—	—	—	—	1	—	—	—	—	—	MV; in wet humus layers	Common
Scirtidae													
Cyphon spp	1	3	1	2	1	2	6	3	9	15	1	A, larvae; MV, adults	Some local; some common
Dryopidae													
Dryops spp	—	—	—	2	1	2	1	—	—	—	—	AV; in all kinds of hydrophilous locations	Generally rare or insufficient known
Rhizophagidae													
Rhizophagus bipustulatus (F.)	—	—	—	—	—	—	—	1	—	—	—	W; under bark, all types of trees	Unknown (common in UK)

Table 1 (contd): Insect taxa from Column B1 samples, Tumbeagh Bog, Co. Offaly.

Family/species	1	2	3	4	5	6	7	8	9	10	11	Habitat	Status in Ireland
Scarabaeidae													
Aphodius sticticus (Panz.)	—	—	—	—	—	—	—	—	—	1	—	F; woodland preferring	Unknown (locally common in UK)
Phyllopertha horticola (L.)	—	1	—	1	1	—	—	2	—	—	1	T; at roots, on flowers etc., in meadows	Very local
Chrysomelidae													
Plateumaris affinis (Kunze)	—	1	—	—	—	—	—	—	—	—	—	M; associated with *Carex* spp	Unknown (RDB UK status: Notable B)
P. braccata (Scop.)	1	—	—	—	—	—	—	—	—	—	—	M; associated with *Phragmites australis*	Unknown (RDB UK status: Notable B)
P. discolor (Panzer)	—	3	3	4	—	3	4	2	6	5	—	M; associated with *Eriophorum* and among *Sphagnum*	Common
P. sericea (L.)	1	—	—	—	—	—	—	—	—	4	3	M; associated with *Carex* spp, *Typha, Iris, Scirpus*	Common
Plateumaris/Donacia sp.	—	1	—	—	1	—	—	—	—	—	—	M; various wetland plants	Generally common
Phaedon sp.	1	—	—	—	—	—	—	—	—	—	—	MB; various hydrophilous locations	Some common; some rare
Phyllotreta sp.	—	—	—	1	1	2	3	2	1	2	1	DTB; various crucifers	Some very local; some common
Altica sp.	—	—	—	—	—	—	—	1	—	1	1	M; mostly *Calluna/Erica* spp, wetland plants	Generally common; some rare species
Chrysolina sp.	—	—	—	1	1	—	—	—	—	—	—	TMB; various habitats from wet to dry	Many very rare; others common
Chaetocnema concinna (Marsh.)	—	—	—	3	—	1	—	—	—	—	—	MBT; various herbs	Common
C. subcoerulea (Kuts.)	—	—	—	—	—	1	—	—	—	—	—	M; reed beds, sedges	Unknown (RDB UK status: Notable B)
Chaetocnema sp.	—	—	1	—	1	—	—	—	1	—	1	MBT; various herbs, tend to be hydrophilous	Some common; some very rare
Curculionidae													
Apion sp.	—	—	—	1	—	—	—	—	—	1	—	MT; various herbs	Generally common
Rhinoncus sp.	—	—	—	—	—	—	—	2	—	—	—	MBT; various herbs, near lakes, riverbanks	In UK restricted generally to northern locations
Micrelus ericae (Gyll.)	—	10	8	3	—	5	1	1	—	2	—	M; drier heaths, bogs, woodland turf on *Calluna*	Common
Ceutorhynchus sp.	1	—	—	—	—	—	—	—	—	—	—	MT; various herbs	Generally common
Bagous spp	—	2	4	4	5	1	3	5	4	3	2	M; wetland habitats, various plant species	Unknown (generally rare, endangered and extinct in UK)
Rhynchaenus spp	1	2	1	2	—	—	—	1	3	1	—	WM; leaf-miner of various tree/shrub species	Generally very local; some common
Total number of individuals	11	53	27	58	38	77	66	62	44	84	24		

Table 2: Insect taxa from bog body samples, Tumbeagh Bog, Co. Offaly (see Table 22, p. 156, for sample source). Nomenclature follows Lucht (1987). The key (after Robinson 1991) is as follows: A = aquatic; B = bankside; C = carrion; D = disturbed or bare ground; F = foul (dung); M = marsh (fen/bog); T = terrestrial; V = decaying plant matter; W = woodland. RDB = Red Data Book.

Family/species	1	2	3	4	5	6	7	8	9	10	11	Habitat	Status in Ireland
Carabidae													
Carabus sp.	1	—	—	—	—	—	—	—	—	—	—	BMW; often hygrophilous	Common
Nebria brevicollis (F.)	—	—	—	1	—	—	—	—	—	—	—	MW; prefers woodland and moisture	Common
Trechus rubens (F.)	—	—	—	—	—	1	—	—	—	—	—	MW; moisture and shade loving	Local (RDB UK status: Notable B)
Trechus sp.	—	—	—	—	—	—	1	—	—	—	—	MW	Generally common
Bembidion sp.	—	—	1	—	—	—	—	—	—	—	—	TM	Common
Pterostichus minor (Gyll.)	—	—	1	—	—	1	1	—	—	—	—	MB; both wooded and open	Common
P. strenuus (Panzer)	—	1	1	—	—	—	—	—	2	2	—	BMW	Common
Pterostichus sp.	—	—	1	—	—	—	—	—	—	—	—	MBV	Common
Cymindis vaporariorum (L.)	—	—	—	—	—	—	—	—	—	—	1	M; *Sphagnum* bogs, wet moorland, sandy soils	Very local (RDB UK status: Notable B)
Dysticidae													
Agabus bipustulatus (L.)	—	—	—	—	—	—	—	—	—	—	1	A; eurytropic	Common
sp.	—	—	—	—	—	—	1	—	—	—	—	A	Generally common
Hydroporus ferrugineus Steph.	1	—	—	—	—	—	—	—	—	—	—	A; acid preferring, but also pools	Unknown (RDB UK status: Notable B)
H. longulus Muls.	—	—	—	—	—	2	—	1	—	—	—	A; springs, bogs	Local (RDB UK status: Notable B)
H. marginatus (Duft.)	1	—	—	—	—	—	—	—	—	—	—	A; stagnant or running water	Occasional (RDB UK status: Notable B)
H. melanarius Strm.	—	1	—	—	—	—	—	1	—	—	—	A; bog pools, leaf-rich woodland pools	Common
H. morio Aube	—	2	—	—	—	—	—	—	—	—	—	A; stagnant waters, small vegetated ponds, temporary pools	Common
H. nigrita (F.)	—	—	—	1	—	—	—	—	—	—	—	A; stagnant water, acid preferring	Common
H. obscurus Strm.	—	—	—	—	—	2	—	1	—	—	—	A; acid water, *Sphagnum*	Common
H. planus (F.)	—	—	—	—	—	—	2	—	—	—	—	A; vegetation-rich pools, woodland pools, mineral substrate	Common
H. umbrosus (Gyll.)	—	—	1	—	2	—	—	—	2	—	—	A; fen species, leaf-rich woodland pools	Generally common
Hydroporus spp.	1	—	3	1	—	2	—	—	1	2	—	A	Generally common
Graptodytes granularis (L.)	—	—	—	—	2	2	—	—	—	1	—	A; swampy areas of bogs, pools, fens	Occasional (RDB UK status: Notable B)
Hydraenidae													
Hydraena sp.	—	—	—	—	—	—	—	—	—	—	1	A	Some local; some common
Ochthebius minimus (F.)	—	—	—	—	—	—	1	—	—	—	—	A; flowing and stagnant water	Common
O. nanus Steph.	—	1	—	—	—	—	—	—	—	—	—	A; marsh and coastal species	Occasional (RDB UK status: Notable B)
Hydrophilidae													
Helophorus sp.	—	—	1	—	—	—	1	—	—	—	—	AV	Generally common
Cercyon sp.	—	—	1	—	—	—	—	—	—	—	—	VFC	Generally common
Laccobius sp.	—	1	—	—	—	—	—	—	—	—	—	A; streams, ponds, ditches, bog pools	Generally local
Enochrus cf. *testaceus* (F.)	—	3	—	—	—	—	—	—	—	—	—	A; shallow, vegetation-rich pools	Occasional
Enochrus spp (at least three species)	18	13	19	12	3	17	14	1	3	8	—	A - pools, detritus ponds, fens	Generally local, occasional or rare

Table 2 (contd): Insect taxa from bog body samples, Tumbeagh Bog, Co. Offaly

Family/species	1	2	3	4	5	6	7	8	9	10	11	Habitat	Status in Ireland
Leiodidae													
Agathidium sp.	1	—	1	—	—	—	—	—	—	—	—	VW	Generally common
Staphylinidae													
Acidota crenata (F.)	—	—	—	—	—	1	—	—	—	—	—	VTM; hygrophilous	Local
Anotylus nitidulus (Grav.)	—	—	—	1	—	—	—	—	—	—	—	VFC; moss, decaying vegetation, dung, carrion	Common
Lathrobium spp	3	3	—	—	2	3	1	—	—	—	—	V; eurytropic	Common
Stenus spp	—	—	1	—	—	—	—	—	—	—	—	TM; hygrophilous	Some very local; some common
Drusilla canaliculata (F.)	—	—	—	—	—	—	—	—	—	—	1	MW; predatory on ants	Common
Aleocharinae gen. et. sp. indet.	1	1	—	—	1	—	—	—	—	—	—	Various	Some local; some common
Scirtidae													
Cyphon spp	—	—	—	—	—	2	1	1	1	2	—	A, larvae; MV, adults	Some local; some common
Scarabaeidae													
Aphodius sp.	—	—	—	—	—	—	1	—	—	—	—	F	Generally common
Phyllopertha horticola (L.)	—	—	—	—	1	—	—	—	—	—	—	T; at roots, on flowers etc. in meadows	Very local
Chrysomelidae													
Plateumaris discolor (Panzer)	—	2	2	—	2	3	4	3	3	2		M; associated with *Eriophorum* and among *Sphagnum*	Common
P. sericea (L.)	—	—	2	—	4	3	—	—	2	—		M; associated with *Carex* spp, *Typha*, *Iris*, *Scirpus*	Common
P. discolor (Panz.) /*sericea* (L.)	3	—	—	—	—	—	—	—	—	—	—	M; various wetland plants	Common
Plateumaris sp.	—	—	—	3	—	—	—	—	—	—	—	M; various wetland plants	Generally common
Phyllotreta spp	—	—	—	—	—	2	—	—	—	—	—	DTB; various crucifers	Some very local; some common
Altica sp.	—	—	—	—	—	—	—	—	1	—	—	M; mostly *Calluna/Erica* spp, wetland plants	Generally common; some rare species
Chaetocnema concinna (Marsh.)	—	—	—	—	—	—	—	—	1	—	—	MBT; various herbs	Common
C. subcoerulea (Kuts.)	—	—	—	—	—	—	—	3	1	—	—	M; reed beds, sedges	Unknown (RDB UK status: Notable B)
Chaetocnema spp	—	—	—	1	—	—	—	—	—	—	—	MT; various plant species	Some common; some very rare
Curculionidae													
Apion sp.	1	—	—	—	—	—	—	—	—	1	—	MT; various herbs	Generally common
Micrelus ericae (Gyll.)	—	—	—	—	—	3	1	—	—	—	—	M; drier heaths, bogs, woodland turf on *Calluna*	Common
Total number of individuals	31	28	35	19	12	43	35	11	19	21			

Appendix 2